Posthegemony

Posthegemony

Political Theory and Latin America

JON BEASLEY-MURRAY

University of Minnesota Press
Minneapolis • London

Excerpt from *Canto General* by Pablo Neruda copyright 2010 Fundación Pablo Neruda. From Pablo Neruda, *Canto General,* translated by Jack Schmitt (Berkeley: University of California Press, 1991); reprinted with permission.

Published by the University of Minnesota Press
111 Third Avenue South, Suite 290
Minneapolis, MN 55401-2520
http://www.upress.umn.edu

Library of Congress Cataloging-in-Publication Data

Beasley-Murray, Jon, 1969-
Posthegemony : political theory and Latin America / Jon Beasley-Murray.
p. cm.
Includes bibliographical references and index.
ISBN 978-0-8166-4714-9 (hc : alk. paper)
ISBN 978-0-8166-4715-6 (pb : alk. paper)
1. Political science – Latin America. 2. Political science – Philosophy. 3. Latin America – Politics and government. I. Title.
JA84.L3B43 2010
327.1′14098 – dc22 2010032928

Printed in the United States of America on acid-free paper

20 19 18 17 16 15 14 13 12 11 10 10 9 8 7 6 5 4 3 2 1

To Ruth Beasley-Murray
and to the memories of George Beasley-Murray,
Maelor Griffiths, and Mavis Griffiths

Contents

Introduction

A User's Guide

> *In this book there are two texts which simply alternate; you might almost believe they had nothing in common, but they are in fact inextricably bound up with each other, as though neither could exist on its own, as though it was only their coming together, the distant light they cast on one another, that could make apparent what is never quite said in one, never quite said in the other, but said only in their fragile overlapping.*
>
> —Georges Perec, *W*

> *One beginning and one ending for a book was a thing I did not agree with.*
>
> —Flann O'Brien, *At Swim-Two-Birds*

Definitions

There is no hegemony and never has been. We live in cynical, posthegemonic times: nobody is very much persuaded by ideologies that once seemed fundamental to securing social order. Everybody knows, for instance, that work is exploitation and that politics is deceit. But we have always lived in posthegemonic times: social order was never in fact secured through ideology. No amount of belief in the dignity of labor or the selflessness of elected representatives could ever have been enough to hold things together. The fact that people no longer give up their consent in the ways in which they may once have done, and yet everything carries on much the same, shows that consent was never really at issue. Social order is secured through habit and affect: through folding the constituent power of the multitude back on itself to produce the illusion of transcendence and sovereignty. It follows also that social change is never achieved through any putative counterhegemony. No amount of adherence to a revolutionary creed or a party line could ever be enough to break things apart. The fact that now people no longer believe in radical change as they may once have done does not mean that everything will carry on much the same. Social change, too, is achieved through habit and affect: through affirming the constituent power of the multitude. But change is not a matter of substituting one program for another. This book offers no blueprint, because the multitude betrays the best-laid plans.

By "hegemony," I do not mean mere domination. To say "posthegemony" is not to say that domination is at an end. Command and control, exploitation and oppression, still manifestly continue. If anything, they are now more savage and more pernicious than ever as the state increasingly permeates everyday life and as politics becomes "biopolitics." Nor by hegemony do I mean the concept in International Relations of a single dominant world power. It may be that such a power no longer exists, but this is more a symptom of posthegemony than the main issue.[1] By hegemony I mean the notion, derived from the Italian Marxist Antonio Gramsci, that the state maintains its dominance (and that of social and economic elites) thanks to the consent of those it dominates. Where it does not win consent, this theory suggests, the state resorts to coercion. By contrast, in stressing the role of habit (rather than opinion) I point to processes that involve neither consent nor coercion. A focus on habit enables us to grasp the workings of the habitus: a collective, embodied feeling for the rules of the social game that is activated and reproduced beneath consciousness. And in stressing the role of affect (rather than emotion) I turn to other feelings: the impersonal and embodied flow of intensities that undermines any concept of a rational subject who could provide or withdraw his or her consent. But in stressing the notion of the multitude (rather than the people) I show that subjectivity continues to play a vital role: the multitude is the subject of a constituent power that is prior to the constituted power of the state and the sovereign. Habit, affect, and the multitude are the three components of a theory of posthegemony. All three are responses to the puzzle posed by the seventeenth-century philosopher Benedict de Spinoza: "No one has yet determined what the body can do."[2] Habit describes the way in which bodies act out the regular and repetitive activities that structure daily life. Affect indicates the power of a body (individual or collective) to affect or be affected by other bodies. And the multitude encompasses an expansive collection of bodies that, in organizing itself so as to increase its powers of affection, constitutes society and drives time onward. All three terms, moreover, refer to immanent processes: they incarnate a logic from below that requires neither representation nor direction from above. Or rather, they undo the spatial metaphor of "above" and "below." They are sufficient unto themselves. So although we may think about posthegemony negatively, in terms of flight or exodus from the current order of things — moving beyond ideology, escaping social constraints — the real question concerns the reverse process. What is the origin of the wrinkles in immanence that give rise to the illusion of transcendence, the fiction of hegemony, the presupposition of the state, and the presumption of a social pact? Why do we stubbornly take these effects for causes? For in fact what we most immediately perceive are bodies, with their habitual movements, their affective intensities, and their multitudinous interactions. Posthegemony is an attempt to rethink politics from the ground up, rooted in the material reality common to us all.

I am not the only person to have advanced a concept of posthegemony, though this book is the first to define it at such length and in these terms. Sociologist Scott Lash, for instance, argues that "power now . . . is largely *post-hegemonic*" and suggests that "cultural studies should look mostly elsewhere for its core concepts."[3] But Lash's conception of posthegemony is purely temporal: he argues merely that power is *now* posthegemonic. My aim is a more comprehensive critique of the idea of hegemony and of the cultural studies that, as Lash rightly but too reverently observes, it defines. Likewise, theorist Nicholas Thoburn contends that social theory has to take account of the fact that the concept of civil society (for Gramsci, intimately linked to the notion of hegemony) no longer holds.[4] My criticism of the notion of civil society is again more wholesale: I argue that it has always been an accomplice of state containment, a means to stigmatize affect and the multitude as somehow barbarous and apolitical. By contrast, political theorist Benjamin Arditi is skeptical of the proposition that the era of hegemony is at an end, but he argues that politics is, perhaps increasingly, not simply about hegemony. Arditi points to two forms of posthegemonic politics: the exodus or defection of the multitude; and the viral politics of informal networks. (I see no significant distinction between the two.) Both are "ways of doing politics that bypass the neo-Gramscian logic of hegemony and counterhegemony characteristic of most of what is usually inventoried under the name of 'politics' today." For Arditi, posthegemony supplements but does not replace politics as "usual." If anything, in his view posthegemony reinforces the concept of hegemony, by giving it "an outside to define it."[5] My disagreement with traditional politics, however, is again more sweeping: I argue that it offers at best a temporary palliative, at worst a fatal distraction from the real workings of power and domination.

My understanding of posthegemony is, like Arditi's, related to debates within Latin American studies about the political and theoretical limits to the concept of hegemony rather than simply about its contemporary obsolescence. In his 1990 book *Modernism and Hegemony*, the Marxist cultural critic Neil Larsen engages with both the "crisis of representation" in modernist aesthetics and the "crisis of hegemony" that has long seemed to plague Latin America. He argues that this supposed crisis of hegemony is in fact merely its inversion: it is a hegemony enshrined in cultural goods rather than political discourse that thereby "render[s] visible what is hidden in the posthegemonic conditions of the center," that is, that aesthetics can no longer be a refuge from "the real space of hegemonic state power."[6] Larsen does not develop this concluding and rather gnomic hint that the collapse of the state, its inability to articulate a coherent or convincing discourse, is really its expansion into culture as a whole, its disarticulated diffusion throughout what was once imagined to be civil society. Five years later, however, critic George Yúdice takes up the term "posthegemony" as part of a qualified defense of civil society. Likewise observing "a weakening of the articulation of national discourse and state apparatuses," Yúdice argues that "we might say that, from the purview of the national proscenium, a posthegemonic situation holds." Again, posthegemony in this instance means mostly that hegemony is no longer tied to the state; but it also implies that hegemony has expanded well beyond national boundaries, "to naturalize global capitalism everywhere."[7]

I agree with Larsen and Yúdice that today power is obviously at work everywhere, that representation has collapsed, and that the state is effectively dissolved into what was once known as civil society. But this means that civil society, which is defined by its distinction from the state, has now withered away.[8] This diffuse ubiquity of politics is what, following the French philosopher Michel Foucault, I term "biopolitics." It is not the expansion of hegemony but its evacuation. More clearly than ever, power works directly on bodies, in the everyday life that once appeared to be a refuge from politics. Yet for Larsen and Yúdice, posthegemony is ironically hegemony's triumph: hegemony is everything and everywhere. I argue that it is this misconception that lies at the root of cultural studies, encouraging a populism that equates the state's dissolution in the everyday with its disappearance altogether.

Discussion of posthegemony within Latin American studies took a new turn following an engagement with subaltern studies. Despite adopting the Gramscian concept of the "subaltern" with alacrity, refashioning it to refer to nonelite members of colonial and postcolonial societies, the South Asian historians who formed the subaltern studies group in the 1980s took issue with what for Gramsci was the related notion of hegemony. For the group's founder Ranajit Guha, for instance, the subaltern is inconstant and unpredictable and refuses to admit the existence of any single sphere (secular, religious, or nationalistic) within which hegemony could be sought or won. Hence "the swift transformation of class struggle into communal strife and vice versa" for which the best-intentioned narrative of solidarity can offer "only some well-contrived apology or a simple gesture of embarrassment."[9] Guha suggests that the subaltern inevitably turns its back on or betrays any putative hegemonic project: it refuses to give consent to consent. If hegemony is the struggle to gain consent, it requires the prior, implicit agreement that it is consent that is at issue in political struggles. Hegemony itself has to become dominant. As Guha argues in *Dominance without Hegemony*, this implies an equation between civil society, the nation, and the state: an echo chamber within which the terms of struggle are more or less predetermined.[10] But the subaltern always disrupts the boundaries of any such delimited space. Subalternity deconstructs hegemony: as postcolonial critic Gayatri Spivak consistently argues, the subaltern is the mute and impossible remainder that always undoes hegemony's claims.[11]

In books published in 2002 and 2001 respectively, Latin Americanist cultural critics Gareth Williams and Alberto Moreiras redescribe subaltern remainder in terms of posthegemony. In Williams's words, posthegemony "permits us to give a name to hegemony's subaltern residues, negative languages, fragmentary responses, cultural leftovers, and fissured experiences." He continues: "Posthegemony, in this sense, is no longer a name for the hegemony of transnational capital, but the name of those 'places in which hegemony ceases to make sense.'"[12] Or, in Moreiras's version, the realization that hegemony can never exhaust the "infinitude of the social" enables "a radical opening to the subaltern position, calling as such for the permanent destabilization of hegemonic ideology and the passage to a thinking beyond hegemony."[13] Posthegemonic subalternism, in this account, maintains a vigilant and unceasing critique of power on the basis of hegemony's inevitable failures. It warns against the hegemony of hegemony: against, that is, any belief in hegemony's promises that it may one day become total, its fiction of an all-inclusive pact. In reality, Williams and Moreiras suggest, the more that hegemony expands, the more its perimeter is violently and viciously patrolled by state forces. As hegemony approaches its limit, the disjuncture between hegemon and subaltern is all the more arbitrary, all the more the site of conflagration and genocide.

Where I differ from Williams and Moreiras is that I am not content with deconstruction, with posthegemony as permanent critique or labor of the negative. Subalternism holds on to a distinction between inside and outside, and so perpetuates the fundamental binarism of both hegemony and civil society: a differentiation between hegemon and subaltern, civil and fanatic. Subaltern studies still believes in a social contract designed to separate civilization from barbarism, even if it champions the nether side of that distinction and refuses any myth of closure. To put this another way: Gramsci always conceded that hegemony was necessarily incomplete. And in the Argentine Ernesto Laclau's reelaboration of hegemony theory, what matters is what he calls the incommensurability between a hegemonic signifier that aspires to represent the whole of society and the real that always recedes from such claims to universality. The difference between hegemony theory and subaltern studies is simply that the political polarity is inverted: whereas Gramsci and Laclau would insist that politics means playing the game of hegemony, Spivak, Williams, and Moreiras question the rules of that game by pointing to the aporetic excess for which it can never account. But they seldom doubt the game itself. (Hence Moreiras, in his more recent book, *Línea de sombra,* now describes his project as *para*hegemonic.) By contrast, then, in my conception posthegemony goes beyond the wreckage of any hegemonic project. I aim to redescribe and reconstruct an image of society that no longer depends on that society's own self-portrayal. My project is constitutive as well as critical. Central to this work of redescription and reconstruction is the concept of the multitude, which I take from Italian political theorist Antonio Negri. The multitude, Negri argues, preexists modern society, as "the conjunction of persons who inhabited a pre-social world that had to be transformed into a political society,"[14] haunts its institutions, and then returns in modernity's death throes. It is both excessive and foundational. The multitude is an agent of violent transformation and also the constitution of what is to come. Perhaps posthegemony can affirm its constituent power.

Structure

Before constitution, critique. This book has two parts. The first is a critique of cultural studies on the one hand, and the social scientific discourse of civil society on the other. I suggest that cultural studies' reductive definition of politics in terms of hegemony, with its insistence on culture as discursive articulation, substitutes culture for the state and therefore also confuses culture and state. This is true even of a more idiosyncratic definition of hegemony, such as that of anthropologist William Roseberry, who rejects hegemony as consensus but still stresses that hegemonic projects aim to construct "a common discursive framework."[15] At its limit, the logic of hegemony simply identifies with the state by taking it for granted. My argument proceeds by way of a history of cultural studies, to show how and why hegemony theory became its distinguishing feature, as well as through a close reading of Laclau, the foremost theorist of hegemony. I then examine the way in which a focus on civil society excludes culture from the political in the name of rational discourse. At *its* limit, however, civil society theory is overwhelmed by the affects it sets out to exclude. Here my argument works through an account of the discourse of new social movements and democratization to explain how and why the venerable concept of civil society has been revived over the past twenty-five years, as well as by way of a close reading of Jean Cohen and Andrew Arato, the most thorough theorists of civil society. What cultural studies and civil society theory share is an emphasis on discourse and on transcendence. They fail to confront immanent processes: either the embedded institutional structures that underpin discourse (in the case of cultural studies) or the affective flux that escapes it (with civil society theory). Moreover, neither are concerned with the means by which the state, or state effects, are constituted. Social science straightforwardly assumes that all politics is state politics, and posits civil society as the portal through which social movements must pass. Cultural studies simply forgets about the state, and so lets it in by the back door, while transfixed by its fetishized substitutes.

My critique of cultural studies and civil society is also, pragmatically, that they mimic the structures of power that they set out to understand. These are the structures that have been paradigmatic in twentieth-century democratic societies: populism and neoliberalism. Cultural studies is, effectively, populist. Civil society theory is, for all intents and purposes, itself neoliberal. Despite the best intentions of their practitioners, neither can be the standpoint from which to launch a critique of, respectively, a populism that claims culture can substitute for the state and a neoliberalism that purports to exclude culture from its domain. At best they can offer distorted glimpses of a politics beyond populism or neoliberalism, for instance in cultural studies' concern for everyday life or civil society theory's anxious fixation on social movement fundamentalism. Only posthegemony, with its understanding of what I call the double inscription of the state (as both immanence and transcendent quasi-cause), provides a foothold from which the unsaid as well as the said of these political formations can be observed and analyzed.

The book's second part turns to affect and habit as forms of (dis)organization beneath and beyond discourse, and so beyond the conceptual apparatus of cultural studies and civil society theory. Affect and habit are the basis of posthegemony. I examine French philosopher Gilles Deleuze's conception of affect, for which immanence is generally a space of liberation, and then sociologist Pierre Bourdieu's conception of habitus, for which it is social control that is immanent and all the more effective as such. Though these two approaches appear to be opposed, I argue that they are complementary, not least because each opens up to the other at critical moments: Deleuze's theory of affect when it has to account for the suicidal state, and Bourdieu's theory of habitus when social crisis reveals the potential creativity of resistance. Together, Deleuze and Bourdieu point to the need to take account, first, of the state's double inscription and, second, of the various possible modes of immanent organization. In conclusion, I suggest that Negri's theory of the multitude helps explain the state's doubleness: multitude and state incarnate a sometimes complicitous confrontation between constituent and constituted power. Yet the multitude is also a social subject that constitutes itself through resonance and repeated encounters on the plane of immanence, offering the prospect of forms of community that might do without transcendence, that is, without either the state or sovereignty. I warn, however, that the multitude may turn bad and ultimately become indifferent to the Empire that it confronts. The concept of "corruption" that Negri employs to differentiate the two is in the end insufficient. Against Negri, then, I argue for a distinction between good and bad multitudes. I further caution that even should the multitude fully emerge, autonomous and unlimited, we may hesitate at the end of history that would result. Hence, inspired by the Irish novelist Flann O'Brien, I offer two endings: a conclusion that meditates on uneventful eternity and death, and an epilogue that rejoices in insurgent history and life.

We may or may not want to embrace posthegemony as a political project for what Negri prophesies will be a future constituent republic. But posthegemony as analysis offers a new understanding of the constitution of the present and of the origins and the limits of politics and political theory. It offers new tools for political and historical investigation. My move from critique to constitution contends that these three theorists (Deleuze, Bourdieu, and Negri) can be productively combined to trace a social and historical plane of immanence, a political and social theory that would reject, and yet also explain, transcendence at every point. This is the book's affirmative project, its elaboration of a theory of posthegemony that rereads social processes in terms of affect, habit, and the multitude. Posthegemony encompasses populism and neoliberalism, but it also goes beyond them, and beyond even modernity's contractualist tradition of which the current so-called left turns (Chávez, Morales, . . . Obama?) constitute the apogee and last gasp. It outlines a path through the everyday biopolitics that structures our long postdisciplinary interregnum. For we are indeed now moving beyond the period in which the state is constituted by means of double inscription and entering a period in which immanence is (nearly) all, an epoch now posthegemonic in the temporal sense, beyond even the fiction of hegemony.

Latin America . . . and Beyond

Parallel to its theoretical argument, this book engages with Latin American social, political, and cultural history. This history is arranged as a series of case studies, each of which resonates with a specific aspect of the theoretical argument. My historical narrative moves from intensive moment to intensive moment rather than following a strict narrative teleology. It jumps from decade to decade. The case studies may perhaps be read separately, skipped, or, better still, supplemented or replaced by other cases that readers may wish to bring to and test with the theoretical matrix of posthegemony: if not El Salvador, then Colombia, say; if not Chile, then Poland; if not Argentina, then the United States. Running through these plateaus are several recurrent concerns: first, Latin American left movements from populism to Maoism, national liberation movements, new social movements, neopopulism, and the left turns; second, the role played by cultural genres such as film, television, *testimonio*, and the novel in Latin American societies; and third, the models of social structure found in Argentina, Peru, El Salvador, Chile, and Venezuela, and the relations between culture and politics in each. Throughout the book, theory and history are interwoven, even as each remains distinct and relatively autonomous. Within each chapter the historical and theoretical arguments are woven together via a mechanism of textual differentiation, in which the historical material bearing on Latin America appears in a different font. This arrangement is not to indicate any hierarchy of the theoretical over the empirical; indeed the historical and cultural could be viewed as the infrastructure for the theoretical, which the reader may or may not wish to peruse. The stories from Latin America include vignettes that have their own specific importance: for instance, the assault on a San Salvador hotel that was the real hinge between the Cold War and the Age of Terror; the Chilean shopping malls that reveal the true architecture of neoliberal consumerism; or the Gabriel García Márquez story that is a telling parable of bare life. In short, "you might almost believe," as French novelist Georges Perec notes in another context, that the two levels of text "had nothing in common, but they are in fact inextricably bound up with each other."[16]

A history of the contract also runs through my historical case studies. We see right at the outset of modern imperialism instances of contracts and compacts that fail to have their purported effect, not least the pact in the dark as the conquistadors read the so-called *Requerimiento*, designed to justify colonization to the natives, while its putative addressees were fast asleep in their beds. The pact does not establish the social relation it claims: that will have to be established by some other means, in this case by force. I analyze the theory of the contract in my concluding chapter, but the intervening historical analyses also involve failed pacts: a series of attempts to bind culture to state, or to secure the legitimacy of the state, that endlessly break down. Peronism, in chapter 1, is a compact between people and nation that is (almost) all-encompassing, that tries to sweep the people up in its promise of populist love that would come to stand in for the state, which spectacularly fell apart in the mid-1970s. Neoliberalism, illustrated in chapter 2 in its fatal dance with Peru's Sendero Luminoso during the early 1980s, is likewise expansive in its attempt to cement the whole of society to the state, but shatters in its encounter with the affect that it would abolish from civil society. In chapter 3 and its focus on the Salvadoran national liberation movement at its peak in the offensive of 1989, I examine insurgency and terror as the absolute limit of societies of control. The example of Chile in chapter 4, and its early 1990s transition from dictatorship to postdictatorship, considers everyday life and biopolitics, suggesting resonance and *conatus* (or striving) as concepts through which to understand the relation between culture and state, social movement and reproductive project. The concluding chapter revisits these case studies to recapitulate the crisis of the social contract in parallel with a theoretical argument concerning the multitude, the ambivalent and treacherous social subject that refuses all pacts and all solidarity. In the Epilogue, Venezuela's 1989 Caracazo and then the coup and countercoup of 2002 show how the multitude breaks even the contracts offered by Latin America's most successful pacted democracy and by its most promising instance of the current left turns, preferring unrepresented, perhaps unrepresentable, insurrection.

These case studies exemplify both the discontinuous history of state projects to bind the multitude and the unbroken red thread of the multitude's ever-expansive constituent power to which the state reacts. They point toward a history of the Latin American multitude through modernity: from the near mutiny on Columbus's first voyage of 1492 to the *chavista* counter-counterinsurgency of

2002. This history might also encompass indigenous revolts during the colonial period, the wars of independence in the 1820s, or late nineteenth-century immigration and urbanization. Among more recent movements, one might consider the Zapatista uprising in Mexico or the *piqueteros* in contemporary Argentina. This would be an underground, alternative history of Latin America that would tell of insurgencies but also the stratagems by which hegemonic projects have attempted to turn those insurgencies to the advantage of the state: from the New Laws of the Indies, the Bourbon reforms, or the postindependence settlement, to the twentieth-century history that is more fully outlined here. It is precisely such mechanisms of reactionary conversion — of culture into state, affect into emotion, habit into opinion, multitude into people, constituent into constituted power — that are the ultimate interest of this book.

This is a book about political theory and Latin America, not political theory in Latin America or Latin American political theory. Its juxtaposition of the two terms is not quite contingent, not quite necessary. In one sense, its analyses of Latin American history and politics are interchangeable, almost disposable. In another sense, they anchor the theoretical argument. In still another, they contaminate and decenter it. The theory of posthegemony draws from but is also tested by Latin American history. Deleuze, Bourdieu, and Negri are European theorists, but European theory's passage through Latin America relocates and dislocates that theory. Passing such theory (and the theory of posthegemony) through other contexts would dislocate it in other ways, forcing revision and reappraisal. At the same time, at least one of my examples is not strictly Latin American at all: for all Columbus's bluster in front of his crew on October 10, 1492, he had not yet "discovered" the continent that would become the Americas. Indeed, the term "Latin America" would not be coined for another 350 years, and even now one would be hard-pressed to define its limits. Part geographical, part political, part cultural, Latin America overspills its bounds: is Belize Latin America? Québec? Miami? Lavapiés, Madrid? The Gaucho Grill, Manchester? Elsewhere I argue that Latin America becomes viral, diffusely global, in contemporary postmodernity.[17] But the history of the conquest, of the colony and its immense transatlantic trade, of populism and neoliberalism, shows that Latin America has always been global, has always directly affected and decentered the global system. The Latin American multitude goes beyond regional borders to infiltrate the metropolis.

Perhaps posthegemony starts in Latin America, or in discussions of Latin America, but that is no reason for it to stop there. After all, most everything begins in Latin America: modernity, nationalism, the industrial revolution, among other world-historical processes.[18] The theories that are the object of my critique — cultural studies and civil society theory — also have a hidden Latin American history. Returning the theory of hegemony (via Laclau) and the theory of civil society (via Cohen and Arato) to a Latin American milieu repositions those theories in the contexts for which they are most adequate. I give those theories their best shot: not only do I choose what I claim are their strongest and most developed articulations (in Laclau and in Cohen and Arato), I also test them in contexts that should be favorable to their assumptions. Hence the choice of locations in which to test the theory of posthegemony: if posthegemony can do a better job of explaining the Central American liberation movements (the point of entry for cultural studies in Latin America) and the transition from dictatorship in the Southern Cone (favored locale for civil society theory), then it is all the more adequate to explain other conjunctures. This is why I am happy to leave, say, *zapatismo* or the *piqueteros* out of my analysis, even though these are the movements that have to date most attracted scholars who work with theorists such as Deleuze and Negri.[19] I take for granted that posthegemony best explains these phenomena, if it also best explains the FMLN and the Chilean new social movements. In other words, although the theory of posthegemony arises from a specific Latin American context, it is not beholden to any one location. It is, I hope, portable. With every iteration, however, the theory is bound to change. Something always escapes!

Christophe Colomb appaise une revolte à bord (Christopher Columbus puts down an attempted mutiny). Nineteenth-century French lithograph. Courtesy of the Library of Congress Prints and Photographs Division, negative no. LC-USZ62-20454.

Prologue

October 10, 1492

When we reach the sea we'll build a bigger boat and sail north to take Trinidad away from the Spanish Crown. From there we'll go and take Mexico from Cortez. What a great betrayal that will be. We will then control all of New Spain. And we will stage history as others stage plays.

—Aguirre, *Wrath of God*

The Fiction of Hegemony

Even empires seek validation. No power can subsist on coercion alone. Hence Antonio Gramsci's famous distinction between "hegemony" and "direct domination": hegemony is "the 'spontaneous' consent given by the great masses of the population to the general direction imposed on social life by the dominant social group," and direct domination is exercised by "the apparatus of state coercive power which 'legally' enforces discipline on those groups which do not 'consent' either actively or passively." Hegemony, in fact, is primary: for Gramsci, power is grounded in consent, and force is employed only secondarily, "in moments of crisis and command when spontaneous consent has failed." Coercion supplements consent, rather than vice versa. Hegemony is, in Gramsci's view, the bedrock of social order. It is through the pedagogical activities of intellectuals in civil society that the state maintains its grip over the exploited, and the dominant group cements the "prestige" that it "enjoys because of its position and function in the world of production."[1]

At first sight, the *Requerimiento* that justified Spanish claims to the Americas is a classic illustration of the relation between hegemony and coercion. Formulated in 1512 or 1513 by legal scholar Juan López Palacios Rubios, the *Requerimiento* ("Requirement" or "Summons") was a text to be read by the conquistadors when they encountered indigenous peoples. The document filled a hole in Spain's legal claim to the New World, complementing and rationalizing the traditional European law of conquest. It outlines the case for the Empire's legitimacy, based on the papal donation of the New World to Castile in 1493, by way of a brief history of God's creation from Adam to the Spanish monarchs Fernando and Juana. Above all, it offers its indigenous addressees a choice: submit, or face violent subjugation. "Wherefore as best we can, we ask and require you," the declaration states, "that you consider what we have said to you, and that you take the time that shall be necessary to understand and deliberate upon it." Its audience is then to "consent and give place that these religious fathers should declare and preach to you the aforesaid." Should, however, they refuse their " 'spontaneous' consent" to occupation and Christian preaching, the indigenous are to expect the worst: "We shall powerfully enter into your country, and shall make war against you in all ways and manners that we can."[2] This is hegemony as a pedagogic enterprise designed to legitimate power, backed up by the threat of coercive discipline: the *Requerimiento* appears to encapsulate Gramscian theory in a nutshell.

On closer examination, however, Spanish practice had little in common with hegemony theory. The indigenous were seldom if ever given any real opportunity to consent. Most obviously, the *Requerimiento* was written in Spanish, a language that they did not speak. How would they agree to what they could not comprehend? Even where there was some attempt at translation, "the interpreters themselves did not understand what the document said."[3] Moreover, as historian Lewis Hanke notes, the circumstances in which it was spoken "might tax the reader's patience and credulity, for the Requirement was read to trees and empty huts when no Indians were to be found. Captains muttered its theological phrases into their beards on the edge of sleeping Indian settlements."[4] Sometimes the invaders read the document only after they had already made prisoners of the natives. At best the exercise devolved into a dialogue of the dumb, as when the Zuni Indians in what is now New Mexico responded to the reading with a ritual of their own, laying down "a barrier of sacred cornmeal" to prevent the Spaniards from entering the town.[5] No wonder historian Henry Kamen calls "the final result . . . little more than grotesque"; he reports that even the document's author "realized it was farcical."[6] Spanish chronicler Gonzalo Fernández de Oviedo is said to have commented to his compatriot Pedrarias Dávila that "these Indians have no wish to listen to the theology of this Requirement, nor do you have any obligation to make them try and understand it."[7] Contrary to claims that the *Requerimiento* was an instance of "Spanish rulers requir[ing] subject peoples to reiterate and reaffirm Spanish hegemony on a regular basis,"[8] in fact here hegemony is not at issue. The indigenous never had the option to consent; they were in no position to reaffirm anything.

Affects and Habits

Despite its transparent fictiveness and patent absurdity, the *Requerimiento* still served a purpose. For it was aimed not at the indigenous, but at the Spanish. Under the guise of an appeal to the consent of the subjugated, it shaped the habits and affects of the subjugators. The very fact of its redundant reiteration reveals that it was an exercise in habituation. And it was repeated for the Spaniards, not for their victims, who heard it only once, if at all. Each time the conquistadors recited the ritual declaration, their desires were synchronized and unified as part of a joint project. Rather than a gesture of incorporation, the edict was an act of constitution. Its confident self-justifications obscure the fact that it was needed only because the imperial state was so weak. It enfolded these European adventurers' often excessive energies into an enterprise directed as though from above. The *Requerimiento* had nothing to do with any putative hegemonic project; it was a properly posthegemonic mechanism. It worked all the better precisely because it appeared to be part of a campaign, however ridiculous and ineffective, to win hearts and minds, precisely because its object seemed to be elsewhere. The Spaniards could feel superior to the dumb Indians who did not know what had hit them, but they themselves were as much in the dark as anybody else. The *Requerimiento* functioned far beneath consciousness or ideology.

Bartolomé de las Casas, the sixteenth-century Dominican priest and defender of the indigenous, provides one version of the *Requerimiento* ritual. He tells us that when the Spaniards

> learned that there was gold in a particular town or village... [they made] their way there at dead of night, when the inhabitants were all in bed and sound asleep and, once they got within, say, half a league of the town itself, read out the terms of this edict, proclaiming (and only to themselves): "Leaders and citizens of such-and-such a town of this Mainland. Be it known to you that there is one true God, one Pope, and one King of Castile who is the rightful owner of all these lands. You are hereby summoned to pay allegiance, etc. Should you fail to do so, take notice that we shall make just war upon you, and your lives and liberty will be forfeit, etc." Then, in the early hours of the morning, when the poor people were still innocently abed with their wives and their children, they would irrupt into the town, setting fire to the houses and burning the women and children alive and often the men, too, before the poor wretches realized what was happening.[9]

Asleep in their beds, at dead of night, with the Spaniards half a league away, the indigenous are literally kept at a distance. Cultural critic Alberto Moreiras describes the *Requerimiento* as "differential inclusion"; but here the indigenous are not included at all. The native inhabitants can neither accept nor reject the choice that the Spaniards offer. They are beyond the pale of any possible community. Everything takes place before consciousness can take hold, "before the poor wretches realized what was happening." The invaders are speaking "only to themselves." But the mechanism in which they are participating depends no more on their understanding than it does on that of their victims. Moreiras points out that the indigenous inhabit a space that is "already marked by death and remains as such illegible."[10] The *Requerimiento*, too, is illegible, however much it is read: it defies interpretation, as if to show that its meaning is of little consequence.

Subalternist historian Patricia Seed shows that the *Requerimiento* drew heavily on the Islamic tradition of *jihad*, or holy war; it was a hybrid text that "often led to considerable incomprehension by traditional Christian observers both inside and outside Spain." Unheard by its notional addressees, and almost as mystifying even to those who pronounced it, the edict's manifest content is beside the point, just as "whether the Spanish conquerors believed in it or found it personally compelling or convincing was irrelevant."[11]

The text appears to seek consent and so to expand the community of believers, but those to whom it offers that possibility remain out of earshot, while those who are already within the circle are there regardless of any beliefs they might hold. The *Requerimiento* is comparable to the Bible proffered before the Inca Atahualpa in Cajamarca as the conquistador Gonzalo Pizarro advanced in his conquest of what is now Peru. The indigenous emperor threw the book to the ground because it did not "speak" to him; this sacrilege toward the holy word was taken by the Europeans to be proof of his barbarism and justification for bloodshed. Yet, as cultural critic Antonio Cornejo Polar observes, the Bible would have been equally illegible to most Spaniards, including Pizarro himself, not least because it was written in Latin.[12] The book was more fetish than text, a shibboleth whose signification was purely incidental. Neither the Bible nor the *Requerimiento* were documents that demanded interpretation; they were instead touchpapers for the violent explosion of imperial expansion, code words in the "protocol for conquest" enacted by the Spaniards in the dark.[13]

Las Casas had no illusions about the Spaniards' motivations: they were driven by the search for gold. This was no civilizing mission. Indeed, the Dominican's complaint was that the *Requerimiento* bore no relationship to the reality of Spanish practice. Las Casas was hardly an anti-imperialist. If anything, his campaign was for the Spanish state to give substance to the fiction of hegemony.[14] For Las Casas, the scandal was the unbridled desire that reduced the conquistadors to savages more dangerous than the indigenous peoples themselves; their "blind and obsessive greed" made them "more inhumane and more vicious than savage tigers, more ferocious than lions or than ravening wolves."[15] But he failed to see that the *Requerimiento* channeled that affect. It placed the lust for gold under the sign of a narrative of progress, and more importantly it unified the conquistadors, huddled together in an alien landscape. The act of reading helped bind the affect mobilized in their hunt for gold, counteracting that affect's centrifugal tendencies by organizing it as part of an ecclesiastical, imperial, and monarchical hierarchy before the men were let loose as a war machine "irrupt[ing] into the town."

The *Requerimiento* consolidates relations between the Spanish conquistadors after the fact of domination; it embodies them as agents of the state, as subjects of constituted power. Everybody knows that the text itself is unpersuasive! Instead of persuading the colonized, it works on the colonizers to establish a common habitus that lies beneath ideology and beneath hegemony. As the invaders repeatedly intone these words that they themselves barely understand, they become habituated to a ritual through which the Spanish state, even at great distance, seeks to regulate their activities. Its men will at least have been singing from the same hymnbook, whatever their beliefs about or consent to the claims made in the hymns themselves. This is "dominance without hegemony," in subaltern studies theorist Ranajit Guha's words, "the fabrication of a spurious hegemony"[16] that nobody believes, but that serves (thanks to the notarization and record keeping that the edict itself demands) to emplot Latin America within a historical narrative generated by the European state. The subalterns will, simply, be eliminated, their culture excluded from the ambit of a Christian universe defined in terms of the centrality and rights of the Catholic monarchy. But the indigenous are never really a threat to those rights: the danger lies within, from the possibility that the conquistadors themselves might (as depicted in Werner Herzog's film *Aguirre, Wrath of God* [1972]) establish a counterstate on American soil. Behind the *Requerimiento* is the fear of betrayal, of sedition, of the threat posed by the men-at-arms who purportedly represent the Crown abroad.

The Multitude and the Pact

Postcolonial studies focuses on the relation between colonizer and colonized, between Empire and its outside. It thereby takes the state, and what goes on inside, for granted. Empire encounters the subaltern at its limit, but it already carries a multitude within. The agents of imperialism are as much escaping state control as expanding it. Colonialism's weak point is always the passage between center and periphery, metropolis and colony. The Spanish Empire was forced to establish an immense bureaucratic apparatus to guard this intermediate space, threatened constantly by piracy, fraud, desertion, and mutiny. The name given to this bureaucracy was the Casa de Contratación: the "Contraction House," or Office of Contracts. The European state depended on a diffuse group of adventurers and ne'er-do-wells to expand its sphere of influence until it covered the entire known world; but it had simultaneously to reign in this renegade subjectivity, to maintain the bounds of the social contract. Empire stretched the state to its limit: the Crown's gravest problem was always its "inability... to control events from a distance."[17] The multitude, a motley crew that resisted authority, representation, or leadership, constituted Empire but also undermined the very power that it brought into being.

Christopher Columbus was a Genoese adventurer who believed he had visionary inspiration. For over a decade, he hawked his idea for an expedition over the Atlantic to a variety of private and public interests. In the end, he won the backing of the Spanish monarchy, but his enterprise was essentially a private one. Spain itself barely existed as a modern nation-state: the crowns of Castile and Aragon had come together with the wedding of Ferdinand and Isabella in 1469, but it was only with the "reconquest" of Andalusia and the expulsion of Jews and Moors from the Iberian peninsula two decades later that the state could even aspire to the fantasy of territorial integrity and ethnic and cultural homogeneity. Columbus gained royal approval for his voyage just days after the king and queen rode into Granada in triumph in January 1492. This year of settling boundaries was also a year of great movements of peoples, "swarms of refugees." Jews who were camped around the ports and on seagoing vessels were given the order to "leave port on August 2, 1492, the day before Columbus set sail."[18] In the early morning of August 3, as Spain consolidated its territorial and ethnic limits, Columbus's small fleet—the *Niña*, *Pinta*, and *Santa María*—constituted a seemingly insignificant line of flight westward. Something always escapes.

Columbus's crew had reason to flee. Tradition portrays them as convicts motivated by the royal pardon they received for signing up.[19] Historian and sailor Samuel Eliot Morison plays down this account of a crew "composed of desperate characters, criminals, and jailbirds," but he does confirm that at least four of the men had indeed been reprieved from death row by enlisting.[20] Even the full-time seafarers among them operated at the margins of the law. Columbus's main associate, Martín Alonso Pinzón, who captained the *Pinta* while his brother Vicente took charge of the *Niña*, had "like many other mariners... occasionally engaged in piracy as well as legitimate trade."[21] This was an expedition packed with potentially unruly subordinates, exacerbated by an imbalance between crew and officers in that each ship's crew was exceptionally large, perhaps double the normal complement.[22] In any case, Columbus had trouble with his men from the start. Even before they set sail, several of the crew on the *Pinta* "had been grumbling and making difficulties," and were suspected of sabotaging the ship at the Canaries.[23] Once underway, the admiral was increasingly worried about a possible mutiny, and with good cause: Las Casas reports that as early as September 24, when they were almost exactly in mid-Atlantic, some of his crew argued "that the best thing of all would be to throw [Columbus] overboard one night and put it about that he had fallen while trying to take a reading of the Pole Star with his quadrant or astrolabe."[24]

The voyage is longer and farther than any of the men had expected. From early on, Columbus is aware that the sheer extent to which they are collectively venturing into the unknown is a likely cause for dissent. From September 9 (just three days after leaving the Canaries) he maintains a double log, with "two reckonings, one false and the other true," of the distance traveled each day, because he is worried that his crew might "take fright or lose courage if the voyage were long."[25] Only landfall will resolve the men's concerns, yet land is frustratingly elusive. Expectation runs high, however. From September 14 Columbus reports that there are many sure signs of land, provoking a veritable interpretosis: there are no innocent objects in the Atlantic traversed by this convoy. On September 16, seeing "many patches of very green seaweed, which appeared only recently to have been uprooted[, a]ll considered therefore that they were near some island." Likewise, a live crab on September 17 can be taken to be "a certain sign of land." On September 25, both Columbus and the crew are convinced that land has been sighted. They fall on their knees to give thanks to God, but "what they had taken for land was no land but cloud." A week or so later, these "many signs of land," previously heralded by Columbus with enthusiasm, have to be discounted as the crew lobbies for the expedition to return to investigate.[26] Columbus rejects their proposal, and insists that they continue on westward. Historians William and Carla Phillips argue that he must have wanted "to maintain his authority over the captains and their crews. . . . Allowing side excursions in search of islands would diminish the aura of certainty that he had been at pains to protect."[27] Previous voyagers (notably Bartholomew Dias rounding the Cape of Good Hope in 1487) had been forced by their crews to abandon further exploration; Columbus, too, is now seriously running the risk of mutiny.

As October arrives, the situation deteriorates. By October 1 there is a discrepancy of 121 leagues between Columbus's "true calculation" of the distance they have traveled and "the lower figure... shown to the men."[28] By October 11 that discrepancy will have risen to at least 195 leagues, or almost a quarter again of the extent that the men are told they have traveled. Yet even the phony log shows that the fleet has sailed much farther than Columbus had predicted. In this context, what Morison calls the "incipient mutiny" of late September develops fast: "Columbus and the Pinzons needed all their moral force and prestige to prevent outbreaks or even mutiny."[29] On October 6, in an "acrid interview,"[30] Martín Pinzón himself questions the route they are taking, suggesting they should veer farther south, but Columbus countermands his associate. One version of the admiral's log has him reporting: "My decision has not pleased the men, for they continue to murmur and complain. Despite their grumblings I held fast to the west."[31] The same day, in response to the near-mutinous atmosphere, with the crew of the *Santa María* demanding that the fleet turn for Spain, he summons a council of his captains; both the Pinzón brothers are persuaded to support the decision to continue.[32] October 7 brings another false sighting of land, and Columbus changes his bearing slightly to the south. Two days later he tacks north. But by October 10, "the men could bear no more; they complained of the length of the voyage."[33]

In Morison's words, "October 10 was the most critical day of the entire voyage, when the enterprise came nearest to failure," as "all the smoldering discontent of the men flared up into open mutiny." Columbus "encouraged them as best he could": he held out "high hopes of the gains they could make" and "he added that it was no use their complaining, because he had reached the Indies and must sail on until with the help of Our Lord he discovered land."[34] Perhaps it was the multiple signs that led Columbus to claim that they had already "reached" the Indies, though if the signs could have been believed they would have seen land long before. Perhaps he was also referring to the fact that, by any measure, the fleet was now more than 800 leagues from Spain, and he had repeatedly declared that land would be sighted at 750 leagues. But these arguments were now wearing thin. Even the ships' captains were turning against their admiral. "The mutinous crewmen began to rattle their weapons."[35] The admiral had to forestall panic among his crew, on whom he was totally dependent. There was no one more vulnerable than Columbus, as he himself would later lament loudly and persistently.

Columbus makes a pact with his men. The compromise he suggests is that "they would continue on their westward course for two more days (or three or four; accounts vary). If they had not found land at the end of that period, they would turn back."[36] The precise details of the agreement are sketchy: it is omitted from the admiral's log and will become a bone of contention in a long-running court case years later in which the Crown will try to argue for the Pinzón brothers' share of the voyage's success.[37] Some accounts claim that it is Columbus who has to be encouraged to continue, and others that the Pinzón brothers are fully part of the mutiny. What is clear is that only this last-ditch attempt at compromise keeps the voyage going on October 10, 1492, and that there are good reasons why even Columbus might be losing heart. But an indication of the type of pact he might have made comes from the admiral's second voyage, in 1494. Then, he and his men are reconnoitering the coast of Cuba until, "fed by frustration and fantasy," Columbus gives up when he begins to suspect that it is not in fact part of the Asian mainland. This realization would threaten his cherished belief that he had indeed found a new route to the East Indies. So he again attempts a contract with his crew. "He called upon the ship's scrivener," Fernández-Armesto reports, "to record the oath of almost every man in the fleet that Cuba was a mainland and that no island of such magnitude had ever been known.... They further swore that had they navigated farther they would have encountered the Chinese." If the men break their oath, they face dire consequences: "a fine of ten thousand maravedis and the loss by excision of their tongues."[38] If they refuse to abide by Columbus's fantasy, the crew lose their place within this newly constituted imperial order and are cast into mute subalternity.

On October 10 of the first voyage, the fictions validating Columbus's control are breaking down: he has given his men a false account of the distance traveled and has argued that they have already reached land, but the crew are no longer so prepared to swear agreement. They are an unruly multitude on the verge of overthrowing their master. His skin is only saved when, late the following night, the fleet finally makes landfall. Now the constitutive tension of Empire can be displaced elsewhere. Perhaps others will have better luck imposing the fiction of a contract, the illusion of consent. Or perhaps the slippage between constituent and constituted power will remain an open if unacknowledged wound throughout modernity.

Part I

CRITIQUE

1

Argentina 1972: Cultural Studies and Populism

> *The most successful ideological effects are those which have no need of words, and ask no more than complicitous silence. It follows, incidentally, that any analysis of ideologies, in the narrow sense of "legitimating discourses," which fails to include an analysis of the corresponding institutional mechanisms is liable to be no more than a contribution to the efficacy of those ideologies.*
>
> —Pierre Bourdieu, *Outline of a Theory of Practice*

> *In Argentina, the people are what they are but rarely what they seem. Our country is not knowable on the basis of the forces that meet the eye but through the sources—always disguised and underground—that feed those forces.*
>
> —Tomás Eloy Martínez, *The Perón Novel*

Hegemony theory has become the ubiquitous common sense of cultural studies. This first chapter is a critique of both by means of an examination of their shared populism. After defining and historicizing the field, I embark on a close reading of the Argentine theorist Ernesto Laclau, whose version of hegemony theory is the most fully developed and influential for cultural studies. Laclau's definition of hegemony is embedded in a series of reflections on populism, especially in his earliest book, *Politics and Ideology in Marxist Theory*, and in his latest, *On Populist Reason*. I trace the development of Laclau's theory, showing how from the start it simply mimics the logic of populism. Laclau sets out to differentiate between a left populism and a populism of the right, a distinction that would be essential for cultural studies to make good on its political pretensions, but ultimately he fails to establish such a difference, even to his own satisfaction. I then move to the relationship between populism and the state to show, again through a reading of Laclau, how hegemony theory and cultural studies alike repeat the populist sleight of hand in which a purported anti-institutionalism in fact enables the state apparently to disappear. Hegemony stands in for politics, and screens off the ways in which states anchor social order through habituation, under the cover of a fictional social contract. Throughout, in counterpoint, I offer an alternative account of the Argentine Peronism from which Laclau's theory stems.

Defining Cultural Studies

Cultural studies resists definition. As Cary Nelson, Paula Treichler, and Lawrence Grossberg state in the introduction to their landmark collection *Cultural Studies*, "it is probably impossible to agree on any essential definition or unique narrative of cultural studies." Cultural studies is, they continue, "a diverse and often contentious exercise, encompassing different positions and trajectories in specific contexts, addressing many questions, drawing nourishment from multiple roots, and shaping itself within different institutions and locations." But cultural studies' indeterminateness, they argue, is also its strength. Indeed, flaunted and celebrated in their description, its diversity is portrayed as essential: "Cultural studies *needs* to remain open to unexpected, unimagined, even uninvited possibilities. No one can hope to control these developments" (emphasis added). Though they claim that cultural studies "cannot be just anything," by stressing its uncontrolled mutability, Nelson, Treichler, and Grossberg forestall efforts to define or delimit the enterprise that they are introducing.[1]

Resistance to definition, however, is itself a defining trait: cultural studies is defined first of all by its mutability. This in turn accounts for a second characteristic: though it may not be pinned down by any one "unique narrative," cultural studies is indeed narrated; it is a repertory of stories. In the words of Stuart Hall, a key player in the field's development, "cultural studies is a discursive formation" that "has multiple discourses; it has a number of different histories." Moreover, Hall observes that telling the tale of cultural studies often involves "speaking autobiographically," not so much to assume the authority of experience as to invoke the inconstancy of memory and anecdotalism. "I'm going to tell you about my own take," Hall recounts, "not because it is the truth or the only way of telling the story. I myself have told it many other ways before; and I intend to tell it in a different way later."[2] As Nelson, Treichler, and Grossberg put it, cultural studies is "constantly writing and rewriting its own history in order to make sense of itself, constructing and reconstructing itself in response to new challenges." They claim that this means that "cultural studies is always contextual," but it is better described as always contextual*ized*.[3] Cultural studies' characteristic diversity demands metanarratives through which the story of its resistance to definition can be repeatedly replayed, reemphasized, and redefined. For Richard Johnson, formerly the director of the Birmingham Centre for Contemporary Cultural Studies, "cultural studies should be recurrently reinvented."[4] By definition, then, the metanarratives of cultural studies have always to be declared incomplete: they imply ever new narratives and the possibility that everything about the story they tell can be rewritten. Everything, that is, except its infinite openness to rewriting. So Nelson, Treichler, and Grossberg can confidently predict the unpredictable: "It is fair to say, then, that the *future* of cultural studies will include rereadings of its past that we cannot yet anticipate."[5]

One story told about cultural studies begins in 1950s Britain, and with the literary critic Richard Hoggart, the historian E. P. Thompson, and above all the critic and theorist Raymond Williams. Emerging from the British "New Left," the publication of Hoggart's *The Uses of Literacy* in 1957, Williams's *Culture and Society* in 1958, and then Thompson's *The Making of the English Working Class* in 1963 collectively heralded a new set of intellectual and political concerns. These authors broke from the condemnation of mass culture prevalent in literary studies, from a focus on the economic or the elite in history, as well as from the orthodoxies of any established political party. Their small group of intellectuals and critics believed that "any political project for socialism had to connect with immediate experience or lived 'culture' of ordinary people whose action ought to count in politics."[6] Putting culture and "ordinary people" at the center of their political concerns, Hoggart, Thompson, and Williams proposed an expanded definition of culture (no longer simply high culture) as well as an expanded conception of politics (no longer simply formal politics). Culture is a "whole way of life," Williams argued; it is also a "whole way of struggle," responded Thompson.[7]

Many early cultural studies practitioners were located at the margins of established institutions; discussion took place in new journals such as the *Universities and Left Review*. But in 1964 Hoggart founded the Centre for Contemporary Cultural Studies at the University of Birmingham, giving cultural studies an institutional base. The Centre, from 1968 under Stuart Hall's directorship, trained a generation of graduate students and led cultural studies in new directions, especially in its 1970s heyday. Students undertook ethnographic accounts of popular and working-class culture (such as Paul Willis's *Learning to Labor*). The Centre pioneered studies of the mass media. There was increased attention to race and gender.[8] Continental theory had a significant impact: first the work of Louis Althusser and Jacques Lacan, disseminated through the *New Left Review* and the film studies journal *Screen*, changed and to some extent split the field; then, from the mid-1970s, readings of Gramsci had a decisive influence on Hall and the Centre. The late 1970s "*Screen* / Centre debate" pitted a psychoanalytic and poststructuralist "screen theory" against the Centre's Gramscian and ethnographic "culturalism."

By the 1980s, cultural studies was flourishing. Hall moved to the Open University, reaching out to new, nonacademic audiences with critiques of Thatcherism and the politics of post-Fordism and postmodernism. Cultural studies' founders, such as Williams and Thompson, were now well-known. The Centre's work attracted growing interest, and its former students were making names for themselves in their own right. Interest came particularly from the United States: in the 1980s, cultural studies crossed the Atlantic. With its popularization and Americanization, much of its specific political context and rationale was lost. As it expanded, the field became attractive to publishers, who put out increasing numbers of cultural studies texts, a far cry from the Birmingham Centre's mimeographed working papers. This success caused some anguish; for instance, Hall warned of the "danger in the institutionalization of cultural studies in this highly rarified and enormously elaborated and well funded professional world of American academic life."[9]

But if cultural studies became less immediately political in its discussions of postmodern culture and readings of Madonna or Rambo, it did give more formalist or ludic approaches to culture a critical edge that they had lacked. Talk of class and socialism may not have translated easily to United States environs. But the Gramscian concept of hegemony, especially as retheorized in Ernesto Laclau and Chantal Mouffe's *Hegemony and Socialist Strategy*, certainly did. American cultural studies soon spoke the vocabulary of power in terms of hegemony and counterhegemony, resistance, transgression, and subversion.

Cultural studies is now global. Beyond the United States, it spawned a distinctive strain early on in Australia, then also in other Anglophone countries. The late 1990s saw the *European Journal of Cultural Studies*, major international conferences of cultural studies in places such as Finland, and soon the *International Journal of Cultural Studies* and the International Association of Cultural Studies. There are journals or edited collections of Spanish Cultural Studies, French Cultural Studies, Latin American Cultural Studies, and more. And while the fervor of the mid-1990s may now have died down, if anything this is further evidence of institutional success: academic job postings ask for expertise in cultural studies almost as a matter of course. The vocabulary of cultural studies has found a place in disciplines from literary studies to sociology, art history to anthropology. Cultural studies has even impacted the public sphere, not least thanks to a generation of undergraduate students who took up work in the media and advertising. The British art theorist Adrian Rifkin gives the example of the children's television program *Teletubbies*, which he tells us is made by "people one had taught or had been friends of people one had taught or whatever. . . . One of the great achievements of cultural studies, if you like, is *Teletubbies*."[10]

It is easy to lament the decline and banalization of cultural studies: from *The Making of the English Working Class* to the making of *Teletubbies*. But a populist championing of the "ordinary" has always been at its heart. This embrace of the everyday has gone hand in hand with a characteristically populist suspicion of academic institutions. Richard Johnson, who took over at the Birmingham Centre after Hall's departure, recalls that "In CCCS, a distance from the academy was often linked with an affinity for other forms of knowledge and culture, especially with popular or 'commonsense' forms."[11] If there is any consistent thread in the history of cultural studies, it is its populist impulse. It is thanks to this populism that cultural studies has been so flexible, so hard to pin down, and therefore also so successful. Its populism has helped provide cultural studies, even at its most celebrated, with an aura of embattled rebelliousness. In this chapter I examine the populism of cultural studies, and its effects. Through a critical reading of Laclau's influential work, I focus on the relation between hegemony theory and populism. And I show how the favored political conceit of a struggle for hegemony, far from being a mark of radicalism, in fact ensures that cultural studies remains blind to its own limitations and renders its purported anti-institutionalism vapid.

A specifically Latin American cultural studies is now in vogue, although still controversial. There is the *Journal of Latin American Cultural Studies* and there are various centers and graduate programs in the subject, such as at the University of Manchester. Representative samples of the field include Mabel Moraña's collection *Nuevas perspectivas desde/sobre América Latina* and Ana del Sarto, Alicia Ríos, and Abril Trigo's *The Latin American Cultural Studies Reader.* Here, concepts and references derived from U.S. and U.K. cultural studies (and also from continental theory and postcolonial theory such as subaltern studies) meet a tradition of Latin American writing on culture that could be traced through figures such as Octavio Paz, Antonio Cornejo Polar, Angel Rama, and Roberto Schwarz or, earlier, José Carlos Mariátegui, José Enrique Rodó, and Domingo Sarmiento. This mixture is in some ways natural: cultural studies and the Latin American tradition of cultural reflection overlap in that both employ expanded conceptions of culture and politics. Cultural studies' concern with hegemony resonates powerfully in a Latin American context where politics and culture have long been obviously intertwined. On the other hand, Latin American thought has also been preoccupied with issues less prominent within cultural studies, above all the question of national or regional identity. Moreover, most Latin American intellectuals explicitly repudiate populism. This is the basis on which the Argentine Beatriz Sarlo, for instance, whom others often associate with cultural studies, in fact disowns it as a "neopopulism seduced by the charms of industrial culture."[12] But it is the provenance of cultural studies, the narrative that locates its origin in Europe or North America, that has raised most hackles. As the literary and political theorist Alberto Moreiras observes, resistance to cultural studies is framed as "a defense of the national or the regional order against an interference that could only be understood as neocolonial, since it emanated from a transnational space that was hegemonized by the U.S. metropole." What matters for its critics is not what cultural studies is, but where it comes from and its institutional implications. This explains the counterintuitive fact that so many of those who oppose cultural studies have been "intellectuals whose credentials as thinkers in the tradition of cultural studies are impeccable."[13] Moreover, and despite explicit repudiation, their resistance often repeats populist gestures, albeit in the service of what Moreiras terms "a sort of antipopulist populism" whose trait is a nostalgic investment in a long lost "national-populist state." In short, the premises of Latin American resistance to cultural studies are a defense of national and regional tradition against unfamiliar and exotic imports, and a rejection of the metropolitan academy in favor of a broader range of writers and thinkers. This opposition therefore ironically mimics cultural studies' own valorization of the everyday and suspicion of the academic. No wonder the debate exhibits so much "babelic confusion."[14]

Latin American cultural studies can and should be the site of a more substantial encounter between the cultural studies tradition and a Latin Americanism that poses new challenges to that tradition. Latin American cultural studies should prompt a crisis and critique of both Latin Americanism and cultural studies. Such a Latin American cultural studies still has to be constructed. Moreiras's work is one of the few indications of what such a double critique would involve; this book aims to be another.

Mutable and narrated, cultural studies is above all *articulated*. Hence its affinity with the theory of hegemony, which can be defined as at root a theory of articulation and its political effects. Articulation is both connection and discursive expression: articulated literally means "jointed" (as in an articulated lorry or truck), but it has come to mean "pronounced distinctly," "uttered," or "expressed in words." Cultural studies mutates because its elements are constantly connected in new ways and to new positions and experiences; it establishes a sense of continuity as its various disjoint histories are narrated and discursively expressed. It is no surprise, then, that cultural studies should so successfully endure, spread, and replicate: cultural studies is the very picture of hegemony itself. As the theorist and philosopher Simon Critchley explains, "the key term in the theory of hegemony . . . is the notion of *hegemonic articulation*."[15] Hegemony, too, is "conjunctural," in Grossberg's words, a "struggle to articulate" and "a matter of the articulated relations" that "is never securely achieved."[16] Hegemony theory is concerned with the ways in which such discursive articulations bind, however tenuously, discrete units to form an ordered social whole. Hence critic Jennifer Daryl Slack's concise definition of hegemony as "a process by which a hegemonic class articulates (or coordinates) the interests of social groups such that those groups actively 'consent' to their subordinated status." Hegemony is a process of articulation, and cultural studies, narrativized as an articulated project, mimics the process by which hegemony is achieved, as cultural studies itself understands it. Cultural studies is itself, then, a "rearticulation of articulation," a kind of second-order hegemony.[17]

Cultural studies' mimicry of the workings of hegemony is no accident: its practitioners often express their rueful admiration for the hegemonic projects they aim to contest. Cultural studies manifests an ambivalent regard for the successes and attractions of the modern and postmodern culture industries. The cultural studies critic is often dancing in spite of him or herself.[18] Grossberg takes to task "critics [who] often ignore popular culture's immediacy, its physicality, and its fun: its very popularity."[19] Cultural studies wants to be like the customary objects of its critique: it wants to be popular, as they are; it seeks to become hegemonic. Some critics introduce a concept of "counterhegemony" to suggest that the hegemony that cultural studies (or the left) desires is distinct from the hegemony it opposes. Richard Johnson, for instance, conjures up the notion of a "political, critical, or revolutionary consciousness or counterhegemony, a universal or expansive opposition by which subordinated majorities transform the social order."[20] Johnson invokes Gramsci, but in fact the Italian theorist never uses the term "counterhegemony." There is no counterhegemony, opposed to hegemony; it is but another version of hegemony, another appeal to the popular.

However much cultural studies envies and mimics the hegemony that it claims to oppose, Nelson, Treichler, and Grossberg insist that it is a political enterprise as well as an intellectual one, and that it is located firmly on the left. They quote approvingly media critic James Carey's judgment that cultural studies leads "to a revolutionary line of political action or, at the least, a major project of social reconstruction."[21] For a disenchanted, post-Marxist West, cultural studies inherits Marxism's position as social conscience of the academy and as inspiration for struggles beyond it. Yet cultural studies rejects Marxism's focus on the working class and gives up on revolution in favor of Carey's "social reconstruction." The turn from Marxism is more pronounced now that cultural studies has become (itself) popular and as it has become institutionalized, especially in the United States. Cultural studies is therefore post-Marxist in two senses: it draws on Marxist categories (ideology, commodification) and theorists (Gramsci, Althusser); but it also replaces Marxism as the academy's preeminent radical theoretical and critical perspective. Populism replaces Marxism, as though one were the natural continuation of the other.

Alongside a critique of cultural studies and hegemony theory, in which I emphasize their shared populism, in this chapter I examine what is perhaps the most successful populist movement of all time: Peronism. There have been few if any political movements with more popular appeal. For over half a century, Peronism dominated Argentine political and cultural life; arguably, it still does. Its founders, Juan and Evita Perón, continued to exert enormous influence even long after their deaths, in 1974 and 1952 respectively. Indeed, especially in Evita's case, but also during Juan Perón's long exile from 1955 to 1973, their cultural importance was only accentuated by physical absence. Yet Peronism remains in many ways an enigma, a phenomenon hard to pin down. As historian Robert Crassweller states of Perón himself, "the parade of Peróns is endless." Crassweller adds that "one is tempted to conclude that... he was many persons – and therefore none."[22] Likewise the movement he founded: Peronism has been variously located across the political spectrum, from fascism to revolutionary socialism; Peronism's economic policies have included both classic protectionism and (with Carlos Menem, Argentina's president from 1989 to 1999) market-driven neoliberalism. In tune with this mutability, Peronism has been endlessly narrated, in a plethora of styles and hues, from Jorge Luis Borges and Adolfo Bioy Casares's "La fiesta del monstruo" to Tim Rice and Andrew Lloyd Webber's international hit musical *Evita.*[23]

There is no single good history of Peronism. A decent introduction is in Luis Alberto Romero's *A History of Argentina in the Twentieth Century,* while the best source for Perón's first presidency is probably Félix Luna's three-volume *Perón y su tiempo.* An army colonel, Perón came to prominence as secretary of labor in the military government of 1943 to 1945, a position from which he cultivated the unions and the workers' movement. Forced to resign and arrested in early October 1945 by an army leadership concerned about his growing popularity, Perón was freed after a multitudinous demonstration in his favor on October 17. But this demonstration did more than just free Perón; it is Peronism's founding moment and, in Romero's words, "inaugurated a new way of participating in politics through social mobilization." In power, after elections in 1946 that Perón won handsomely, Peronism was characterized by assiduous cultivation of its popular base, often through mass rallies and the rituals of mobilization, but also through policies directed at ensuring full employment and an improved standard of living for the regime's working-class base. Perón's (second) wife, María Eva Duarte, or Evita, became the movement's figurehead and mediator. Evita was adored by a working class that identified with her "plebeian voice," but she was vilified by a "polite society" for whom she symbolized all that was barbarous in "the regime's demagogic excesses."[24] Evita died, young, of ovarian cancer in 1952. Amid escalating conflicts with the church and the army, Perón was overthrown and exiled in 1955. For almost two decades, successive governments (military and civil) attempted to extirpate his memory from Argentine political culture. But Peronism's social base remained strong and in fact expanded in the late 1960s, as a generation of young radicals pursued revolutionary third-worldism in its name. Faced with growing social tensions, the rise of armed groups, and economic crisis, the government of General Alejandro Lanusse called for elections in 1973 and lifted proscriptions on political activity, paving the way for Perón's triumphant return. Perón's second presidency, however, was a failure. After a brief truce, violence flared up again, and the Peronist movement started to tear itself apart. Perón died in 1974 and his third wife, Isabel, became president. But she failed to curb the crisis and was deposed in the 1976 coup that ushered in a murderous military regime that would last until 1983. The first postdictatorship government was led by the Radical Party, but Peronism returned to power, albeit in rather different form, with the neoliberal president Carlos Menem from 1989 to 1999 and with a succession of administrations from 2001. As of 2010, Argentina's current president is also a Peronist: Cristina Fernández de Kirchner.

Peronism, too, is the very picture of hegemony. Its long-lasting ability to secure popular consent contrasts starkly with the coercion employed by Argentina's various military regimes. More than that: Peronism is the model for hegemony in that Laclau's theorization of the concept emerges from his analysis of Peronism. As Simon Critchley acknowledges, "Ernesto in English *sounds like* high theory. But Ernesto's theory is highly dependent upon the dynamics of populism in a South American context, obviously in Argentina—of which he has a perfect intuitive understanding."[25] Given the importance of the concept of hegemony, and above all Laclau's formulation, for cultural studies, a detour through Peronism maps out what I have elsewhere called a "secret history of cultural studies."[26] Reaching out to the global periphery but touching at the very heart of cultural studies, this secret history reframes hegemony theory. Yet in this chapter I also question the extent to which the theory explains even Peronism. Critchley's comment that Laclau's is an "intuitive understanding" of populism already indicates another approach. Instead of seeing it as a matter of hegemonic articulation, Peronism's hold is better attributed to the way it organizes intuition, instinct, and affect. Rather than an articulate appeal to ideology, Peronism is a prime example of the institutional inculcation of habit.

Cultural studies, hegemony, populism: these are slippery terms. But they are slippery in similar ways and for similar reasons. They are also circular: cultural studies turns to hegemony theory so as to secure its sense of radicalism and thereby to ward off the accusation of populism; but it occludes the fact that its theory of hegemony is premised on populism. Cultural studies has been elaborated around a populist desire (and a populist anxiety) that is at times repressed, at times expressed, but seldom theorized. Any theory of populism has been blocked by cultural studies' own populist impulses. In the rest of this chapter, by means of a close reading of Laclau's theory of hegemony, I pursue the question of cultural studies' populism, to pin down both populism and cultural studies. Laclau articulates the problem and challenge for cultural studies: to produce a theory and critique of populism; and to distinguish its political impulse and strategies from those managed by the state, by constituted power. I argue, however, that in the end Laclau, too, elides the question of the state, falling into the populist trap of substituting culture for the state, and hegemony for any other conception of politics.

Jim McGuigan, one of the few critics to consider the relation between cultural studies and populism, argues that "*a non-populist cultural studies is very nearly a contradiction in terms:* it is an academic game which might do better calling itself something else." He suggests that "the field of study is unintelligible without recognition of its populist impulses."[27] But a consideration of the consequences of cultural studies' populism does more than merely explain an academic movement that happens to be currently in vogue. It is also a step toward investigating the structure of the social field, and the relation between culture and politics more generally. For although cultural studies has become the vehicle for intellectuals looking to reinvent a certain image of the left, oppositional and engaged, its populist inclinations afford it little purchase against a new right, one of whose defining characteristics is often a rejuvenated populism. My argument, then, is in some ways similar to that of postcolonial theorist Timothy Brennan in *Wars of Position:* that left and right are increasingly blurred following what he terms the "turn" to theory of the late 1970s (when Laclau began his theoretical career with *Politics and Ideology in Marxist Theory*). But where Brennan's diagnosis is that today's leftist intellectuals have adopted an anarchist antistatism, I argue that in fact they occlude the state, taking it for granted in typical populist fashion. Indeed, my reading of Brennan's own case studies is that the right is aware that hegemony is not at issue; the left has been losing the culture wars because it is not yet posthegemonic. The left believes its own rhetoric; the right does not. Cultural studies emerged in the shadow of first Macmillan and then the ascendancy of Thatcher and Reagan: is it but a reflex of their populist discourse, or can it provide a critique of its own conditions of production? I have argued elsewhere that cultural studies needs to take the risk of becoming *un*popular, and should therefore turn from the people to the perspective of the multitude.[28] This is the approach that I develop further in this book's final chapter.

Populism is always a pleasing gesture, and so a temptation. But if those currently involved in cultural studies would resist that temptation, they may have to think seriously, as McGuigan suggests, of abandoning cultural studies as it is presently constituted. Cultural studies' theory of hegemony offers ever more critical targets and ammunition in the field of culture, but it fails to note the systemic relations between culture and the state, between ideologies and their "corresponding institutional mechanisms," in social theorist Pierre Bourdieu's phrase.[29] It misses the extent to which culture itself operates as a screen, a fetishized substitute, for the political logic of command. It passes over the ways in which power is entrenched as an affective relation, or as habit. Partaking in rather than criticizing a fetishism of culture, cultural studies is oblivious to, and even helps to hide, a recent vast expansion of political and state control. In the end, both the political populism of the right and the academic populism of the left perform the same function: they uphold a fiction of hegemony that perpetuates the dream of a harmonious social compact.

A Progressive Project: Populism

"Populism," writes political scientist Paul Taggart, "is ubiquitous in modern politics.... It permeates representative politics as a potential force." The "irony," he continues, is that "the impulse for populism comes from frustration with representative politics." Indeed, Taggart locates this frustration at the heart of the matter: "At its root, populism, as a set of ideas, has a fundamental ambivalence about politics, especially representative politics.... Populism is reluctantly political."[30] Populism is therefore a political antipolitics, or a politics expressed in antipolitical ways. Social theorists Yves Mény and Yves Surel describe this antipolitical negation that emerges from the heart of the political as "the pathology of democracy." Yet they hesitate over whether populism is disease, symptom, or cure, for at the same time they describe it as "one possible reaction to the malfunctioning of the political system."[31] Populism arises from a dissatisfaction with existing politics, but also as an attempt to fix its representational failures. Hence Mény and Surel define populism in terms of three successive rhetorical moves: first, it demarcates a fundamental cleavage between "the top and the bottom, the rich and the poor, the rulers and the ruled," in short, between "the good, wide, and simple people" and "the corrupt, incompetent, and interlocking elites"; second, "elites are accused of abusing their position of power instead of acting in conformity with the interests of the people as a whole"; and third, populism then insists that "the primacy of the people has to be restored." Direct democracy is encouraged: "The ideal populist political system comes close, at least on paper, to a 'pure' democratic regime where the people are given the first and final word."[32] So populism combines: a framework of an overriding distinction between people and elite; an analysis that presents this distinction as antagonism rather than mere difference; and a gesture of solidarity with the people, against the elite.

Mény and Surel, like Taggart, stress populism's complexity and contradictions; they are disquieted both by its premises and by its effects. By contrast, Jeffrey Bell, a critic rather more in sympathy with populism's claims, is refreshingly succinct: "Populism," he tells us, "is optimism about people's ability to make decisions about their lives."[33] Expressed like this, populism is simply a matter of common sense and faith in the common sense of others. What cultural studies scholar could disagree? Yet the simplicity of Bell's definition obscures the real difficulty of locating populism on the political spectrum. It so happens that Bell's book is a polemic against the "liberal elites" who, he claims, have made "relativism the core of American moral culture." Hence Bell praises Ronald Reagan's presidency for its steadfast anticommunism, its fiscal conservatism, and Supreme Court appointments that enabled "the restoration of popular control over community standards."[34] Bell locates himself firmly on the neoconservative right; cultural studies by contrast overwhelmingly locates itself on the left. But there is not much distance between Bell's optimistic confidence in the people's ability to decide and Raymond Williams's declaration that his working-class "family and family friends" possessed "as much natural fineness of feeling, as much quick discrimination, as much clear grasp of ideas within the range of experience as I have found anywhere."[35] Williams shared few, if any, of Bell's specific political positions, but populism blurs such distinctions.

Latin America is the great cradle of political populism. What political historian Jorge Castañeda describes as Latin America's "populist epoch" dates from the 1920s or 1930s (Peru's APRA party was founded in 1924; Gertulio Vargas acceded to the Brazilian presidency in 1930) to the 1970s, when it was curtailed by the rise of military dictatorships.[36] Postdictatorship leaders, however, have often also been cast in a (neo)populist mold, from Menem in Argentina to Peru's Alán García or even Venezuela's Hugo Chávez. More broadly, Michael Conniff argues that "in the long view" of the region's politics, "populists were the most characteristic leaders" of the twentieth century.[37] "Populism," social theorist Alain Touraine suggests, "has always been the great Latin American temptation." Touraine argues that this is because it "represent[s] a desire for change within continuity, without the violent rupture that both socialist and capitalist processes of industrialization experienced."[38] An additional attraction is that populism purports to solve the problem of national identity, while leaving that identity inchoate and somehow beyond representation. Identity has been a central postindependence political and philosophical concern for the region: Latin America's cultural roots are variously European, indigenous, and African, and the vast majority of its inhabitants are mixed or "mestizos" of one sort or another, while it has at different times been under the sway of Spanish, Portuguese, French, British, and now U.S. political and cultural influence. In the search to resolve this complex and contradictory hybridity, it is small surprise that Latin America has been a laboratory for the most significant experiments in populism. Populism promises simple answers to simple questions of allegiance and belonging: are you with the people or with the elite?

Peronism follows the classic dualist model described by the Spanish political scientist Sagrario Torres Ballesteros when she argues that "what matters" in populism "is the confrontation between the 'people' and the 'antipeople,' the struggle between 'poor and rich,' 'exploiters and exploited. . . .' All populist rhetoric revolves around the 'people/anti-people' antagonism."[39] Hence Peronism, according to the movement's "Twenty Truths" promulgated in 1950, "is essentially popular. Any political lobby is anti-people, and as such not Peronist."[40] For Peronism, the antipeople was at first "the communist camp and red socialism."[41] Increasingly, however, it was also defined in terms of imperialism and its oligarchical agents within Argentina, the "enemies of the people."[42] Perón warns against the "traitors and foreign agents" who thrive "wherever there is colonization." Describing the military regime that had overthrown him, Perón says that "this is the treacherous gang; none of them give a damn about the country. . . . The People are Olympian in their scorn for each and every one of these vermin, who are a scourge on the country."[43] The antipeople had sold the country and its economic assets to foreign interests and ensured the destruction of national industry "to serve foreign interests and to fulfill debts incurred to those who financed the revolution," primarily (Perón asserts) British capital. By contrast, "counterpoised to all the powers of the anti-fatherland is the true Argentine People."[44] Perón continually returns to the theme. In 1972, shortly before his return to the country, he is still denouncing "foreign agents within Argentine society," that is, "the bad Argentines themselves who join forces with imperialism to defend their own shameful interests to the detriment of the Nation they claim to serve." Theirs is a "power usurped from the People" and their deceit a "fraud against the People." But the repression that the people and the unions have to endure has been "a real test" that has, Perón argues, "proved that they possess the virtues required of men who struggle for their real liberation."[45]

In Peronism, the people's ultimate identification is with the movement itself. Solidarity is the ultimate value: "For a Peronist there can be nothing better than another Peronist."[46] "True patriotism," Perón assures his followers, "is love of the community." This is "a community characterized by justice and solidarity, in which every individual can count on the help that others are able to provide, and support them in turn in their times of misfortune."[47] In this community, all differences melt away: "For Peronism, there is only one class of men: those who work.... In the New Argentina the only ones to be privileged are the children."[48] This is an organic, organized community that elicits an affect that can do without either ideology or discourse. As true patriotism is "a kind of love," according to Perón, "either you feel it or you don't.... So there will be no need for speeches, symbols, or ceremonies." This affect then induces Peronist habits: "When this community is in danger, there will be nobody who does not feel the inclination and the need to defend it against its enemies external or internal." In short, "egoism does not exist" for a Peronist.[49] The individual is dissolved into a crowd in which all are the same, united in a common movement; he finds his "historic destiny by way of the State, to which he belongs."[50] Identification with the movement becomes, in populism, identification with constituted power.

For McGuigan, what he calls "cultural populism" is "the intellectual assumption... that the symbolic experiences and practices of ordinary people are more important analytically and politically than

Culture with a capital C."[51] There is no doubt that cultural studies is populist in this sense. Cultural studies, first, expands the terrain of investigation from the elite culture that had been the traditional concern of the literature departments from which it generally emerged. Second, this shift is driven by the desire to validate nonelite cultural forms, and so to underline the worth of the "ordinary." "Culture is ordinary," declared Raymond Williams in 1958, "that is the first fact." Culture is not, then, the exclusive preserve of a minority; it is not what the nineteenth-century poet and critic Matthew Arnold defined as the "best which has been thought and said."[52] Cultural studies breaks open the canon and is as happy to discuss jazz as to analyze Shakespeare. For Stuart Hall and Paddy Whannel, writing as early as 1964, jazz was "popular in the sense of being *of the people*." It followed that "the jazz ethos" was "tolerant and nonconformist," associated with "lively, radical and creative groups of young people [who] in quite different cultures have, during the short period of its history, found in it a common, international language."[53] Some critics took to studying jazz alongside Shakespeare.[54] More often, and as media scholar John Hartley comments, "despite misgivings about commercial or mass culture," cultural studies has looked "for Shakespearian quality in the works — and the audiences — of popular culture."[55] Cultural studies returns the concept of culture to the people, and enthusiastically champions a broader conception of culture against the notion of culture as a minority pursuit of the "cultured."

Cultural studies is also populist in a stricter sense. Most of its practitioners regard their vocation as being in some way political, and see the movement to open or break traditional canons as of more than merely academic interest. The shift to something closer to an anthropological definition of culture is envisaged as a blow (however small) against an elite that has monopolized our conception of culture in the West and gained undue power in the process. This is a theme that unites cultural studies scholars of all generations and on both sides of the Atlantic. In Williams's foundational *Culture and Society*, "the development of the idea of culture has, throughout, been a criticism of what has been called the bourgeois idea of society."[56] For the doyen of U.S. cultural studies, Lawrence Grossberg, what matters are "the ways in which popular culture and daily life can become the battlegrounds for real struggles over power [and] also how they are articulated to broader struggles in the social formation."[57] And perhaps most emphatically of all, Stuart Hall famously declared that popular culture was "one of the places where socialism might be constituted. That is why 'popular culture' matters. Otherwise, to tell you the truth, I don't give a damn about it."[58] Cultural studies paints itself as an oppositional practice, driven by a democratizing impulse. It shares this impulse with the parallel moves on the part of feminist, African American, and Latino/a scholars (among others) who study "minority" cultural production as a means to open up the academy and by extension other institutions that consecrate and conserve culture (museums, publishing houses, and so on), welcoming voices that have hitherto been excluded and unheard. But if identity politics argues for the specific history and experience of particular groups (women, African Americans, Latinos/as), cultural studies has a broader remit. Above and beyond identity or even class, cultural studies declares its commitment to the *people*.

So beyond its choice of popular texts and practices to study and its oppositional stance toward elite definitions of culture, even toward dominant culture as a whole, cultural studies is also an affirmative politics of solidarity with the "people." This solidarity is often aesthetic, as in Grossberg's emphasis on the "fun" of popular culture.[59] But it is just as often explicitly political. For Williams, solidarity is a value found in and vital to the "common culture" that he claims is latent in working-class experience. "The idea of community" developed by the working class is itself an "idea of solidarity." "A culture in common," Williams argues, "will be a very complex organization, requiring continual adjustment and redrawing. At root, the feeling of solidarity is the only conceivable element of stabilization in so difficult an organization."[60] More recently, the Birmingham Centre graduate and critical race theorist Paul Gilroy likewise finds "spontaneous tolerance and openness" to be the hallmarks of "the underworld of Britain's convivial culture" and the basis for a possible "cosmopolitan solidarity."[61] But solidarity is not simply a goal for cultural studies. In ethnographic works, it is premise and method, as the boys who are Paul Willis's subjects tell him "you were someone to pour our hearts out to.... Anything that happened you'd understand.... You listen to us, you want to know what we've got to say."[62] And solidarity is also motivation: as Hall describes the aim of the Birmingham Centre, "we were trying to find an institutional practice in cultural studies that might produce an organic intellectual," that meant producing intellectuals aligned "with an emerging historic movement."[63]

From Williams to Hall, to Willis, Gilroy, and Grossberg, then, cultural studies goes further than McGuigan's merely "cultural" populism. From Williams's argument for a "common culture" premised on "the idea of solidarity" going beyond both "mass" and "class," to Hall's directive that cultural studies should be "transmitting [its] ideas, that knowledge, through the intellectual function, to those who do not belong, professionally, in the intellectual class," to Grossberg's call "to construct a 'we' that can represent and speak for and across different identities and groups, a collective identity which transcends differences": the populism of cultural studies is also insistently political and consistently the very image of classical political populism.[64] Grossberg even suggests that "perhaps the Left needs to be less suspicious of the media's power to construct charismatic leaders who can call forth and mobilize those affectively charged places that will pull people out of their everyday lives."[65] Like classical populism, the political project of cultural studies resides in its attempt to construct a popular cross-class alliance against an illegitimate elite. Cultural studies takes as its task the identification and encouragement of popular resistance and mobilization from below, bringing together the disparate identities and ideological elements (for Grossberg, also affective investments) that constitute the people and honing their antagonism toward dominant ideology.

The conditions were ripe for cultural studies to take on populism as its guiding spirit. Laclau argues that "the emergence of populism is historically linked to a crisis of the dominant ideological discourse which is in turn part of a more general social crisis."[66] Such was indeed the context for the emergence of cultural studies, which took place in the wake of the left's defeats and the post-1956 discrediting of Marxism, on the one hand, and in a climate of anxiety over Britain's deindustrialization and loss of Empire on the other. For Hall, cultural studies' conditions of possibility were the postwar "manifest break-up of traditional culture" and "the cultural impact of the long-delayed entry of the United Kingdom into the modern world."[67] The subsequent institutional expansion of cultural studies came during the generalized climate of crisis (oil crisis, currency crisis, debt crisis, unemployment crisis) of the 1970s and the early 1980s, for which the ideological discourses then current could provide neither explanation nor answer. Finally, cultural studies achieved global reach in the shadow of the end of the Cold War and in the vacuum left by the collapse of the ideological dichotomy between communism and Western liberalism. Repeatedly, however, cultural studies has been confronted, and indeed outplayed, by the success of populist projects articulated by the right: the neopopulism of Blair and then Bush in the late 1990s and, especially, after 2001 and, before that, what Hall called the "authoritarian populism" of Thatcher and Reagan.

Peronism anticipates the "Third Way" politics of New Labour. Indeed, however much it is premised on an overriding binary distinction between people and antipeople, populism generally presents itself as beyond such dichotomies. Peronism, for instance, gathered up a series of referents, such as the poor (the so-called *descamisados*), workers, youth, and women, each of which was defined by opposition (to the rich, the bourgeois, the old, the male). But these referents became the "people" only as they were then articulated into a system of equivalences with Peronism, a term otherwise outside of referential discourse: Peronism referred to no one single thing, but to the conjunction of many referents, what Laclau and Mouffe term a "chain of equivalence."[68] Beyond any single binary opposition (though present in them all), because its own articulations were contingent rather than necessary, Peronism could position itself as a third term or horizon for all such either/or logic. This then was the Peronist "Third Position," expressed in slogans that followed the rhythm of "neither/nor, but," such as "Neither Nazis nor fascists — Peronists" or "Neither Yankees nor Marxists — Peronists."[69] Laclau terms this process "the social production of 'empty signifiers,'" whereby one term, here "Peronism," defined in its relation to a chain of equivalences among a set of disparate terms, appears to transcend and so establish itself outside of the signifying system itself. Laclau argues that particularly in the 1960s and early 1970s, from his Madrid exile, Perón, "careful not to take any definitive stand . . . was in ideal conditions to become the 'empty signifier' incarnating the moment of universality in the chain of equivalences which unified the popular camp."[70]

In exile, Perón shifted positions constantly, according to circumstance. The enemies of the people took ever different form, depending on who was listening. The substance of Peronism itself became indeterminate, though it retained the same referent both in Perón's own name and charisma, and in the notion of an ideal, unbroken movement toward an unnamed historical destiny (and Perón's ever-imminent personal return). Equivocation could be presented as constancy. Peronism was therefore able to legitimate and support multiple political inflections from the far right (Perón's fascist elements), through reformism, to the revolutionary left (the Peronist Youth and its armed groups). The fact that anyone could be part of the coalition meant also that no one was essential to it. As to whether Peronism was a movement of the left or of the right: it was both. (And it was neither.) Peronism's ambiguity was further accentuated by the fact that the figure of Evita was always available as a second pole for identification: from the guerrilla version of Evita as rebellious incarnation of the Peronist left, as in the chant "If Evita lived, she would be a Montonero!" to her right-wing portrayal as the image of fidelity and subservience to patriarchy. The Evita who "renounced all ambitions and all pretensions to bureaucratic office and institutionalized power,"[71] and so opposed all constituted power, was counterpoised to the Evita who was the eternal president's eternal wife, and so functioned as that power's buttress.

The height of Peronist hegemony could come only while Perón himself was out of power; in this sense, hegemony and power are opposed rather than mutually reinforcing. Perón's exile enabled an unrecognized complicity between those making opportunistic use of Perón and those whom Perón manipulated to maintain his own authority. In the early 1970s, Perón endlessly played off the Peronist Youth (and associated guerrilla movements) against the trade union stalwarts and vice versa. In 1972 and early 1973 Peronism's hegemony was almost complete: Perón's absence allowed for multiple identifications and for the movement to fabricate an image of the Argentine people as whole, homogenous, and united. But only in exile could Perón maintain his position as empty signifier. On his arrival home it became evident that, in Laclau's words, "the chains of equivalences constructed by the different factions of his movements had gone beyond any possibility of control — even by Perón himself."[72] The day of his return to the country, June 20, 1973, as he was due to land at Buenos Aires's Ezeiza Airport, up to four million people came out to greet him. In the tumult, violence erupted between sections of the Peronist left and the Peronist right. Young militants were cut down by gunfire directed by the union old guard. Peronism's capacity to absorb and neutralize contradiction had reached its limit. After an uneasy coexistence, during which the left refused to believe that their leader could betray them, Perón himself finally condemned the Peronist Youth at a mass rally they had organized for May 1, 1974, expelling those who, it turned out, had only been contingently incorporated.[73] But they could still appeal to (the ghost of) Evita. Tomás Eloy Martínez's *The Perón Novel* centers on the massacre at Ezeiza and is a study of Peronism both as an open field of identification and affiliation, and as a decisively violent moment of closure. The massacre as Perón reentered Argentine history reveals the state violence that ends interpretation and establishes the antipeople once more. Perón's return meant the return of history to Peronism, the fragmentation of hegemony given the need to reestablish a state.

Throughout, Peronism flirted with what Moreiras defines as "the death of politics": politics, he argues, is "the negotiation of difference";[74] yet Peronism annulled difference, at the same time as it also asserted differences so radical that they were nonnegotiable. Cultural theorist John Frow's critique of Laclau's valorization of populism is based on a similar premise, that its organizing " 'structure of feeling' . . . [is] the building of a space of equivalences held together by the absolute otherness of the opponent; the repression of difference; the politics of the Imaginary."[75] Populism claims to renovate politics, but in fact it destroys it. Likewise, hegemony is at best a distraction from the political, when it is not simply a renunciation; at worst, it screens it off, rendering it entirely opaque. The violence that is all too often politics' hard truth then comes as a terrible surprise.

Populism allows, indeed encourages, a slippage between left and right, freedom and discipline, openness and closure. The challenge for any putatively progressive populism, as cultural studies would like to be, is to distinguish itself from the populism of the right. Absent such a differentiation, populism is always liable to lose its progressive impetus. This is the trajectory that literary and cultural theorist Catherine Belsey foresees for cultural studies, as she fears that its "great strength" has come "to seem like a constraint. The strength was its popularising impulse; that impulse is now in danger of settling down as populism; and, as we in the UK found out in the Thatcher years, populism can too easily turn into conservatism."[76] But, as I have been arguing, cultural studies has always been populist. Hall admits that even the British New Left of the 1950s was already populist in what he calls "the 'Narodnik' sense of 'going to the people' and in terms of what they/we might become." The New Left's populism turned particularly around the Campaign for Nuclear Disarmament (CND), which Hall describes as "a popular movement with a clear radical thrust and an implicit 'anti-capitalist' content ... but lacking a clear class composition and appealing to people across the clear-cut lines of traditional class identity or organizational loyalties." Hall insists, however, on a distinction between this populism and "the Thatcherite sense of massaging popular consent by cynical appeals to what the people are said by their betters to want."[77] Again, as with Belsey, the reference to Thatcherism: it is not that cultural studies suddenly became populist; rather, Thatcherism served as a warning of populism's potential dangers. Yet Hall's own work elsewhere shows that Thatcherism was rather more than the "massaging [of] popular consent"; he here falls back on a logic of false consciousness that cultural studies otherwise repudiates. Such an easy distinction hardly resolves the question of what a Narodnik "going to the people" might entail; indeed, this has been an ongoing anxiety for cultural studies.

Cultural studies has always been at least half-aware of its own populist impulses, and if it were not, there have been plenty of critics to remind it of them.[78] In response, there have been various attempts to formulate a distinction between the populism of cultural studies and other populisms. Cultural theorist Ken Hirschkop, for instance, defends what he terms Williams's "complex populism" against "a simple populism, of the kind now habitually resisted," but without explaining what makes the one complex and the other simple, except for the observation that Williams shuns "the notion of a 'national' interest."[79] Yet nationalism is hardly the defining feature of right populism and has in any case arguably been embraced, however ambivalently, by cultural studies scholars such as Gilroy with his celebration of "Britain's convivial culture." McGuigan, on the other hand, defends a "critical populism" against "an *uncritical* populist drift in the study of popular culture." A critical populism, he claims rather vaguely, would arise from a "greater dialogue between mainstream cultural studies ... and the political economy of culture."[80] Sociologist Ben Agger, meanwhile, insists that cultural studies does not go far enough and argues for "the real populism of a modernist cultural theory that recognizes the colonization of popular culture by elitist imperatives of control and consumption."[81] Yet there has never been any shortage of conservatives who would happily go along with Agger's crusade: among the modernists, the likes of T. S. Eliot, for instance.

It is Stuart Hall whose response to the triumph of right-wing populism is the most illuminating. Hall saw in Thatcherism a crystallization of the problems of cultural studies. He realized that cultural studies' established theories could not account for Thatcherite populist success, while the right was stealing a march on both cultural studies and the left. Cultural studies, which had attempted to address the failure of prior left projects for radical change, was now faced with a successful hegemonic shift engineered by the right and, after 1979, from a position of state power. As Hall put the problem in the mid-1980s, Thatcherism had "set out to and has effectively become a populist political force, enlisting popular consent among significant sections of the dominated classes." It had done so "through a combination of the imposition of social discipline from above . . . and of populist mobilization from below."[82] The right was proving far more successful on what this New Left considered its own natural terrain. Thatcherism had succeeded where the Birmingham Centre had failed: "We never connected with that rising historic movement," Hall conceded by the 1990s;[83] but Thatcher did. Above all, Thatcherism presented a theoretical as well as a political challenge, demonstrating as far as Hall was concerned the need to turn to hegemony as the key notion for any understanding of power. Indeed, "Thatcherism gives you a better understanding of what the struggle for hegemony is about than almost anything one has seen in the politics on the left."[84] Thatcherism was authoritarian, yes; but it was also and most importantly hegemonic. More: it offered the clearest model of a successful hegemonic project.

No wonder Hall suggests that "make no mistake, a tiny bit of all of us is also somewhere inside the Thatcherite project."[85] Thatcherism interpellated cultural studies twice over: first, by appealing to a sense of antagonism against the status quo; and second, by offering a paradigm of hegemony achieved. No wonder also that Laclau's work on Peronism (which most attracted Hall) and his later work with Mouffe (which fed the translation of cultural studies to the United States) seemed so useful, defining as it did the stakes of a left populism and refining the theoretical analysis of hegemony. Laclau too, after all, was intent on defining and reclaiming a left populism in the face of a seductive but intimidating political counterexample. Yet as cultural studies followed Laclau on the path of hegemony theory, Hall's focus on the state could be forgotten (eventually, even by Hall himself) along with his argument that "the moment of the passage of power into the State and its condensation there into a definite system of rule is a critical historical moment, representing a distinct phase."[86] An exclusive concern with culture soon masked any interest in the state, in what a populism in waiting (such as cultural studies) could learn from a populism in power (such as Thatcherism).

A Theory of Hegemony: Laclau

Since the late 1970s, hegemony has been the master trope of cultural studies. In *Subculture*, which theorist Fredric Jameson notes is probably cultural studies' single most influential text, Birmingham Centre graduate Dick Hebdige states simply that the "theory of *hegemony*... provides the most adequate account of how dominance is sustained in advanced capitalist societies."[87] Or as Simon Critchley argues, "hegemony is the logic of the political, it's what is at the heart of the political, because that is the way power is organised." Critchley locates hegemony also at cultural studies' heart: "Cultural studies is a political project. The political project turns around the use of the category of hegemony."[88] Hegemony was, furthermore, the cornerstone of the post-Birmingham cultural studies' pedagogic project, the key concept for Open University course U203, on "Popular Culture," written by Tony Bennett, Stuart Hall, and Paul Willis among others. Five thousand students took this course between 1982 and 1987, and David Harris argues it "had as great an influence as the Birmingham Centre." Harris describes the cynical epiphany of the cultural studies student who discovers "with relief that 'hegemony can explain everything.'"[89] For Hall it was an "enormously productive" concept.[90] The theory of hegemony resolved the tensions that had plagued cultural studies during the 1970s and prepared the way for the field's 1980s expansion.

Cultural studies' embrace of hegemony theory is usually described as a "turn to Gramsci" that ended a ten-year engagement with

Althusser.[91] In Chantal Mouffe's words, "if the '60s had been the era of Althusserianism, the '70s was the era of Gramscianism."[92] And it is true that Gramsci was crucial as Hall and others at the Birmingham Centre tried to get to grips with the rise of Thatcherism and to transcend the debate between "culturalism" (à la Williams and Thompson) and "structuralism" that had polarized the field by the late 1970s. In his 1980 article "Cultural Studies: Two Paradigms," Hall argued that "the line in Cultural Studies which has attempted to *think forward* from the best elements in the structuralist and culturalist enterprises" was one that picked up on "some of the concepts elaborated in Gramsci's work."[93] The idea of hegemony was, as it were, in the air; it had been invoked by Althusser and, separately, already been introduced to cultural studies by Williams (in his 1973 essay, "Base and Superstructure in Marxist Theory"). But the version of the concept that Hall championed was not Williams's; nor was it exactly Gramsci's. Mouffe herself, with her 1979 collection *Gramsci and Marxist Theory*, was, as Brennan observes, key in packaging Gramsci for cultural studies. But even before that, it was her partner who was more influential still. As media theorist Colin Sparks notes of Hall's analysis of Thatcherism, "the theoretical point of reference which Hall used to argue for this position is explicitly drawn from Laclau. It is *his* notion of hegemony and of the construction of 'the people' which, with some small reservations, Hall employs throughout his work in the 1980s" (emphasis added).[94]

Laclau's version of hegemony is the single most influential formulation for the development of cultural studies. Laclau's hegemony theory is also, by some distance, the most fully developed and the least reliant on some vague "common sense." Hegemony is the focus of his and Chantal Mouffe's best-selling 1985 work *Hegemony and Socialist Strategy*, a book that "triggered a series of significant transformations of both political and theoretical debates on the left" and "place[d] Gramsci at the center of American and British cultural theory."[95] However, in what follows I focus mainly on Laclau's first book, published in 1977 and now long out of print, *Politics and Ideology in Marxist Theory*, because this is the text that particularly influenced Hall and that shaped the direction of cultural studies. Even in the mid-1980s, Hall insisted, "I still prefer *Politics and Ideology in Marxist Theory* to *Hegemony and Socialist Strategy*."[96] Moreover, *Politics and Ideology* also offers a theory of populism and attempts, more thoroughly than any cultural studies text, to resolve the dilemma of how to distinguish between a populism of the left and a populism of the right, and so to legitimate left populism as a political practice. Ultimately, Laclau's project is a defense of populism; his is a theory of hegemony (and of politics) that is modeled on populism, as is more visible than ever with the more recent (2005) publication of *On Populist Reason*. Hegemony, cultural studies, populism: these three slippery terms meet at the nexus that is Laclau's theory of hegemony. Given the intimate relationship between populism and cultural studies, it is no wonder that cultural studies scholar Angela McRobbie should suggest that Laclau provides the field's "theoretical underpinning."[97]

Any analysis that relies upon the concept of hegemony inevitably partakes of a populist politics. Hegemony shares with populism (and indeed, with politics itself in Laclau's analysis) the fact that it is predicated on the constitution of popular subjects. As I argue in what follows, Laclau's initial concern as he refines his concept of hegemony is to differentiate between left and right populism; in his work subsequent to *Politics and Ideology*, however, he abandons that attempt and ends up validating populism as a whole, at first implicitly and later explicitly. But from the outset his analysis is so bound up in its object that it is in no position to offer a critique. Most seriously, like populism Laclau's theory of hegemony evades the question of the role of the state: the state is both present and absent, fetishized and ignored. In Laclau, this evasion is possible in part thanks to his conflation of the difference between linguistic and nonlinguistic elements of what he declares is an all-embracing "discourse." Substituting hegemony for politics and silent about institutional power, the theory of hegemony effectively becomes an antipolitics.

Latin Americanists and cultural theorists alike often forget Laclau's Argentine origins. Yet he himself states that "the years of political struggle in the Argentina of the 1960s" remain his primary context and point of reference. "When today I read *Of Grammatology*, *S/Z*, or the *Écrits* of Lacan," he claimed in 1990, "the examples which always spring to mind are not from philosophical and literary texts; they are from a discussion in an Argentinian trade union, a clash of opposing slogans at a demonstration, or a debate during a party congress."[98]

In the same interview, Laclau recalls his political past, first as a member of the Partido Socialista Argentino, then later with the nationalist Partido Socialista de la Izquierda Nacional, a party that entered into a strategic alliance with Peronism on the basis that populism had started an anti-imperialist revolution under "bourgeois banners." An analysis of Peronism grounds Laclau's theory in *Politics and Ideology,* but he returns to the example of Peronism elsewhere, too, for instance in *Emancipation(s),* and most recently and most emphatically in *On Populist Reason.* It should be obvious, therefore, that any discussion of Laclau's concept of hegemony, let alone his theorization of populism, ought to set it beside a critical examination of the Peronism from which it springs. Yet in Critchley and Marchant's *Laclau: A Critical Reader,* beyond an invocation of Argentina in the introduction's opening pages, and Marchant's brief quotation of the passage I have just cited, not one of the contributors mentions Latin America, let alone Peronism or Perón. Even Marchant moves quickly on: "In his political biography, it *may have been* the experience of demonstrations and party congresses which taught Laclau his 'first lesson in hegemony,' but in his intellectual biography it was of course Gramsci's work that provided him with the means to articulate his practical experience" (emphasis added).[99] Meanwhile, only one of the collection's fifteen essays so much as cites *Politics and Ideology.*

Argentina is the bedrock of Laclau's theorization of hegemony. Where Gramsci had been prompted by his experience and observation of Italy, particularly underdeveloped southern Italy and so the European semiperiphery, Laclau's thought comes from an engagement with Argentina's complex place in the global system. In the early twentieth century, thanks to nascent industrialization, profitable agro-export, and the impact of mass immigration from Europe, Argentina's economic and social standing was similar and indeed in some respects superior to that of European countries such as Italy (from which many of its immigrants had in fact come), Belgium, or Norway. Despite their country's long-term economic decline over the twentieth century, Argentines have often felt themselves closer to Europe and North America than to their Latin American neighbors. In *Hegemony and Socialist Strategy,* Laclau and Mouffe appear to exclude "the periphery of the capitalist world" from their analysis, because there the constitution of popular subject positions prevails over what they call democratic struggles. They seem to assert, in short, that hegemony and populism are mutually exclusive. But their claim that it is in the metropolis where hegemony is the order of the day, while in the periphery more archaic populist logics predominate, is rather undermined by their observations on the rise of Thatcherism and Reaganism, formations that are both populist and apparently hegemonic, and also firmly located in the "First World."[100] Indeed, *Hegemony and Socialist Strategy*'s disdain for populism is an aberration. In Laclau's *On Populist Reason,* populism is very explicitly the model for hegemony: the periphery is therefore implicitly the guardian of the political, and the danger now is that in the metropolis "the Third Way and the 'radical centre'" may be "substituting administration for politics" and so eliminating possibilities for hegemonic articulation.[101]

Mapping hegemony theory back onto an analysis of Argentine history is no simple matter, not only because of the changes within that society since the 1940s, but also because Laclau's views about the geopolitics of hegemony theory have wavered over the past thirty years. But the exercise is worthwhile because Laclau's own procedure is often to treat individual case studies with extreme brevity, offering at most a page or two on (say) Chartism in Britain or the fate of Kemalism in Turkey. It is worth seeing whether or not his theory of hegemony can be put to a more sustained examination of what, in Peronist Argentina, should be its favored territory. My aim is to show that hegemony theory fails even in its best-case scenario.

Hegemony theory is intended as a response to the failure of determinism: the fact that what classical Marxism terms an ideological superstructure does not, at least in any simple way, reflect an economic base; that however much change might be to their benefit, it is only *in extremis* that people rise up against a system that oppresses them; and that society somehow coheres, despite its internal contradictions. In Laclau and Mouffe's words, the genealogy of the concept of hegemony is "an expansion of what we could provisionally call a 'logic of the contingent,'" from Luxemburg and Lenin to Sorel and Gramsci. The theory of hegemony aims to understand and account for contingency, and so takes its distance from reductionist explanations. Gramsci, Laclau and Mouffe argue, shows the way toward a fully developed theory of hegemony, in that he demonstrates the contingent and constructed nature of any "historical bloc" that unites different interests and so constitutes a hegemonic formation. But he did not go far enough, they contend, in that he believed that there was a "*single* unifying principle in every hegemonic formation, and [that] this can only be a fundamental class."[102]

Laclau and Mouffe lay siege to what they term "the last redoubt of essentialism: the economy." *Hegemony and Socialist Strategy* goes beyond Gramsci (and Marxism), to argue that it is not the economy (or indeed any other external principle) that determines political subjectivity; it is "the logic of hegemony" itself, as "a logic of articulation and contingency" that "come[s] to determine the very identity of the hegemonic subjects." Hegemony arises from the contingent articulation of discursive elements (both linguistic and nonlinguistic) according to the twin principles of equivalence and difference. Specifically, a successful hegemonic project presents a variety of different elements as equivalent in their mutual antagonism toward some other element or elements. A hegemonic formation consists in the articulation of a historical bloc whose unity is not pregiven but constituted in and through the very process of its articulation on an "antagonistic terrain."[103] What has to be stressed is that this definition of hegemony arises directly, in Laclau's case, from a consideration of populism. For populism refutes class reductionism; populism constructs novel political subjectivities; and populism, too, articulates the social field around a fundamental antagonism. These are the issues that Laclau addresses in *Politics and Ideology*, laying the ground for his later work with Mouffe on hegemony, in which populism as such fades into the background.

First, populism demands a theory of contingency, because in populism the links between political ideologies and economic interest are clearly broken. We understand why the rich might vote for the right or the poor commit to the left, but puzzle over why rich and poor should come together to support populist movements whose policies may lie either on the right or on the left. As Laclau explains, "it is easy to see, then, why a conception that makes *class reduction* the ultimate source of intelligibility of any problem has met with particular difficulties in the analysis of populism." Populism illustrates the error of traditional Marxism's class essentialism. For populism has no necessary class basis: left movements such as Maoism and right movements such as Nazism (not to mention formations such as Peronism that contain both left and right elements) all exhibit populist features. This, then, makes for "the impossibility of linking the strictly populist element to the *class* nature of a determinate movement" and prevents any simple evaluation of populist movements according to their class orientation.[104] More recently, Laclau has observed that populism is also "the locus of a theoretical stumbling block" for political theory in general. As there is no single set of features (either ideological elements or class components) common to the variety of movements that have been labeled populist, the term has been denigrated, and essentially abandoned, for its irreducible "vagueness" or "imprecision."[105] But "vagueness" is just another indication of the contingency that has to be explained rather than condemned or ignored. Hegemony theory promises such an explanation.

Second, populism constructs novel political identities. If analysis of populism cannot fall back on an appeal to preconstituted identities, such as classes, it must consider the ways in which identities are created through populist discourse itself. The "people," for Laclau, is a political subject constructed in and through populism, rather than a subject that preexists and expresses itself through populist politics. The process by which such subjectivities are produced is what Laclau terms "articulation." I have already noted that articulation is key to the concept of hegemony (and also to cultural studies), but what is important here is the way in which Laclau develops the idea by working through a theory of populism. If "ideological and political levels" cannot be reduced to "relations of production" (and ideological positions cannot simply be inferred from economic interests), then they must, Laclau says, be articulated. Thus "classes exist at the ideological and political level in a process of articulation and not of reduction." Through articulation, diverse ideological contents (which have no necessary class basis) are drawn together in the service of class interest to form what is, already in *Politics and Ideology*, termed a hegemonic formation: "The dominant class exerts its hegemony" first and foremost "through the articulation into its class discourse of non-class contradictions and interpellations."[106] Laclau later abandons what is here still the trace of economic determination (for which "relations of production maintain the role of determination in the last instance"), leaving only the contingent articulation of discrete elements in a "chain of equivalence."[107] But the logic of hegemony is in place: the articulation of discursive elements, substituting equivalence for heterogeneity, so that a social subject emerges as their unifying principle — all this is already present in Laclau's early work on populism.

Third, we have seen that antagonism is central to populism. *Politics and Ideology* outlines two fundamental principles of social antagonism: one sets classes against each other and is determined by the mode of economic production; the other arises from "the complex of political and ideological relations of domination constituting a determinate social formation." It is this second antagonism that sets the "people" against the "power bloc," and so creates the division around which populism revolves. Like class conflict, it too has to be articulated; it is not simply expressed, but is constructed discursively. Populism accentuates the conflict between people and power bloc, presenting "popular interpellations . . . in the form of antagonism and not just difference." As opposed to transformism, in which a dominant class neutralizes dissident popular elements, accommodating at least some of their demands, populism polarizes the social field. Thus "populism starts at the point where popular-democratic elements are presented as an antagonistic option against the ideology of the dominant bloc."[108] Subsequently, Laclau and Mouffe drop any notion of a fundamental class antagonism and indeed abandon the notion of any preexisting antagonisms at all ("any position in a system of differences . . . can become the locus of an antagonism"). Moreover, they argue that transformism, a characteristic of developed societies, merely "displace[s] the frontier of antagonism to the periphery of the social."[109] Most recently, however, Laclau returns to the fundamental difference between hegemony, whose logic is now explicitly populist, and what he now terms "administration," which he sees as effectively antipolitical: he warns against "Third Way" attempts "at substituting administration for politics."[110] "The political operation par excellence," he claims, "is *always* going to be the construction of a 'people' " (emphasis added) in that "constructing a 'people' also involves constructing the frontier which the 'people' presupposes" and so initiates "a new hegemonic game." Again, "the construction of the 'people' is the political act par excellence — as opposed to pure administration" because the former articulates antagonism, while the latter dissolves it.[111] As Laclau has developed his theory of hegemony, it has become more rather than less populist.

Contingency, articulation, and antagonism: these are the lessons Laclau draws from his analysis of populism; he then applies them to his developing theory of hegemony. Indeed, even Laclau's initial description of populism as "the presentation of popular–democratic interpellations as a synthetic–antagonistic complex with regard to the dominant ideology" could already equally be a definition of hegemony.[112] Populism and hegemony are, for Laclau, essentially the same. And now he claims that "populist reason" is "*political* reason *tout court.*" Or as he puts it elsewhere, "does not populism become synonymous with politics? The answer can only be affirmative."[113] Populism is hegemony is politics!

Laclau's analysis of Peronism in *Politics and Ideology* is surprisingly brief. He spends more time on the liberal order that preceded Perón's rise to power than on Peronism itself, which he sees as in effect a rearticulation of the elements that had condensed in oligarchical liberalism between the 1860s and the 1920s. Initially, the nineteenth-century oligarchy's "ideological hegemony over the rest of the country was minimal" and it resorted to force to ensure its dominance. Gradually, however, liberalism neutralized the threats posed variously by the Radical Party, right-wing nationalism, and the working class, by articulating some of their demands in concert with the liberals' own political agenda. The success of this project was curtailed only in the 1930s, as the world depression caused a "crisis of transformism" such that "the oligarchy could no longer tolerate the generous redistributive policies characteristic of the Radical governments and had to ban the middle classes from access to political power." This led to a "scission between liberalism and democracy," which Perón exploited by rearticulating the same basic components that had characterized liberal hegemony, but now in the service of antioligarchical populism.[114] Peronism took preexisting demands for democracy, industrialism, nationalism, and anti-imperialism, highlighted "their potential antagonism" toward liberalism, and encouraged the emergence of a "new historical subject," the people, opposed to the oligarchy. For Laclau, it was the "attempt to distinguish between liberal ideological forms and real democracy" that "dominated the whole of Peronist discourse." Like all populisms, Peronism promised to reform a corrupt political system. However, antiliberal antagonism had to be confined "within limits imposed by the class project that defined the regime." Peronism's popular-democratic elements could not be fully expressed, at least while Perón remained in power. After the regime's fall in 1955, these limits were breached, "popular ideology became increasingly anti-liberal, and in the most radicalized sectors increasingly fused with socialism." Peronism could now take the form of a specifically left populism. Upon Perón's return to power, "successive attempts to turn the clock back and to articulate popular-democratic ideology in a form assimilable by the bourgeoisie all failed" and "the regime of Isabel Perón collapsed into repressive chaos."[115]

Laclau has remarkably little to say about Peronism's "class project." Despite showing how Argentina's nineteenth-century oligarchs took on the mantle of liberalism, and thereby demonstrating the contingency of the relationship between ideology and class, once he moves to a discussion of Peronism itself he treats liberalism as though it were simply inherently bourgeois. As class does not really enter into his discussion, Laclau's later abandonment of the notion of a fundamental class antagonism hardly affects his analysis, except insofar as he therefore also jettisons the attempt to locate Peronism on the political spectrum of left versus right. In his brief discussion of Peronism in *Emancipation(s),* Laclau shifts from a focus on Perón's rise in the 1940s to an analysis of the "universalization of [Peronism's] popular symbols" during the 1960s and 1970s, now however without claiming any fusion between populism and socialism. Rather, his interest is in how Peronism exemplifies the logic of the "empty signifier," that is, the tendential emptying and transcendence of one element within a given signifying chain. That element was Perón himself, during his exile, who became "the 'empty signifier' incarnating the moment of universality in the chain of equivalences which unified the popular camp." But, again, the collapse once Perón returns to power in 1973: the chain of equivalences breaks down; hence "the bloody process which led to the military dictatorship in 1976."[116] In this shift in focus between the two books, from the 1940s and 1950s (when Perón was in power) to the 1960s and 1970s, Laclau manages to occlude the role of the state in Peronist politics, implying that populist hegemony (even hegemony per se) is necessarily anti-institutional, perhaps also necessarily imaginary, shipwrecked on the assumption of state power.

In *On Populist Reason,* Laclau does revisit Perón's first administration, but only to describe its logic as what he now terms precisely "administration" (and had previously called transformism), rather than hegemony. Laclau now argues that by the 1950s Peronism was hardly populist at all, as it tried "to overcome the dichotomic division of the political spectrum through the creation of a fully integrated differential space." "The image of the 'organized community' " replaced the figure of the *descamisado,* and "the need to stabilize the revolutionary process becomes a leitmotiv of Peronist discourse." Following Perón's downfall, this call for restraint failed, and what Laclau terms "the new Argentinian populism" emerged. Earlier, Laclau had described this phenomenon as a fusion of populism and socialism; now he describes it as promoting an "anti-system popular and national identity," encouraged by the deliberate ambiguity of Perón's "multilayered" messages, which "allow[ed] for endless interpretations and reinterpretations."[117] Hence, once more, "the demand for Perón's return to Argentina became an empty signifier unifying an expanding popular camp." Peronism began "dangerously bordering" on the possibility of its "tendentially empty signifier becom[ing] *entirely* empty." This would be something like an absolute hegemony, for which any link, however contradictory, could be added to the equivalential chain; but it was also extremely precarious. Laclau then replays the familiar story of Peronism's inability "to hegemonize the totality of his movement" once in power, and the chaos and collapse that ensued.[118]

By focusing on this "new Argentinian populism" of the 1960s and 1970s and emphasizing its incompatibility with state power, Laclau neglects his own observation that Peronism also had "a strong statist component."[119] He has to split the "new" Peronism from the Peronism that had been in power for a decade. It is as though only the late Peronism were hegemonic, or indeed populist. But in fact the early Peronism never really disappeared: it had built or dramatically reshaped institutions (the Evita Perón Foundation, the Trade Union Federation [CGT]) whose impact endured for decades, habituating a generation of working-class Argentines to the feeling that they belonged to a Peronist project that almost preceded politics. Laclau's suggestion that Peronist love did not "crystallize in any institutional regularity" takes the movement's splits (for instance between the Montoneros and the CGT) as an excuse not merely to pass over the existence of Peronist institutions, but also to imply that Peronism and institutionalization were somehow radically incompatible.[120] This repeats the mistake of the radical Peronists of the 1960s (when Laclau was himself a militant), who were so brutally proven wrong by Perón and the movement old guard after 1973. Indeed, there is arguably no institution in Argentina so durable as the Peronist party apparatus itself, which continues on into the present, however much its ideology has changed in the meantime. Rather than ignoring the state, then, we need to acknowledge that Peronism was always, from its inception, split in ways that hegemony theory is simply unable to grasp. I have stressed the importance of habit and habituation for the Peronist movement; in my final chapter, I return to the split within Peronism, its double register, which I explain in terms of a tension between popular form and the formless constituent power of the multitude that gives it life.

Populism, for Laclau, infuses all political processes, and indeed comes to be identified with "political reason *tout court*." As such, it can no longer be denigrated or ignored. But how then to distinguish between populisms? What differentiates a populism of the left from a populism of the right? Which is also to ask how left hegemony differs from right hegemony, the hegemony of the dominant from the hegemony of the dominated (or the would-be dominant). In *Politics and Ideology*, the key is class. The contradiction between people and power bloc is ancillary to the contradiction between classes. Together they make up the "double articulation of political discourse," and both need to be specified to describe adequately any given political formation. But as social formations are ultimately subordinate to the mode of production, class is paramount. There can be a populism of the left and of the right in that the antagonism between people and power bloc can be articulated by either the dominant or the dominated class. There is therefore both "a populism of the dominant classes and a populism of the dominated classes."[121] In the former, the dominant class articulates populist (popular-democratic) demands; in the latter, it is the dominated. Differences between populisms, from fascism to Maoism, depend on their ultimate class articulation.

Though class politics is (at this stage of his thinking) the priority, Laclau argues that populism is more than a necessary inconvenience. It is also a positive goal: "The struggle of the working class for its hegemony is an effort to achieve the maximum possible fusion between popular-democratic ideology and socialist ideology." The working class becomes hegemonic by being also populist. Populism, precisely because it is hegemony itself, is no distraction or deviation from socialism. Far from it: "A 'socialist populism' is not the most backward form of working-class ideology but the most advanced—the moment when the working class has succeeded in condensing the ensemble of democratic ideology in a determinate social formation within its own ideology." In that hegemony is the aim of any left movement, populism must be its ultimate destination: "In socialism, therefore, coincide the highest form of 'populism' and the resolution of the ultimate and most radical of class conflicts."[122] Populism fully stands in for hegemony. Thus in *Politics and Ideology*, Laclau validates the populist character of contemporary social movements while providing, with his appeal to class as the ultimate principle, a means to distinguish between populisms. This would appear to be the theory of hegemony that cultural studies demands: a theory that could simultaneously validate and criticize its populist impulses on the basis of theoretical analysis beyond the domain of popular culture itself. No wonder it was taken up so eagerly by Hall and others at the end of the 1970s.

With *Hegemony and Socialist Strategy*, however, in line with and influencing shifts within cultural studies during the 1980s, Laclau and Mouffe reject the idea that class struggle determines the form of hegemonic articulations. The emergence of the so-called "new social movements," from feminism to environmentalism or queer activism, expresses "that rapid diffusion of social conflictuality to more and more numerous relations which is characteristic today of advanced industrial societies." I will discuss the new social movements in the context of civil society theory in my next chapter; here it is sufficient to note that Laclau and Mouffe argue that society is now riven by multiple antagonisms and that any of the new subjectivities that arise as a result may determine the "nodal point" of a hegemonic bloc. In Laclau and Mouffe's post-Marxism, class is deprived of any epistemological or ontological privilege. The totality of social struggles is then the struggle for radical democracy that, they argue, constitutes the ever-expanding horizon of politics. As a hegemonic project expands to articulate the demands of more social groups, and as social differentiation produces and abstracts more such groups and demands, it necessarily becomes more democratic. The criterion by which to judge hegemonic articulations (which are progressive, and which are reactionary) becomes therefore their potential to expand the logic of the social, to achieve "a maximum autonomization of spheres on the basis of the generalization of the equivalential-egalitarian logic."[123]

Purportedly this struggle for what Laclau and Mouffe term "radical and plural democracy" thus "finds within itself the principle of its own validity," but it easily slides into a celebration of the diversity that is (they themselves argue) an inevitable consequence of modernization. Hegemony comes to the fore as modernization brings about a more differentiated society: "The hegemonic form of politics only becomes dominant at the beginning of modern times" and subsequently, inevitably, undergoes a "constant expansion," tending to approximate the social totality.[124] As Critchley observes, there is therefore a normative (and political) deficit in Laclau and Mouffe's theory of hegemony: by stating "in a quasi-functionalist manner that 'the democratic revolution' and 'radical democracy' are descriptions of a fact, . . . one risks collapsing any *critical* difference between the theory of hegemony and social reality which this theory purports to describe." Hegemony theory "risks identification and complicity with the dislocatory logic of contemporary capitalist societies."[125] This is precisely the risk that cultural studies runs.

In *Hegemony and Socialist Strategy* Laclau and Mouffe banish populism to the premodern backwaters of European feudalism and the global periphery. But the most cursory glance reveals that Peronism (in power and out) expanded the logic of the social, and so advanced radical democracy in their terms. Peronism's success depended upon its power to cultivate the new subjectivities thrown up by Argentina's rapid early twentieth-century modernization.[126] A good example is the way in which it encouraged women to become political actors: Perón's government expanded the electoral franchise to women in 1947; Evita herself was of course a key political figure; and more generally, as historian Daniel James comments, "during the crucial decade from 1945 to 1955 Peronism, through its political and cultural institutions, both mobilized and legitimized women as actors within a newly enlarged public sphere."[127] It is then no great surprise that, with Isabel Perón, Peronism should have given us the Americas' first woman president (and now, with Cristina Fernández de Kirchner, the first country in the hemisphere to have had *two* women heads of state). Moreover, especially through Evita's welfare policies, Peronism also validated daily life as a legitimate arena for political demands, confounding liberalism's conception of public (masculine) citizenship. In this as in other examples (such as the student movement of the 1960s), far from being hostile to the new social movements, Peronism nurtured and encouraged them. Even today, as Argentine historian Javier Auyero reveals, the memory of Peronism continues to resonate powerfully through the "problem-solving networks" of contemporary shantytown politics.[128] In practice at least, the Peronist masses were never as homogenized or dedifferentiated as Laclau and Mouffe might imagine: arguably, Peronism constructed and articulated a whole series of new social actors in precisely the radical democratic manner that Laclau and Mouffe envisage. In line with their conception of a radical democracy, Peronism emphasized the openness of the social, while maintaining the constitutive antagonisms of populism. More to the point, however, Peronism constituted the ground of (particularly working-class) Argentine politics. It shaped an incorporated common sense or habitus from which political identities could emerge, and against which politics itself could be assessed. In Auyero's words, Peronism "remains the standard against which a government and its representatives and policies are judged."[129]

In his most recent work, and now more explicitly than ever identifying it with hegemony, Laclau raises again the problem of populism's ambivalence. He refers to the "entirely opposite political signs" of distinct populist movements, but provides no grounds for such a classification, for distinguishing between left and right.[130] How after all do such signs differ from the signs deployed by and in political discourse itself? If these signs are indeed part of the discourse articulated by populist movements, then their meaning is surely dependent on their articulation and cannot be determined in advance by any political calculation: Laclau would be the first to argue that the political valence of a given statement or demand is determined only by the hegemonic structure within which it is articulated. If, by contrast, they are some type of metasign transcending the political, then they are illegitimate impositions supplementing the theory, a matter perhaps of common sense: *of course* we know that (say) Mao was on the left and Hitler on the right. But that begs the question of more difficult populist movements, such as Peronism. Hence Laclau can distinguish between left and right by abandoning his theory of hegemony and appealing to an extratheoretical common sense; from within the theory itself, he is condemned to repeat the populist gesture that blurs all such distinctions.

Ultimately, Laclau's political project is undermined by his portrayal of society as an all-encompassing discursive web, the meaning of whose terms (because they are always meaningful, representational) is dependent upon the various struggles and articulations that constitute it. Labeling fascism "right-wing" or Maoism "left-wing" has no special weight, except insofar as such labels are articulated as part of a hegemonic project that itself determines their value. In the end, Laclau gives up: he resorts to warning against the danger that hegemony might come to an end, replaced either by administration, and so absolute integration, or by the millenarianism of absolute rupture. But both extremes, he also claims, are "actually unreachable."[131] As such, it is hardly worth warning against them; the theory's political import disappears. At this stage, a cultural studies that views its mission as political might be tempted to salvage the concept of hegemony by returning to what Laclau had abandoned in his shift from the Marxist populism of *Politics and Ideology* to the post-Marxism of *Hegemony and Socialist Strategy* and then the conflation of populism with politics of *On Populist Reason*. This would entail returning either to class struggle or to the antagonism between people and power bloc, to a Marxist essentialism or to a more thoroughgoing and more combative populism. In the following section, I examine these options and consider Laclau's approach to populism's supposed anti-institutionalism, its denunciations of the state.

Populism and the State

The state is the unacknowledged center of Laclau's theory of hegemony. In *On Populist Reason*, he defines "social demands" as the "smallest unit" of political analysis. But these demands are addressed to some preexistent structure, an "institutional system," "the dominant system," or an "institutional order," that is presupposed in and through their articulation. These "democratic demands" are "formulated *to* the system *by* an underdog of sorts."[132] Laclau's examples of such institutional systems include the "local authorities" from which people might seek a resolution to housing problems or, elsewhere, the "city hall" that could improve transport networks.[133] His historical case studies all involve nation-states. If "a demand is always addressed to someone," that "someone" is always, for Laclau, an institution already in a position to respond.[134] Indeed, the demand itself recognizes the constituted power of the system that is addressed: "The very fact that a request takes place shows that the decisory power of the higher instance is not put into question."[135] But nor does Laclau himself ever question the power of the state as "higher instance"; he, too, insists that social demands can be satisfied, and satisfied fully. He takes the state for granted, and never interrogates its power.

When a demand is satisfied, it disappears: it "ceases to be a demand." When it remains unsatisfied, however, it gains "discursive presence." Unmet demands engender the people and power bloc as partners in an antagonistic relation: they accumulate, and an equivalential relationship is established between them; "they start, at a very incipient level, to constitute the 'people' as a potential historical actor." Thus emerges "an internal antagonistic frontier separating the 'people' from power."[136] But this antagonism also displaces the object of its address. When "an extensive series of social demands" remains unfulfilled, these "popular demands are less and less sustained by a preexisting differential framework: they have, to a large extent, to construct a new one." Hence "the identity of the enemy also depends increasingly on a process of political construction." That enemy may be given any of a number of names, such as "the 'regime,' the 'oligarchy,' the 'dominant groups,' and so on." And as Laclau points out, names retrospectively constitute their referents: "The name becomes the ground of the thing."[137] But what is important is the displacement, by which a discursive antagonism replaces an institutional relation. The enemy constituted through populist discourse *stands in* for the state itself.

At the same time, the populist leader, or rather the tendentially empty signifier that is populist articulation's nodal point, comes to incarnate the sovereign. First the leader is identified with the group: "The equivalential logic leads to singularity, and singularity to identification of the unity of the group with the name of the leader." The more successful this process, the more the populist leader can claim to represent the social whole, the "populus." Of course, in that a populist movement emerges in opposition to the state, this constitution of a "signifying totality" has to be distinguished from "actual ruling": the latter would require institutional power, the power to satisfy or deny social demands. But to the extent that a hegemonic project can persuasively claim to represent a "people," its leader can claim to embody the popular sovereignty denied by an illegitimately dominant "enemy." Indeed, for Laclau, it is the logic of populism, with its production of empty signifiers, that constructs sovereignty itself, defined as the "void [that] points to the absent fullness of the community."[138] The principle of populism's transcendent "empty universality" is also the principle that forms sovereign power. And on this basis, the populist leader demands that his sovereignty be recognized, that he correct the system's representational deficit and assume the mantle of the state.

These, then, are populism's characteristic moves regarding the state. First, it displaces the state through the construction of a discursive antagonist. In the process, institutional power, the power to grant or deny demands, is replaced by an image of power, projected onto an enemy declared illegitimate; the stakes of the political game become representational legitimacy rather than the satisfaction of demands. Second, the populist leader assumes representational transcendence and demands the right to be named sovereign and so, in turn, to take the place of the state. All this is accomplished by means of a sleight of hand that substitutes hegemony for other forms of politics, and sovereignty for any other conception of power. Hence populism can gain institutional power while still maintaining an anti-institutional critique directed at the forever displaced objects of its antagonistic discourse. But instead of offering a critique of this process, Laclau mirrors it, accepting that hegemony is indeed politics *tout court*. As I will show, this is true even in *Politics and Ideology*, despite its ostensible Marxism and antistatism.

In *Politics and Ideology*, Laclau invokes a number of different names to describe the dominant pole in a given social formation. Most often it is the "power bloc" (sometimes "the power bloc as a whole"), but not always. Compare the following three descriptions of the same basic antagonism: "the 'people' / *power bloc* confrontation . . . a synthetic–antagonistic complex with regard to *the dominant ideology* . . . antagonism toward *the State*" (emphasis added). For good measure, in this brief passage Laclau also refers to "an antagonistic option against *the ideology of the dominant bloc*" (emphasis added).[139] He is indifferent as to whether the dominant pole is a bloc, an ideology, the state, or some combination of the three; these names are for all intents the same. Further on, with a single phrase he naturalizes the articulation that treats these terms as if they were equivalent: "To the extent," Laclau argues, "that popular resistance exerts itself against a power external and opposed to 'the people,' that is to say, *against the very form of the State*, the resolution of 'the people'/power bloc contradiction can only consist in the suppression of the State as an antagonistic force with respect to the people."[140] To say "a power external and opposed to 'the people' " is also "to say . . . the very form of the State," which is also to say "the State as an antagonistic force."

Laclau constructs a veritable chain of equivalences with the state, displacing its properties onto a series of other names: the form of the state is equated with the state; the state with an antagonistic force; the state with the power bloc; the power bloc with "a power external and opposed to 'the people.' " Laclau's indifference to names is not inconsequential: it enables him to justify populism in this text, as we have seen, by claiming that "in socialism . . . coincide the highest form of 'populism' and the resolution of the ultimate and most radical of class conflicts." For it is because its "*class interests* lead it to the suppression of the State as an antagonistic force" that the working class is "the only social sector which can aspire to the full development of 'the people'/power bloc contradiction, that is to say, *to the highest and most radical form of populism.*"[141] Again, "that is to say." Again, the slip between "the State as an antagonistic force" and the "power bloc." And so the final equivalence: "The highest and most radical form of populism" is socialism.

Laclau had embarked on his discussion of populism in *Politics and Ideology* by stressing the distinction between class struggles and popular struggles. Here, however, the two coincide. Laclau had also been at pains to refute the class reductionist argument that classes are simply represented at the cultural or political levels, but suddenly the proletariat's objective "class interests" are now directly identified with the antagonism between people and power bloc. Laclau had distinguished between discursive articulations of a vague external power (the oligarchy, traitors, and foreign agents), and opposition to the very form of the state (if this is indeed the essence of socialism): indeed, distinguishing between power bloc and state enabled his distinction between left and right populisms, in that left and right would construct distinct images of power, in line with their differing articulations of class antagonism. Yet he now annuls these differences and ascribes a single essence to populism: populism is essentially "against the very form of the State" insofar as it is "against a power external and opposed to 'the people.' " This identification of power bloc with state should be interrogated by any critical analysis of populism, not assumed by the casual phrase "that is to say" that takes for granted the equivalences populism itself works so hard to establish.

In his early, Marxist, phase then, Laclau argues for a socialist populism through a double equivocation conflating the double antagonism that, he himself argues, structures social totality: first he identifies socialism with antagonism toward the (very form of the) state; second he claims that populism is also inevitably against the state. He can then claim that the two are (in their highest forms) one, despite his initial descriptions of socialism as a class antagonism and populism as an antagonism toward the power bloc. Laclau's argument is plainly and unreflectively populist, again according to his own definitions. For Laclau has shown how populism mobilizes antistatist sentiment only to demobilize this social energy by presenting the abstract figure of the power bloc as the object of this conflict, substituting discursive antagonism for antiauthoritarian struggle. Laclau repeats this move in his slip between power bloc and state, his substitution of the "form of the State" for state structures. He confuses what political theorist Philip Abrams terms the "*idea* of the state" with the "state structure" itself.[142] The various institutions that compose the state are conflated with the image of its sovereignty. Or as John Frow puts it, "What is at stake [for Laclau] is not directly the power bloc but rather a particular discursive *representation* of the power bloc." And as Frow goes on to argue, the result is a characteristically populist "drastic simplification of the political space."[143]

In practice, Laclau's own analysis of Peronism ultimately depends on a consideration of state structures and state power: Peronism's distinguishing feature turns out to be a form of neutralization that "consisted essentially in allowing the persistence of various 'elites' which based their support of the regime upon antagonistic articulating projects, and in confirming State power as a mediating force between them."[144] It is the state, then, that anchors the populist project. Institutional mediation compensates for unresolved discursive tensions and fissures. Indeed, rather than being a "starting point for a scientific study of political ideologies," as he claims in *Politics and Ideology,* Laclau's analysis of Peronism might direct renewed attention to the ways in which social order is in fact secured beneath discourse, and in the teeth of the manifest failure of hegemonic projects. We need to address the inarticulacy of power, its direct application on bodies through habit and affect. For finally even Laclau has to concede that the Peronist state "coalesced very few ideological symbols" and relied on structural mechanisms instead. Peronism resists the ideological analysis that hegemony theory asserts: Laclau argues that its "renowned ideological poverty and lack of official doctrine" can be explained only "by this mediating character of the State and Perón himself."[145] I will argue in my final chapter that what is going on here is the conversion of constituent into constituted power that constructs the illusion of mediation.

The importance of the state to Peronism is so obvious as hardly to require mention were it not for Laclau's contention of populism's essential antistatism. The Argentine sociologist Guido Di Tella, for example, is one of many to observe how in Perón's first administration "the State increased its role substantially" in the economy, in line with its policy of Import Substitution Industrialization.[146] The sociologist and historian Juan José Sebreli emphasizes Peronism's subordination of legislative and judicial power to the state and, in similar vein, Luis Alberto Romero describes the state under Perón in terms of "a restructuring of democratic institutions and a subordination of constitutional powers to the executive branch, where the leader resided."[147] The Peronist state absorbed and ignored ideological contradictions, becoming "a mixed brew of everything that took Perón's fancy, a capacious cauldron to which he always added his personal seasoning regardless of previous ideological commitments, and unconcerned about any contradictions between words and actions."[148] It was thanks to its capaciousness and expansiveness, and despite its authoritarian tendencies, that the Peronist state could encourage a "highly vigorous democratizing movement," coordinating a "singular form of democracy" by mobilizing civil society as an extension of state logic.[149] Peronist society as a whole was organized around and permeated by a state that was increasingly biopolitical in its constant presence in everyday life. The sociologists Juan Carlos Portantiero and Emilio de Ipola therefore describe Peronism in terms of its coordinated "state fetishism."[150] As I discuss below, cultural critic John Kraniauskas adds to this observation with his discussion of Evita's specifically fetishized role. Elsewhere, de Ipola's critique of Laclau argues that the state not only mediates discursive claims, but also secures ground won apparently through hegemonic struggle.

"After his electoral triumph," de Ipola points out, "Perón had not only implanted his hegemony in the field of the popular: he then controlled also the material means to maintain and consolidate that hegemony." De Ipola's conclusion stresses the "link between the *relations of power,* crystallized in apparatuses, hierarchies, and practices that legitimate or disqualify social actors, allowing them to speak or reducing them to silence, and the *relation between the discourses themselves.*"[151] But Laclau conflates apparatuses and discourses, presenting an expanded concept of discourse that fails to distinguish between signifying and asignifying elements.

Many critics have denounced Laclau and Mouffe's abandonment of class and their denial of economic determination.[152] But the problem with Laclau's position appears equally in his earliest work, which does indeed argue for the priority of class and the fundamental importance of the economy. The basic flaw in hegemony theory is not its underestimation of the economy; it is that it substitutes culture for state, ideological representations for institutions, discourse for habit. Hegemony theory is a conceptualization of politics as populism that never escapes its own populist grounds and is therefore destined to repeat a characteristic sleight of hand, "that is to say," that gives us a series of displacements effected through a chain of assumed equivalence. This same sleight of hand now marks cultural studies, undermining its potential for critical analysis. The dream of abstracting some radical impulse from populism's anti-authoritarian and rebellious sentiments is shipwrecked on the fact that, under the guise of subversion, populist movements only ever construct and consolidate sovereignty, authorizing a people whose rebelliousness never rises above sentimentality.

Populism, as exemplified by classical political movements such as Peronism and contemporary intellectual tendencies such as cultural studies, and as theorized by Laclau, entails a systematic set of substitutions. It presents us with people instead of classes (or multitude), gestures instead of analysis (or struggle), morality instead of politics (or ethics), sentiment instead of affect (or habit), socialized identities instead of social forces (or preindividual singularities), transcendence instead of immanence (or quasi causes), unity instead of multiplicity (or contingency), the body of the sovereign instead of the power of the state (or constituent power). As John Kraniauskas observes of such populist moves, quoting Freud on fetishism, in each case "*something else has taken its place, has been appointed its substitute*, as it were, and now inherits the interest which was formerly directed to its predecessor."[153] Through these serried substitutions, populism constructs a drastically simplified image of social space. What has been substituted is quickly forgotten, erasing also the process that has constructed this falsely straightforward scenario of easy dichotomies, crystal-clear antagonisms, and well-worn assumptions. It is true that these disavowals conserve some remainder of what has gone, but theoretical analysis must move beyond the mere examination of such symptoms, which is all that cultural studies and hegemony theory can provide.

Above all, populism presents us with hegemony instead of any other conception of politics, and portrays the state's expansiveness as though it were cultural subversion or a flourishing civility. In the name of a purported counterhegemony of antiauthoritarian sentiment, populism's self-erasing state logic permeates and coordinates everyday life. In a relatively early article tracing Marxist theories of the state, Laclau himself equivocates on this point. He notes that state logic has come to organize society as a whole: "The form of the state defines the basic articulations of a society and not solely the limited field of a political superstructure"; but he immediately disavows this insight by claiming that "political struggle has passed now to extend to the totality of civil society."[154] This merely repeats the populist substitution: the state is conflated with civil society, political struggle with sovereign command. Hegemony theory can only glimpse and then foreclose the state. So long, therefore, as political analysis remains confined to the theory of hegemony, as contemporary cultural studies does, it will remain confined to a logic of populism unable either to differentiate itself from the populism of the right or even to recognize and so criticize the transformations and substitutions that populism demands and entails. Yet it will be anxiously haunted by the reminders of what has been lost: the traces of the state; subaltern excess. Rather than fixating on discursive articulations within civil society (a concept I examine in more detail in the next chapter), we might do better to reexamine the differential interimbrication of culture and state. Or rather, we might again see the state as what has to be explained, in its dependence on but distinction from the affective performativity and cultural habit that sustain it.

Beyond Cultural Studies: Habit

Populism structures both hegemony theory and cultural studies. Indeed, it gives cultural studies what little coherence and consistency that discipline has. The attractions and seductions of this populism are clear: it provides a broad terrain of activity and analysis, expanding the sphere of politics from the formal arena of debate and policy-making to the swathe of everyday practices that constitute culture. Populism promises to open up another front for a politicized undertaking that has lost its way with the decline of Marxism. It seems to ring true in a context in which the cultural economy is taken as seriously as any other sector of the economy, in which the sound bite dominates while traditional political allegiances wither, in which the media are more extensive and more influential than ever, in which subjectivity is molded ever more by taste and consumption, in short in which, as Fredric Jameson puts it, " 'culture' has become a veritable 'second nature.' "[155] At the same time, in this same context, populism is also a source of anxiety and uncertainty. Its uselessness as a political compass is evident as soon as one withdraws from the passion and fervor that the populist impulse itself inspires. After all, for example, is not the antiglobalization critique of Americanism, along the lines of the French activist Jose Bové's campaign against McDonalds, as populist as the celebration of U.S. popular culture and taste upon which so much of McDonalds' own image and advertising depend?

One response might be to argue that populism is less compass than weathervane: simply a more or less neutral reflex, an inevitable accompaniment to political activity. In some ways, this is Laclau's position: politics is inconceivable without populism; so although populism has no predetermined political valence, it should be welcomed rather than denigrated. What would be important therefore would be to differentiate between populisms, between populism as a progressive project and populism as the ground for conservative reaction. There are, however, two problems with this position: first, as I have shown, the difficulty of resolving to any satisfaction how to distinguish between left and right populisms; and second, more importantly, that populism itself does political work. By presenting hegemony as the only conceivable form of politics, populism helps conceal other modes of political command or struggle. It enables a series of substitutions that fetishize culture at the expense of institutions, and establish transcendence and sovereignty in place of immanent processes or micropolitical struggles. Populism simplifies the double register through which the social coheres. It does this by obscuring the mechanisms through which transcendence is produced from immanence, subjective emotion from impersonal affect, signifying discourse from asignifying habit, people from multitude, and constituted from constituent power, precisely because it is one of those mechanisms. The task of posthegemony theory is to uncover what has been obscured in these substitutions and to outline the means by which its suppression has been achieved, enforced, naturalized, and legitimated. In sum, social order has to be disarticulated to reveal both its mute underside and the process by which it has been ventriloquized, made to speak but in another's voice.

Above all, hegemony theory presents social order as the result of either coercion or consent. Dominance is achieved, it suggests, either by imposition from above or through agreement from below. People are either overpowered by a transcendent state, or they willingly subscribe to a dominant ideology. But pure coercion is unthinkable, so hegemony theory posits that there is always at least a residue of willed acquiescence. People stick together, forming societies and submitting to their laws, because in one way or another they think the same things, in the same ways. Hence the culturalism of cultural studies: communities achieve consistency and coherence through a shared set of beliefs and ideologies. Hegemony theory is the last gasp of the contractualism that has justified the bounded forms of modern social formations since at least the sixteenth century. However modified, it is still a rationalism: people give up their consent because it seems reasonable to do so, given what they know and believe (even if those beliefs are themselves ideological or irrational). But this dichotomy between coercion and consent is misguided and debilitating.

Ask a populist subject "why?" and a response is seldom forthcoming. Peronism shows that populist politics are structured by habit, rather than belief. So in *Resistance and Integration,* Daniel James reports that he "was constantly struck by the seemingly unquestioning identification, particularly amongst militants, of working-class activism, resistance and organization with being a Peronist." Peronism, he continues, "seems to have become almost an accepted part of working-class 'common sense' in the 1955–73 period." James shows Peronism's lack of any persistent ideological affiliations, and so refutes the "pervasive form of explanation...which has emphasised the continued adherence of workers to populist ideology."[156] Workers' identification with Peronism was fluid, mutable, and inarticulate, especially during Perón's long exile: "Peronism had become by the late 1950s a sort of protean, malleable commonplace of working-class identification." James therefore turns our attention from ideological interpellations to "the ontological status of the working class," picking up on Raymond Williams's notoriously underdeveloped concept of "structures of feeling" and Pierre Bourdieu's concern with the structuring of "private experience" through an embodied habitus.[157]

James's subsequent book, *Doña María's Story,* continues this focus on Peronism's embodiment in the Argentine working class, examining the physical monuments and architecture of the working-class town of Berisso, and so the unspoken political geography of a "profoundly Peronist place." He analyzes the testimony of Peronist activism as a performance whose "final coherence" is at best "elusive," showing how it is elaborated around an affective kernel of "ultimately indigestible feelings" that can never fully be narrativized, that "must simply remain in tense coexistence within the story" told about it. Peronism's structure of feeling is in tension with the ideological articulation that its hegemonic project imposes. Peronism attempted to resolve this tension through a "melodramatic fix" that would harness the energy of plebeian affect to reinforce its characteristically populist dualisms.[158] We see the same narrative appropriation of habit and affect in Auyero's *Poor People's Politics,* for which Peronism is embodied as a performance that is "taken for granted, unreflective, and outside the realm of discursive consciousness." Peronism's affective register, its adherents' surrender to an "imaginary 'bond of love,'" is only later overcoded by ideology.[159] Contemporary shantytown activists' political practice is a mode of "performing Evita" that faithfully mimics Eva Perón's own role within Peronist dramaturgy. Or consider Kraniauskas's description of Evita as fetish: "the paradoxical structure of Peronism's political negation of modernity—simultaneously mobilizing and demobilizing the working class and women—is written right into her body, which itself becomes literally 'seized by meaning' and by a love that is not, quite, patriotic."[160] Seized by meaning and seized by love: this is populism's double register.

Evita Perón on the balcony of the Casa Rosada, October 17, 1951. Juan Perón holds her weakening body and also hides behind it.

Peronism employed imagery, technology, and dramaturgy to demarcate its proper spheres of social, symbolic, and physical space. Its paradigmatic orchestration of a primal populist scene took place in Buenos Aires's central square, the Plaza de Mayo, in front of the presidential palace or "Casa Rosada" from whose balcony Evita and Juan addressed the masses below. In its rallies, Peronism staged the social collectivity, the people in its positivity, as presumed subjects and objects of a mutual and reflecting gaze between leader and mass. It was Evita's image above all, on the balcony with "her arms . . . always raised, encouragingly, in a gesture of love,"[161] that, as anthropologist Julie Taylor suggests, "functioned as intermediary between Perón and his people, between governmental machinery and governed masses."[162] For Kraniauskas, as Evita mobilized and organized popular affect, she "invades the political space of the state" and becomes a "hybrid figure, emerging at the interface of the cultural and the political, where the logics of education and entertainment fold into the logic of the State, making the latter a peculiar kind of stage and of Eva Perón herself, a peculiar kind of fetish." The Peronist regime referred its followers back to the October 17, 1945, demonstration that founded its power, rewrote its plot by constructing Evita as its central organizing principle, and engrained its version of that mythic event into their bodies. In the process, Kraniauskas notes, the state disappears as "(a conservative military) *anxiety* produces a *substitution* . . . through *disavowal* (the containment of working-class and female 'barbarism')."[163] Kraniauskas comments that it is when Evita becomes embalmed body that her functionality is perfected; but alive, Evita was already half cadaver. See the famous image of the last October 17 celebration that she attended, in 1951: Evita was by then almost completely incapacitated by cancer; Perón is seen behind her, supporting her dying body but also sheltering behind it. Historian Mariano Plotkin's analysis of the annual celebrations and re-creations of October 17, and of the regime's similar use of May Day parades, concludes that "toward the end of Perón's regime . . . May Day and the Seventeenth of October were no longer popular festivals, but highly ritualized celebrations organized entirely by the state."[164] Both present and absent in these performances, propping up and protected by its fetishized substitute, the Peronist state produced its people and, reciprocally, its own sovereignty, which was then encrusted within the habit of being Peronist. In my final chapter I will return to this scene, to uncover the constituent power of the multitude that underlies it. Ultimately, the Peronist state revealed itself to be remarkably fragile, for all the technological apparatus it employed to sustain the fetish. In one of Evita's very few public outings just weeks before she died in July 1952, to attend her husband's reinauguration as president, her body was held up by a support made of metal and wax, hidden under a flowing fur coat. And famously, following the coup that overthrew

Perón in 1955, her corpse set off on a long, mysterious journey that led to an unmarked grave in a Rome cemetery. Something always escapes.

In the end, populism, and so also cultural studies, is an antipolitics. No wonder cultural studies has been derided for its complicity with the status quo, however radical its rhetoric. It is not so much that its practitioners are victims of bad faith. It is that cultural studies takes hegemony at its word and so misses the ways in which hegemonic processes stand in for the other, more complex, means by which dominance is asserted and reproduced. If there is anything that can be salvaged from populism, it is its antipathy to representation. In the second half of this book, in a discussion of nonrepresentational and unnarratable affect, habit, and the multitude, I outline a theory of posthegemony that can better account for dominance and social order. We need such a new theory because cultural studies merely reinforces sovereignty, by shoring up the strange notion that power comes from above and that the only options for the dominated are negotiation or acquiescence. It is blind to the ways in which state institutions emerge from immanent processes and secure their legitimacy well below consciousness, with no need of words. So long as cultural studies continues to take these processes for granted, then all its articulate verbosity is no more than a form of complicitous silence.

2

Ayacucho 1982: Civil Society Theory and Neoliberalism

To make war, one must be a philosopher. C. Gonzalo poses battles politically, not technically.

—Sendero Luminoso, quoted in Gustavo Gorriti, *The Shining Path*

It is a question of effecting groupings of powers, *and these are what constitute affects.*

—Gilles Deleuze and Félix Guattari, *A Thousand Plateaus*

Civil society theory has flourished in the social sciences in recent decades and enjoys great influence with nongovernmental organizations, social-democratic think tanks, and the like. This second chapter is a critique of that theory and the practices it fosters, arguing that it assumes a liberal compact that is too easily overtaken by its neoliberal radicalization. I first discuss the various definitions of civil society and the reasons for the concept's popularity: it names a sphere of mediation between state and market, private and public, and also brings with it an aura of normativity. Who would not want a more "civil" society? I go on, however, to criticize the term's deployment, through a close reading of political theorists Jean Cohen and Andrew Arato. Their theorization of civil society reveals the concept's profound ambivalence: it is presented as a moderating, mediating force, but depends upon what they call the "democratic fundamentalism" that drives the social movements that constitute civil society itself. For all that these movements are championed as the expression of democratic rejuvenation, they are to be policed and curtailed to protect both state and market in the name of political and economic efficiency. I argue that the neoliberal state outflanks civil society theory with a cult of transparency that bypasses mediating institutions and breaks down the boundary between society and state. Neoliberalism and its diffuse sovereignty herald a revolution in reverse, a fundamentalism purged of affect. But that repressed affect always returns, and in counterpoint I offer an account of the Peruvian Maoists Sendero Luminoso and their relations with the neoliberal regime of Alberto Fujimori. Sendero's baffling ferocity challenges any theory of civil society and provides a foretaste of the global war on terror that we are all living through now.

Defining Civil Society

Like cultural studies, civil society resists definition. Michael Edwards calls it "a concept that seems so unsure of itself that definitions are akin to nailing jelly to a wall"; he cites another account that calls it "a woolly expression for woolly-minded people." Yet Edwards comes not to bury the concept but to praise it. He is, after all, director of the Ford Foundation's "Governance and Civil Society" program and is more than aware of the term's currency among nongovernmental organizations such as, precisely, the Ford Foundation. Edwards's aim is to rejuvenate and refine the concept of civil society, to ensure its continued viability. He is therefore "happy to be called a 'civil society revivalist.'" Civil society is, he claims, for all its uncertainty or woolliness, the "'big idea' for the twenty-first century."[1] We are already mired, however, in circularity. For there is something self-serving about the Ford Foundation's advocacy of this "big idea," when by almost any definition such a body is itself an integral part of civil society.

The concept of civil society gathers together all those organizations, associations, and movements that mediate, formally or informally, between private and public, state and market, particular and universal. Whatever its precise boundaries (and this is where the slipperiness enters in), whatever the spheres or institutions with which it is said to be in contact, and whatever its exact function, civil society is generally agreed, from Hegel or Tocqueville onward, to be an *intermediate* sphere. Along with nongovernmental organizations and foundations, other associations today commonly thought to constitute civil society include voluntary groups, charities, pressure groups, social organizations and clubs, as well as (more controversially) trade unions, political parties, religious organizations, some business organizations, and even the media. This is such a broad-ranging collection that it is sometimes hard to distinguish civil society from the public sphere or even society as a whole. Indeed, as we will see, often civil society theorists expend most effort and energy in limiting the concept, in ensuring that it does not break its bounds. After all, if it is to be an intermediate sphere, then civil society has to be located in between some other entities that can be distinguished from it.

The concept of civil society has a distinguished history, whose origins date as far back as Aristotle's discussion of *koinōnia politikè* (κοινωνια πολιτική) at the outset of *The Politics*. Aristotle characterizes the *polis* as a political community, "the state as an association" as one modern translation has it.[2] But this phrase has also been rendered variously as *societas civilis, civill societie, bürgerliche Gesellschaft,* and *societé civile.* The French political scientist Dominique Colas traces the term and its translations from Aristotle to Lenin via Luther, Spinoza, Leibniz, Kant, Hegel, and Marx. The American John Ehrenberg likewise emphasizes the idea's classical heritage (from Cicero as well as Aristotle), and its Christian articulations (via Saint Augustine).[3] U.S. theorists tend to point to the influence of the early nineteenth-century French writer Alexis de Tocqueville: according to Edwards, it is "Tocqueville's ghost that wanders through the corridors of the World Bank."[4] The key moment in the term's evolution, however, is Hegel's emphasis on the *bürgerliche* or *bourgeois* to refer not to society as a civic whole, but to one element within a complex system of differences. Hegel was the first to distinguish civil society from the state; in Aristotle the two are conjoined. But Hegel was suspicious of any notion that civil society could be autonomous and believed that it should be firmly subordinate to constituted power.

Today, commentators prefer to stress how the state bends to pressures from civil society. So, as the philosopher Lawrence Cahoone observes, "contemporaries who use 'civil society' are in the odd position of using Hegel's term, but not his meaning."[5] When, after a long period of neglect, it was resurrected in the 1970s and 1980s, the concept of civil society was to designate a site from which to transform or reign in the state. It was revived as a way to understand struggles in Eastern Europe and Latin America in which social groups first opposed authoritarian states and then, in the various democratic transitions from dictatorship, set to consolidating and "deepening" democracy. Analysts praised civil society as a source of normative democratic values. From these dictatorial and post-dictatorial contexts, the term spread to considerations of Western Europe and the United States as well as to Africa, Asia, and the Middle East. It has been enthusiastically adopted by nongovernmental agencies and aid workers; in political theorist John Keane's words, "the language of civil society is now more widely used than ever before in the history of modern times."[6] The term's ubiquity, the fact that it is often invoked if seldom questioned, characterizes what I call civil society discourse. Civil society theory, by contrast, is the attempt by theorists such as Cahoone, Colas, Edwards, Ehrenberg, and Keane to make sense of and systematize the disparate uses that cohabit in this discourse.

The idea of civil society is popular today thanks also to a slippage between descriptive and normative meanings: between civil society as the name for one part of a social whole (the Hegelian sense), and *civil* society as an ideal polity that would be characterized by civility rather than arbitrary violence or bureaucratic rationality. The normative meaning is closer to Tocqueville's use of the term. Hence for neo-Tocquevillians, the tendency to form associations uncoerced by the state is itself an unalloyed good. "Civil society as the good society," as Edwards puts it, is envisaged as "a reservoir of caring, cultural life and intellectual innovation . . . nurturing a collection of positive social norms."[7] In this conception, civil society takes on substantive content as well as a functional role: not only is it an intermediate sphere, defined therefore by what it is *not;* it is also a realm whose particular character results from the qualities of the groups that constitute it, and which is defined therefore by what it *is*. Here civil society theory overlaps with the theory of "social capital" as outlined in works such as political scientist Robert Putnam's influential *Bowling Alone*, which laments the decline of "voluntary associations and the social networks of civil society" in the contemporary United States.[8] Putnam is concerned with all types of association, from Rotary Clubs to bowling leagues; but civil society discourse usually focuses on the so-called "new social movements," which are likewise envisaged as contributing to overall social well-being.

New social movements (also, as we have seen, championed by Laclau and Mouffe) develop out of the social protests and identity politics of the 1960s. They are not strictly political, according to one of their most important theorists, the French sociologist Alain Touraine: traditional political parties "call for the seizure of state power. A social movement, by contrast, is civil and is an affirmation rather than a critique or a negation."[9] The new social movements are the lifeblood of civil society: it is their emergence, Touraine argues, that leads to "the growing importance of 'civil society,' or in other words of a new type of political action that is both less organized and less continuous than that of parties and unions."[10] The new social movements give civil society positive content, flesh out what would otherwise be an obscure and ill-defined term, and (civil society theorists tell us) make it worthy of our approbation and encouragement.

Latin America was, with Eastern Europe, one of the regions in which the contemporary renaissance of civil society discourse first took hold. The concept came to prominence in the 1980s in analyses of the opposition to authoritarian rule in the Southern Cone (Chile, Argentina, Uruguay, and Brazil). The concept was particularly popular in Chile and Brazil, where sustained pressure from opposition movements was claimed as a factor in the military's withdrawal from power. For Brazil, political scientist Alfred Stepan quotes the sociologist and politician Fernando Henrique Cardoso's observation that "the whole opposition . . . was being described as if it were the movement of Civil Society"; Stepan goes on to comment that " 'civil society' became the political celebrity of the abertura," or opening.[11] The transitions to democracy in these countries (with elections in Argentina in 1983, Uruguay in 1984, and Brazil and Chile in 1989) led to further interest in the concept, as civil society was considered crucial for consolidating or deepening the democracy formally secured at the ballot box. Political scientists Guillermo O'Donnell and Philippe Schmitter, for example, argue that the return of democracy entails a "resurrection of civil society."[12] But while space opened for civil society as repression lifted, participation within its constituent organizations often declined. As many of those who had theorized civil society in opposition later gained political power in posttransition governments (most notably Cardoso, Brazilian president from 1995 to 2003), they became anxious to improve relations between civil society and the state so as to ensure democratic legitimacy. By 1998, at the second Summit of the Americas in Santiago de Chile, the hemisphere's heads of state pledged to "promote, with the participation of civil society, the ... institutional frameworks to stimulate the formation of responsible and transparent, non-profit and other civil society organizations."[13] The then president of Chile, Eduardo Frei, wrote in the preface to the Summit's subsequent publication that "civil society's participation in the decision-making process is vital to the strengthening of democracy and the development of our peoples.... I am convinced that only insofar as civil society is directly and effectively involved in life will democracy fully become a reality."[14] At the same time, analysts began discussing civil society in regional and even global terms: scholars Sonia Alvarez, Evelina Dagnino, and Arturo Escobar noted, also in 1998, that "conservative and progressive analysts and activists alike tend overwhelmingly to sing the praises of civil society's democratizing potential on a local, national, regional, and global scale."[15] By the turn of the century, talk of civil society had comprehensively permeated political and social discourse in Latin America.

Over time, the role envisaged for civil society in Latin America has changed, particularly its relationship to the state. At first it was to be the springboard for opposition to the authoritarian state; later it was to be a partner for the democratic state; most recently, it has been seen as a site from which to protest the neoliberal state's withdrawal from its social responsibilities. The Chilean philosopher Martín Hopenhayn, for instance, sees civil society and the new social movements as responding "to the crisis of modernization in Latin America without identifying with neoliberalism."[16] Throughout, however, the concept's definition has remained more or less constant, a sign perhaps of its capaciousness. Civil society is consistently seen as an intermediate sphere, though the demands and pressures that it channels may vary; and, more emphatically than for discussions of civil society elsewhere in the world, in Latin America the new social movements are described as civil society's most significant actors. New social movements are harbingers of civil society as the good society. Indeed, for Hopenhayn, it is because they inhabit civil society's intermediate sphere that they gain emancipatory power: thanks to "their marginal or interstitial space within society and with regard to the State and the market," he declares, these movements "can materialize 'counterhegemonic' logics where solidarity, resistance, cooperation, autonomy and/or collective participation predominate.... They constitute themselves as small 'promises of emancipation' in the eyes of critical theory."[17] Civil society is to instantiate theory's critical desires.

Cultural studies, too, is concerned with what Touraine terms "new type[s] of political action."[18] Indeed, there are plenty of continuities and similarities between cultural studies and civil society theory, though there are also significant differences. The two share above all the impulse to turn from the formal political sphere of parties, state, government, and administration. Both choose instead to focus on a sphere that they regard as relatively autonomous: culture in one case, civil society in the other. Insofar as they take account of the state, at issue is either its impact upon this other sphere or the ways in which it is influenced in turn. Equally, both cultural studies and civil society theory are concerned with community or the various possible formations of communities imaginable within this nonstate realm. They set their face against the individual as much as they turn from the state. Insofar as psychology is at issue, it is the psychology of groups rather than a more general psychology of "man." Finally, both cultural studies and civil society theory present themselves as progressive theories, although the one is post-Marxist and the other more clearly social democratic.

Culture and civil society overlap, and so therefore do the ways in which they are theorized. Indeed, cultural studies and civil society theory meet in the same nexus where populism meets neoliberalism; both ultimately underwrite the same hollow fiction of a social pact. On the other hand, the differences between cultural studies and civil society theory include the fact that where cultural studies stresses antagonism (the conflict between people and power bloc), civil society theory emphasizes mediation (communication and checks and balances). Civil society theory tends toward formalism, projecting ideal types of democratic regimes against which existing regimes are measured (often statistically); it flirts with both normativity and universalism. Cultural studies prefers narrative and thick description and to shirk explicit discussion of norms. This difference between narrativity and formalism reflects a disciplinary distinction: cultural studies is strong in the humanities; civil society theory in the social sciences, particularly within political science. Cultural studies is also usually localist or nationalist, where civil society theory tends to the international and the global.

Cultural studies and civil society theory are distinct but complementary discourses and should be examined in parallel. Cultural studies, a discourse of antagonism rooted in the humanities that provides generally narrative explanations within a national frame, is the other side of the coin to civil society theory, a discourse of mediation emerging from the social sciences that provides generally functionalist or statistical accounts within a global frame. In each case, however, a purported project of the left echoes rather than engages the dominant paradigms of governance: technocratic neoliberalism and media-savvy neopopulism, increasingly combined in diverse regimes of popular managerialism (of which Blairite New Labour is perhaps exemplary). I showed in my last chapter how cultural studies is unable to escape, and so critique, its own populist desires. In what follows, I argue that neoliberalism is a response to and radicalization of civil society discourse.

Through an interrogation of political theorists Jean Cohen and Andrew Arato's theory of civil society, I show how advocacy of democratic expansion soon switches to an anxious patrolling of social movement "fundamentalism." Civil society theory comes to support the state's project to contain democratic radicalism; it turns against democratic movements, purportedly in the name of democracy as some kind of higher good. Despite its emancipatory and oppositional aura, the concept of civil society becomes part of the toolbox of governmentality. It is perhaps no wonder that Michael Edwards is also now director of the "Governance" program at the Ford Foundation: civil society and governance go hand in hand. Civil society theory plays into the hands of technocratic neoliberalism, providing faint hope with what is at best a naïve vision of democratization as self-limiting radicalism. For neoliberalism seeks to implement a transparent and perfectly functional civil society. Neoliberal technocrats are as scathing about the traditional political processes and institutions (parties, unions) as are advocates of new social movements. But new social movements add little in the way of transparency or efficiency, so neoliberalism institutes a quasi-direct democracy of opinion polling and media saturation that dissolves the boundaries between state and civil society and does away with social movements. Civil society theory is caught in the paradox that it relies on the enthusiasm of social actors for its appeal and credibility, but it is forced to stigmatize that same enthusiasm as "democratic fundamentalism" in order to maintain the complex hierarchy of separate spheres upon which civil society depends. Neoliberalism resolves that paradox in a smooth, featureless space that dissolves all mediations: nothing should stand in the way of a perfect communication between citizens and the state. In the process, civil society disappears, subsumed within the state's machinery to replace multiplicity and singularity with unity and consensus. The dreams of liberal rationality and communicative action are conflated and superseded.

In tandem with my general critique of civil society theory as a discourse of governmentality that ultimately colludes with neoliberal practice, I specifically criticize the way in which civil society and new social movements came to be presented as the progressive motor of Latin American democratization. I focus on how Peru's Maoist guerrillas Sendero Luminoso (Shining Path) figure as the horizon of Latin American civil society discourse, destabilizing overconfident characterizations of new social movements. And I explore the continuities between civil society theory, Sendero, and neoliberalism, as well as the rise of technologies of immanence and immediacy, through an examination of the regime that effectively defeated Sendero, the government of Alberto Fujimori. Sendero, stigmatized as a repository of barbaric affect and feared as a highland counterstate, stands at the mute limits of both civil society and the neoliberal state. Sendero haunts civil society discourse in Latin America: analysts endlessly and anxiously refer to Sendero as the fundamentalism that threatens any conception of civil society as an intermediate sphere incarnating the good society of persuasion, consensus, and differentiation. But this specter consistently returns, hinting at a fundamentalism at the heart of new social movements and neoliberalism alike. Civil society theory is therefore unable to account either for the terror at its margins, or for the social movements themselves, which are not so "unaffected" after all.

One instance of civil society boosterism is *Utopia Unarmed,* the influential 1993 book written by Mexican political scientist (later his country's foreign minister) Jorge Castañeda. A bestseller outside as well as within the academy, Castañeda's text helped frame a rethinking of the Latin American left; it reevaluated national liberation movements and advocated moderate state intervention in the economy and welfare projects. Castañeda offers an unabashed social democracy. As in *Compañero,* his subsequent book on Che Guevara, he bids a fond farewell to all that the Latin American left held dear for most of the twentieth century.[19] Yet his enthusiasm for civil society won plaudits from leftist critics such as Duncan Green, who suggests that Castañeda proposes "one of the most ambitious" attempts to formulate an alternative to neoliberalism.[20] No longer, however, are such alternatives to involve gaining and exercising state power: "Here, then, is the first democratic order of battle for the left: to encourage every conceivable expression of civil society, every social movement, every form of self-management that Latin American reality generates."[21] This is the radicalism of civil society discourse. But it is very much what Cohen and Arato term a "self-limiting radicalism."[22] For there is a definite limit to the range of "conceivable" expressions of civil society: Castañeda locates the notoriously violent and ruthless Sendero Luminoso at the horizon of all leftist reformism; Sendero serves as a warning for any who choose not to rethink a democratic alternative. "The condition for the renewed viability of reformism in Latin America," he argues, "lies inevitably in the threat of something worse. Since it cannot be revolution as such—the way Cuba was for nearly twenty years—it must be different, yet terrifying nonetheless. This is the syndrome of Sendero Luminoso." If not reform, then Sendero. For Castañeda, Sendero is both the outcome of neoliberal social disintegration ("the new bane of Latin America") and the epitome of a left that refuses to reform. Sendero is the fundamentalism that haunts civil society's radicalism. Sendero "can certainly instill fear in the hearts and minds of many": a fear of the neglected masses, should they not be harnessed to a new program of reform, and of the recalcitrant left, should it continue with its fanatical excesses.[23]

For all that has been written about Sendero, the movement is still for the most part little understood. The best English-language introductions to the movement are the Peruvian journalist Gustavo Gorriti's *The Shining Path* (a narrative account of the insurgency in the early 1980s) and historian Steve Stern's collection, *Shining and Other Paths* (particularly on Sendero's history and political context). Sendero exploded from the remote Andean province of Ayacucho in 1980, and grew in strength and size until 1992, when it rapidly declined after the capture of leader Abimael Guzmán. I have no desire to romanticize Sendero, or to advance its cause: the movement was undoubtedly vicious and deservedly (almost) friendless. At the same time, I am not interested in demystifying it, either. Stern declares that "the agenda of [his] book is to move 'beyond enigma,' "[24] but enigma was part of Sendero's strategy: its militants worked hard to maintain their invisibility, mysteriousness, and unrepresentability. Demythologizing them too fast prevents us from understanding their hold over their own recruits and, more importantly, also over the imagination of middle class and urban Peru in the late 1980s and early 1990s. Gorriti's book, written in the midst of that period, conveys quite viscerally just how "the insurgency's very obscurity seemed to add to its power."[25] Moreover, because "enigma, exoticism, surprise" condition the ways in which the group is (mis)perceived and (mis)understood,[26] stripping them of that enigma prevents us from seeing how they figured not only within Peru, but also in the discourse of Latin American political and cultural theory more generally. Again, I am concerned precisely with the ways in which Sendero serves as a limit, an inassimilable presence haunting both neoliberalism and civil society theory.

Fundamentalism constitutes the limit or horizon for both civil society and neoliberalism. Civil society theory constantly invokes but then represses its other side: a fundamentalism stigmatized for its affective, irrational, culture-bound qualities. The concept of civil society marks off fundamentalism as other in order to reinforce the rationality of an expansive state. It tries to reconstruct the social pact, no longer through affect but despite it. As a result, however, it expels affect and culture from its analyses. Neoliberalism, too, has to discard affect as an opaque, irrational, and unrepresentable obstacle to its reductive mechanisms of rational calculability. But affect returns as terror, or as a counterstate to disrupt the principle of state unity. In my next chapter I return to terror and what is ignored or repressed by both neoliberalism and civil society theory: the irreducible affective relations that sustain and subvert social order. But to think affect, we will need new theoretical tools. Civil society theory can tell us little about the fundamentalisms that it so vigorously attempts to govern and excise.

A Progressive Project: New Social Movements

Civil society is projected as a means to rejuvenate politics, to dispel the threat of antipolitical reaction. In a context defined by the decline of the traditional left and the end of both "actually existing" socialism and revolutionary utopias, by the rise of technocratic neoliberalism and fear of a disempowering globalization, by the increasing blandness and sameness of major political parties and widespread public apathy toward formal political processes, civil society has appeared to provide at least some cause for optimism. Commonwealth scholars Barry Knight, Hope Chigudu, and Rajesh Tandon, for instance, worry about a "yawning gulf between political institutions and their citizens.... With the social contract in jeopardy, we risk falling prey to the forces of barbarism." Strengthening civil society, the intermediate sphere between citizens and institutions, is our only hope if we are to ward off barbarism and cement the social pact: "Civil society functions," they claim, "as a metaphor for 'hope for a better world....' Indeed, our view is that it is impossible to separate the idea of civil society from the idea of progress toward a better world."[27] Activist author David Korten offers a similar solution to much the same concerns. Noting the failure of "our dominant institutions," he argues that "it is left to civil society to expose the causes of the institutional dysfunction and to define and pursue alternatives." Korten is positively ebullient about the prospect of "globalizing civil society," which he identifies with "the emergence of a new global awareness and sense of solidarity that is joining people from every part of the planet in the task of creating a new global civilization grounded in peace and cooperation."[28] Civil society promises the utopia of a civilization based on peace, not war.

Other analysts, even self-proclaimed civil society revivalists, are more cautious. Edwards, for instance, recognizes that since the September 2001 attacks on New York and Washington, and subsequent U.S. and British intervention in Afghanistan and Iraq, civil society has lost some of its cachet. The national security state and those who protest it are equally suspicious of the concept: the former for the possibility that civil society harbors subversion; the latter for the ways in which the post-Kosovo conflation of humanitarianism and bellicosity has, in radical journalist Naomi Klein's view, "embedded what is called 'civil society' into part of the war machine."[29] The state is both more distrustful and more untrustworthy than ever, while protest movements (from Seattle to La Paz) are more confrontational or cynical about the promises of NGOs and the like. Yet Edwards draws inspiration from the vitality of the World Social Forum and from the sight of millions demonstrating against the Iraq war, which he claims "provide a useful reminder that mass protest on the basis of human community may yet generate the foundation for alternative forms of politics and a new kind of society."[30] For Edwards, then, despite these protestors' suspicions of civil society, they are acting out its presuppositions by coming together as a social movement, however transient. They are part of civil society whether they know (or like) it or not.

In Latin America, civil society is often simply equated with democratization: to strengthen civil society is automatically to expand and deepen democracy. Civil society is given an emancipatory aura, dressed in the rhetorical flourishes of the old left, as in Castañeda's invocation of a "first democratic order of battle for the left: to encourage every conceivable expression of civil society."[31] This is rhetorical shorthand, a gesture toward the new rather than a serious attempt to think through possibilities for self-management. Yet Castañeda is not alone in his clarion call for the rejuvenation of Latin American civil society, and this sense of engagement is not merely a result of martial metaphors ("order[s] of battle"). Sociologist William Robinson's laudatory account of the São Paulo Forum is in the same vein. The Forum is a broad coalition of leftist Latin American groups and parties; indeed it is practically a "Who's Who" of the Latin American left, from Brazil's PT (Lula's Workers' Party, which originally convoked the Forum) to the Nicaraguan Sandinistas, the Salvadoran FMLN, and the Cuban Communist Party. Writing in 1992, Robinson commends the Forum's belief that "the correlation of social forces in civil society is at least as important as who actually holds power, maybe more so."[32] Indeed, Robinson seems to suggest that civil society can simply be divorced from the state, which can be left to its own devices; the PT, now in power, would presumably no longer agree.

Though the São Paulo Forum embraces almost the entire spectrum of the Latin American left, Sendero Luminoso has always stayed away from this or indeed almost any other coalition. Pacts or contracts are anathema to Sendero. Sendero differs markedly from a group such as the FMLN: the FMLN was a broad "front" uniting numerous parties and tendencies; Sendero, by contrast, was the residue of a series of factional divisions.[33] The Partido Comunista del Perú–Sendero Luminoso (or Peruvian Communist Party–Shining Path), to give it its full name, was an offshoot of the Partido Comunista del Perú–Bandera Roja (PCP–Red Flag), which itself had splintered from the Peruvian Communist Party proper. As the Peruvian Truth Commission puts it, Sendero emerged from "a long process of dogmatic purification." Indeed, by Sendero's foundation in 1970, only twelve militants remained in founder Guzmán's Ayacucho faction, and the party had no more than fifty-one members in total in all Peru. It is as though it had to begin with something like a degree zero of extension, so as to ensure it was untainted by association with any other group. Sendero took little or no part in the "great social mobilizations" of the late 1970s against the military regime of General Francisco Morales Bermúdez, refusing for instance to participate in the national strikes of 1977 and 1978. Sendero "stayed on the margins and even opposed mobilizations that it considered manipulated by 'revisionism,' the term it employed to describe the 'Unity' Communist Party (PCP-Unidad) and the rest of the parties on the left, which it viewed as obstacles to the development of the revolution."[34] Far from seeking alliances, Guzmán deemed further purification necessary in 1980, on the eve of battle. Before initiating the "people's war," he called a Central Committee meeting, which lasted from March 17 to the end of the month, and then a Military School from April 2 to April 19, for which criticism and "self-criticism" were paramount. As Gorriti reports of a typical day's activities in the Military School, Guzmán urged his cadres to "clean out the 'colossal mountain of garbage' . . . left behind by the ideological struggles within the workers' movement. The task of ideological policing lasted all day and concluded, inflexibly, with another round of self-criticism from those members of the wretched historical detritus."[35] There is little in the way of discussion or negotiation here. In place of extension, intensity. And if civil society theorists exclude Sendero, in turn Sendero decisively turns its back on civil society.

Social movements are at the heart of claims for civil society as a progressive project. Civil society is, for political scientist Joe Foweraker, "the cradle of such collective identities"; reciprocally, these "active and diverse groups...act as 'schools of democracy'" and give life and substance to what would otherwise be an empty structure.[36] Civil society, for its enthusiasts, is more than simply a buffer against the immediate claims of either the market or the state and more also than a mere vehicle for protest. As a diverse collection of organizations and associations, civil society offers, it is argued, new ways of thinking and experiencing sociability, conviviality, and connectedness. For Edwards and others, the concept presents new modes of doing politics, more flexible, creative, and democratic than those hitched either to the traditional institutions of the state or to the atomization of the market. Social movements are to "constitute the laboratories in which new experiences are invented and popularized. Within these local laboratories, movements utilize a variety of means of communication...to question and transform the dominant codes of everyday life."[37] Civil society is the intermediate sphere for the articulation of demands to the state, but it is also a communicative medium within which social movements construct, live out, and express new collective identities. It is in this sense that Cahoone suggests that civil society "is, if you will, a form of life."[38]

Social movements, and particularly the "new" social movements, are the agents that are to shape and transform civil society. For William Robinson, they have already effected a "revolution" in civil society.[39] For Cohen and Arato, "social movements constitute the dynamic element in processes that might realize the positive potentials of modern civil societies."[40] Similar sentiments surround descriptions of a "movement of movements" that gives life to the so-called antiglobalization protests and the World Social Forum, as detailed in social theorist Tom Mertes's *A Movement of Movements*. The Brazilian Emir Sader's contribution to Mertes's collection is critical of the concept of civil society (because he sees it as ignoring the role of the state), but he goes against the grain of the antiglobalization movement's own conception of its political role: no less a body than the World Social Forum describes itself as "an open meeting place for reflective thinking...by groups and movements of civil society that are opposed to neoliberalism."[41] Social movements and civil society go hand in glove: analysts point to the plethora of new social movements as evidence of contemporary civil society's dynamism, and to bracket off any vestigial conservative elements (more traditional associations and "old" social movements).

The radical potential of civil society, we are told, is unleashed by its newest, emergent forces.

New social movements encompass the post-1960s countercultural opposition (such as antiwar and antinuclear activism), pressure groups (environmental, animal rights, or AIDS activism), groups premised on identity politics (feminism, the lesbian and gay movements), as well as now the "antiglobalization" movement. For Touraine, the rise of many diverse new movements in the past forty years responds to the advent of postindustrial or "programmed" society. Whereas the principal site of domination and resistance in industrial society was the factory, and so the central struggles concerned class and labor, in postindustrial society "political action is all-pervading: it enters into the health service, into sexuality, into education, and into energy production."[42] Social movements are products of modernity, perhaps even of postmodernity, rather than resistant elements of a previous order. They arise from "a weakening of traditional cleavages in which people are freed from traditional ties of class, religion, and the family."[43] They disrupt the notion that modernization necessarily implies an undifferentiated "mass society" and increased homogeneity. Social movements embody the paradox that postindustrial society allows new forms of creativity and novel experiments in identity-formation at the same time as it brings new modes of control, more extensive regimes of bureaucratic rationalization. Their emergence is part of what in chapter 4 I describe as "biopolitics."

At stake in the new social movements' struggles, Touraine argues, is first and foremost "self-management."[44] The movements take advantage of the communicative possibilities offered by technological change (telephone, fax, and now e-mail and the Internet) while fending off the threats of surveillance and control brought by these same developments. "Struggles over quality of life issues," write globalization theorists John Guidry, Michael Kennedy, and Mayer Zald, imply "movement goals toward the rearticulation of identities and the elaboration of identities denied by systemic constraints."[45] Movements are *social* or even cultural before they are political: the new social movements renovate civil society as one renovates a house; they inhabit civil society rather than being merely represented within it. This is "civil society as an ordinary *lebensraum*."[46] Social movements, it is argued, are autopoietic or self-making, seeking space within an ever more expansive civil society to vindicate and consolidate the ways of life they incarnate, and to demand the state's support and succor. Hence Touraine's conclusion that "a social movement . . . is an affirmation rather than a critique or negation."[47]

Rather than elaborating universal demands or aiming to smash or capture the state, new social movements prefer to seek the state's protection or legitimation for the spaces they have carved out within civil society. Whereas traditional political parties claimed to speak for a plurality of subjects in a single voice, representing them across a broad range of issues, new social movements are more limited in their composition and in the issues they address. As so many of the new social movements are the expression of who people are (identity politics) or where they happen to be (neighborhood organizing), they promise a quasi-natural participation in the political, a promise accentuated by the apparent everydayness of their typically small size and antibureaucratic workings. Social movements engender new habits, a "second nature" to be preserved from incursions by the state. In Cohen and Arato's terms, these movements "operate on both sides of the system/lifeworld divide," intervening in the strategic projects of political and economic society, but rooted in a Habermasian "lifeworld" devoid of bureaucratic rationality.[48] They come to seem organic, embedded in the soil of life itself; they are, after all, the "grassroots."

In Latin America the label of "new social movement" is often applied to indigenous organizations, ecclesiastical base communities, squatters' movements, peasant cooperatives, and so on. The concept is particularly associated with those groups that took over the role of opposition to authoritarian regimes after the repression of political parties or trade unions: relatives of the disappeared, neighborhood soup kitchens, and human rights organizations, for instance. Some movements, particularly Latin American feminists and gay and lesbian campaigners, draw on the example and resources provided by similar organizations in Europe and North America. Others arise from the distinct problematics not only of dictatorship and resistance, but also of the extremely rapid modernization and urbanization that have affected much of the region in the past forty years. "In the new situation," theorists Arturo Escobar and Sonia Alvarez declare, "a multiplicity of social actors establish their presence and spheres of autonomy in a fragmented social and political space. Society itself is largely shaped by the plurality of these struggles and the vision of those involved in the new social movements."[49]

As anthropologist Orin Starn observes, new social movements are generally assumed to be outlets for social protest. But this is a dubious generalization. Starn comments that in Escobar and Alvarez's collection on Latin American social movements, "not a single essay considers drug gangs, conservative civic movements, soccer hooligans, neo-Nazi skinheads, faith healers or evangelical churches."[50] The same, one might add, is true of books such as geographer David Slater's *New Social Movements and the State in Latin America* or sociologist Susan Eckstein's *Power and Popular Protest.* Eckstein frames her collection in terms of the "coordinated and overt nonviolent forms of defiance" on the part of "the politically and economically weak."[51] But this ignores the conservatism inherent in some social movements, particularly as they grow in strength: if they so zealously guard their newly won identities from the intrusions of the state, why should they not also react against threats real or perceived from other, perhaps more progressive, movements within civil society itself? As Starn goes on to argue, the general silence around civil society's conservative or reactionary elements "operates to preserve both the pleasing ring of insurgency to the labels 'popular initiatives' and 'social mobilization' and the simplified picture of the dispossessed as always in feisty opposition to the state, the ruling classes, and the powers that be." But acknowledging this would threaten the notion of an organic society of the oppressed. Starn argues for a more nuanced approach that notes both that conservative movements have progressive aspects and that even the most cherished vehicles of popular protest can and do reproduce relations of domination. Yet Starn is not so nuanced when it comes to Sendero, taking at face value their own claims of "absolute . . . certainty" to characterize the guerrillas only in terms of "myopic inflexibility."[52] He seems to accord Sendero a homogeneity that he is quick to unravel in other movements. Again, Sendero serves as the limit of analysis, even in the context of a subtle account of groups such as the *rondas campesinas,* the often state-organized civil defense patrols that competed with Sendero for support in highland Peru.

Is Sendero a new social movement? Slater comments that "on most counts Sendero Luminoso is not a 'new social movement,' certainly not in relation to the way this category has been discussed."[53] Sendero is usually contrasted with movements such as the *rondas,* because of the latter's political stances (pragmatic), formal organization (unhierarchical), and undogmatic willingness to enter into coalitions with the state as well as with other popular groups.[54] Sendero has confounded those who have tried to understand it in ideological terms, as social movement new or old whose goal would be to advance some doctrine or program. It refused to define itself. For most of the insurgency, Sendero issued no manifesto, made no demands, gave no interviews, and shunned any conventional conception of the public. It foreclosed the possibility of any negotiated political resolution. Sendero has bemused or shocked those who see it as an irrational deviation from the political, as a mystical death cult or barbarous terrorism. Or rather, Sendero bemused at first, opening its campaign in Lima by stringing up dead dogs in shrouds daubed with the eccentric slogan "Teng Hsiao-ping, son of a bitch."[55] Shock took over as the war advanced and as the violence became more frequent if no more explicable. But however much Sendero came to condition Peruvian political discourse, there was no space within that discourse to talk about Sendero. Sendero was pure terror. Peruvian historian Nelson Manrique notes the implicit convention that one "categorizes [Sendero] as terrorist. When the discussion reaches this point, apparently it is impossible to say anything more without running the risk of being considered at best an appeaser of Sendero, if not a covert Senderista."[56]

Some do view Sendero within the framework of the new social movements. Slater's collection has an essay on Sendero, as does Eckstein's. In the former, Dutch researchers Vera Gianotten, Tom de Wit, and Hans de Wit attribute the movement's growth to the lack of competing movements in the city of Ayacucho, a town "without an organized peasant and labour movement."[57] In the latter, analyst Cynthia McClintock separates out Sendero's early mobilization from what she claims was a later hardening when, "after the onset of the Peruvian military's counterinsurgency offensive in 1983, Sendero's dedication seemed to become fanaticism and brutality."[58] Political scientist Cyrus Zirakzadeh likewise attempts to distinguish a social-movement Sendero from a fanatical Sendero: "It never developed a consistent position... but vacillated during the late 1980s between peaceful infiltration within popular associations and violent destruction of rival organizations."[59] Meanwhile, Calderón, Piscitelli, and Reyna present Sendero as a new social movement, albeit "striking, absolute, cruel, and disconcerting." But they suggest that Sendero is more symptom than actor, though its actions are what make it so "striking": "The movement reflects the complex processes of exclusion and disintegration occurring in Peruvian society." "Sendero Luminoso is strong," they claim, "because the Peruvian working class is weak."[60] Again, Sendero is a warning of the consequences of a vacuum in civil society. It is the limit, the "disconcerting" image of a false movement, to be warded off at all costs.

Sendero encouraged the view that it was a limit movement: it has always shown intense hostility toward other Peruvian social movements, as was epitomized in its infamous 1992 assassination of María Elena Moyano, a community organizer in a Lima shantytown. This hostility upsets the assumption that social movements can quasi-naturally enter into coalition, an assumption that rests on the fundamental premise that Latin American societies really are organic wholes. Sendero challenges such organicism. It claims that the social movements, especially those supported by NGOs, are foreign incursions into the Peruvian political scene: "From Sendero's sectarian point of view, organizations that support grassroots groups represent an attempt on the part of the imperial powers . . . to strengthen the chains of capitalism in rural Peru."[61] On the other hand Sendero never claims to be natural, to be part of the grassroots. From its initial gesture of inscribing Maoist slogans on the corpses of Lima's animal population, Sendero has always presented itself as somehow uncannily out of place.

There is something ambivalent about new social movements. On the one hand, they are to be the vehicle and catalyst for democratic participation. What Knight, Chigudu, and Tandon term "citizens' organizations" are, they argue, "the bedrock of civil society." The task of "reviving democracy" is to "appeal to their self-interest and to show them ways in which they may increase their power." Only then will formal "representative democracy" be fleshed out and given substance, and so be transformed into a "participatory democracy" that could integrate civil society as the "arena where the common good is negotiated, intense deliberation and dialogue take place and diversity is celebrated." Politics is here conceived as a process of continual negotiation (according to the lifeworld's logic of communicative reason) to build consensus among diverse social actors. Civil society would be the space within which the terms, strategies, and actions of power are debated, contested, or approved by social movements that represent and are inhabited by the various elements and identities of an increasingly modern and differentiated society. The new social movements vitalize civil society and ensure, we are told, that "democratic states will regain much of the legitimacy that they have lost."[62] Yet on the other hand, social movements also threaten civil society. Encouraging their participation and mobilization, to "show them ways in which they may increase their power," risks promoting movements that may not stop at respectful consensus. What if participants take too seriously the agency ascribed to them? They may not wish to stop short at the boundaries of civil society. Why should the force and vitality of a mobilized social movement be appropriated by the state for its own legitimation? The social flesh that gives substance to campaigns for a more direct democracy may turn monstrous (multitudinous), and refuse containment. Here the "hand" of social movements rips the constricting "glove" of civil society. Social movements, in short, give life to civil society but also press against its limits, endangering its role as intermediary to power.

A Theory of Civil Society: Cohen and Arato

For "an age when totalizing revolutionary utopias have been discredited," Jean Cohen and Andrew Arato offer the "self-reflective and self-limiting utopia of civil society." Drawing on the vitality of new social movements, impelled by the fact that the concept of civil society is "in fact the major category of many of the relevant actors and their advocates from Russia to Chile, and from France to Poland," they present civil society as a progressive project, and emphasize its utopian dimensions.[63] Further examination, however, reveals an anxious attempt to patrol civil society's boundaries. The limits of this supposedly "self-limiting" utopia are in fact imposed upon social movements by the theory that claims these same movements as inspiration. A close reading of Cohen and Arato's insistence on the autonomy of state and market, allegedly in the name of civil society's own autonomy, demonstrates the paradoxes of civil society theory: a theory of democracy becomes a discourse of governmentality and control that sets the constituted power of state and market institutions against the democratizing force of social movements. Civil society theory comes to blows with civil society discourse, extirpating from the latter all traces of what it stigmatizes as "fundamentalism." In place of fundamentalism, Cohen and Arato privilege efficiency: forced to choose, civil society theory sides with the instrumental logic that it purportedly opposes.

I focus on Cohen and Arato's formulation of civil society theory because I accept their claim that "despite the proliferation of this discourse, and of the concept itself...no one [had] developed a systematic *theory* of civil society" before them. They argue, for instance, that for all its importance "Touraine's work points us in the right direction, but he does not offer a *theory* of civil society."[64] Cohen and Arato set out to provide contemporary civil society discourse with a theoretical basis, and theirs undoubtedly is a significant theorization of civil society. Though the German philosopher Jürgen Habermas is their primary influence, they also engage with or draw on Hannah Arendt, Carl Schmitt, Michel Foucault, and Niklas Luhmann, among many others. Published in 1994, their book has perhaps had less influence than it deserves in part because it is so rigorous and academic (in short, difficult). It is out of tune with the pragmatic and untheoretical (and sometimes self-serving) tendencies more common in the civil society discourse of foundations and aid agencies. Activists often disdain theorizing as impractical and overintellectual, as though political action were simply a matter of common sense; but given that contemporary neoliberalism also relies on presenting itself as second nature, as beyond question, such a refusal of theoretical reflection can only be self-defeating. It should not be theory as a whole that is at issue, but this theory in particular. It is, however, a theory that should be examined, understood, and respected. I focus on Cohen and Arato's work, therefore, also because it is the most consistent, thorough, and coherent theory of civil society to date. If there are problems in their work, these are problems afflicting the very best theory of civil society.

As with Laclau and Mouffe's theory of hegemony, a submerged Latin Americanism runs through Cohen and Arato's book. Citing particularly the work of Guillermo O'Donnell, Alfred Stepan, and Fernando Henrique Cardoso, they note that Latin American debates about civil society are "the richest, most open-ended and most synthetic" of the discussions that have returned the notion of civil society to the contemporary sociotheoretical map. Yet Latin America soon drops off this map: later only Eastern Europe is mentioned as providing "the world-historical impetus to revive the category" of civil society.[65] No doubt Cohen and Arato's occlusion of Latin American contributions to civil society discourse arises largely from their unfamiliarity with the original Spanish texts, though their overall project of relegitimating civil society as a concept for the West also requires a certain silencing of non-Western discourses. More importantly, it is perhaps another instance of Cohen and Arato's ambivalence about the social actors they discuss. They claim both inspiration and distance: inspiration in that by invoking actually existing social movements, such as those that brought down authoritarian regimes in the Southern Cone, they can assert that they are "not speaking in a void"; distance in that they reject what they call the "democratic fundamentalism typical of collective actors based in civil society." The price they pay, they admit, is that they lay themselves open to criticism for their "soulless reformism."[66]

Cohen and Arato define civil society as an intermediate sphere "of social interaction between economy and state, composed above all of the intimate sphere (especially the family), the sphere of association (especially voluntary associations), social movements, and forms of public communication."[67] They emphasize civil society's modernity and self-limitation. Civil society is modern because it is a product of modernization's differentiating tendencies, which give rise also to the distinct subsystems of economy and state. It is self-limiting because it respects the differences between these subsystems, and maintains its (relative) autonomy from them. Following the differentiation of economy and state, civil society emerges as a reciprocally differentiated space, site of interaction, mediation, and communicative action. Economy, state, and civil society: this is the fundamental Hegelian division. It is also the basic schema invoked by social movements: Cohen and Arato claim that they are in tune with the "contemporary collective actors" that themselves establish this tripartite model, as "by 'civil society,'" they "have in mind a normative model of a societal realm different from the state and the economy."[68]

But the three-part division of economy, state, and civil society, while "fundamental," is insufficient to describe the complexity of modern social formations. Civil society is the nexus for multiple mediations and interactions that are part of what Cohen and Arato term "a fabric of societal intermediations." So, for instance, in addition to the state there is also a "political society" that mediates between civil society and the state; and as well as the economy there is an "economic society" that mediates "between civil society and the market system."[69] State, political society, civil society, economic society, and market: Cohen and Arato's model now has five components. But the complexities do not stop there, in that civil society is itself internally differentiated. Its functions are split between intervention in other subsystems on the one hand, and defensive integration and self-conservation on the other. Further, Cohen and Arato invoke the Habermasian distinction between lifeworld and system: civil society connects the communicative, quasi-organic, interactions of the lifeworld with the systemic attributes of the state and the economy, whose subsystems are guided by the rationalized media of power (within political society) and money (for economic society). Mediation goes every which way. At the porous border between lifeworld and system, civil society can be where institutions encroach upon the lifeworld: these are the "negative dimensions of civil society," which its defenders should guard against. It can also, of course, be the site from which social movements "exert pressure for inclusion" and "influence . . . within political (and economic) society" through "receptors" within these subsystems that "can, within limits, be added to and democratized."[70] "Receptors" are elements unusually open to the communicative logic of the lifeworld, and the points at which the system includes social movements. So the subsystems are split, too, between their more coldly rationalized elements, and their receptive nodes, open to the influence of a civil society conveying another logic, derived from the lifeworld.

Cohen and Arato's full social architecture therefore comprises: a quasi-organic (but partially or potentially rationalized) lifeworld; a rational–bureaucratic system made up of the state, the market, and attendant subsystems of political and economic society (with their receptive and nonreceptive elements); and civil society as space apart, interstice, communicating vessel, and multivalent conduit. Civil society connects these diverse spheres. But it also keeps them separate. For Cohen and Arato, it is as important to preserve social boundaries as to bridge them. Invoking Habermas again, they argue that " 'the utopian horizon of civil society' . . . is based on preserving the boundaries between the different subsystems and the lifeworld." Civil society has to defend the lifeworld from the incursion of instrumental reason. But instrumental reason has also to be protected from the overeager interventions of civil society. The encroachment of system upon society should be limited; but civil society, too, should be self-limiting. Any scope for mediation is surprisingly restricted. Indeed, for Cohen and Arato, the "logic of democratic association" turns out to be but an "emergency break" *(sic)* on the "logics of money and power," waiting for an emergency whose lonely hour, it seems, never arrives.[71]

However much store Cohen and Arato set by civil society, they allot it remarkably little scope for influencing either politics or the economy. Despite "the obvious permeability of political and economic institutions to societal norms" in theory, in practice the boundaries of civil society are remarkably watertight. Cohen and Arato are at pains to protect the state from overenthusiastic social demands, by maintaining a rigid distinction between civil and political society. They repeatedly reject any radical democratic proposal that would fuse civil society and the state: "It would involve such an *overburdening of the democratic process* that it would discredit democracy by associating it with political disintegration or by opening it to subversion through covert, unregulated strategic action" (emphasis added). It would be all too much. Moreover, civil society is no more prepared to take the strain of overzealous intervention into the political sphere: any dedifferentiation, threatening the autonomy of the two spheres and making the state immediately accountable to civil society, "would deprive civil society of time resources for democratic deliberation and decision making." Indeed, Cohen and Arato's view on the prospect of civil society taking on an expanded role in ensuring the political system's democratic accountability is downright dystopian: extending "the (communicative) logic of democratic association" to the state would be, they claim, "conducive to short- and long-term dysfunctional side effects and pathologies."[72] The chances are slimmer still that civil society, in Cohen and Arato's conception, could affect the economy. Though they continue to claim that "the political public is an open structure because of its permeability to general social communication," they are forced to "admit that it is difficult to apply the same conception to economic society, where conditions of publicity and therefore the possibilities of democratization are even more restricted." Any possible social movement intervention into the workings of the economy is endlessly deferred and subject to doubt: social movements engage in a "politics of influence targeting political (and *perhaps* economic) insiders"; they "target political society (and will *one day perhaps* target economic society as well)" (emphasis added). A more democratic economic society remains a theoretical possibility, but right now it is bracketed off: literally, Cohen and Arato place it in parentheses. Economic processes are separated out, inscrutable and inviolate. In sum, against the pathological specter of direct democracy, they hold that "modernization depends on the differentiation of modern economy and state"; excessive dedifferentiation is "incompatible with . . . the presuppositions of modern democracy."[73] In Cohen and Arato's conception, civil society's "self-limiting utopia" is rather more self-limiting and rather less utopian than one might initially have imagined.

Cohen and Arato's strictures are presented as a defense of democracy. But this defense is paradoxical: democracy is to be defended against democratization, against social movements taking the promise of their empowerment too literally, too seriously. The state and the market are never to be fully democratized. At best there are "forms of democracy adequate" to these subsystems. Social movements are to be content with an "adequate" democracy. They should not take up the burden of undue influence: separating out economic and political society from civil society ensures that "communicative interaction is unburdened from the task of coordinating all areas of life."[74] Civil society should remain an intermediate sphere separate from, but also attendant on and subservient to, state and market. Civil society should, in brief, know its place. By implication, that place is also bounded by the nation: a civil society that consents to back off from intervention in political society is tied to political society and its institutional support, the nation-state. Implicit in Cohen and Arato's discussion of citizenship, legality, and identity, and part and parcel of their conception of modernity, is that civil society should be a national civil society. (Reciprocally, calls for a global civil society are also calls for a global state, as in proposals such as journalist George Monbiot's *The Age of Consent*.) They hem civil society in on all sides; yet Cohen and Arato present themselves as its supporters!

Cohen and Arato attempt to dampen the enthusiasm of civil society's democratizing impulses in the name of modernity and from fear of fundamentalism. There is something deeply conservative about their attempt to safeguard modernity. Political modernization can be guaranteed, they suggest, only by upholding the relative autonomy of the state and political society. Economic development can be safeguarded only by insulating the economy and economic society from social demands. Civil society mediates between these spheres, but its task is above all to defend the integrity of the lifeworld. Systemic reason is to be spared full democratization; communicative reason is to be relieved of the burden of implementing full democracy. Everywhere, in Naomi Klein's phrase, there are more fences than windows; this is modernity's rather anxious defensive compact.[75] Any threat to this order threatens modernity as a whole: Cohen and Arato stigmatize such threats by labeling them fundamentalist, a term they apply both to the traditionalist "fundamentalism of false communities" and to innovative demands for radical democracy, that is, the "revolutionary fundamentalism" of the "total politicization of society." Both fundamentalisms, the traditionalist and the revolutionary, are antimodern: premodern or "primitivist" on the one hand; postmodern on the other. It is, however, the revolutionary demand for immediacy and immanence, against differentiation and the protection of state and market from civil society's demands, that most threatens "the universalist tradition of cultural and political modernity." Civil society is only modern if it is a "lifeworld capable of rationalization." "Democratic fundamentalism," which resists and overcomes rationalization, and which refuses to differentiate between civil and political society, would overwhelm the state and lead, Cohen and Arato imply, to anarchy.[76]

The identity of the fundamentalists themselves is never precisely specified. It is as though fundamentalism were strangely omnipresent: haunting civil society, never settling in any one location. A desire to breach the boundaries separating civil, political, and economic society could arise at any point, from any part of civil society. If anything, fundamentalism is to be expected. However much it may be hoped that modern social movements "are no longer motivated by fundamentalist projects of suppressing bureaucracy, economic rationality, or social division," in practice such views are "*typical* of collective actors based in civil society" (emphasis added).

Everyone is a potential fundamentalist. "Democratic fundamentalism" is the everyday but false consciousness of social movements. This is no barbarism at the gates of civil society; it is the enemy within, the pathogen carried in the cells of the social movements themselves. The concept of civil society has, then, to be "reconstructed" to protect it from its own most fervent supporters, to ensure that it remains "usable."[77] A usable concept of civil society would ensure that instrumental reason still held sway over communicative logic. But social movement fundamentalism arises from the very popularity of the concept of civil society and the promises of empowerment that it offers. Hence the double-edged sword of participation: without participation in and from civil society, the state loses legitimacy; so civil society has to be encouraged. The more people who take part, the better, but it is all too "easy for such actors to slip into fundamentalist postures." Fundamentalism is civil society run amok, unreflectively celebrated by "the theoretical defenders of civil society who see democratic publics, intact solidarities, and forms of autonomy everywhere." Fundamentalism is central for Cohen and Arato because it is dangerous and ubiquitous, but also because it is entrenched in civil society discourse itself. The "imagery" of civil society articulated by social actors is "not really adequate . . . to the most important constraints on collective action."[78] Civil society theory, in Cohen and Arato's hands, is now directly opposed to civil society discourse as championed by the new social movements themselves.

The truth of civil society theory is that it imposes a series of boundaries, drawing on the force of social movements to legitimate political order, but restraining that force at the point at which it might challenge the state. Tendencies that might overspill or dissolve those boundaries are ostracized as fundamentalist. Dominique Colas's genealogy of the term demonstrates that whenever the concept of civil society is invoked, it always depends upon the demarcation of a fanaticism that is its other. The concept of civil society founds and maintains a "regulated system of differences." Systemic differentiation has to be regulated, its borders anxiously patrolled against the threat of fanatical dedifferentiation. Colas details the various distinctions secured by the idea of civil society over the long history of the term's use: civil society has been counterposed to the people, the City of God, the state of nature, and (in its most recent incarnation) the state. In all its guises, however, civil society invokes "the flexible management of multiplicity, heterogeneity."[79] The concept manages multiplicity by imposing representation, by "translat[ing] force into signs," and thereby establishing politics as "a noisy theatricality like an essential 'demonstration' of the belief in the effectiveness of representation." By contrast, "for the fanatic" (and Colas has little sympathy for fanaticism), "representation is always a parasitic excrescence" and "mediation is a loss of strength or meaning that necessarily entails a degradation." Civil society is threatened not by the other elements within the system of differences that it establishes (such as the state), but by a constituent power that would abolish all distinctions and all mediations. From Martin Luther and the early modern battles against religious radicalism to the very literal fences constructed to protect world leaders in Davos and Genoa in the present, civil society is haunted by the fear of what Colas calls "the multitude triumphantly imposing its unmediated will."[80]

What distinguishes civil society theory today is that with the emergence of "democratic fundamentalism," fanaticism is now a component part of civil society. Fanaticism is no longer simply the other, external to modernity. In the early sixteenth century Luther could denounce the iconoclasts and Anabaptists as heretical sects who had misinterpreted his teaching, and assert that "crushing the fanatics was vital for the very existence of civil society."[81] This history of the Anabaptist rebellions and their violent suppression is marvelously told in *Q*, a novel written by Italian anarchists under the pseudonym "Luther Blissett." They certainly are alert to the continuities between, say, Münster in 1535 and Genoa in 2001. But crushing the fanatics is no longer an option. Fanaticism and civil society are now practically indistinguishable. To mobilize the forces of civil society, in the name of the state's legitimation, is at the same time to summon forth the fanaticism that threatens to abolish both civil society and the state. The more that civil society expands, the more it incorporates fanaticism and the "revolutionary fundamentalism" that so perturbs Cohen and Arato. The more that social movements and groups are integrated into civil society, the more differentiated and complex civil society becomes, and so the more that civil society incarnates a pure, immediate multiplicity that would destroy the entire system of differences. Civil society's triumph is also its downfall: it gives expression to emergent subjectivities that, now empowered, threaten to annihilate civil society from within. Civil society loses its capacity to regulate difference and multiplicity. Civil society discourse therefore has to stir up fear of fundamentalisms that are not or cannot be incorporated within civil society itself. The image of a fanaticism beyond its borders wards off the more pressing danger of fundamentalism within. The name given to this new fanaticism is "terror."

The influential Mexico-based anthropologist Néstor García Canclini invokes Cohen and Arato to advocate a market-based version of civil society and to demonize fundamentalism. As cultural theorist George Yúdice observes, García Canclini identifies "a bipolar divide between negotiation and fundamentalism" in Latin American popular culture.[82] Confronted with this choice, García Canclini opts unequivocally for negotiation. He argues that subaltern resistance is doomed, because the market is "stronger than the difference of the subalterns or marginalized groups."[83] Such groups need to accept the market and ally themselves with the state which, though weakened, can still shelter some forms of cultural specificity. Civil society is the midpoint between the two, and so the site of accommodation to the market on the one hand and negotiation with the state on the other. García Canclini gives civil society a culturalist and consumerist twist, premised upon the market enabling what Yúdice elsewhere glosses as "consumption as a 'means of thinking' " and upon the state virtuously regulating the trade in cultural goods. Again, however, the state is the prime beneficiary: "Communities of consumers" will provide the "cultural adhesive" legitimating a renovated social pact.[84] This is García Canclini's version of "regional federalism," a project in some ways now being put into effect with the current Latin American left turns. But again, civil society has to be protected even from its advocates: too often, García Canclini argues, the term "is used nowadays to legitimize the most heterogeneous agendas of groups, non-governmental organizations, private corporations, and even individuals." Seeking to refine and restrict the concept, he turns to Cohen and Arato for its "best reformulation."[85] He draws a line in the sand: social groups open to negotiation are to be set apart from those that tend toward fundamentalism; the fundamentalists no longer belong.

Sendero provides García Canclini with the exemplary image of fundamentalism, beyond the pale of possible political positions. Even banished from sight, however, Sendero continues to trouble his political project. Sendero is a symptom of the neoliberal breakdown that leads to (para)ethnic fundamentalism: as "peasant and urban economic conditions have deteriorated," García Canclini argues, "the segregationist fundamentalism of ethnic or paraethnic movements such as Sendero Luminoso only makes it more difficult to implement integration projects." Blocking integration, Sendero prevents the realization of a multicultural civil society. Or rather, it reveals the limits of integration and multiculturalism; it is inassimilable. But García Canclini warns that fundamentalism wears many masks, appearing even "in the guise of Latin Americanism." He launches a critique of magical realism, on the grounds that it "freezes the 'Latin American' in a premodern sanctuary and sublimates this continent as the place where social violence casts its spell through the affects."[86] It is against this enchanted, affected version of the region that García Canclini proposes the concept of civil society, which would presumably be characterized by disenchantment and realism. There is, however, something fantastic about the picture he paints: for instance, Sendero is hardly an ethnic movement, and very far from magical realism's vision of Latin America as a place of primitive enchantment. But everything lumped together as fundamentalism and affect has to be banished to the margins and excluded from view, so it is no surprise that it should also be subject to such mischaracterizations. Sendero becomes inconceivable and unknowable for a civil society discourse that so anxiously wishes to distinguish its own incipient fundamentalism from that incarnated by Sendero. Fundamentalism has to drop out of discourse altogether, to become part of the nonnegotiable real, sacrificed for the sake of an increasingly fantastic realism. For if fundamentalism were but one discourse among others, then it could enter civil society, its differences relative and negotiable. To prevent this from happening, it is expelled to the perimeter where all differences are annulled and all mediations abolished, and where the distinction between referent and sign is iconoclastically erased. And this in the name of a discourse that refuses to portray Latin America in terms of subaltern abjection! For García Canclini, Sendero incarnates Latin American fundamentalism, the affect and terror at civil society's margins against which his rationalism, otherwise always ready to negotiate, turns its back. But Sendero's unrepresentability haunts Latin American conceptions of civil society, frustrating attempts to extirpate it. García Canclini's

Hybrid Cultures ends with the question of "how to be radical without being fundamentalist."[87] He might equally ask how to be radical without being Sendero; for if Sendero is nothing else, it is radical.

In Peru, above all, Sendero's presence was spectral but no less frighteningly real. Unseen, the insurgents could be anywhere. Just as Abimael Guzmán was frustratingly elusive for the Peruvian security services, so also with Sendero's militants: their eyes and ears were everywhere, but even the bodies of fallen combatants were removed from the scene of battle before the security forces arrived. All they left behind was an affective trace. Peruvian filmmaker Francisco Lombardi's *La boca del lobo* (1988) portrays the state's paranoia and paradoxically puts Sendero's invisibility on display.[88] The movie shows a detachment of the Peruvian army sent to a remote Andean village. They wake up after their first night there only to discover that at some point, someone, without disturbing the guards, has replaced the Peruvian flag that was flying high above their billets with Sendero's red flag, its hammer and sickle. The soldiers search for who could be responsible, but Sendero are never seen: the guerrillas constitute the absolute horizon and limit of visibility in the clear Andean air, the real whose insistent but invisible ubiquitous presence threatens order and internal coherence. Suspicion and self-doubt eat away at the forces supposedly ensuring national security: the commanding officer breaks down under the strain, orders a massacre of the villagers, and then loses control even of his own men.

At the war's outset, Sendero quickly turned its spectrality into strategic advantage. They soon demonstrated that they could operate virtually with impunity in the city of Ayacucho, as well as in the countryside. As early as March 1982, they attacked the city's jail, taking the security forces completely by surprise and freeing almost 250 prisoners. In the face of withering fire, the Civil and Republican Guard blockaded themselves into their barracks. "On Ayacucho's streets," Gorriti reports, "mobile Shining Path teams dedicated themselves to hunting down the isolated policemen serving as sentries.... In less than thirty minutes, the Shining Path had established complete control over Ayacucho." An hour or so later, the Sendero fighters had already disappeared back to the countryside ("they vanished on the road to Huancavelica"), but the damage had been done and the "siege of Ayacucho" had begun. In December of that year, the bridge linking Ayacucho with the neighboring provinces of Andahuaylas and

A hammer and sickle flag has appeared from nowhere in the middle of the night; Sendero Luminoso's name is not quite erased from the wall behind. Film still from *La boca del lobo* (directed by Francisco J. Lombardi, 1988); courtesy of the director.

Cusco was dynamited. Two days later, the city's mayor was shot and seriously wounded; when the doctor who had been treating him left the hospital, on his car's driving seat "he found a written note: 'The people have a thousand eyes, a thousand ears.' "[89] Sendero's mobility, the fact that it could turn up anywhere, at any time, contrasted with the immobility of a petrified police force who had been "undermined morally, not defeated in battle." The policemen's only movement was the jitters: "Fear of an attack like the one that had taken place in March was intense.... Few officers dared walk on foot at night – even downtown – for fear of the trembling trigger fingers of their own men." And the jitterbug: "In a not entirely incomprehensible paradox, the discotheques were filled to capacity." That same year, Sendero's siege of Lima also began: "On December 3, the Shining Path celebrated the exalted Guzmán's birthday.... A simultaneous blackout darkened Lima and Ayacucho. On San Cristóbal Hill, which overlooked colonial Lima, and on Ayacucho's La Picota Hill, hundreds of cans with burning material inside drew a fiery hammer and sickle in the blackness."[90] National and provincial capital alike were confronted by a burning presence, uncomfortably close and (not quite) visible at their margins.

The paradox of civil society theory is that the fundamentalism it disdains has given soul, promise, and hope to social movements and so to the civil society that it sets out to praise. Social movements mobilize people by offering them empowerment, expansiveness, and collective influence; they promise participants that (in the slogan of the World Social Forum) "another world is possible!" People join up to do away with the noisy theatricality of representational politics. Cohen and Arato admit that by contrast their own project, with its emphasis on limitation and systemic management, may appear "deficient in its motivational ability." They are sensitive to the charge of "soulless reformism."[91] Civil society theory is dry and affectless compared to the inspirational force of social movements and their democratic fundamentalism. This absent affect shadows Cohen and Arato's text: they have eliminated desire from civil society, but recognize that civil society is nothing without it. In its place, all Cohen and Arato can offer is efficiency. In the end, they prefer efficiency to affect, and governability to democracy. So, for example, "the need for steering mechanisms for the state and the economy must be respected if we expect them to function efficiently." Opposing civil disobedience that would target economic society, they assert that "economic efficiency should not be sacrificed *in toto* to democratic pressure."[92] Modernity's compact of limitations subjects democracy to efficiency rather than vice versa. You might not like it, Cohen and Arato imply of their conception of civil society, but at least it works.

Neoliberalism and the State

As efficiency becomes its principal rationale, civil society becomes a subsystem of what Cohen and Arato term the "*steering performance* . . . [of] system rationality." Efficiency trumps democracy, albeit tempered by legitimacy. Civil society resolves the dilemma faced by "bureaucratic–authoritarian regimes," that they "never manage to solve their problems of legitimacy."[93] The result is managerialism: civil society becomes an auxiliary component of the state's self-guidance mechanism. An expanded civil society, in short, is subsumed by a still more expansive neoliberal state. A new state form emerges, whose technocratic legitimacy rests on an image of transparency and accountability that bypasses parties, politics, and even social movements in favor of immanent investment in civil society. The forms of the state's expansion are novel: they include opinion polling, mediatization, surveillance, as well as the proxy state institutions of NGOs and charitable organizations. Civil society and the state merge, and civil society's mediating function becomes rationalization, a far-reaching mechanism for the production of consensus. Cultural particularities are filtered, sorted, negotiated, and finally eliminated. Heterogeneity becomes unity; multiplicity and singularity are reduced to identity. Civil society and the state, a single assemblage whose operations lie well beneath ideology, strip culture of its irrationalities and fold back its force as the power of management. Neoliberal regimes silently and efficiently transform constituent into constituted power, consolidating their claims to a monopoly on violence.

Neoliberalism is more than simply a set of economic policies, though that is how it is usually defined, as a conjunction of neoclassical economics and monetarism. The neoliberal economic agenda, codified as the so-called "Washington Consensus," is premised on stabilization, structural adjustment, and export-led growth, and its implementation calls for privatization, deregulation, reducing subsidies, cutting tariffs, and generally encouraging market solutions over state intervention.[94] But an exclusive focus on economics occludes the fact that, above all, neoliberalism ushers in a new state form. British prime minister Margaret Thatcher famously summarized her own version of neoliberal doctrine as "rolling back the frontiers of the state," but neoliberalism is better understood as a radical reconstruction of the state's contours. Neoliberal states relinquish direct control of the economy, but are highly interventionist in other arenas. Indeed, "freeing" the economy involves direct and often controversial action to break the powers of those institutions that are vying for power with the state. In Thatcherism's case, the paradigmatic confrontation involved the political mobilization of the police against the National Union of Mineworkers' 1984 strike. The fact that neoliberalism was first tried and tested under a military dictatorship, in Augusto Pinochet's Chile, demonstrates that it is hardly incompatible with a strong state; indeed, its "shock doctrine" requires it.[95] But Pinochet's dictatorship or Thatcher's authoritarianism are only the early stages of neoliberal ascendancy, in which initial resistance is overcome. Neoliberalism comes into its own in transitional, postauthoritarian societies, under the banner of consensus and with the promise of a renovated social pact.

The state brooks no competition; it has to be singular and all-encompassing. "In the end," sociologist Max Weber tells us, "the modern state controls the total means of political organization, which actually come together under a single head."[96] Never has this been truer than of the neoliberal state, despite its apparent reticence. Following German legal scholar Carl Schmitt, political theorist Giorgio Agamben describes "the dominant paradigm of government in contemporary politics" as a "state of exception" in which the law is suspended, and so the boundaries between state and society ("between law and the living being") radically breached.[97] This is the state's own brand of fundamentalism, its own excessiveness. Yet, again following Weber, if the state is defined by its monopoly (its monopoly on "the means of organization" but also on "the legitimate use of force"),[98] it is not simply "in the end" that it acquires such monopoly. The state always has this monopoly, at least ideally: its very definition depends on its uniqueness; there can be no half measures within the territory that it controls. Philosophers Gilles Deleuze and Félix Guattari argue that "the State was not formed in progressive stages; it appears fully armed, a master stroke executed all at once. . . . It is the basic formation, on the horizon throughout history."[99] With the neoliberal "state of exception," the state's fully armed ideality is apparently realized; history's horizon rushes up to meet us. The state is everything, or so it would have us believe.

Peru's experience of authoritarianism differs from that of Southern Cone countries such as Brazil and Chile, and its postdictatorship history has been anomalous and disorderly. Sendero took advantage of this chaos and also made it much worse. The military regimes of, first, General Juan Velasco Alvarado (1968–75) and, then, General Francisco Morales Bermúdez (1975–80) were corporatist, left-leaning, and progressive: Velasco, for instance, initiated one of Latin America's most ambitious land reform programs. The military did not destroy public institutions; indeed, in some cases it strengthened them. But not for long: as political scientist Philip Mauceri argues, "the transition to democracy largely provided a framework for the military to extricate itself rather than providing a strong institutional framework for a new democratic order." This would not, however, become evident for some years. Mauceri comments that "the marvel perhaps was not that that structure would be easily swept away twelve years later, but that it lasted as long as it did."[100] The first head of state after the 1980 transition was Fernando Belaúnde, who had been the president ousted by the 1968 coup. By contrast with the protectionist positions he took in the 1960s, in his 1980–85 administration Belaúnde reversed some of Velasco's reforms, further accelerating the trade liberalization that Morales Bermúdez had already initiated. But the economy soon entered into crisis, the national debt spiraled upward, and the Sendero rebellion took hold and rapidly grew out of control. Alan García's presidency of 1985 to 1990 was the last hurrah of Latin America's historic populist parties: with García, APRA (the American Popular Revolutionary Alliance) finally took power, over sixty years after its 1924 foundation as perhaps the region's first mass populist movement. García's presidency was, however, by almost any standards a disaster: despite initiating an increasingly dirty campaign of counterinsurgency in the highlands, he failed to contain Sendero; hyperinflation only worsened Peru's economic crisis; and García himself left office in disgrace, soon to face charges of massive corruption. (He has since, however, returned to power as though redeemed by his subsequent years in the political wilderness.) With APRA thrown out of office, a vacuum ensued. The party system had by now effectively disintegrated, paving the way for the 1990 presidential contest that culminated in a face-off between the renowned novelist Mario Vargas Llosa and a then-unknown university professor by the name of Alberto Fujimori. Against all expectations, Fujimori won.

The best accounts of Fujimori's regime include anthropologist Carlos Iván Degregori's *La década de la antipolítica,* sociologists Julio Cotler and Romeo Grompone's *El fujimorismo,* and, for its economic policies, economist Efraín Gonzales de Olarte's *El neoliberalismo a la peruana.* Fujimori was an outsider to the Peruvian political scene and had campaigned on a more or less populist platform. Once elected, however, he revealed himself an ardent neoliberal. Gonzales de Olarte points out that the reforms that Fujimori initiated almost as soon as he took office were "an extreme model of efficiency-driven adjustment" in line with "a radical model of the 'Washington Consensus.'" He also argues that the new regime engineered a "divorce of economics from politics," as "active intermediaries such as political parties... employers' or workers' organizations" either disappeared or lost all influence.[101] But bypassing such groups is the politics of neoliberalism: stripping politics of its mediating bodies fully fits with radical changes in the economic sphere. Degregori rightly sees Fujimori's regime as "the end of the Creole Republic." But to term it also "the apotheosis of antipolitics" is to define politics solely in terms of the mechanisms bequeathed by traditional republicanism and, more generally, by modernity's model of separation of powers, formal representation, active interest groups, and clear limits between civil and political society. What Degregori describes is in fact better understood as a new mode of (antipolitical) politics. "Opposed to any form of organization," Degregori explains, "the anti-politician preferred to preside over an amorphous country, based on an alliance of de facto powers: the intelligence services, the armed forces, the media, and technocrats linked to international financial organizations." This permeation of society by state characterizes what in chapter 4 I describe as biopolitics. But a shift to biopolitics brings its own dangers for constituted power. Degregori goes on to note that these same "de facto" powers later had pause for thought, as they "began to see this formerly obscure ex-agronomist acquiring ever more life of his own, redolent of multitudes."[102]

Fujimorismo often strangely mirrored Sendero, supposedly its sworn adversary. Indeed, Degregori suggests that Peruvian society in the 1990s was built on a common philosophy articulated most clearly by Abimael Guzmán, in the one interview he conceded the press (the so-called "interview of the century") in 1988. Here, Guzmán declared that "Senderistas were 'prepared to do anything and everything. Anything, without exception.'"[103] This was a declaration of fundamentalism, no doubt, but one shared and amplified by Fujimori. "What effect," asks Degregori, "does this philosophy have on a country that lacks institutional brakes? Anything goes. Anything can be bought, anything sold.... Anything and everything in the name of the cult to utilitarianism and efficiency."[104] This willingness to do anything relates to another fundamentalist trait shared by both Sendero and *fujimorismo:* their refusal to enter into alliances. As Grompone puts it, "the regime managed without seeking support for its reforms from social coalitions, which would necessitate political negotiations, and to appeal instead to a passive consensus, directed from the seat of power. In fact what was proposed was to bypass any pacts." Instead of political representatives, Fujimori's government relied on political "operatives," conduits immediately and directly in touch with civil society. They mirrored, Grompone tells us, Sendero's cadres: "Both sides understood that what was at stake were problems 'of life and death.'"[105] Of "bare life," as Giorgio Agamben would have it.[106]

If anything, Sendero and *fujimorismo* were adversaries precisely because of their similarities. Both aimed to construct a new state, disputing the monopoly of legitimate violence and in the process destroying any possibility of a functional civil society along classical lines. As anthropologists Deborah Poole and Gerardo Rénique indicate, by the late 1980s Sendero had established a counterstate in the areas under its control, building "a new moral order in the countryside. Theft, adultery, wife-beating, corruption, failure to cooperate in communal work projects and other moral infractions were severely punished by flogging and occasional executions." Poole and Rénique observe that "during [the] early years many peasants viewed the PCP-SL positively as a source of the moral order and security that the Peruvian state had for centuries failed to provide."[107] Sendero was less antistate than a parallel state, aggressively seeking to legitimate its violence and exploiting historic weaknesses in the Peruvian state's claims to legitimacy or monopoly. Civil society breaks down when split between two states, two competing poles of potential negotiation and legitimation. In response, some demanded greater representativity on the part of the "official" state, better adequation between state and civil society. Writing in 1991, lawyer and journalist María del Pilar Tello claimed that "the whole of civil society appears more and more lucid in its demand that the State represent the national community and its interests on top of the party interests of the State government."[108] Calling for a representativity beyond party and sectoral differences, Tello points to a crisis of state legitimacy that was both effect and cause of the Sendero rebellion. The entire system of representation had broken down, fragmented into two (or more) parts. The state can do without parties, but cannot stand threats to its unity and monopoly. Within months, Fujimori reacted, not perhaps in the way that commentators such as Tello might have imagined: his response to this legitimation crisis would be to declare a coup against his own regime and to absorb civil society fully within the state.

Neoliberalism demands that civil society provide ever more legitimation ever more immediately and directly. The state and civil society should be completely transparent to each other. Transparency is neoliberalism's key value, going hand in hand with governance. So Michel Camdessus, managing director of the International Monetary Fund from 1987 to 2000 (the IMF's longest-serving chief official), declared to "Transparency International" his belief in "the central importance of transparency and good governance in achieving economic success."[109] Transparency International itself is, it declares, "the global civil society organisation leading the fight against corruption, bring[ing] people together in a powerful worldwide coalition."[110] It defines corruption as "the abuse of entrusted power for private gain" and produces an annual "Corruption Perception Index," statistically documenting on a ten-point scale which societies it believes are the most transparent (in 2009, New Zealand, which scored 9.4 closely followed by Denmark with 9.3) and which the least (Afghanistan and Somalia with 1.3 and 1.1 points respectively). The workings of government and business are to be transparent to civil society. Equally, however, neoliberal practice insists that society be transparent to business and government. Business must have immediate access to information about consumer behavior, while government needs to be able to sound out its citizenry as efficiently as possible. Transparency is aimed at literally disarming social movements: Camdessus's example of the "positive effects" of the IMF's initiatives, which he himself terms a "revolution," involves unions "giv[ing] up the idea of a general strike."

With social transparency elevated to the acme of public virtue, opinion polls in all their many current incarnations come to the fore as the prime mechanism of governance and control in public and private sectors alike. Constant surveys eliminate the residual autonomy and texture of civil society, and public opinion becomes directly assimilated to both state managerialism and private profit. Many of the companies specializing in the variety of polling devices now in use also provide their services to business as "market research," and vice versa. Politics becomes market research as market research becomes a particularly valuable tool for politicians. Both thrive on surveys, focus groups, brand analysis, even corporate ethnography and social semiotics: business and politics are increasingly built on the same basis. The thickness and texture of civil society disappear, as the state moves to an apparently direct relation with the public. Transparency is promoted through the technocratic conversion of disparate affects (the way things make us feel) into statistical opinions (what we think about them) that can justify a single set of policies, a single outcome for the governmental client. Pierre Bourdieu points out that the social scientific survey, on which technocracy's production of public opinion is based, proceeds "as if it had already resolved the essential problem of politics, namely, the question of the transmutation of experience into discourse, of the unformulated ethos into a constituted, constituting logos."[111] Yet polls are too often taken at face value by researchers, and their rationale is seldom questioned. Much social science, after all, is premised upon unconditional belief in such surveys. When the tools of social science are taken up by power, there is little that the statistic-minded scholar can do but applaud this incorporation of social scientific calculation into governance.

There is nothing passive about the recording technologies that underpin an age of transparency. They effect real transformations, changes in state for the state's unchanging benefit. They bridge what Bourdieu describes as the "radical discontinuity" that separates "ethos and logos, practical mastery and verbal mastery."[112] Opinion polls and other such instruments of technocratic observation are apparatuses of capture converting qualitative difference into quantity: they produce a statistical striation of social space that reduces experience to opinion and people to pop-sociological epithets ("soccer moms," "Essex man") so as to calibrate endlessly comparable differences. Multiplicity is replaced by simple multiplication. Once different sectors of society are compared, they can also be represented and appropriated. The state becomes what Deleuze and Guattari term a "form of expression" for the disparate elements that it has captured in its all-observing gaze.[113]

Polling goes hand in hand with the mediatization of politics under neoliberalism. These media take new forms; the classic critique of the spectacle, for the way in which it turns viewers into passive subjects, is now outdated. Cinematic spectators may have been blinded or distracted at the apogee of historical populism. But in the televisual age of neoliberalism, participation is all. We are endlessly encouraged to vote: for Pop Idol or American Idol, and a myriad other reality programs. George Orwell would never have imagined Big Brother converted into an interactive fantasy in which it is the television audience that determines events on the omnipresent small screen (to evict or save a housemate), rather than the other way around. But the incitement to join in does not merely affect so-called reality television: British TV constantly exhorts its audience to "press the red button on your remote control" or "send us an SMS message," urging viewers to provide feedback and commentary immediately and directly. Participating viewers produce a stream of real-time opinion that can then be run along the bottom of the screen, like a stock market ticker, while a politician is interviewed or breaking news is broadcast. Meanwhile politicians themselves, on the sofas and comfy chairs of the daytime discussion shows, enter the nation's living rooms to chat, mug of coffee or tea in hand, about ever more everyday topics: their favorite football teams, recipes, and health tips. And all this is to say nothing of the Internet or the blogosphere, Twitter or Facebook, and the ways in which they, too, foster the sensations of transparency, immediacy, accountability, and the blurring of boundaries between economy, state, and civil society.

Opinion polls played a central role in Fujimori's political survival. Especially after he dissolved Congress in an "autogolpe," or self-coup, public opinion was the mainstay of his administration's legitimation: a public opinion constituted solely through the polls. Fujimori's neoliberal reforms faced resistance from both chambers of Congress, which were controlled by opposition parties. On April 5, 1992, therefore, he suspended the constitution, dissolved both the Chamber of Deputies and the Senate, and had prominent opposition figures and journalists arrested, "the culminating response of an attempt to restructure the state and its relations with society."[114] As Poole and Rénique report, in subsequent weeks "Peruvians were subjected to an avalanche of opinion polls, most purporting to demonstrate massive public backing for Fujimori's coup. Most were simple 'yes' or 'no' polls, suggesting widespread support."[115] Fujimori then paraded these polls before the Organization of American States (meeting soon thereafter in the Bahamas) to secure international as well as national legitimation for what he had done. As political scientist Catherine Conaghan puts it, "It is not unusual for coups to be made in the name of 'the people.' What was novel about Peru's Fuji-golpe was that the assertion could be tied to a body of 'scientific' data."[116] Poole and Rénique go on to comment that the polls revealed "the potency of Fujimori's 'anti-political' and 'anti-establishment' stance."[117] But again, the regime was only "anti-political" inasmuch as it had almost fully converted the complex relations between culture and the state into a managerial discourse interior to the state itself; all mediating institutions could be pushed aside because Fujimori could claim, through polling, direct access to the public mind. The one book on Peruvian opinion polls, sociologist (and subsequently head of the Peruvian electoral commission) Fernando Tuesta Soldevilla's *No sabe/no opina,* is mainly concerned with their representativity and their treatment in the press. In an interview, however, Tuesta partly confirmed what was commonly rumored, that Fujimori worked closely with an Argentine polling company headed by one Saul Mankewich.[118] Subsequently it emerged that Mankewich was being paid $2,000 per month for his work on Fujimori's 2000 reelection campaign.[119] In biographer Luis Jochamowitz's words, Fujimori's "fondness for political marketing is no secret; the polls have become, with him, a theme of frequent discussion."[120] As these are unpublished polls, they are not discussed in Tuesta's book. But it is invisible polling that truly permeates neoliberal social order.

There is no poll more invisible than that conducted by the intelligence services. The MRTA hostage crisis and its resolution in the spring of 1997 provide an object lesson and metaphor for the combination of political polling, intelligence gathering, and mediatization that characterized Fujimori's regime. The Movimiento Revolucionario Túpac Amaru (Túpac Amaru Revolutionary Movement) was the other, much smaller, guerilla movement active in Peru during the 1980s and 1990s. It was, however, quite different from Sendero: in the tradition of classic Latin American guerrilla groups, similar to and affiliated with the FMLN and other darlings of the 1980s left, its followers aimed to create some public space for negotiation, even if this had to be taken by force. In December 1996, disguised as waiters, a group of fourteen MRTA militants infiltrated and then overran a reception at the Japanese ambassador's residence in Lima, taking hundreds hostage, many of whom were prominent figures from Peru's social, business, and political elite. The MRTA held seventy-two of these hostages for four months, in a drama played out daily on Peru's television screens (and also in the eyes of world opinion). The guerrillas were happy to create a spectacle and bask in its limelight; the crisis was their soapbox. TV crews were even invited into the residence for interviews with the armed group's leaders. Fujimori, on the other hand, insisted that negotiation was impossible; talking was not an option. When the polls indicated that the time was right, he instead implemented a technocratic solution to eliminate this blockage to the state's expansion and transparency. The MRTA was all too visible, and Fujimori's security forces undermined them literally as well as metaphorically, digging subterranean tunnels that permeated the ground beneath the hostage-takers. Using sophisticated listening devices, unbeknownst to the camera-friendly militants, the state was quietly listening in on their overconfident volubility from under their very feet. Finally, in a special operation that was broadcast live to the nation, the forces of order emerged from their tunnels and stormed the compound, killing all the guerrillas. The victorious state then allowed itself the luxury of teaching potential militants a visual lesson: images of the MRTA members' corpses, and of Fujimori inspecting the scene, were repeatedly replayed on the nightly news. The exercise depended, however, on an invisible penetration of the social bedrock, on a surreptitious sounding out of everyday routines in the residence above.

Media politics under Fujimori took both overt and covert forms. For the importance of TV talk shows and the culture of so-called "vedettes" (showgirls) during the 1990s, see not only Degregori's *La década de la antipolítica* but also media scholar José Luis Vargas Gutiérrez's *Adiós a la vergüenza,* journalist Carlos Chávez Toro's *Susy Díaz,* and Romeo Grompone's *Fujimori, neopopulismo y comunicación política.* "In his marketing strategy," Grompone tells us, "Fujimori starts from the idea that people's reference point is television and the opportunities they have for direct contact with the president."[121] Chávez Toro focuses on the election of a vedette, Susy Díaz, to Congress in 1995. Díaz won a significant share of the vote, and more in absolute terms than almost sixty other elected members of Congress. Asked the reasons for her success, she answered that "the people have voted for me because I am a transparent person."[122] To the same question, sociologist José María Salcedo's response is that "it is because in Peru the category of professional politician has disappeared. The distance between those who know and those who don't know about politics has vanished."[123] Anyone could be in politics, so long as they were transparent enough. Degregori, meanwhile, is quick to point out the similarities between talk show culture and Sendero: "One of Sendero's most terrifying slogans was the Foucauldian 'the party has a thousand eyes, a thousand ears.' A TV channel has a thousand eyes and ears, too: electronic ones. Placing hidden cameras in the most unexpected places... is a perverse erasure of the separation between private and public."[124] But the most telling evidence of the imbrication of politics, media, and intelligence came with the scandal of the so-called "Vladivideos." In late 2000 it emerged that Vladimiro Montesinos, Fujimori's right-hand man and head of the Peruvian National Intelligence Service, had secretly videotaped thousands of his meetings with military, commercial, and political contacts. These videos recorded a series of illegal financial transactions, including outright bribes accepted by opposition members of Congress and by the proprietors of several Peruvian television stations. The scandal brought down Fujimori's government, but not before making crystal clear the complete infiltration of state, market, and civil society. In the end, none of this was too surprising. As Degregori comments, "corruption had become the only institution. All the other institutions had become mere façades."[125] Corruption kept the state going; but it was also eating it away from within.

State and society, and their mutual relations, have been transformed over the past twenty or thirty years. Opinion polls take popular representativity to an extreme, holding out the dream of a direct expression of popular will: a utopia of direct democracy that would replace the mediated representations and the mediating institutions (political parties and social movements alike) of formal democracy. Any such institution has its own weight and relative autonomy and thus, from the perspective of neoliberalism, distorts the political process, either through bureaucracy or through corruption. In the interests of transparency, such institutions are subject to constant scrutiny and demonization. The discourse of scandal becomes ubiquitous: even minor peccadilloes are magnified by a press and a political establishment determined to eliminate any remnant of opacity, any obstacle to the smooth and transparent operations of a technocratic direct democracy. Corruption fights corruption: an unbounded flow of knowledge, wealth, and desire (insider trading, bribery, and sexual affairs, but also television, marketing, and the popular press) is simultaneously obstacle to and vehicle of neoliberalism's self-realization.

The state too is caught up in such flows: it does not so much shrink, as neoliberal ideology would have it, as slip its bounds and invest society as a whole. It totalizes, legitimating itself through a direct and total coincidence with the social, thus erasing any distinction between state and civil society. The most radical elements in the new social movements have long tried to break down these barriers between state and civil society: neoliberalism takes up their fundamentalism, but on the state's own terms. Sovereignty becomes dispersed and decentered, but at the same time all the more entrenched in everyday life. Italian philosopher Paolo Virno terms this a "counterrevolution" or "revolution in reverse" whereby social demands are appeased but inverted.[126] The state's response to a constituent power that it brands fundamentalism is a new form of sovereignty: Empire. All limits are abolished, but in the process multiplicity is reduced to unity, singularity to identity.

No matter how many inputs civil society has, how many different voices enter the general hubbub, everything becomes one. It is ironically by taking up civil society's most radical demands that the state maintains its monopoly. Civil society transforms multiple inputs into a single output (policy), and the state then intervenes into civil society to stratify and so contain the force of its social movements. The state differentiates and classifies: by recognizing some individuals as citizens and others not, for instance; or by marking off the insane, the educated, the criminal, and so on. But these differences are subject to a single principle of sovereign unity, identity, and legitimacy. The state lies behind modernity's multiple differentiations. It is a machine to produce difference, but it depends upon civil society's hyperrepresentational assemblage to produce its own overarching identity. In other words, the multiple negotiations within civil society become the components of an eminent unity that then overcodes differences according to a single legitimate and legitimating principle. But something always escapes.

Beyond Civil Society: Affect

Neoliberalism takes civil society discourse to its limit. Many left and social democratic intellectuals champion civil society to counter the ascendancy of neoliberalism. But at the same time they often betray their ambivalence and their distrust of the concept and even of democracy as a whole. Political scientists Catherine Conaghan and James Malloy, for instance, argue that "democrats must make and remake civil society to prevent the realization of Tocqueville's worst fears," that is, "the potential of democracy to devolve into new insidious forms of domination."[127] It is as though there were a battle over the soul of civil society. In its neoliberal incarnation, civil society no longer looks much like civil society as it has been imagined or theorized, because there is no role for parties or other mediating institutions and because the complex architecture of liberal limitation has been erased. Functional efficiency has replaced any Tocquevillian normativity. This is a more perfect, or at least a more perfectly functional, civil society: fundamentalism has won out as the last barriers to communication fall and as the division between state and society is more permeable and diffuse than ever. But this is a dispassionate fundamentalism. A new breed of intellectual comes into play: the technocratic manager, political operative, special advisor, or marketing guru, with his or her ear permanently to the ground. These spin doctors try not to stick out above what is by now a torrential flow of information. As all distinctions disappear, striated space becomes smooth, and everything is a matter of blending in. September 11, 2001, for instance, becomes simply a "good day to bury bad news" in the notorious phrase of the British political advisor Jo Moore. Politics is now the art of desensitization. This is a cold world, from which all sentiment and affect is, ideally, excluded. But that repressed affect is bound to return.

Neoliberalism's affectlessness contrasts sharply with populism's passion. In other ways, neoliberalism and populism are very similar. Both, above all, are born out of a frustration with political representation. Both construct a direct relation or pact: between state and society or between leader and people. Both reconstitute a social contract eroded by unruly elements (a multitude) that threaten to exceed and overcome the state or the nation. They both engender new habits that harness dissident energies to constituted power. No wonder that neoliberalism often takes neopopulist form. In neoliberalism, however, immanent infiltration trumps all alliances; populism, by contrast, may operate through intermediary institutions such as trade unions. Populism's pact is sealed via an affective affinity that obscures the state and holds it at arm's length; neoliberalism excludes all affective relations to impose the state's hitherto unimagined universality. Populism substitutes culture for the state, while the neoliberal state excludes culture in the name of a hyperrational civil society. Hence the disparate moods of the two regime forms: neoliberalism's coldness and cruelty on the one hand and populism's ecstatic love on the other. Hence also their very different dramaturgies: replacing the theatricality of traditional liberalism, populism is cinematic; neoliberalism is televisual. Populism is incarnated bodily, its crowds gathered in the central plaza facing the projected image of the charismatic leader. Under neoliberalism, space is privatized, individuals are cloistered in living rooms or aptly named "dens," and the social is calculated in line with statistical ratings on a piece of paper or spreadsheet reviewed by a leader without qualities.

It would be hard to imagine a regime less embodied in its leader than Fujimori's. From the outset, in the 1990 election campaign, this shy agronomist and mathematician defeated the flamboyant Mario Vargas Llosa without ever trying to imitate the novelist's style. Fujimori's public image was consistently muted, his reticence popularly attributed to his Japanese heritage and the myth of Asian inscrutability. But his stubborn undemonstrativeness could equally be interpreted as the result of social awkwardness, the fact that he never quite fit in. Populist leaders, too, are often outsiders, but they prefer to put their antiestablishment credentials on dramatic display: for instance, Evita Perón's every effort was to produce the effect (and affect) of natural and spontaneous emotion, however much in fact her ailing body was propped up by makeshift technology. In contrast to the volubility of a populist leader, who is always perorating from the balcony, Fujimori kept his counsel. In Degregori's words, "he governs in silence. A silence that provides a sense of relief after the verbal excesses of previous years; moreover it proves its utility for the tactic of the ambush, one of his preferred forms of doing politics."[128] As if to compensate for his outsider status, rather than standing out or standing up, Fujimori aimed always to blend in. On his numerous visits to provincial communities around the country, he would take on local dress (a poncho and woolen hat, for instance, in the highlands) rather than bringing with him the pomp of presidential office. Fujimori turned his "lack of character," "unease in speaking," and "lack of charisma" to his advantage. With Fujimori's election, "the era of voting for the 'master,' for the 'exemplary father' was at an end"; in a form of "electoral narcissism," people were now voting for themselves.[129] No wonder Jochamowitz should entitle his biography of the president *Ciudadano Fujimori,* "Citizen Fujimori." Whereas a populist leader incarnates popular aspirations, the neoliberal leader tries to disappear into the crowd.

Again, we see a strange affinity between *fujimorismo* and Sendero. Abimael Guzmán, who also started off as an obscure academic, likewise turned reticence and silence into a virtue. Before his capture in 1992, Guzmán had the reputation of forever being just out of reach, consistently evading capture by the narrowest margin. He was everywhere but nowhere: rumor often had it that he was in fact dead; Sendero's maximum leader left only semilegible signs of his spectral presence, such as a bag of personal effects found discarded after an attack in Ayacucho.[130] British novelist Nicholas Shakespeare's *The Dancer Upstairs* centers on the paradox of the guerrilla leader (a fictionalized version of Guzmán) who is nowhere, everywhere, and in front of his pursuer's eyes all at the same time. Inscrutable and uncommunicative, his principle is that "if you wanted to be effective, you'd leave no trace." The revolution's mastermind "had dismembered and scattered his body, and now thrived like a monstrous Host in the heart of anyone invoking his name."[131] And yet, like Poe's purloined letter, he is in plain view, living above the studio where the novel's detective protagonist takes his daughter for ballet lessons and falls for her teacher. When in 1991 the Peruvian state captured a videotape of Guzmán dancing to "Zorba the Greek," it was proudly displayed on national television as a publicity coup. The images of the clumsy and apparently drunk former professor lumbering around to the music gave him a sense of physical presence. Ironically, at the time Guzmán was in fact less present than ever: owing to health problems aggravated by altitude, he was seldom able to travel to the Andean regions where Sendero had the most power and support. Guzmán was no Che Guevara. He could never project himself at his people's side in the populist manner and instead is represented in Sendero iconography as the teacher, the bookish pedagogue, finally as the incarnation of a form of thought (*pensamiento Gonzalo*) that allied him, as the "fourth sword of Marxism," with a parade of dead foreigners (Marx, Lenin, Mao).

Civil society theory and neoliberalism alike set out to exclude affect, passion, and the body from politics. In their place, they propose statistical articulation and hyperarticulacy. Affects are replaced by reasons (by Reason) as answers are solicited to the questions of management and state direction. Opinions hold pride of place in society's constant self-interrogation, which contrasts so baldly with populism's barely articulable ontology of habit. If populism is apolitical, its antipolitics is very different from neoliberalism's. Populism is an underarticulate disposition of the body, an incorporated common sense, as opposed to neoliberalism's overarticulate frame of mind, its deracinated opinion. Neoliberalism excludes any affective sense of bodily location. It is not that populism, with its material, bodily grounding, is somehow more natural than neoliberalism. Neoliberalism's stress on transparency enjoys a very similar aura of incontrovertibility, as though it harnessed a spontaneous effusion of popular opinion, varnished with the sense of rightness that rationalization and reason bring. Moreover, as neoliberalism's techniques of surveillance and observation are so in harmony with a whole range of social scientific methods and ideologies, it gains additional purchase in that its constitutive distortions mirror those of its social scientific observers. The state processes and ultimately dispenses with experience and affect to construct the realm of managerial reason. Normally this procedure passes more or less unnoticed, but when the constituent force of this excluded affect reappears, it does so with a vengeance.

Sendero combines affect and reason with peculiar intensity. From the outside it always appeared bloodthirsty, mysterious, and irrational. Sendero militants seemed to be motivated perhaps by archaic prejudice, perhaps by sheer hatred and *ressentiment.* Everything about the movement was excessive and disturbing. But political scientist David Apter comments that "just as there are reasons of state, so there are reasons of the anti-state," however much the latter appear to be antireasons.[132] Indeed, as Degregori explains, Sendero is better understood as what, taking the phrase from nineteenth-century poet Manuel González Prada, he calls a "divine cult to reason."[133] Its ecstatic rationality slides easily into rational ecstasy and back again. Hence Degregori argues that to understand Sendero, we should "invert Pascal's phrase, 'the heart has reasons of which reason is unaware,' " and say of Sendero's leading group that "reason has passions of which the heart is unaware." Sendero is a "hyperrationalist movement" that "develops and draws out" extraordinary passions.[134] It amplified the passions of its adherents, but it also drew out unsuspected passions from society at large. At the peak of the insurgency, nobody could be sure of the line between reason and affect, rationality and madness. Sendero encouraged its followers to embark on a paranoid search for order, but at the same time it revealed the paranoid structure of civil society as a whole.

The modern, developmentalist state inadvertently spawned and nurtured the passions that drove those who would become its most tireless enemies. Sendero's cradle was Ayacucho's University of Huamanga, reopened in the late 1950s. In particular, the movement was always strongest in the university's Faculty of Education. The state held out education as the vehicle of progress and raised enormous expectations about the transformations that lay ahead. The university would bring modernity to this rural backwater in the Andes. Education offered a form of salvation, a means to escape; if there was any millenarianism or messianism in Sendero, this was its source. As Degregori puts it, "Andean peasants . . . flung themselves into the conquest of 'progress.' " They searched for the knowledge and truth that would set them free; and "those who made it to university would have to go further and search out, by dint of great effort, something beyond truth: *coherence.*" For Degregori, Sendero militants, especially its leadership in the early stages, were driven by this state-sanctioned love of truth and coherence: "And when they think they have found them, they are capable of the greatest violence in order to defend and impose them."[135] Their violence provoked consternation and horror in Peruvian civil society; but it merely reflected the structural (and often enough also actual) violence that had long patrolled the boundary between center and periphery, civilization and presumed barbarism. Again, Sendero held up a mirror to civil society, revealing its translations between affect and reason, and unveiling the terror that secures its simulacrum of a social pact. Sendero "affected" civil society, reintroducing affect into its rationalizations. It provides the limit of civil society theory, the unaccountable distortion at its horizon. And precisely because its hyperrationality is illegible to the state, Sendero is also a brick wall, a screen, an empty signifier upon which others project fearful and shadowy images (not least, of Peru's indigenous majority) in an inverted reflection of Sendero's rational purity, its all-consuming joy.

Sendero tipped reason over into madness. Like the paranoid whose obsession with interpretation and connection soon constructs a hyperreal edifice that no longer bears much relation to the real itself,

Sendero passed through rationality to delirium but also demonstrated the delirium that underlies rationality. With Sendero, ideological reason was cultivated and transformed such that it no longer had a communicative function. In its abstract rigor and autonomy, an ideology that lays claim to the scientific tradition came close to a surreal poetry that is both horrifying and sublime: "[The people's] blood will rise like pulsing wings, and that bruised flesh will turn into the powerful whips of vengeance, and muscles and action will turn into a steel battering ram to destroy the oppressors, who will be irretrievably smashed."[136] Language becomes pure affect. Sendero's language is the expression and sign of purity, foretelling the joy of those who share in that spotless clarity and instilling fear into those it defines as radically other. It never attempted to convince or persuade. The passions of reason mimic the reasons of the heart in a reciprocal reinforcement that requires no justification. This is barbarous indeed, but Sendero equally shows up the barbarity of the constituted, official state and its mechanisms of subalternization. Sendero seeks no negotiation because it poses only one question: Are you loyal to this vision of revolution? Or as its militants put it to María Elena Moyano: step aside or be eliminated. While the neoliberal state has a panoply of polls and calls for managerial support, Sendero, which managed only the revolution, reduced this discourse to the single question: yes or no? Increasingly, however, the same is true also of the contemporary state, affected by a war against terror that is now global. It, too, asks little more than that we be either for it or against it.

Though Sendero's discourse becomes sublime and sublimely horrifying, we should avoid describing Latin American reality as abject difference. This is neither the *"noche obscura"* of novelist Joan Didion's *Salvador,* nor the revolution from the Incan South of journalist Simon Strong's *Shining Path.*[137] Sendero incarnates the apotheosis of reason, plucked straight from the finest Western philosophical tradition of Kant (subject of Guzmán's thesis) and Marx. More generally, all civil societies are "affected." Neither the Peruvian nor more generally the Latin American experiences are aberrant. As I will suggest in chapter 3, all social formations are structured through affect, by the reasons of the heart and the passions of reason. Sendero shows how affect is a constituent element of any social formation, that necessarily disrupts the working of any civil society. Any attempt to set limits to this constituent power is doomed to failure, not least in an era of biopolitics in which neoliberal Empire has already pulverized the carefully constructed barriers of liberal modernity. Sovereignty is more precarious than ever, and rightly so. Which is not to say that we should support all its adversaries: Sendero's line of flight soon became suicidal as well as homicidal; it became entranced by death rather than life. As historian Alberto Flores Galindo tersely comments, in reaction to a 1988 Sendero killing: "Socialism is a wager on the side of life, not that of death. Its objective is not simply the destruction of a state and the liquidation of class domination but also and above all the construction of new social relations that should and can be developing in the present."[138] The problem posed by Sendero, and other similar movements, is why such constituent power turns back on itself and how hope and expectation become death and conflagration.

With the crisis of the state, and the dissolution of any boundary between state and civil society, affect comes to the fore. Paranoia flourishes in the face of constant surveillance, but equally the tides of policy ebb and flow with changes in popular sentiment. The extent to which social relations are structured in terms of affect rather than (or on another level from) discourse becomes clearer. Other social logics begin to emerge in eddies and whorls, and fundamentalisms thrive as the mechanism of representation passes its sell-by date. Civil society theory aims to restore order, and at the same time holds out the hope of reform by returning a sense of rationality and agency to subaltern subjects. If traditional left politics had assumed a vanguard role for intellectuals, who are to awaken and educate the masses, a focus on new social movements emphasizes rather the myriad negotiations and initiatives performed by subaltern subjects. No doubt this has been a progressive move to counter the view that peasants, the indigenous, and others are formed by premodern communities bound by atavistic tradition and superstition. An emphasis on subjectivity is a welcome corrective. Yet it is as though subalterns were presented as perfect rational choice actors, conforming to the most ideal of Western liberal paradigms of reason. Presenting them as rational actors of this type deculturates and depoliticizes such agents by presenting them "as if they were outside culture and ideology."[139] The price subalterns pay is that their activities are recognized only so long as they accord to a notion of reason imposed upon them; only, that is, so long as efficiency and modernization continue to be the ground of civil society. Such actors are to be ascribed agency, but on the terms of the social theorist. Anything outside that framework becomes invisible, and the democratic task becomes to substitute a rational civil society for affective and cultural relations seen as distorting its managerial transparency. But an insistence on transparency heralds a massive expansion of the state, a politics futilely focused on the wholesale elimination of culture and corruption. Neoliberalism takes over where civil society theory leaves off, only to founder on the terror that lurks at its margins and haunts society as a whole.

Civil society is enlivened by the fundamentalism that civil society theory subsequently seeks to curtail. But in the context of a global war on terror, fundamentalism has the upper hand: whether that be the fanaticism that is pledged to bring down the state, or the state's own brand of now decentered sovereignty. A multitude confronts Empire and yet, as I argue in my concluding chapter, there is less than ever to choose between them. But surely there is some alternative to the fundamentalisms of a Sendero Luminoso or an al-Qaida on the one hand, or of neoliberalism's diffuse forms of command and control on the other. There is no point returning to the deadening restrictions and careful regulations of the liberal contract. And populist hegemony is also but an illusion, a misleading sleight of hand. Could there then be a fundamentalism driven by vitality, affirmation, and life, rather than the death drive of mutual immolation? Refusing the constrictions and antidemocratic democracy of civil society theory, we might reconsider the immediacy of social movements in their excessive and passionate demands. *Encore un effort.* Néstor García Canclini asks how to be radical, without being fundamentalist. We might do better to look for a good fundamentalism, a good multitude. With that in mind, I turn now from critique to constitution.

Part II

CONSTITUTION

3

Escalón 1989: Deleuze and Affect

From the edge of the gully, the "Ciguanaba," bathed in moonlight, gives the prearranged signal: a long, thundering peal of laughter: ha ha ha ha HA. . . . Just behind her, the "Cipitío," in a comandante's beret, grasps his gun and fires off his own gleeful cackle: hee hee hee hee HEE.

—Colectivo "Huitzilipochtli,"
El "Cipitío" en el Salvador Sheraton

We will say of pure immanence that it is A LIFE, and nothing else. . . . A life is the immanence of immanence, absolute immanence: it is complete power, complete bliss.

—Gilles Deleuze, *Pure Immanence*

The Return of Affect

The Marxist critic Fredric Jameson famously senses a "waning of affect in postmodern culture." He argues that "the great modernist thematics of alienation, anomie, solitude and social fragmentation and isolation" have now "vanished away." Jameson claims that postmodernism offers "not merely a liberation from anxiety but a liberation from every other kind of feeling as well, since there is no longer a self present to do the feeling." He adds, however, that feelings have not entirely disappeared: it is just that they "are now free-floating and impersonal and tend to be dominated by a peculiar kind of euphoria."[1] Hence, he argues elsewhere, the sensation of "relief" as postmodernism heralds what feels like "a thunderous unblocking of logjams and a release of new productivity."

This relief, Jameson continues, is an effect of our distance from production; it is a symptom of our "economic impotence."[2] Now that all trace of production has been effaced from the commodity, consumers can surrender to the narcotic delights of postmodern *jouissance*.

But since the exuberant 1980s, when Jameson's essay was originally published, or even the 1990s, when it was revised and republished as part of his book *Postmodernism*, anxiety has surely returned with a vengeance. We may be no less impotent, yet fear and even terror rather than euphoria define the age inaugurated by the September 2001 attacks on New York and Washington. Affect is back (if it had ever really gone away). Affect has also returned as an object of study: critics such as Corey Rubin and Joanna Bourke have written specifically on fear; theorists such as Teresa Brennan, Antonio Damasio, Brian Massumi, and Eve Sedgwick have reconsidered affect more generally.[3] There is even talk of an "affective turn."[4] Critics disagree, however, on the terminology they employ and their definitions. Affect, emotion, feeling, passion, sensation: these terms often overlap and are used by some interchangeably, but by others to refer to very different concepts. Jameson, for instance, contrasts affect, which he defines as subjective feeling, with the "free-floating and impersonal" feelings that "it might be better and more accurate to call 'intensities.'"[5] Feminist theorist Brennan, on the other hand, distinguishes the physiological from the linguistic: affects "are material, physiological things," whereas "feelings are sensations that have found the right match in words."[6] Neurologist Damasio invokes a similar distinction, but what Brennan terms affect he terms emotion: "Emotions play out in the theater of the body. Feelings play out in the theater of the mind."[7] Philosopher Massumi defines affect as impersonal intensity, by contrast with emotion, which he calls "qualified intensity," that is, "the sociological fixing of the quality of an experience which is from that point onward defined as personal."[8] And queer theorist Sedgwick, finally, following psychologist Silvan Tomkins, separates affects and drives: both are "thoroughly embodied," but "affects have greater freedom with respect to object."[9]

My use of the term "affect" (and of the related term, "emotion") is closest to Massumi's. Moreover, like him I draw on French philosopher Gilles Deleuze to flesh out a politics of affect that resonates with posthegemonic times. Massumi argues that Deleuze's theory of affect "holds a key to rethinking postmodern power after ideology," and he proposes therefore "an affective theory of late-capitalist power."[10] I go further, to argue that we need an affective theory of power per se. Affect is central to the understanding and elaboration of posthegemony, alongside the concepts of habit (affect at standstill) and multitude (affect become subject), which I develop in subsequent chapters. Yet I also argue that the Deleuzian conception of affect is insufficient, indeed that it falls prey to traps similar to those that befall hegemony theory, in that on its own it cannot distinguish between insurgency and order, ultimately between revolution and fascism. Still, affect is where posthegemony theory must start. Feeling is a gateway to the immanence of politics (and to a politics of immanence).

Deleuze's definition of affect derives from the seventeenth-century philosopher Benedict de Spinoza. Spinoza's philosophy is centrally concerned with the relationships between bodies, which can be human bodies but also body parts, things, and collectivities. As Spinoza declares in the opening to his discussion of emotions in the *Ethics*, "I shall consider human actions and appetites just as if it were a question of lines, planes, and bodies." For "the whole of nature" consists of "bodies [that] vary in infinite ways." And the human body, for instance, comprises many other bodies, requires still other bodies for its preservation and regeneration (through, say, food or shelter), and in turn "can move and dispose external bodies in a great many ways."[11] So bodies continually affect and are affected by other bodies. Indeed, a body is defined by its potential to affect or to be affected, by its powers of affection; some bodies have much greater powers to affect other bodies, and no two bodies affect others in precisely the same ways. Moreover, this capacity for affection is in constant flux, depending upon a whole history of interactions. If I am well-nourished, for instance, I may have a greater power to affect other bodies than otherwise; if I have fallen from or collided with some other body, I may have less power of affection. In short, affect is a way of redescribing the constant interactions between bodies and the resultant impacts of such interactions. Every encounter brings with it some kind of change: as Deleuze explains, the result is "an increase or decrease in the power of acting, for the body and the mind alike"; affect is variation, "a variation of the power of acting." When our power of acting (of affecting and being affected by others) increases, we feel joy; when it decreases, we feel sadness. So there is a basic distinction between "joyful passions" and "sad passions."[12]

Affect is, for Deleuze and Spinoza, an index of power: we may feel pain (a sad passion) when our power of acting diminishes; we may feel pleasure (a joyful passion) when it is enhanced. In turn, a body's power is itself is a function of its affective capacity or receptivity, its power to move or be moved by others. And as its power changes, so does its very essence: increases or decreases in a body's power, changes in its affection, determine its ability to further affect and be affected, to become another body (more or less powerful). Affect marks the passage whereby one body *becomes* another body, either joyfully or sorrowfully; affect always takes place *between* bodies, at the mobile threshold between affective states as bodies either coalesce or disintegrate, as they become other to themselves. Hence, Massumi argues, affect constitutes an immanent and unbounded "field of emergence" or "pure capacity" prior to the imposition of order or subjectivity. It is another name for the continuous variation that characterizes the infinite encounters between bodies, and their resultant displacements and transformations, constitutions and dissolutions. It is only as affect is delimited and captured that bodies are fixed and so subjectivity (or at least, individual subjectivity) and transcendence emerge. But as this happens, affect itself changes: the order that establishes both subjectivity and transcendence also (and reciprocally) converts affect into emotion. The myriad encounters between bodies in flux come to be represented as interactions between fixed individuals or subjects, and affect becomes qualified and confined within (rather than between) particular bodies. This qualification of affective intensity is its "capture and closure"; Massumi suggests that "emotion is the most intense (most contracted) expression of that *capture*."[13]

As affect is transformed into emotion, it founds sovereignty. Deleuze and his coauthor, the psychoanalyst and activist Félix Guattari, provide an example taken from the stage to illustrate the capture and so subjection of affect. In opera, the "romantic hero," that is, "a subjectified individual with 'feelings,'" emerges from (and retrospectively orders and envelops) "the orchestral and instrumental whole that on the contrary mobilizes nonsubjective 'affects.'" But this orchestration of affect, its transformation into emotion, is also immediately political: the "problem" of affect in opera is "technically musical, and all the more political for that."[14] The same mechanisms orchestrate subjectivity in politics as in the opera house. Massumi identifies some of the ways in which contemporary regimes exploit "affect as *capturable* life potential."[15] He details how Ronald Reagan, for instance, put affect to work in the service of state power, conjuring up sovereignty by projecting confidence, "the apotheosis of affective capture." Reagan "wants to transcend, to be someone else. He wants to be extraordinary, to be a hero." But ideology had nothing to do with this arch-populist's transcendence: "His means were affective." Rather than seeking consent, Reagan achieved the semblance of control by transmitting "vitality, virtuality, tendency."[16] Affect, then, is more than simply an index of the immanent, corporeal power of bodies whose definition mutates according to their state of affection; it is also what underpins the incorporeal or "quasi-corporeal" power of the sovereign whose empirical body, in Reagan's case, crumbles before our eyes. In this double role, as an immanent productivity that also gives rise to transcendent power, affect is "as infrastructural as a factory." Like labor power, it is a potential that can be abstracted and put to use, a "liveliness" that "may be apportioned to objects as properties or attributes," an "excess" or "surplus" that "holds the world together."[17]

Just as Latin America has long supplied raw material to feed the global economy, so the region has also been exploited for its affective potential. Gold, silver, copper, guano, rubber, chocolate, sugar, tobacco, coffee, coca: these have all sustained peripheral monocultures whose product has been refined and consumed in the metropolis. And parallel to and intertwined with this trade in consumer goods is a no less material affective economy, also often structured by a distinction between the raw and the refined. After all, several of these commodities are mood enhancers, easily confected into forms (rum, cigarettes, cocaine) that further distill their affective powers. Others have inspired their own deliria: gold fever, rubber booms. But there has always been a more direct appropriation and accumulation of affective energy: from the circulation of fearful travelers' tales describing cannibals and savages to the dissemination of "magic realism" and salsa, or the commodification of sexuality for Hollywood or package tourism. Latin America marks the Western imagination with a particular intensity.

And the figures who stand in for the region are therefore distinguished by their affective charge: the "Brazilian bombshell" Carmen Miranda, for instance, her headdresses loaded with fruit signifying tropical bounty, functioned in films such as *Week-End in Havana* (1941) and *The Gang's All Here* (1943) as a fetishized conduit for the exuberance and sexiness that Hollywood captures, distils, and purveys as "Latin spirit." At the same time, and despite the elaborate orchestration typifying a Carmen Miranda number, some disturbing excess remained, not least in the ways in which Miranda's patter upset linguistic convention. She blurred English and Portuguese and dissolved both, (re)converting language into sounds that were no longer meaningful, only affectively resonant. In film scholar Ana López's words, "Miranda's excessive manipulation of accents... inflates the fetish, cracking its surface while simultaneously aggrandizing it."[18] So there is a complex relationship between Latin affect and Western reason: both reinforcement and subversion. Cuban anthropologist Fernando Ortiz suggests that at stake in the exploitation of Latin affect is a colonial pact with the devil: he says of tobacco and chocolate from the Americas, as well as Arabian coffee and tea from the Far East ("all of them stimulants of the senses as well as of the spirit") that "it is as though they had been sent to Europe from the four corners of the earth by the devil to revive Europe 'when the time came,' when that continent was ready to save the spirituality of reason from burning itself out and give the senses their due once more."[19] An economy of the senses saves reason, gives it a shot in the arm, but also demonstrates reason's addicted dependence upon sensual as well as spiritual stimulation.

There is, then, a politics of affect; perhaps there is no other kind. We have seen how, in excluding affect from their calculations, both neoliberalism and civil society theory find themselves surprised by its often violent resurgence with the contemporary crisis of the state. Populism and cultural studies, on the other hand, are so fully affected, so invested in affective relations, that they succumb to the lure of the state as fetish and abandon critique. Ignoring or repressing affect and wallowing in it or taking it for granted have ultimately the same effect: affect remains a mystery; politics is rendered opaque. The return of affect demands an adequate conceptualization of affect's politics, and of its relation to the state.

Deleuze's theory of affect promises such a conceptualization, and so a better understanding of affect's role in both order and insurgency. It also enables us to rethink the very notion of the "return" of affect, with its implication that at some point affect had been lost to history. Far from it: there is an entire history of affect; or rather, history too is entirely affected. History is often cast as a narrative that emphasizes regularity and predictability: in Massumi's words, it comprises a set of "identified subjects and objects" whose progress is given "the appearance of an ordered, even necessary, evolution . . . contexts progressively falling into order."[20] But this appearance is conjured up by the same political operation that qualifies the prepersonal multiplicity and mobility characteristic of affect. Narrative history is the by-product of a process that selects, confines, and captures an affective flow that is in fact unpredictably mobile and in continuous variation. In Deleuze and Guattari's terms, "all history does is to translate a coexistence of becomings into a succession."[21] In this translation, affects become emotions, singular collectives become identifiable individuals, and the state arises, imposing its order upon culture. The affective, now constituted as the emotional, is represented as reactive, secondary, the essence of passivity: events provoke sadness, happiness, or whatever. Affect's primacy and excess is translated into the secondary residue that is emotion.

History has to be remapped in view of the affective flux that resonates through (and resists) its linear orderings. One starting point is to note how history is both marked and produced by affect and how historical changes are registered directly on and in the body. It is because it is imprinted on, as well as generated by, the body that, as Jameson notes, "history is what hurts."[22] Attempts to eliminate affect, either directly through its suppression or indirectly through the recuperation of those "affected" into the striations of disciplinary systems, although never fully successful, register as a recomposition of bodies: their incarceration in institutions, their normalization in society; or their subalternization, their dispersion and mutilation beyond the bounds of the social contract. Changes in prison demography or in the numbers or types of felons sent to the gallows, for instance, mark the imposition and expansion of the wage relation as surely as do unemployment statistics or the redeployment of workers along a factory production line.[23] History impacts on bodies immediately. Even the terms "mark" and "impact" are misleading: it is not that bodies are history's recording surface and affect its ink; we need to break from the representational logic that characterizes hegemony theory. Rather, immanence is the key to understanding affect. Affect is not what happens to a body, but part of a process by which a body becomes other to itself. History is no more or less than the recomposition or movement of bodies, a series of modulations in and through affect. Anything else is mere tableau.

We start with emotion, with our common emotions such as happiness or fear. Political theorist John Holloway suggests that "the beginning is not the word, but the scream."[24] Affect can be reread back through emotion, and so reinserted into history and politics. After all, emotion is a form of affect (*formed* affect), and the emotional individual is always on the verge of being overwhelmed, and so desubjectified, by an affect that goes beyond all bounds. For, however much affect is confined, something always escapes: "Something remains unactualized, inseparable from but unassimilable to any *particular*, functionally anchored perspective."[25] Individuals risk being carried away, losing their wits or their senses to become possessed by affect. For Massumi, "that is why all emotion is more or less disorienting, and why it is classically described as being outside of oneself."[26] Hence emotion frequently appears excessive and inappropriate; affect constantly threatens to reappear, to take over. And no wonder emotion is so often gendered, viewed as feminine: sweeping away fixed identities, affect initiates what Deleuze and Guattari term a "becoming," a becoming-woman or a becoming-minoritarian. Affect sweeps subjects away from normative models (man, state, human) and toward their counterpoles (woman, nomad, animal). In Deleuze's words, "affects aren't feelings, they're becomings that spill over beyond whoever lives through them (thereby becoming someone else)."[27] Affect gathers up singularities and partial objects, bodies of all shapes and sizes, and redistributes and recomposes them in new, experimental couplings and collectivities. Insofar as we let this happen, we liberate ourselves — from our *selves*. Carried away, we (but no longer "we"; someone else, some other collectivity) increase our power to affect and be affected. Flight is not a sign of weakness; it is the line along which we gain powers of affection and experiment with new "ways in which the body can connect with itself and with the world."[28]

This chapter's case study is El Salvador's FMLN (Frente Farabundo Martí para la Liberación Nacional, or Farabundo Martí National Liberation Front), the guerrilla group that waged war on the Salvadoran state in the 1980s until the peace accords of 1992, after which it became a conventional political party. My focus is on the FMLN as an insurgent organization. Rather than recuperating it as part of civil society, or seeing its struggle as predicated on some hegemonic project, I emphasize the consequences of clandestinity and so unrepresentability, and armed force and so terror, to show how the FMLN occupied an affective line of flight. This redescription of the FMLN aligns it more with a group such as Sendero than with (say) the Madres de la Plaza de Mayo or other so-called new social movements. At the same time, there is something savage ("fundmentalist") in all subaltern movements, even those that do their best to stake out a position within civil society or to submit to the logic of hegemony. These efforts at participating in the game of hegemony are always failures, at least in part, in that subalternity necessarily implies a (non)location outside of the circuits of civil society and rational discourse, outside of hegemonic projects. And there is always something terrifying about such an outside; but also something joyful, and it is this joy that inspires militancy, a becoming-other by becoming part of the movement. For the FMLN, affect was both a weapon and the site of an inhabitation at odds with the logic of hegemony. As such, the FMLN is an archetype of the nomad "war machine" valorized by Deleuze and Guattari. As we will see, however, the FMLN was not the only subaltern subject in the Salvadoran war: the state too becomes subaltern, becomes nomadic, in the death squads and in the activities of at least some parts of its armed forces, most notably the dreaded Atlacatl Brigade.

The Salvadoran civil war lasted from 1980 to 1992, and was one of the hemisphere's most prolonged and intense conflicts. But while much was written about the situation at the time, since the peace accords the country has mostly dropped off the agenda for academia and the media alike. A good introduction and overview to the country as a whole as well as to the civil war is historian Aldo Lauria-Santiago and anthropologist Leigh Binford's collection *Landscapes of Struggle*. Lauria-Santiago and Binford's theoretical frame is, they claim, "the complex and contradictory operations of hegemony and counter-hegemony." But they themselves admit that, even on their own terms, hegemony theory hardly helps explain Salvador's twentieth-century history: "The country's authoritarian legacy" makes for at best "a condition of 'weak hegemony.'"[29] Hegemony therefore functions as a deus ex machina in their account: the concept is sometimes invoked, loosely defined as "a system of beliefs and practices that favor dominant groups and that serve as frames that shape people's lived experience," but more often passed over in silence.[30] In practice, hegemony theory proves a poor guide to the Central American conflicts, and even where the concept is used with more consistency and rigor, as for instance in the discussion of testimonial literature by critics such as John Beverley, it leads (as I argue at more length in my concluding chapter) simply to misreadings and misunderstandings.

The FMLN emerged in 1980 as a coalition of five armed groups, most of which had been founded in the early 1970s. Galvanized by brutal state repression in the late 1970s and early 1980s, and building on the mass protests against which that repression was directed, they hoped to provoke a general insurrection with their so-called "final offensive" of January 1981. After all, other successful revolutions (most notably the 1979 victory of the Sandinistas in Nicaragua) had, at least in their final phases, been relatively rapid affairs. Both the Nicaraguans and the Cubans urged the FMLN to adopt a similar insurrectional strategy, and to do so quickly before Reagan assumed the U.S. presidency: "A quick insurrection would present the new administration with a fait accompli, an irreversible situation."[31] But despite some local victories, overall the 1981 offensive proved a failure, and soon both the FMLN and the Salvadoran armed forces dug in for a longer conflict. Indeed, in the first few years of the war (1980 to 1984), FMLN strategy stuck more or less to patterns of conventional warfare. With the Salvadoran armed forces "occupied in static defense of infrastructure," the guerrillas consolidated and expanded their territorial control in the countryside, "building a quasi-regular army" of battalions and brigades concentrated in large camps. In these early years, the FMLN sought primarily "a military resolution to the conflict," combining fixed battles and assaults on towns and villages, in an almost permanent series of minor offensives, with economic sabotage that sapped the Salvadoran state's ability to respond.[32] The rebels enjoyed significant success in this period: most analysts concur that had the guerrilla coalition been able to unify politically and militarily in time, and so had in fact their "final offensive" come earlier, they probably would have succeeded in overthrowing the Salvadoran state. Even without that decisive victory, by the end of 1981 "the FMLN had indisputable control over at least a quarter of the national territory," and this in what is (after the small island nations of Barbados, Haiti, Saint Lucia, and Grenada) the most densely populated country in the Americas.[33] Even the vehemently anti-FMLN analysts José Angel Bracamonte and David Spencer concede that the guerrillas were "without any doubt... the best militarily developed insurgent movement in the history of the American continent."[34]

It soon became clear that the Salvadoran revolution would prove a "long war" (to use political historian James Dunkerley's phrase) in more ways than one: not only could it trace its inspiration back to the 1930s when a Communist uprising was bloodily repressed by the oligarchic state, it would also become one of the hemisphere's most sustained guerrilla insurgencies. By the mid-1980s the FMLN strategy's unsuitability for such a long war was apparent. Hugh Byrne records that by the end of 1983, "the guerrillas were winning the war. However, the FMLN had military weaknesses. Its concentration of forces made the insurgents vulnerable to the assets of the armed forces, particularly helicopters, aircraft, and artillery." Byrne goes on to observe that "a quasi-regular war played to one of the strengths of the ESAF [El Salvadoran Armed Forces]: its access to sophisticated equipment and extensive funds to wage a high-technology war." From 1984, the FMLN therefore switched tactics. The rebels divided into smaller and more mobile units. They dispersed their forces throughout the country, only "concentrating them for strategic actions, particularly at night for short periods." Guerrilla units combined military and political functions, "working to build political support among the population."[35] Though significant parts of the country (particularly in the departments of Chalatenango in the west, Morazán and Usulatán in the east, and around the Guazapa volcano just to the north of the capital, San Salvador) remained beyond the permanent control of the Salvadoran state, in this new deterritorialized warfare the rebels were always on the move, or ready to move. Civilians, too, learned to flee – not least after the December 1981 massacre at El Mozote, a small village in Morazán, in which the army killed those who, when the guerrillas fled, had stayed behind in the expectation that their noncombatant status would protect them. Many sought refuge in Honduras and refugee camps such as Colomoncagua and Mesa Grande just over the border. However, given these camps' proximity to rebel-dominated zones in El Salvador, there was much traffic to and fro. Another massacre, at the Río Sumpul in May 1980, was an attempt by a combination of Salvadoran and Honduran armed forces to prevent such movement: at least six hundred *campesinos* were killed trying to cross the river as the Hondurans forced them back to face their Salvadoran pursuers. What emerged therefore was a transnational population simultaneously in resistance and in exodus. While the state tried to reinforce borders, slow down transport, and trap guerrillas and civilians alike in repeated "hammer and anvil" operations, those who inhabited a zone such as northern Morazán were in "a condition of permanent flight."[36]

Affect threatens social order. A focus on the apparatuses of capture that confine affect and on the lines of flight that traverse them, along which affect flees, enables a redescription of both social struggle and historical process. Resistance is no longer a matter of contradiction, but rather of the dissonance between would-be hegemonic projects and the immanent processes that they always fail fully to represent. This dissonance results from an incompatibility between state and war machine, sovereignty and subalternity, emotion and affect, however much the former also overlap and indeed rely upon the latter. Moreover, in and through affect other modes of community and coexistence are envisaged and practiced. So in what follows I investigate Deleuze's conception of affect as resistance, as a political alternative to state hierarchy. Particularly, I read back from our dominant contemporary emotions — the modulated nervousness and fear that now grip us, the carefully calibrated public anxiety that results from "affect modulation as a governmental-media function"[37] — to analyze the terror to which the contemporary state claims to respond. The state identifies in terrorism a mode of organization that is radically different and upsetting to its forms of order. The state intuits that terror threatens the very division between inside and outside upon which hegemony theory and civil society theory both depend. Hence, although the discourse on terror invokes a radical distinction between civilization and its barbarous others, in the end terror undermines such certainties, opening up a line of flight that undoes all binaries.

Deleuze theorizes affect, and the relationship between affect and the state, without either assimilating affect to state logics of normalization or assuming that the affective is simply supplement or excess. Rather, he describes a dynamic relationship between a nomad war machine characterized by affect and a state apparatus that seeks to eliminate that war machine's affects and energies by (trans)forming and stratifying them. Deleuze focuses on what the state excludes and represses; he demands that we confront immanence on its own terms, showing its distinction from transcendence (as well as the latter's dependence on the former). This is the basis for a theory of posthegemony: an analysis of culture that accounts for the state without subordinating itself to its logic and that can therefore chart the historical vicissitudes of the relations between nomad and state; an analysis of the double inscription of politics, as well as of the disparities between its two registers. Yet the danger is that this doubleness is now collapsing: the state itself is now becoming terrorist, and so diffusely nomadic; sovereignty is increasingly affective rather than merely affect's parasite. Deleuze and Guattari acknowledge that "the State apparatus *appropriates* the war machine, subordinates it to its 'political' *aims* and gives it war as its direct *object*."[38] But the suicidal, fascist state goes beyond any rationality of "aims" or objectives. And especially in posthegemonic times, with the so-called society of control or "control society," the state is ever more immanent. The state has to be explained twice: as it is instantiated in affects and habits, as well as in its projection as transcendent sovereignty. Again, distinguishing immanence and transcendence (affect and the sovereign state) is but a first step for posthegemonic analysis.

Affect as Immanence

Deleuze's entire philosophical project is premised on an affirmation of immanence, and a refusal of all transcendence. In theorist Michael Hardt's words, Deleuze "limits us to a strictly immanent and materialist ontological discourse that refuses any deep or hidden foundation of being."[39] He turns to Spinoza, whom he and Guattari term "the prince of philosophers" precisely because "perhaps he is the only philosopher never to have compromised with transcendence and to have hunted it down everywhere."[40] And if it is from Spinoza that Deleuze draws his conception of affect, this is because the Spinozan conception of affect offers a path toward immanence, leading from immediate encounters between bodies to a fully impersonal "plane of immanence." As commentator Gregory Seigworth summarizes, "there is not one type of affect in Spinoza, but two (*affectio* and *affectus*), and then not only two but, before and beneath them both, a third...and then,...not just three but a multitudinous affectivity beyond number (a plane of immanence)." *Affectio* is "the state of a body as it affects or is affected by another body"; *affectus* is "a body's continuous, intensive modification (as increase-diminution) in its capacity for acting"; affect proper then is "pure immanence at its most concrete abstraction... affect as virtuality"; and Seigworth quotes Deleuze's definition of the plane of immanence as "the immanence of immanence, absolute immanence: it is complete power, complete bliss."[41] So, just as affect itself can be read back through emotion, here is a progression: from the actual interactions of bodies as they always overflow any set identities; to the ever-changing essence of any body or combination of bodies, defined by their power to affect and be affected; and on to an ever more expansive conception of immanence itself, as pure virtuality. We have a program of study, from emotion, to affect, to bodies and collectivities, to immanence; and perhaps a political program, too.

But if we are continually surrounded by and immersed in (immanent to) the mechanisms and flows of affect, it can still stubbornly appear that transcendence is the only game in town. In philosophical terms, Platonism has still to be overthrown. In political terms, the state continues to claim transcendence and thereby sovereignty—although other figures, "the body of the earth, that of the tyrant, or capital" also establish themselves by "appropriating for [themselves] all surplus production and arrogating to [themselves] both the whole and the parts of the process, which now seem to emanate from [them] as a quasi cause."[42] A quasi cause acts *as though* it inhabited the empty dimension that constitutes transcendence, and also then *as though* it were the source of what in *Anti-Oedipus* is designated "desiring-production." Causes are presented as effects, and vice versa. Representation is posited as ulterior reason, and lack as the key to desire. Thus the state consolidates its power, allocating and distributing lack within and beyond the territorial boundaries it thereby secures, denying any power to the immanent affectivity of bodies as they affect and are affected by each other. Hegemony is substituted for politics; constituted power, with its reliance on negation and judgment, for the affirmative constituent power embedded in affective encounters.

The state is an "apparatus of capture" that transforms affect into emotion, multiplicity into unity, intensity into the extension of territorial Empire. This is the state's "incorporated, structural violence."

And against (but also prior to) the state is arrayed a nomad war machine for which "weapons are affects and affects weapons."[43] Deleuze and Guattari argue that the nomad is fundamentally separate from and exterior to the state: "In every respect, the war machine is of another species, another nature, another origin than the State apparatus." Just as the state, however warlike it may be, defines itself against war, against and in fear of a "war of all against all," so the war machine repels the state: "Just as Hobbes saw clearly that *the State was against war, so war is against the State*, and makes it impossible." Deleuze and Guattari conclude that "war is . . . the mode of a social state that wards off and prevents the State."[44] The state and the war machine are also differing modes of community. Whereas the state privileges and incarnates form (and so identity, fixity, definition), "the regime of the war machine is on the contrary that of *affects*, which relate only to the moving body in itself, to speeds and compositions of speed among elements." Whereas the state subjects bodies to identity, fixed (often, incarcerated) and defined according to (static) categories, "affects transpierce the body like arrows, they are weapons of war."[45] Against the striated space of categorization, of bounded differences, the nomad war machine organizes itself within a smooth space of continuous variation, of endless modulation: *affectus* tending toward immanence. Politics is no longer a matter of the consent and negotiation implied by the hegemonic contract; it is a (non)relation or incompatibility between processes of capture and affective escape.

The FMLN became ever more flexible, mobile, and nomadic so as to maintain its challenge to the Salvadoran state. It abandoned ideological as well as military rigidity, even largely abandoning ideology *tout court*. For Bracamonte and Spencer, it was its "lack of ideological trappings [that] allowed the FMLN to continually develop successful tactics that worked to near perfection."[46] In place of ideology, affect. Joining the FMLN involved not the adoption of any specific set of beliefs, but a change in affective state; indeed, it involved a shift from the individualized subjectivity associated with opinion as well as emotion, to the depersonalized commonality characteristic of affect. Guerrilla *testimonios* indicate the trauma and the intense affective charge of the transition to clandestinity. The subject of one such account, Ana María Castillo (Comandante Eugenia), explains how becoming-guerrilla is a form of social death: "You . . . will leave your family, your friends, and it's inevitable that some of your loved ones will die. Perhaps they'll kidnap your relatives to test if this'll lead them to you. You won't be able to do anything about it." Dialogue and discourse with the rest of the world, or the world left behind, become impossible: "You'll even see people you know in the street, and your heart will be in your mouth with the desire simply to say hello, but you won't be able to. You'll have to pass by on the other side . . . and that'll hurt you."[47] Clandestinity entails radical separation, and the guerrilla returns only as specter. She can see and (here, at least) be seen, but cannot look back and cannot speak. She is suffused with desire (as well as hurt), but also helpless, desubjectified, strangely passive: "You won't be able to do anything about it." Her motives will have to go unrecognized, taken to be snobbery ("perhaps they'll think 'How stuck up Eugenia's become' ") or treachery: "All my worker comrades will be left believing absolutely anything, even that I may have betrayed them. That I've gone who knows where."[48] She has gone, and if she is brought back, it will only be as a corpse: "They won't take me alive."

If the transition to clandestinity is a scission, a becoming-spectral, for the guerrilla it is also a passage to bodily union. Going underground is an immersion in materiality that desubjectifies the guerrilla as he or she becomes immanent to the struggle and to the revolutionary movement. Charles Clements, a pacifist U.S. doctor who spent a year with the FMLN around the Guazapa volcano, notes this emphasis on the corporeal in a conversation with the guide who leads him to the war zone. Asked "¿Por qué un gringo se incorporó?" Clements comments that "the question puzzled me. I didn't understand the verb. '¿Qué quieres decir por incorporarse?' (What do you mean by 'incorporate'?) I asked. He explained to me that when you join the struggle, you 'incorporate' with the guerrillas — literally, I suppose, to join their body." Despite himself and his sense of difference — because is a gringo, a doctor, and a pacifist — Clements later realizes that he too has incorporated, has joined the social body and lost his sense of individuality: "I had altogether ceased to be Charlie Clements."[49] For Clements, this realization provokes a profound sense of crisis. His aim had been to keep neutral, to keep his distance. But in the Front, the "Zone" that the FMLN traverses, desubjectification and an immanent immediacy that destroys all distance are inevitable. And for the fighters, incorporation fulfills a desire to be subsumed in the collectivity:

alongside the hurt and perhaps terror involved in inhabiting spectral excess, there is also the joy of commitment, of being fully enfolded within the struggle.

A community gathers on the line of flight, the *guinda* or forced march that defined life in the FMLN's liberated zones. For internationalist guerrilla Francisco Metzi, these tension-filled voyages were "exceptional times for fraternity. They were when we came closest to a truly Communist way of being."[50] Undoubtedly, they were associated with particularly intense fears, as the insurgents abandoned entrenched positions and were at their most vulnerable while on the move. But Belgian priest Roger Ponceele notes that they also occasioned intense happiness: "We are ever more mobile. . . . We are always en route to somewhere else. . . . As I go along I am always giving thanks to God."[51] Be it fear or happiness, the *guinda* resonated with an affective intensity that enabled new ways of being together. Above all, flight required ingenuity or daring: there was constant creativity in the attempt to come up with new ways to slip through (or make porous) the boundaries that parceled up the territory. These frontiers could come and go as an outcome of military maneuvers. Often, the Salvadoran armed forces attempted a pincer move, and a column of guerrillas and civilians had, at dead of night, to become invisible and pass through enemy lines. At other times, the boundaries to be infiltrated were political, geographical, or infrastructural: they included national borders and highways, such as the Panamericana that splits El Salvador west to east, the road north that bisected the conflictive zones of Guazapa and Chalatenango, or the "black road" dividing Morazán in two. Chronicler José Ignacio López Vigil's *Rebel Radio* describes the challenges involved in such border breaching: "The idea was to march all night to reach the Black Road. . . . That was the edge of the noose. If we could get across the road before dawn, we'd be home and dry. But to do that, we had to move the command post, the radio station, the clinic with the wounded, the explosives workshop — and all the residents of the area!"[52] Breaching these limits was a key experience of the civil war. For clandestine radio operator Carlos Henríquez Consalvi, the black road was "the limit separating life from death."[53] Fleeing across such a boundary involved silence, invisibility, and danger, but also the sense that this was a vital contribution to building a new world. Along the line of flight, voices hush and contact replaces discourse as the collective body of the guerrilla and civilian multitude decomposes and recomposes itself in a veritable exodus:

"One by one, our hands on the backpack of the person in front, holding our breath, we crept past the *cuilios* [government soldiers] and they didn't see us. Later on Rogelio [Ponceele, the priest,] told us that was how the Hebrews marched across the Red Sea to escape from the pharaoh."[54]

The sovereign state constructs a striated space governed by transcendence, by an authority presumed to adjudicate from on high as to who or what belongs where. This entails a series of exclusions as well as categorizations, the better to purge civil(ized) society of affect. A formidable institutional work of marginalization produces the illusion of a rational normativity. The state constitutes its ideal citizenry through a complex process of simultaneously containing and othering those elements that do not conform to its ideal. The mad, the bad, and the sick (for instance) are all excluded in often similar ways, condemned to a maze of bureaucratic (non)spaces: asylums, prisons, hospitals. Nonconformity is marked by terms signifying an affective excess and loss of self-control: lunacy, deviance, hysteria. As Michel Foucault argues, the "abnormal" is made an object of discourse, and as such excluded (objectified, othered), but also bounded or contained, and so recuperated for the sake of legal, medical, and philosophical conceptions of normality, which, further, hold out the possibility of transforming monstrous affect into labile emotion: "Confinement actually excludes and it operates outside the law, but it justifies itself in terms of the need to correct and improve individuals, to get them to see the error of their ways and restore their 'better feelings.'"[55] If the institutions of what Foucault terms disciplinary society effect a more or less precarious internal exclusion — the confined are not quite part of but not quite outside the body politic — they combine but also conflict with more radical exclusions that define the margins of society itself. Many of these forms of othering have archaic roots, such as the ancient Greek punishment of ostracism or the Hebrew ritual of scapegoating, which implied expulsion without recuperation. Within modernity, absolute exclusion tended to be replaced by its relative, recuperable forms. But some modes of radical othering persisted (capital punishment, for instance, albeit in apparently more humane, medicalized garb), while others were newly minted. The most significant modern politics of absolute othering is encountered at colonial boundaries. Strictly, perhaps, these are modernized versions of premodern exclusions, in that the ancient Greeks already left us the legacy of splitting civilization from "barbarism," so called because alien tongues were perceived only as incomprehensible mumblings: ba, ba, ba. But with the growth of European empires from 1492 onward, and the discovery of what Tzvetan Todorov terms "the Exterior other," came the invention of the primitive, to whom were ascribed affects banished from modern societies.[56] In cultural critic Marianna Torgovnick's words, "Europeans were increasingly ghettoizing and repressing at home feelings and practices comparable to what they believed they saw among primitives." Hence the repressed returned, displaced onto the subaltern: "There was still a persistent, residual need for expression. So [these feelings] were projected abroad in a complicated process by which an aspect of the self was displaced onto the Other."[57] Colonialism instituted something like a division of affective labor by which feeling was lodged with the subaltern.

The repressed is also enticing; what is forbidden or displaced is, after all, a desire, which can itself become the object of desire. Torgovnick details how, from within a twentieth-century modernity experienced as homogeneity, standardization, and boredom, Westerners looked to the primitive as the locus of an "ecstasy" that was both "a sign of *eros* or life force" and "a state of excess, frenzy, and potential violence." And although Torgovnick reads this quest as a search for a semireligious transcendence, surely (for instance in her case study of primatologist Dian Fossey) seeking "intimacy with mountains" or "friendship with animals and access to the language of beasts" is closer to an immanent materialism. Moreover, Torgovnick too quickly associates attempts to escape Western normativity with solipsistic mystical experiences, such as those found among New Age movements or even the commodified "generational style" of piercing culture.[58] Not that exoticism should be celebrated.[59] But it can be read as in part a protest, a yearning for escape from the self, or the selves we are permitted by the disciplinary state. Exoticism is a desire, however misplaced, for a form of community that goes against the rational organizations and orderings instituted by the modern state. Again, affect is best understood in terms of its (non)relation with the state: as a refusal that is, at least potentially, the declaration of a guerrilla war.

The persistence of the desire for immanence demonstrates that affect's capture by the state is contingent, partial, and unstable. Captured and (de)formed affect underwrites the state and its claims to sovereignty, but also suggests that other social formations are imaginable: affect is autonomous; immanence does not depend upon transcendence. Immanence preexists social organization, but it has continually to be reinvented through an experimentation that endlessly produces the new. This experimentation in novel modes of being resists the strategies of containment, the attempts to secure social order, purveyed by a state that claims transcendence and fixity premised upon the assumption and negotiation of contractual obligations or hegemonic consensus. Moreover, any such escape is collective. This is not the self-absorbed individual turning on, tuning in, and dropping out. To experiment in modes of being is immediately political, and in new ways: the war machine arrayed against and in defiance of the citizen consumer as much as the state. In fleeing, affect resists or eludes the state's apparatuses of capture, kick-starting the construction of what Deleuze and Guattari term a "body without organs," which leads toward the plane of immanence. What appears at first to be marginal and excessive becomes a force destabilizing individualized and categorical identity, as it carries the bodies it affects along an axis of deterritorialization. Deleuze argues that flight is not negative, for "revolution never proceeds by way of the negative"; it is active, productive, and creative, as "the movement of deterritorialization creates of necessity and by itself a new earth."[60]

Incorporation is experienced as plenitude rather than excess, and it gives rise to guerrilla joy. In *They Won't Take Me Alive,* Eugenia's husband, Javier, says of her death: "I think she died in this fullness. Fully happy. Death merely bestows the crown of heroism upon a life profoundly given over, *without any remainder*" (emphasis added).[61] Becoming-guerrilla is death to one mode of sociality, but rebirth in another. For FMLN combatant Edwin Ayala, "here in the Front you are born again, everything is new, you learn everything, you start on your first steps." So returning to social order could be quite as traumatic as becoming clandestine. Recounting his 1992 demobilization, Ayala reflects on what he will miss about guerrilla life: from singing to making tea on an open fire or constructing air-raid shelters, to the collective affect of "sensing everyone's happiness at the moment of a victory." He contemplates a future of "boredom what with all the hassle of navigating the world of 'civilization' again."[62] At the threshold between what is implicitly "barbarism" and his reinsertion into "civilization," he meets a fallen comrade's mother: "I left the multitude to go up to someone; at first I hesitated, but up I went, it was Leo's mother. Standing before her, I couldn't find anything to say. She was sitting down. So I crouched low and asked, 'Are you really Leo's mother?' "[63] For Ayala, reentering civilian life is a transition from the multitude back to the personal, from silence to a speech that names family ties and social position. From affect to an affectless boredom and emptiness.

Happiness and joy are constant features of guerrilla experience. Happiness arises when combat goes your way, as in Ayala's comment about "happiness at the moment of a victory." Moreover, and however much the FMLN assumed the mantle of principled combatants forced to violence for lack of any peaceful path to social change, there is the joy of seeing your enemy fall. Killing is associated with joyful passions. Combatants only ever express regret over the need to execute traitors from within the guerrilla ranks. A special joy comes when casualties are inflicted on the government's elite battalions—such as the Atlacatl, trained in the United States and responsible for grave human rights violations. And there is little that compares to the happiness that arises when the FMLN blow up Domingo Monterrosa, the colonel who had been responsible for the infamous El Mozote massacre, in which over 750 unarmed *campesinos* died (what "may well have been the largest massacre in modern Latin-American history").[64] After Monterrosa's death, even the noncombatant priest Ponceele expresses a happiness intensifying into a joy that he assumes is shared by all: "I was so happy. You too, surely?... How happy we all were when we heard that the plan that they'd prepared against that man had succeeded!... There were games and dancing. And we were so happy about what had happened!"[65] For López Vigil's *Rebel Radio,* which gives full details of how the operation to kill Monterrosa was executed and exults in its ingenuity, the episode gives rise to communal celebration and ecstasy: "Have you ever heard the Brazilian soccer team score a goal in Maracaná stadium? That's what the yelling was like!... The radio operators, the kids, everyone in the command post in one big cheer, hugging and kissing each other like at a wedding!"[66] Only Francisco Mena Sandoval, a guerrilla *comandante* who had previously been a Salvadoran army officer, and who observes that "Monterrosa, just like myself, was from a humble background," can also see in the colonel's life and death a wasted opportunity: "A good military man, as he undoubtedly was, could play a different role in an Armed Forces that was at the service of the nation and subordinate to civil authority elected by the people."[67] Only Mena Sandoval, whose hybrid of populism and civil society theory limits him to imagining alternative forms of representation, excludes happiness—and affect—from his discourse.

Ponceele consistently returns to a happiness that evades representational logic, that he "cannot describe in words." Beyond the happiness of victory, the guerrilla priest associates this indescribable joy particularly with the constant movement required of life in the liberated zones: both the *guindas* and also the entry into towns freed from government control. When he arrives at a newly liberated town, Ponceele reports again "a great happiness, difficult to describe in words." The mainly rural guerrilla army mingles with the townspeople and an atmosphere of festivity prevails. When the fighting is over "and our army comes in, it's really happy. . . . The *compañeros* wander around happily drinking their soft drinks and often organize a dance. . . . The girls like to dance with a guerrilla, even though the *compas* don't dance well. They play *rancheras* and *cumbias* and it's one big happiness."[68] A sense of carnival accompanies the breaching of barriers as the FMLN demonstrate the permeability of the tenuous border between city and countryside. *Rebel Radio* (a book that throughout emphasizes humor and comic misadventure) likewise stresses the carnivalesque atmosphere attending the guerrillas' entry into town. In an episode not translated in the English edition, we learn that they would put on a show of popular theater called "The Fifth Floor of Happiness": "And the Radio transmitted first the combat and then the happiness."[69] The Fifth Floor of Happiness then becomes the title of Dutchwoman Karin Lievens's *testimonio* of three years with the guerrillas.[70]

Topologically, the distinction between transcendence and immanence is the difference between the empty dimension of hierarchical sovereignty and the n-1 dimensions (a multiplicity stripped only of the transcendent) that define immanence. This distinction often plays out in the conflict between the Maoist guerrilla "fish in the sea" and imperialist air power, or between underground subversion and state monumentality.[71] For instance, tall buildings provoke a kind of fatal attraction for the homeless, mobile components of the nomad war machine. Building upward has marked homogenizing unification from Babel to Petronas. Babel still epitomizes the dream of unimpeded and transparent communication, but it was merely the first such project (and the first such tower) to fall. One hesitates to call Babel "modern," but like the Pyramids its height required the cooperation that ultimately only modernity would perfect. And Kuala Lumpur's city center, site of the Petronas towers, is an "intelligent precinct" set in the world's most ambitious communications project: Malaysia's "Multimedia Super Corridor" (MSC) is an area the size of Singapore that will be fully wired and the site of two new "smart cities," Putrajaya and Cyberjaya, "with multimedia industries, R&D centres, a Multimedia University and operational headquarters for multinationals wishing to direct their worldwide manufacturing and trading activities using multimedia technology." "The future is the MSC," declares its website.[72] Not if the war machine has anything to do with it!

Among the FMLN's most daring accomplishments, and perhaps the civil war's defining moment, was the capture of the San Salvador Sheraton, one of the city's tallest buildings, in November 1989. As López Vigil puts it: "We attacked the big hotel because it was the highest point in the neighbourhood." They were attracted to its height, and so to its commanding position within the fashionable neighborhood of Escalón in which they were launching a counterattack during their November 1989 offensive. But the Sheraton also held a few surprises. The FMLN "had no idea who was inside: none other than the secretary general of the Organisation of American States, Joao Baena Soares, who was in El Salvador to learn about the war and ended up seeing it up close."[73] Still more significantly, staying on the hotel's top floor were twelve U.S. Green Berets, who suddenly became in effect the FMLN's prisoners. The then U.S. president (George H. W. Bush) sent an elite Delta Force special operations team from Fort Bragg, ready to intervene directly in the Salvadoran civil war for the first time. But after twenty-eight hours the guerrillas left the hotel of their own volition. As far as the press were concerned, they simply vanished: "Reporters who approached the hotel just after dawn... said

A guerrilla and a somewhat surprised hotel guest inside the San Salvador Sheraton during the November 1989 FMLN offensive. Photograph by Jeremy Bigwood; courtesy of the photographer.

there was no sign of the rebels."[74] Another report emphasizes the guerrillas' elusiveness ("the rebels were nowhere to be seen") in contrast with the U.S. soldiers' territorial immobility and reliance upon direction from above: "The Green Berets, however, were still behind their barricades. 'We've had no orders so we're staying here,' one of them said to a large crowd of journalists."[75]

The offensive was now over. The FMLN had shown that they could mount and sustain an engagement at the very heart of middle-class Salvadoran society; elsewhere, the government had shown that it had no qualms about bombing its own population, or about murdering some of the country's leading intellectuals, six Jesuit priests at the Universidad Centroamericana. State terror more than matched any "outrageous act of terrorism" (in the words of a U.S. State Department spokesman) that may have been committed by the insurgents.[76] The resulting impasse led to the peace accords that ended the war. But in a twist, and perhaps an anticipation of future wars, future attacks on tall buildings, the incident at the Sheraton, prompted by a decision to escape working-class barrios bombarded from the air, had demonstrated that the almost imperceptible deterritorialization incarnated in exodus can also be the most disturbing form of attack. Slipping through the barrier dividing subaltern from elite, the FMLN destabilized the possibility of maintaining any such division, any such exclusion of culture and affect.

Deleuze and Guattari are not alone in revalorizing affect as a mode (perhaps unconscious, and all the more significant for that) of social critique. A politics of affect has also, for instance, characterized feminism. So literary scholars Sandra Gilbert and Susan Gubar examine representations of the "madwoman in the attic" and argue that "over and over again" women authors of the nineteenth century "project what seems to be the energy of their own despair into passionate, even melodramatic characters who act out the subversive impulses every woman inevitably feels when she contemplates the 'deep-rooted' evils of patriarchy."[77] Likewise, but from a Marxist perspective, critic Terry Eagleton aims to rescue affect from another form of confinement, its aestheticization. He claims that the aesthetic is the privileged means by which affect is purified, submitted to the apparent disinterestedness of liberal ideology, by being transformed into "habits, pieties, sentiments, and affections" and so becoming "the ultimate binding force of the bourgeois social order." But precisely for this reason, art offers a resource for revolution, if it can only be reconnected to a resistant corporality: "If the aesthetic is a dangerous, ambiguous affair, it is because . . . there is something in the body which can revolt against the power which inscribes it."[78] Moreover, affect's ambivalence is thematized by psychoanalysis, for which the affects aroused in mental illness (melancholia, anxiety, and so on) result from a repression whose origin is fundamentally social. And while psychoanalysis has tended to collude in the state's normalizing strategies, other trajectories are imaginable: postcolonial theorist Ranjana Khanna, for example, argues for a "critical melancholia," an "affect of coloniality" that makes "apparent the psychical strife of colonial and postcolonial modernity."[79]

Ambivalence works both ways. As Torgovnick points out, a search for ecstasy also characterizes fascism: "When the Nazis renewed a glorification of the primitive Folk and the primacy of Blood and Land, they unleashed a tidal wave of oceanic sentiment typified by the rallies at Nuremburg. They also produced the devastation of World War II and the horrors of the death camps."[80]

Hegemony theory found its stumbling block in fascism: Laclau was faced with the problem of how to distinguish between left and right populisms, hegemony and "counter"-hegemony, fascism and revolution. As I will show, Deleuze's affect theory also hesitates in the face of Nazism, although by contrast now for fascism's nonhegemonic tendencies, its promotion and inhabitation of a line of absolute deterritorialization. Today, the radical other goes by the name of terrorism. The conflict between transcendence and immanence, the state and the war machine, tall buildings and nomad, affect and (new forms of) normativity, is encapsulated as the "war on terror." The label "terrorism" is instant delegitimation, othering and denying to what it demarcates any rights or recognition. Terror defines contemporary politics, and yet it is negated as nonpolitical, as the affective excess of an irrational "fundamentalism." I suggest that Deleuze allows us better ways to think through the phenomenology and politics of terror, but also that an examination of terror reveals new ambivalences. Terror breaches the boundaries between civility and its other, and therefore helps foment a control society in which the state, too, becomes affective and immanent.

Terror

Terror is now the absolute boundary of civility, marking the ultimate decision: "You're either with us or against us," as George W. Bush declared after the September 11 attacks. This renovated "civilization or barbarism" dichotomy no longer allows for any civilizing project, only a stark choice. Upon the heads of terrorists the "global community" pours all the sobriquets previously reserved for the inmates of disciplinary society's institutions: fanatics, outlaws, and madmen constitute an "axis of evil." They are the ultimate exterior other, the global noncommunity. But the vituperation that terrorists draw perhaps indicates a fear that they have their own community, invisible, inhabiting the pores of our own. Moreover, it suggests that we may all be drawn into this radical immanence, whether we want to or not. Faced with a total war against terror, liberals attempt to renovate a politics of rationalization, under the banner of "understanding." The West today has all the more reason to try to understand its others beyond (and as often as not, also within) its borders; the United States should reflect on how its foreign policy has caused it to be so hated, so despised. A logic of representation returns, giving a face or voice to the invisible plotter. Understanding provides terror's agents with motives and rationale — without of course ever condoning the destruction itself. But the disjunction between understanding and condoning, the fact that understanding motives requires bracketing off terrorist actions, shows that terrorism provides even liberality with its limit, fixed now between understandable motivation and excessive action. Again, a nonrational residue remains, here in the surplus of means over ends. This residue is an affect (for what is terror but affect at fever pitch?) that liberals prefer to ignore.

Liberals and the new illiberal or neoliberal state may appear to be fundamentally at odds, but both agree that terror, the one affect that neither the state nor liberalism has succeeded in assimilating, should be eliminated from discourse and politics. Whereas the state personalizes this elimination, by slowing down the movement of peoples through security or immigration barriers, or by instigating manhunts for demonized individuals (Saddam, Osama, Mullah Omar), liberals attempt to dissociate persons from their actions, seeing those actions only as markers of desperation. Yet the illiberal state is surely correct not to bracket off affect altogether: its single-minded prosecution of the "war against terror" identifies terror itself as the embodiment of nonrecuperable affect, and the state of siege induced by so-called terrorism's invisible forces as what is finally at issue for social cohesion today.

The propensity of cultural studies is to suggest that terrorism is, ultimately, a discursive construction: there is no terrorism in itself, simply the construct of "terrorism," vilifying and preventing us from understanding counterhegemonic forces or marginalized groups (Irish republicanism, Palestinian resistance, Moslems). This argument shrinks from justifying terror, but turns the tables to suggest that terrorism in fact serves the state: terror is the ultimate excuse for discipline, invoked by the state to justify the illiberalism of increased surveillance, detention without trial, and even (in the United States) the possibility of torture. Sociologist Frank Furedi, for instance, argues that "the politics of fear has such a powerful resonance... because of the way in which personhood has been recast as the vulnerable subject," and that in response we should "set about humanizing our existence."[81] There is something to this position. Terrorism does function as a construct to produce docile civil subjects at the same time as it presents us with images of evil masterminds forever beyond the pale. The label "terrorism" has become a potent weapon in the state's discursive arsenal, taken up by numerous nation-states to reframe historic disputes with the new linguistic simplicity of the "war against terror." Yet in reducing once more all politics to hegemony (the attempt to build discursive coalitions, to assert equivalences and construct antagonisms), cultural studies refuses to think affect. It turns everything into a political game, played on the same playing field with a shared playbook.

The illiberal state is, by contrast, right to identify in terrorism a mode of organization that is radically different and upsetting to its forms of order. Terror is not simply one more piece in a war of position, or even some constitutive outside to hegemony *tout court*. Terrorism may be a signifier that has come to prominence (albeit not for the first time) in recent years, but it cannot be reduced to the nominalism of discursive strategies. Terror is also, and above all, a particularly intense configuration of affect. Moreover, the state is right to fear that terror threatens the very division between inside and outside upon which hegemony theory and civil society theory both, at least implicitly, rely. Terrorist movements may mirror modes of organization and representation characteristic of the state, while terror itself may appear (or be painted as) utterly beyond the pale, but ultimately terror works by concentrating, and so intensifying, affective characteristics that can be found in the very pores of all social organization. Terror works on the affective residue that remains from the work of constitution upon which sovereignty depends, returning us to the mobile affective flux that precedes the organization of social hierarchy.

The illiberal state is also right to insist that with terror comes the end of negotiation, the limit of rational discourse. One does not negotiate with terror. But this well-worn cliché, often used to justify state repression (albeit usually without the realization that state repression can reciprocally be taken to justify terror), is well founded only insofar as terror can never come to the negotiating table. Terror may prompt or condition dialogue, but strictly speaking when the negotiating starts, the terror ends. Terrorists who do negotiate undergo a change of state. This is why liberals distinguish "terrorism" or "terrorists," the individuals or movements who take up terror, from the terror itself: one can negotiate with individuals, but not with terror. Hence also the duality that structures so many terrorist groups: Sinn Fein-IRA; FMLN-FDR; ETA-Herri Batasuna;

PLO-Al Aqsa Brigades; the political wing and the military wing. Likewise, even the most repressive state tends to prefer proxies (death squads, secret services) who will invisibly fight its invisible enemies. Neither facet is, in any simple way, a mere supplement, just as neither fully expresses the truth of the other. Sinn Fein is not "simply" the IRA in Armani rather than with Armalites, as Ulster Unionists sometimes argue. Equally, the Armalite has a logic and an affect of its own, and this mute logic deserves its own investigation, because it will never be fully repressed, exorcized, or talked over.[82]

My implicit comparison between the FMLN and al-Qaida, and between the Salvador Sheraton and New York's World Trade Center, may seem surprising. Unlike Sendero, the FMLN were long the darlings of the international left, perhaps the last third-world guerrilla group (excluding the Mexican Zapatistas, whose métier and milieu have never been violence in the same way) to count on widespread networks of international solidarity. Yet there is no point rehashing the hackneyed opposition between "terrorist" and "freedom fighter"; the continuity between the two is more significant. Groups such as the Committee in Solidarity with the People of El Salvador in the United States, or the El Salvador Human Rights Committee in Great Britain, propagated a fundamentally distorted representation of the nature of the Salvadoran war: they portrayed it as always and only the justified struggle of the weak against the strong, in the name of human and civil rights. This representation, by confusing affective force with citizen rights, arguably debilitated the FMLN more than it aided them. The FMLN carved out new spaces of freedom and pioneered practices of innovative creativity. But they were also, and inextricably, agents of terror: a war machine, not a negotiating team. Given the intensive affect that they inhabited and produced, we cannot imagine them as proponents of pluralist liberalism. And equally, by insisting on the centrality of hegemonic struggle (and for all their celebration of subalternity), those who read Central American *testimonios* within the framework of cultural studies missed the plot. For instance, controversial anthropologist David Stoll was surely right to insist that Rigoberta Menchú's *I, Rigoberta Menchú* is a *guerrilla testimonio,* written in support and at the instigation of the Guatemalan Guerrilla Army of the Poor; John Beverley's comment that in fact her book was seen "as a defense of indigenous cultural autonomy and identity politics, rather than left-wing revolutionary vanguardism" merely shows the more or less willful blindness with which the text was read outside of Guatemala, and more generally the almost perverse obtuseness of much of the movement for solidarity with Central America.[83]

Terror comes to us from without, whether we like it or not, and makes us all equal. Terror overtakes us and overpowers us; we are subjected to, not subjects of, terror. We are all victims, rather than agents, and there can be the sense of a savage democracy in victimhood: stockbrokers and merchant bankers can suddenly feel as vulnerable as janitors, no longer masters of the universe. Terror effects a leveling that obliterates individuality. We are all equal because we are all (potential) victims of terrorist violence, and so all subject to terror. We are forced to realize that we are part of a collective, again whether we like it or not. Terror works through random indiscrimination: a whole social order, and all its elements, is under siege. We become synecdoches for that social order: women, children, the old, or the disabled are all (equally) instances of (say) the Israeli state or British imperialism. But therefore terror is never entirely random: it always interpellates. This is terror as a constitutive outside, exposing the presence of the community that it aims to destroy, as though by imprinting its image in negative on our retinas. It brings us together; we are all enjoined to "pull together" in the aftermath. Even those who survive are encouraged, by the state and by terror alike, to identify with the victims: for instance, in the endless *New York Times* obituaries to the World Trade Center dead, which the paper tells us "are really our stories, translated into a slightly different, next-door key."[84] It could have been me, it could have been you; in this, we are indifferent. Love your neighbor, love yourself.

We are also all equal because we have been torn from the order we otherwise incarnate. Disordered, unprotected, or doubting the effectiveness of the protection we are offered, we are now indifferent from the terrorist. Just as the terrorist resides, homeless, uncertainly beyond the limits of the social, so we too now experience, however briefly, something of that existence. This is terror as it (often literally) explodes the border between inside and outside. Hence the aptness of the suicide bomb: a terrifying equalization as the terrorist "takes us with him." But hence too the suspicion that terror sows among the population it threatens. We are encouraged to identify with our fellow citizens (it could have been me), and at the same time to suspect our fellow citizens (it could be you). The terrorist was once and could still appear to be like us. If we are all in a synecdochal relation to the state, then we may have to take the law into our own hands: the man over there with the backpack, is he one of them? Is he with us or against us? Suspect your neighbor (suspect yourself?). Terror is therefore immediately collective, immediately social, while it simultaneously if only momentarily shows us the limits of the social, as the walls come crashing down. Terror conjures up an existence beyond community, but also suggests other forms of community. The terrorist network that infiltrates a state-centered social order posits a stateless, immanent network of cells and nodes, however much a terrorist group may claim to be founding a new (parallel, or mirror) state. For why should the state be inevitable? The community established in and through terror may be invisible or imperceptible, but we are all drawn into it when subject to terror. Part of the romance that inevitably attaches itself to terrorism is found here. Becoming-terrorist means social death, with all the rituals of clandestinity that include a change of name, separation from family and friends, and the burden of secrecy that marks one out from what now appears to be a superficial everydayness. Yet it also means discovering a new, perhaps seemingly more profound, community of conspirators and fellow travelers, safehouses and coded communications. An intensive community replaces an extensive one: social individuality is sacrificed for the sake of a new form of vitality and life, even when that life is devoted to inflicting death.

As it deindividuates, terror debilitates rational thought and language. Psychologist Rony Berger notes that "during a terror attack and immediately thereafter, most people's cognitive functioning is temporarily altered." Survivors report "confusion, disorientation, attention difficulties, lack of concentration, forgetfulness, difficulty in decision-making and impaired judgment."[85] Terror is immediately corporeal rather than signifying or linguistic. It grips the body first; often it paralyzes the body. Terror functions not so much as a thought as (to borrow Massumi's phrase) "a shock to thought." Or perhaps it is a thought that is so excessive that it is itself shocking, unassimilable, and immediately corporeal. It stuns; we catch our breath to call back language. The mouth dries up. In terror, language gives way to mute fear. Alternatively, as part of an intensive feedback loop that stops the body dead and kick-starts it again over and over, as the body simultaneously conserves energy and rushes to produce more, terror induces kinetic hyperactivity: palpitations, shakes, sweats. Sugars flood the bloodstream and muscles tense. Our legs tremble; we go weak at the knees. Terror's intensity leaves the tongue flailing, gabbling. Language gives way to the scream, deformed, asignifying. Long afterward, the body remains hypervigilant and sensitive to the smallest disturbance or noise, easily startled or distracted. Terrorist violence may be compared to language (the anarchist "propaganda of the deed"), but it is always of a different order, an order that subverts and puts a stop to language. Terror in this sense is like pain, which "does not simply resist language but actively destroys it, bringing about an immediate reversion to a state anterior to language."[86] Biologically, terror short-circuits the cortex to affect the limbic system directly. We are reduced, however briefly, to what Giorgio Agamben in *Homo Sacer* terms "bare life," which critic Andrew Norris explains is "mute, undifferentiated, and stripped of both the generality and the specificity that language makes possible."[87]

Terror is also inherently antinarrative. Narrative either precedes terror (as justification or exorcism) or follows it (as resolution or explanation). Yes, narrative *surrounds* terror: acts of violent terror infiltrate discourse, as in the ubiquitous contemporary references to September 11; discourse agglutinates around terror and the terrorist, providing the "oxygen of publicity" that Margaret Thatcher declared the IRA to breathe. Terror demands an explanation, or some justificatory narrative. At times we may find we can talk of nothing else. Yet this is precisely because terror itself produces no narrative and overwhelms all other discourse. The narratives that surround terror function as so many tunes whistled in the dark; they attempt to fill a terrifying void. Terror is like all violence, which, as anthropologist Robert Thornton claims, "necessarily disturbs all structural, causal or narrative sequences and continuities." It prompts and even underwrites narrative but it is always left outside of the histories that it relates: "The act of violence ... requires that a new story be told to explain the loss, to account for the disruption, and to rebuild social relations after its occurrence." As Thornton explains, "this makes violence *appear* to be located at the 'beginning' of new social forms, new behaviours, and new accounts, and thus to *appear* as their 'cause,' but this is a false perception based on the peculiar temporality of violence itself, and its chaotic nature."[88] In terror, violence is fully apprehended as such. Terror shares, then, this "peculiar temporality" beyond and beneath narrative, beyond narrative time. And while stories may help close the wounds that terror opens up, such stories also justify violence, because without it there would be no story.

The FMLN's 1989 offensive, and its occupation of the San Salvador Sheraton, inspired one of Latin America's most interesting testimonial texts: a book that describes itself as a "combination of chronicle and literary collage," a "*testimonio*-document-popular consciousness." *El "Cipitío" en el Salvador Sheraton* begins with the effects of the first sounds of the offensive, the war brought home to the city, on bystanders downtown. The initial response to this bombardment of rocket launchers and artillery is shuddering shock and stasis:

> Saturday, November 11. 0900 (or a little earlier)
>
> Boom! – the first slam; Boom! – two . . . Boom! – three . . . , Boom! Boom! – four . . . five . . . Boom! – six . . . seven . . . eight . . .
>
> The heart trembles with each clout. You can hear the explosions are somewhere in the distance, but that was when the chaos took hold of San Salvador's center. Looks are exchanged and the scene freezes. People stop walking or doing anything. . . . "The marble statues / Are here and there / One, two, and three." Did you hear that, did you hear? asked one of the statues, and the scene unfroze.
>
> I kept on walking, as though I were crossing an icefield. . . .

Speech, seeking confirmation ("did you hear?"), interrupts and displaces the initial shock and terror, but an icefield remains. The book's narrator, a middle-class intellectual sympathetic to the FMLN, goes home to pack his bags and make ready for exile, in some bad faith: "Tomorrow, Sunday 12th, I'm leaving for Mexico. I'll get involved in organizing in favor of Salvadoran culture (ahem)."[89]

As the middle classes make to leave, terrorized in and from their daily routines, the spirits arrive. Though the narrator hopes that in Mexico he will find "a good standard of reporting from the press," the book abandons any simple linear narrative at this point. Rather, it imagines that the guerrilla forces are accompanied by a Salvadoran sprite, the *cipitío,* with his companion the *ciguanaba* (often represented elsewhere as a castrating mother) and associated mythical creatures. It goes on to tell their story interlaced with poetry, newspaper reports, personal testimony, drawings, and photographs of the military action. The narrator's voice is joined by many others: a cacophony of noise, conflicting perspectives, sounds, images, even music as the narrator listens to Holst's "Planets" suite, played by the Berlin Philharmonic. He listens to Karajan conducting "Mars" while, "trembling," he listens to "Mars, conductor of helicopters and tanks, with the force of a cosmic beast, with his hurricanes of fire, his five-hundred-pound bombs and more, falling hard-heartedly over the valley and hills of San Salvador." He struggles to see and understand what is going on, blinded by the "brutal" disinformation of the official networks playing military marches and "Yellow Submarine." He barricades himself in his house, trying to tune in to the guerrillas' Radio Venceremos, but the signal has been jammed. He can give an account of terror's effects but not of events themselves: "We are witnesses, then, mostly to sounds, although to some extent also to sights, because we have touched upon the fear found in the faces of the people." Finally the war has "arrived at the metropolis in this country of *campesinos.*... Until now we had only lived the war through television and rumors."[90] Television and rumor: these are two modes of communication that come to the fore in control society. But whereas the former is "one to many" (however many channels may be available at any particular time, each retains the "one to many" structure), the latter is inherently "many to many" in that it has no single enunciating subject and no single destination. Rumor always circulates, faceless and ever changing shape, in the background and in the pores of society.

El "Cipitío" approximates the mutability and continuous variation of rumor with its collage of elements, some verifiable, others clearly fictional, still others mythically enlarged or distorted. The book portrays the FMLN as similarly circulating and shape-shifting in the pores of society. Proscribed from the official channels of (dis)information, no wonder that the guerrillas inhabit the circuits of rumor, and that their exploits are talked up (or down) and mythicized accordingly. When the offensive moves toward middle-class Escalón, *"Comandante* 'Cipitío'" shepherds the members of the guerrilla band into and out of the Sheraton safely by turning them into a jaguar, a coyote, a deer, a hummingbird, a quetzal, and so on, all of whom travel on a cart that is "invisible to the patrols and the guards" while the Mayan moon Tezcatlipoca obligingly hides behind the San Salvador volcano. The guerrillas fade out of representability. The guards hear the cart's ghostly noise, "ú, ú, ú, ú, ú, ú, ú, ú . . . chiiiiiiír, chir . . . chilín-chilín," but are unable "to figure out where it was coming from." And as discourse is replaced by sound, language is also undermined. Not only do the fighting and the bombardments produce a series of onomatopoeic explosions: "Ra-ta-plan-plan-plan . . . plin . . . pffff . . . boom . . . pffff . . . boom. . . . Over here. . . . Over there . . . boom-boroom . . . ra-ta-pum-boom-boom. . . . On all sides." Further, the discourse of justification and hegemonic projects shows the strain of war, repression, terror, and subversion as it is disrupted and reformulated, deformed: "DemocraCIA: ra-ta-ta-TA. . . . Freedom: boom-boom-boom-boom-boom. . . ." Similarly, the cipitío and the ciguanaba are distinguished less by their language than by their distinctive laughs. The few times they speak, it is either in Salvadoran slang ("¡Ya, pué!" "pues, cipotones") or in an indigenous language, as when they discover the Green Berets' presence in the hotel: "*Comandante* 'Cipitío' let out a shrill hee, hee, hee, hee, HEE . . . and gave out orders and positions. From the lobby the 'Ciguanaba' shouted out in Náhuat 'I am your mother, the woman warrior.' "[91] Spoken in Náhuat by a mythological creature, and so destined to be unheard by its addressees, the ciguanaba's claim posits a subaltern foundationalism. The guerrillas are portrayed not simply as resisting an oppressive state regime, however much this was the basis of the solidarity they garnered internationally. Rather, they are seen as connected to traditions that precede the state, as inhabiting a milieu that lies outside of any state / civil society duopoly. Indeed, even as it infiltrates the metropolis and occupies the heart of middle-class Salvadoran society, the FMLN is never fully of that society. Whether in the "liberated zones" of rural Guazapa, Morazán, and Chalatenango, or in urban Escalón and the Sheraton, the FMLN constitutes an alternative mode of social organization more than any "counterstate." If anything, as the ciguanaba suggests, it is associated with forces that have given birth to the state, only to reject it.

Terror underwrites both reason and unreason alike. Anthropologist Michael Taussig describes how terror demarcates the colonial difference of subalternity. Reworked to construct a colonial "sense" of the distinction between "civilization" and "barbarism," terror "heightens both sense and sensation." So, "if terror thrives on the production of epistemic murk and metamorphosis, it nevertheless requires the hermeneutic violence that creates feeble fictions in the guise of realism, objectivity, and the like, flattening contradiction and systematizing chaos." Colonial reports such as Roger Casement's 1911 account of the Putumayo rubber boom in the Amazon, and testimonial narratives (say, Rigoberta Menchú's *I, Rigoberta Menchú*) are equally "feeble fictions," driven by the terror that provides their raisons d'être only to systematize the chaos that it threatens. At least *testimonio* attempts to present what Taussig notes is "so painfully absent from [Casement's] Putumayo accounts, namely, the narrative mode of the Indians themselves." But claims to give the subaltern voice are problematic: "Rescuing the 'voice' of the Indian" is "the ultimate anthropological conceit," and Taussig refuses the rationalism that grants Western culture the power of representation.[92]

Terror constructs sense and depends upon it, but ultimately it also undoes it as the state becomes indistinguishable from the affect that it apparently repels. In his analysis of colonial terror (and capitalist "primitive accumulation") in the Putumayo, Taussig argues that "terror nourished itself by destroying sense." Terror per se is scarcely imaginable (however much it is felt), and the fact that it is so quickly recontextualized by narrative justification must not make us "blind to the way that terror makes mockery of sense-making, how it requires sense in order to mock it." Taussig sees state terror, the (re)appropriation of terror by the state, as "a colonial mirroring of otherness that reflects back onto the colonists the barbarity of their own social relations, but as imputed to the savagery they yearn to colonize."[93] In the circuit of terror, the state captures the war machine, then goes on to project its own barbarism onto the so-called terrorist, who in turn frustrates such categorization by passing almost invisibly through territorial borders, followed by the state's ever more anxious surveillance. Terror sets up a spiral of immanentization in which origins and causes become increasingly blurred: the state ends up chasing its own tail, frustrated at its inevitable failure to delimit even its own boundaries; confident civilizing missions soon become caught up in messy quagmires, bogged down in jungles, or stranded in the desert. The fiction of a "mission accomplished," or even that such a mission could ever be accomplished, becomes the feeblest narrative of all. As any notion of hegemony breaks down, let alone the distinction between civil society and its outside, it becomes hard to distinguish state from war machine. The state, too, is affected, becoming immanent, becoming imperceptible. In the end, affect alone is an insufficient guide to posthegemonic politics.

Toward Habit

We have seen how, by defining affect as increase or decrease in the power of acting, and as a series of encounters between bodies that involves also a mutation in those bodies, Deleuze opens a gateway to immanence. He contrasts a fluid escape toward the plane of immanence with the static categorizations and insistence on identity characteristic of a state that establishes itself as a transcendent quasi-cause. The state is an apparatus of capture, transforming mobile affect into a set of fixed emotions. Yet there is always some slippage, something excessive even in emotion that threatens to revert to affect and indicates a line of flight along which a nomad war machine (re)constitutes itself. Domination and insurgency can be reread in terms of this perpetual tension between transcendence and immanence, capture and exodus, rather than as a series of competing hegemonic projects or as a dialogue between state and civil society. A community gathers on the line of flight, a community whose principle of organization has nothing in common with the state's territorializing claim to sovereignty: intensely occupying multiple dimensions on the plane of immanence rather than submitting to the empty dimension of hierarchical order, the war machine unsettles and destabilizes all pretension to hegemony. In terror, however, state logic reaches its limit and even begins to dissolve. Terror vividly demonstrates the porousness of the border between reason and affect, and the impossibility of banishing affect altogether. Terror undoes the distinction between inside and outside. But it also problematizes Deleuze's own contrast between state and nomad, immanence and transcendence, between a liberating affect and a stifling regime of emotion that turns around a state fetish.

The distinction between a transcendent state and immanent affect is patent and palpable, but it is ultimately unsustainable. First, transcendence itself is but an epiphenomenon, a (perverse) result of immanent processes. At best the state *claims* transcendence: it acts *as though* it were sovereign; it represents itself as cause by attempting to align with and account for the affects of which it is in fact mere effect. But even the control that it does exercise is not a result of these claims; rather, it is a product of the ways in which the state, too, operates immanently. Second, then, at times of crisis such as in the face of insurgency, the state becomes unabashedly immanent, drawing its own line of flight or absolute deterritorialization. The state always overreaches itself, but it sometimes abandons any claim to transcendence in a suicidal death drive, most clearly in the case of fascism. We see this now almost every day. For third, with the emergence of a society of control or "control society," replacing an earlier disciplinary society, transcendence withers away and yet the state continues business (almost) as usual. We are all these days a little bit affected, a little less secure in our previously fixed subjectivities. But we are nonetheless subjected. Perhaps it is simply that the state is a habit we just cannot break; perhaps the state was always no more (or less) than habitual. In either case, we will have to move toward a theory of habit, rather than rest on an analysis that concentrates solely on an affective war machine set against (emotional) states.

Michael Taussig emphasizes that affect is never simply exterior to the state. He argues that state power, or rather the "magic" by which it conjures up its potent illusion of power, depends upon both terror and death: "The magic of the state is saturated by death." It is less that the state deals out (or even fends off) terror, than that it recodes, redirects, and regulates an affective force that Taussig associates with the popular and above all with spiritism, with communing with the dead. Hence "the outlandish but real possibility that underpinning the legitimacy of the modern state is a vast movement of transposition between the official and the unofficial for which spirit possession is paradigmatic."[94] Language arises in this transposition, because it is also a figuration: the state *represents* society to itself as given, constituted, and hierarchically ordered. So the state mimics spiritism's power, and then appears to give life to those it newly declares to be dead because they lack its revivifying language. The state is dependent upon affective materiality, and "it is, by and large, the poor, especially the urban poor, who fulfill this desperate need for a body. It is these poor whose task it is to supply stately discourse with its concrete referents."[95] Therefore it is not so much that the subaltern is excluded from power. In fact, the state is parasitic upon the power of the so-called "excluded"; it is they who provide it with legitimacy and life, as much as (or even more than) it is the state that denies welfare and recognition to them. The state is a reflex, constituted by and in affect, only to expel any affective surplus to the demonized margins of its territorial and symbolic control. The state excludes culture and affect, categorizing and disciplining it, but as a reaction-formation that depends upon an affective culture that is, in fact, primary.

However much it is accumulated, memorialized, and stratified, intensity replaced by monumentality, the sacred affect appropriated by the state remains inherently unstable. Not only is society under threat at its margins (the terrorist beyond the pale), it is also endlessly subverted at its core. In Taussig's words, "Guarded as it is by unmoving troops in scarlet uniforms and ceremonial swords, it is nevertheless the very nature of the sacred to leak."[96] Civil society would eliminate affect and expel terror to the margins, but it never fully achieves its aim. Even Fredric Jameson, in a remark that has gained less attention than his claim about a waning of affect, argues that in postmodernism, "as throughout class history, the underside of culture is blood, torture, death, and horror."[97] The state leaks, but it also overreaches; its pretensions to sovereignty never fully coincide with its constitution in and through affect. As Foucault meticulously demonstrates in his analyses of micropolitics, power never descends from on high as the principle of sovereignty claims; rather it is always exercised immanently and immediately, on and through the body, in a "multiplicity of force relations immanent in the sphere in which they operate."[98] This noncoincidence between power's self-image and its actualization offers the possibility of escape, of exodus. But sometimes it is the state itself that escapes, with devastating consequences.

For Deleuze and Guattari in *Anti-Oedipus*, "one can never go far enough in the direction of deterritorialization: you haven't seen anything yet — an irreversible process."[99] Yet Deleuze later indicates growing caution or "sobriety." *Anti-Oedipus*'s relatively cavalier spirit, its broad declaration of a new "universal history," gives way to an emphasis on specificity: "There is no general prescription. We have done with all globalizing concepts." Deleuze and his interlocutor Parnet call for an analysis of the dangers, as well as the opportunities, offered by schizophrenizing, deterritorializing strategies. They ask: "How is it that all the examples of lines of flight that we have given, even from writers we like, turn out so badly?"[100] Outlining the various lines of social organization and their politics in *A Thousand Plateaus*, Deleuze and Guattari return to the dangers of deterritorialization on the lines of flight. "It would be oversimplifying," they say, "to believe that the only risk they fear and confront is allowing themselves to be recaptured in the end, letting themselves be sealed in, tied up, reknotted, reterritorialized. They themselves emanate a strange despair, like an odor of death and immolation, a state of war from which one returns broken." Perhaps fascism is to be situated along this line of flight: "Fascism," Deleuze and Guattari now argue, "involves a war machine.... A war machine that no longer had war as its object and would rather annihilate its own servants than stop the destruction. All the dangers of the other lines pale by comparison."[101] The distinction between immanence and transcendence — between affect and emotion, constituent and constituted power — may not be sufficient to differentiate revolution from fascism. Either that or fascism, too, can be revolutionary; and revolution, fascist.

Philosopher Nick Land, a "hard core" Deleuzian who offers a refreshing alternative to the tepid humanist Deleuzianism that has found a home in cultural studies, argues that Deleuze and Guattari's caution represents a catastrophic act of bad faith, a lapse into moralism. For Land, deterritorialization must continue at all costs. In a parody of Foucault's preface to *Anti-Oedipus*, he asks "how do you make yourself a Nazi?" and answers that "trying not to be a Nazi approximates one to Nazism far more radically than any irresponsible impatience in destratification." Land concludes that "nothing could be more politically disastrous than the launching of a moral case against Nazism: Nazism is morality itself."[102] Thus Land denies the possibility of moral resistance to fascism — while posing fascism as an overwhelming moral possibility. Whether or not he would be similarly skeptical of other forms of resistance remains unclear. Land here implies a political response, in that his frame is defined by the very antifascist problematic that constitutes the political for Deleuze and Guattari. Yet in *The Thirst for Annihilation* he refuses the concept of politics, preferring an almost mystical celebration of desiring-production as, simultaneously, creativity and orgiastic death. And in "Meltdown," Land describes politics as "police activity, dedicated to the paranoid ideal of self-sufficiency, and nucleated upon the Human Security System."[103]

For critic Arthur Redding, on the other hand, the analysis of fascism in *A Thousand Plateaus* is potentially more shocking than even Land (himself hardly apocalypse-shy) realizes, in that it points to "the revolutionary nature of National Socialism, a point...which even a philosophy so 'irresponsible' as Deleuze's trembles upon." Moreover, this is fascism not just as the utopian populism suggested by (say) Alice Kaplan in *Reproductions of Banality*, but as a sustained critique of the state form; it is the state's rebellion against its very form as state. Not that this should provoke a celebration of fascism. Rather it suggests the limits of celebration, limits which *Anti-Oedipus* had too easily disparaged. As Redding puts it, drawing on the anarchism of Georges Sorel and Walter Benjamin, we should reiterate that "we are not 'believers.'"[104] Just as cultural studies too often takes its self-imposed duty of solidarity to entail belief in any and all "counterhegemonic" forces, wherever they be found, it is tempting to fall into a similar trap with affect. Even Massumi associates affect purely with vitality: "Affect is vivacity of context," he claims. "Affect enlivens."[105] But we should no more "believe" in the vitality of affect than simply reverse the polarities of the opposition pitting supposedly benevolent states against rebels deemed terrorists. Affect is a "disposition to change"; but change may also be for the worse.[106]

Sympathizers portrayed the FMLN as a counterhegemonic force of national liberation and self-determination, a coalition of the poor searching for their voice in the face of an inflexible state bent on silencing all protest. Latin American cultural studies, predicated on a theory of hegemony that valorizes articulation in the double sense of national-popular coalition-building and discursive voicing, found in such movements a model for its own theorization of counterpower. It is therefore unsurprising that the advance of cultural studies in the United States should be associated with, on the one hand, gestures of solidarity with Central America and, on the other, a discussion of *testimonio* as the medium best suited to the articulation of emergent subjectivities. This chapter has presented a radically different conception of the Salvadoran guerrillas, as a movement of desubjectification, deterritorialization, and affective intensity that preferred silence to discourse, and that systematically evaded and undid any effort of (self-)representation. I have therefore also implied some of the ways in which the FMLN ran the risks of the lines of flight they traversed across the Salvadoran polity: terror as well as liberation lay on these lines; there are at least formal and phenomenological similarities between the FMLN, darlings of the left, and Sendero or al-Qaida, who are nobody's heroes (or nobodies' heroes, in that expressing admiration for Sendero or al-Qaida can convert you into a juridical nonperson). These groups can and should all be considered under the rubric of terror. There is nothing here to celebrate; we are not believers in the FMLN. But there is no need either for the pangs of disappointment that marked Latin American cultural studies after the downfall of national liberation movements. Posthegemony suggests a politics of experimentation rather than solidarity, a politics ever open to the possibility of betrayal, even self-betrayal.

Nor did the forces bent on the FMLN's destruction exactly follow the playbooks of hegemony or sovereignty. It is true that the regular Salvadoran army was almost a parody of state sedentariness: a nine-to-five army that "rarely fought at night" and that "play[ed] their radios so we'll know where they are. If they didn't, we might catch each other by surprise, and they'd have to fight."[107] Yet the war was also one of death squads and special forces, and parts of the army were quick to take up guerrilla methods. Sometimes therefore roles reversed, as Radio Venceremos's Carlos Henríquez Consalvi notes of an incident early on in the conflict: "While the army [was] using guerrilla tactics of movement and infiltration, we [were] acting like a regular army, defending positions."[108] Moreover, as the war continued, the United States helped form and train several elite counterinsurgent units, which were always distinguished from regular army troops, and especially feared by the guerrillas. Above all, part army unit, part death squad, and never fully under state control, there was the battalion that took its name from a mythical indigenous leader: the Atlacatl. Critic Gareth Williams provides a salutary and path-breaking reading of what he terms the "Atlacatl affect." He observes an "astounding symmetry of affective divisions" between guerrilla narratives seeking to harness the power incarnated in dead martyrs for revolution, and the state's "own violent sacrificial dance that was also anchored in the harnessing of the dead. However, in this case it was no longer a harnessing of the dead carried out for insurrectional purposes but rather for insurrection's violent dismemberment."[109] Sustained by a mystique of magical violence, "bloody consumption," and "abject slaughter," the Atlacatl committed some of the civil war's most notorious massacres, including both El Mozote and the murder of the Jesuits during the 1989 offensive—the latter just days before the FMLN invoked their own magical warlike powers in occupying the Sheraton. The Atlacatl and the FMLN are not the same (just as the FMLN and al-Qaida are not the same; we should avoid the game of equivalences), but each participates in the continuum that Williams describes as "the nomadic savagery of subaltern insurrectional commonality."[110] Both the FMLN and the Atlacatl are multitudinous; but, as I explain at more length in my conclusion, we should distinguish also between multitudes. And Williams's constant refrain of "perhaps" cautions us against any certainty as to which are which.

Terror reverberates through contemporary society now more than ever. Affect is the very matter of culture, rather than merely its "underside." As internal borders are dismantled, such that it is hard to distinguish between factory, madhouse, hospital, and everyday life, and as the external border between reason and terror comes under attack, society's increased porousness allows for the capillary circulation of low-intensity affect, ubiquitous and disturbing, and part of a new mechanism of universal control. This at least is what Massumi suggests with his discussion of "*low-level fear*. A kind of background radiation saturating existence." Everywhere we see warnings and dangers: trans fats and second-hand smoke, street crime and AIDS. For Massumi, "fear is the inherence in the body of the ungraspable multicausal matrix of the syndrome recognizable as late capitalist human existence (its *affect*)."[111] Low-intensity fear and high-intensity terror alike differ from fear as it is usually understood, and so also from emotions more generally. We normally admit that there is something that makes us afraid: I am scared of spiders, heights, crowds, or whatever. These fears can be named and categorized: arachnophobia, acrophobia, agoraphobia. They invoke a subject and an object ("I," "spiders"), and indeed help define and delimit the subject ("I am an arachnophobic; that is part of what I am"). They may not be rational, though they may have a rational basis (some spiders, heights, and crowds are dangerous) and they are certainly rationalizable. Treatment strategies and risk management help us deal with such fears, which then function as input variables for a mechanism of risk and calculability. Risk with its associated statistical logic comes to precede and regulate fear: it is risky to walk across the park at night (a number of people have been mugged), so I fear crossing the park, because I fear being mugged. I alter my behavior accordingly, perhaps by walking around the park or by ensuring I start my journeys before sundown. Alternatively, faced with the relevant statistics (in fact, the park is not so risky as I imagine it to be), I can regulate my fear and so reduce the need for behavior modification. With care, I will cross the park. Risk, fear, and regulation combine to produce and manage rational choice.

Rationalizable fear founds state reason and the social contract: fear of the consequences of the "war of all against all" leads, in seventeenth-century philosopher Thomas Hobbes's conception, to an assessment of the reduced risks in cooperation, and the surrender of natural rights to the care of the state as protector. Whereas terror threatens the state and the social order, self-interested fear holds that order together and constructs us as rational subjects bound by mutual contractual obligations. We should all be a little afraid, especially of the sanctions that could result were we to break our side of the contract. Fear is the motor of discipline, the key to subjectification. "Hey, you there!" calls the police officer in Marxist theorist Louis Althusser's account of interpellation, and in that moment, in the recognition that it is me to whom he refers, is born also a fear of what might happen were I to ignore the call.[112] Moreover, fear categorizes social subjects: whether I turn to face the officer or whether I run away, I am equally interpellated; but if I face him, I am the model (of the) citizen, and if I flee I suggest I am a criminal with something to hide. Affect becomes personalized, and it both personalizes and regularizes.

Low-intensity fear, on the other hand, differs from normative fear. Like terror, low-level fear has neither subject nor object; it is ubiquitous and collective. "We" in general are faced by innumerable unspecified threats. Now we are afraid of "whatever." In Massumi's words, "ever-present dangers blend together, barely distinguishable in their sheer numbers... they blur into the friendly side of life.... From the welfare state to the warfare state: a permanent state of emergency against a multifarious threat as much in us as outside."[113] Whereas normative fear is possessed by a subject (*my* fear of spiders), low-level fear possesses and envelops *us*. We are enfolded within affect and become one with it, as all boundaries—between inside and outside, subject and object, or subject and subject—become mutable. This affect is immanent, and we become immanent to affect. The Hobbesian social contract, premised on a distinction between the welfare of the state and the warfare of natural man, dissolves in favor of affective contact, proximity. A host of other low-level affects arise. A generalized fear fades into generalized pleasure or generalized boredom. Whatever! And in boredom, as in terror, we approach the condition of bare life: "We suddenly find ourselves abandoned in emptiness."[114] Fluidity is all. While the self does not disappear altogether, it is decentered: "The self is a process of crossing boundaries."[115] Affect does not necessarily imply homogenization or equalization: fear differs from terror, but as a matter of degree, or intensity; similarly, fear is distinct from pleasure, but the shift between the two involves modulation rather than categorical change. It might be better to say that fear and pleasure are not so much distinct as approximate; one affect can always lead to another.

Guerrilla happiness can quickly turn to fear. In Ponceele's words, "After the happiness comes the fear. Because when we take a town the army goes, but a few days later it almost always tries to take back what it has lost, and the combat begins again. . . . Who is not afraid of war?"[116] The life of a guerrilla is a continual series of modulations; the guerrilla is always *between* affective states and between geographical positions, a vector in the mobile coordinates of political control that constitute (here) El Salvador's war of shifting intensity. FMLN combatants live out an affective continuum that covers the gamut of highs and lows, varying intensities, joy, fear, listlessness, activity. But the 1992 peace accords did not put an end to this mode of inhabiting affect: instead, and rather than marking the return of a social contract, they made the war general. Indeed, some statistics suggest that the intentional homicide rate had *risen* rather than fallen by 1995, to the astounding figure of 136.5 per 100,000 inhabitants, far above "Costa Rica's rate [of] 3.9 per 100,000; the United States', 8.5; Mexico's, 19.4" or even "urban Colombia's, 110.4."[117] Political scientist Mo Hume, who gives a murder rate of "over 100 per 100,000 inhabitants," notes that "one of the most noticeable legacies of the civil war has been the extreme militarization of society. At a conservative estimate, there are some 400,000 – 450,000 arms in the hands of civilians." Hume also reports on the growth of private security firms, increased domestic violence, and the arrival of youth gangs or *maras* such as the Mara Salvatrucha and Mara 18. She quotes an eye-opening estimate that "membership of *maras* outnumbers that of the guerrilla forces during the war twofold." These gangs have "transnational links throughout Central America, Mexico, and the United States."[118] Awash with weapons and with people trained to use them who often also have old (or new) scores to settle, a particularly intense node in an international network of gang violence, and with private security services blurring any line between state and society, El Salvador resonates with anxiety and fear. The civil war ushered in a new, more generalized regime of affect.

The Salvadoran civil war was part of a broader, global transition. Let us return to the FMLN occupation of the Sheraton. As the guerrilla forces quietly slipped away from the scene, and as the fighting across the country began to subside, on the other side of the world the Cold War was ending. The FMLN offensive had taken place in the brief interlude between the fall of the Berlin wall on November 9, and the first collapse of an Eastern European Communist regime (in Czechoslovakia) on November 24. The November offensive ("in all probability, the biggest guerrilla offensive ever mounted against a Latin American government"[119]), and particularly the incident in the Sheraton with which it ended, was a hinge: both the last confrontation of the Cold War era, and the first post–Cold War conflict, a premonition of future actions against tall buildings. In the incident at the Sheraton, the FMLN crossed the boundary that separates subaltern from hegemonic project, but without staking any claims, making any demands, or articulating any particular project. There was no attempt to construct equivalences or antagonisms. One day they simply appeared; shortly thereafter they vanished again. They undercut pretensions to hegemony, providing a foretaste and example of posthegemony. Perhaps, then, San Salvador provided a better indication than Berlin or Prague of how the world would soon look. For all the euphoria of the border-breaching and deterritorialization in Eastern and Central Europe, Central America offered a clearer index of the low-intensity fear and control societies that would emerge from the wreckage of Cold War ideological tussles.

The state now seeks to manage otherness by means of a succession of ever-more scientific designations: in place of stigmatizing madwomen, it diagnoses postpartum depression or bipolar disorder; in place of mere criminality, it sees a gamut of antisocial tendencies. Management becomes more complex, and not simply a matter of repression or sequestration. Normalization strategies range from cocktails of drugs enabling so-called schizophrenics to function beyond the walls of the asylum, to electronic tagging instead of incarceration, or (in Britain) "Anti-Social Behaviour Orders" that restrict not crime but everything from loitering on specific streets to swearing in public. The precise measures imposed are tailored to the individual or locality, rather than applied to an entire category of citizens. In place of generalized abstraction, then, there is increased attention to the specific and the singular. Even, as on London's orbital motorway, the M25, speed limits can be varied automatically by sensors that compute current traffic conditions and optimum flow-rate. Such calculations depend on modes of surveillance and tracking that are more ubiquitous than could previously have been imagined: closed-circuit television is trained to recognize suspicious activity while mobile phones and bus passes leave electronic traces of our every movement, turning familiar, quotidian possessions into our very own electronic tags. At the same time as it pervades everyday habits and practices, the state also intervenes directly on the body. It seeks more than ever to get under our skin, often quite literally as with plans to implant GPS microchips into the flesh of sex offenders on probation. It becomes diffuse, contracting out its operations or encouraging self-regulation, self-medication among its citizenry. Its effects are felt on the field or plane from which everyday behavior emerges. In short, immanently orchestrating and managing bodies' capacity to affect and be affected, while gradually abandoning any universal norm in favor of a continuum of flexible impedances and incitements, the state itself becomes affective.

Deleuze describes the shift from societies structured by bureaucratic "sites of confinement" to societies in which all these "interiors" have suffered a "general breakdown" as a transition from "disciplinary societies" to "control societies." Control societies constitute a "new system of domination" that reconfigures the penal, educational, health, and business systems.[120] Internal limits once divided prison from school from hospital from factory from society at large; now there is only the external limit drawn by the war on terror, and that too is crumbling. At stake in that external limit is the fate of difference and so of identity itself. For within control societies, difference is variable, intensive rather than extensive and subject to constant "modulation" rather than contained within fixed "molds."[121] If the mad, the bad, and the sick walk among us (thanks to care in the community, tagging, outpatient services, and so on), this is because we are all now therapized, criminalized, and medicalized. We are all now expected to be taking Prozac or Ritalin, subject to random search at airports or on trains, and urged to exercise, diet, and keep track of our stress or cholesterol. This is biopower. The end of confinement and discipline hardly signals liberation. Indeed, it is harder than ever to imagine sites from which alternative social logics could be envisaged or established. When we are all equally under police suspicion, then criminality is no longer distinguished from, and so potentially critical of, the norm (as it had been for, say, Jean Genet or Eldridge Cleaver). When we are all half-mad, then there are no more asylums from within which to challenge convention (as, for example, in Ken Kesey's *One Flew over the Cuckoo's Nest*). Likewise, trade unions or student movements have no purchase when factories and schools are no longer spaces apart, when they become simply "transmutable or transformable coded configurations of a single business where the only people left are administrators."[122] The shift from discipline to control goes hand in glove with neoliberalism's elimination of politics by managerialism.

We reject the postulation of a civil society standing up to the state as well as hegemony theory's insistence on populist rearticulations. Yet to see resistance or insurgency as immanent affect escaping stately claims to transcendent sovereignty is but a partial improvement. Not only does affect constitute the state by being captured and transformed into a patriotic (and territorialized, bound) emotion; equally, the state becomes immanent, however destructively, suicidally, or unstably. The "global suicidal state" that theorist Paul Virilio notes emerged after the terrorist attacks on New York and Washington is also a "global covert state."[123] The state can become subaltern, passing beneath visibility, and remain the state. A consideration of affect and of the state's limits shows how the state is a set of immanent, corporeal processes as well as a transcendent institution. Terrorism is always doubled (Sinn Fein-IRA; FMLN-FDR), but so is the state, which is constituted twice, in a double inscription of institutions and affect. And though the institution claims to be affect's source or cause (Evita inspiring the masses' devotion), it is but quasi-cause, for which appearance is all. Affect remains autonomous.

The affective processes induced by or constitutive of the state usually appear to be in synch with the institutional structures by which the state becomes visible. They leak or escape away, but slowly. Only rarely, at moments of crisis, does the state embark on a full-scale (fascistic) line of flight (and revolution). When the "secret state" spawned by crisis outstrips and flees before the visible state of bureaucratic functionality, the state apparatus as a whole teeters on the verge of collapse. Normally, however, the affects engendered in and through the state are low-intensity, humdrum, routine, and unremarkable. They are the habits of everyday life, the glue of social order underlying and resonating with state institutions at a level well below discourse. Deleuze describes this regulated affect as "habit," as the "contraction" that is also "the foundation from which all other psychic phenomena derive."[124] It is "the affect of self by self, or folded force" that generates "subjectivation."[125] But the foremost theorist of this folded force is Pierre Bourdieu, whose work "could be thought of as the negative to Deleuze and Guattari's positive. Reproduction as the negative of becoming."[126] For Bourdieu, reproduction is also an immanent process, grounded in what he terms the "habitus." It is to habitus that I now turn, to the immanent structuring of affect, the everyday resonance with social authority that explains authority's persistence.

4

Chile 1992: Bourdieu and Habit

The social order is merely the order of bodies: the habituation to custom and law that law and custom produce by their very existence and persistence is largely sufficient, without any deliberate intervention, to impose a recognition of the law based on misrecognition of the arbitrariness which underlies it.

—Pierre Bourdieu, *Pascalian Meditations*

To get to know Pinochet, you only have to read his statements . . . his own words say it all.

—Nelson Caucoto, in Luis Alejandro Salinas, *The London Clinic*

The Persistence of Habit

"Tiredness and waiting," observes Deleuze, "even despair are the attitudes of the body." This is the more reserved, soberer side of Deleuze's thought; we are some distance here from nomadic lines of flight. The point is to underscore the Spinozan maxim that "we do not even know what a body can do." As we have seen, the body opens up a world of immanent resistance and exodus: an "imperceptible passage of attitudes and postures to 'gest,'" a Brechtian shock that is "necessarily social and political" as well as "bio-vital, metaphysical, and aesthetic."[1] Yet, "obstinate and stubborn," weary and worn down, often enough the body is simply a creature of habit. At its most reduced, most contracted, affect becomes habit. For instance, the tick inhabits "a world with only three affects, in the midst of all that goes on in the immense forest."[2] It seeks out light, to climb a branch; smell, to detect and drop down on an animal passing below; and warmth, to burrow into that animal's skin. These three affects are an index of the tick's power, what its body can do; and they enable the tick's becoming, its leap and clandestine submergence within a host animal's hide. But these same affects also structure a profound passivity, a "tiredness and waiting" that reaches its apogee in the famous Rostock tick that, as Giorgio Agamben reports, zoologist Jakob von Uexküll "kept alive for eighteen years without nourishment." The tick incarnates the persistence of habit, a captivation or "remaining-inactive" in which everything continues the same.[3]

The world today often seems to consist of little more than the sum of its routines; perhaps this is why it can feel as though history has indeed come to an end. Agamben suggests that we are closer to the tick than ever: "For a humanity that has become animal again, there is nothing left but the depoliticization of human societies." We are hardly even bored any more, for boredom is at least the "awakening of the living being to its own captivation," a realization of our own habituation.[4] On television, we are obsessed with people like us who, as with the Rostock tick, are denied almost all external stimulus (reality TV's *Big Brother*). On the Internet, millions surf listlessly, perhaps with half an eye on webcams of coffee warming or paint drying.[5] Ours is but a bare life, all the more so for the routines that fill it, captivating us as much as the tick is captivated by the meager affects that constitute its plane of immanence. Contemporary culture is pervaded with the sense that most of us are condemned to cubicles and McJobs, a world of blank indifference enlivened only by petty rivalries with coworkers or grievances toward employers. After its initial shock, even terror becomes routine: we adapt to the search procedures of airport security just as British shoppers in the 1970s adjusted to the inconveniences of IRA bomb threats. Few of us really believe either in the threat of terror or, still less, in the measures taken to deter it (which is in part why terror maintains its power to shock, because it is both expected and unexpected); but we go along with the rigmarole, altering our habits accordingly. Our bodies become accustomed to waiting in line, to passing through metal detectors, to iris scans and security pat-downs.

Few of us believe: habit persists even when ideology fades. German philosopher Peter Sloterdijk describes our contemporary condition as "a universal, diffuse cynicism," which is "that state of consciousness that follows after naive ideologies and their enlightenment." The paradigmatic cynic is "an average social character in the upper echelons of the elevated superstructure" who is aware that he or she is exploited at work and alienated by the culture industry, but who continues on nonetheless, in the spirit of "a detached negativity . . . that scarcely allows itself any hope, at most a little irony and pity."[6] Now a host of books, from Timothy Bewes's *Cynicism and Postmodernity* to Wilber Caldwell's *Cynicism and the Evolution of the American Dream*, reinforce the contention that, "over and over, cynicism pops up as a description of our society's problems."[7] Moreover, today this cynicism is more diffuse, no longer restricted to Sloterdijk's "upper echelons." In what is often regarded as a sign of widespread depoliticization, we are all cynical now, thanks to a "mass cultural retreat from politics itself."[8]

Cynicism threatens traditional conceptions of politics. No wonder so many commentators (and politicians, as Bewes documents) consider that their task is to rescue us from our cynical tendencies, to inspire us once again with belief: "Every diagnosis of cynicism renews a call to believe."[9] Critics such as Arthur Redding might assert that we are better off declaring that "we are not 'believers.' "[10] But cynicism also gives criticism pause for thought, in that it leaves little room for a politics of either denunciation or revelation. When we are already "enlightened" without our enlightenment altering our behavior, then a critique of mystifying representations loses its purchase. Ideology is no longer at issue. Social actors are neither persuaded nor mystified by ideology; rather, they are indifferent. As Sloterdijk observes, "the traditional critique of ideology stands at a loss before this cynicism."[11] At the least, the concept of ideology should be reformulated, in line with Deleuze and Guattari's injunction to "revamp" its theory, to take account of the processes that secure social order while bypassing discourse and representation.[12] So, commenting on Sloterdijk's observations, the Lacanian critic Slavoj Žižek notes the failure of Marx's formula for ideology: "They do not know it, but they are doing it." Now that, by contrast, "they know very well what they are doing, but still, they are doing it," Žižek argues that "ideology is not simply a 'false consciousness,' an illusory representation of reality, it is rather this reality itself which is already to be conceived as 'ideological.' " He urges an analysis of how "ideology structures the social reality itself," beneath or despite discourse (in Žižek's terms, beneath or despite the symbolic register).[13] If ideology is no longer a matter of (mis)representation, then it should be reconceived as immanent and affective.

Alternatively, we might dispense with the concept of ideology altogether, in the spirit of Deleuze and Guattari's "there is no ideology and never has been."[14] In this chapter, I turn to French social theorist Pierre Bourdieu's theory of habit as a better model with which to understand social order and control, and as both correlative and corrective to Deleuze's tendency to valorize an immanent affect as opposed to a transcendent state. For Bourdieu, the patterns of behavior that sustain state institutions and enable social reproduction are engrained directly in the body. Bourdieu argues that " 'ideology' (really, by now, we would be better off calling it something else) does not appear as such, to us and to itself."[15] Effects attributed to ideology inhere, rather, in the embodied common sense that constitutes what Bourdieu terms the "habitus." Habitus is generated by the repeated practices that seem commonsensical precisely because they are undertaken without ever coming fully to consciousness; and in turn, it is what generates the habits in which are incarnated an entire disposition toward the world. Habitus is "the social made body," that is, social principles invested directly in the body "below the level of calculation and even consciousness, beneath discourse and representation." In short, habitus is a system of habits, and also a structure that (re)produces habits that tend to be aligned with the social field within which the habitus is formed. Hence the habitus can go without saying, without acknowledgement, in that "when habitus encounters a social world of which it is the product, it is like a 'fish in water': it does not feel the weight of water, and it takes the world about itself for granted."[16]

Habit's persistence, however, also generates its own form of resistance. The first sign of this resistance is inertia: when the social field within which habitus operates differs from the field that formed it, friction results as the old habits no longer fit the new circumstances. Moreover, such dislocation is inevitable, for habitus is *always* a product of past experience, the repository of an embodied, historical memory. There is always some tension or slippage, however slight, between habitus and field. And geographical dislocation or rapid social change may mean that habitus is particularly poorly equipped to deal with its context. Habitual strategies, previously taken for granted, may find little purchase, produce unanticipated effects, or simply be blocked. But old habits die hard. And frustration builds when habits are blocked or repressed. Precisely because habit is the expression of an embodied common sense, changing the social field may come to seem easier or more logical than adjusting our existing habits or adopting new ones. The stage is set for a conservative resistance, conservative because its goal is to preserve or recover the conditions of possibility for the unimpeded performance of habitual activities. There is no reason, however, to imagine that such resistance is necessarily politically conservative. Immigrants, for instance, may bring with them habits forged by radical social moments or may find themselves indisposed to habituate themselves to social conditions that the local population has long tolerated. African slaves in the Americas sustained their resistance to the plantation system in part thanks to the cultural and religious habits that had endured through the middle passage. The shock of old habits meeting new circumstances demands novel and creative strategies, hybrid solutions that change social reality and in turn engender new habits. Habit suggests that things could be different (because they always once were different). Reading Bourdieu somewhat against the grain, downplaying his functionalist tone and scientistic inclinations, I stress a *conatus* or striving specific to habitus. The persistence of habit ensures historical memory, but it is also an ethical claim on the future. Habit is both a reminder of the past and the kernel of what is to come. Hence habit leads us to the multitude: a social subject that gains power as it contracts new habits, new modes of being in the world whose durability is secured precisely by the fact that they are embodied well beneath consciousness.

Latin America is often envisaged as a site of passion and affect, but it is equally often supposed to be a place where nothing ever happens, where the state is characterized by endless bureaucratic delays to which its citizens swiftly become habituated. For all his fame as a novelist of magical realism, and so purportedly of surprise, creativity, and delight, Gabriel García Márquez is as much a writer of habit, tedium, and repetition. *One Hundred Years of Solitude* is an epic without a plot, whose characters are stymied by their propensity to reproduce the attitudes and actions of their forebears. Matriarch Ursula Iguarán notes these insistent repetitions, which enable her to navigate the household even after she loses her sight, as "she discovered that every member of the family, without realizing it, repeated the same path every day, the same actions, and almost repeated the same words at the same hour."[17] Or consider the opening of "No One Writes to the Colonel," in which the colonel of the novella's title makes a cup of that ubiquitous stimulant, coffee, banishing tiredness with caffeine. But he and his wife have ailing bodies: he "experienced the feeling that fungus and poisonous lilies were taking root in his gut"; she "had suffered an asthma attack" the night before and "sip[s] her coffee in the pauses of her gravelly breathing. She was scarcely more than a bit of white on an arched, rigid spine." The pair's deteriorating physical condition is a direct result of their long wait for the colonel's overdue pension: "For nearly sixty years... the colonel had done nothing else but wait."[18]

In what follows in "No One Writes to the Colonel," there is not much action beyond the small routines that occupy the couple in their quiet, desperate poverty. The colonel makes coffee, winds the pendulum clock (a constant reminder of time's passage), sees to the rooster he is keeping for a forthcoming cockfight, picks out his suit, shaves, dresses.... "He did each thing as if it were a transcendent act." But these habits are far from transcendent. Rather, they are the semiautomatic, reiterated reflexes of a life spent waiting for transcendence, for a response from whichever ministry it is that is charged with allocating money to war veterans. Of all the colonel's routines, the most symptomatic is his weekly trip to greet the mail launch, follow the postman to the post office, and watch him sort the mail, hoping for a letter from the pensions office. Always in vain: "As on every Friday, he returned home without the longed-for letter."[19] Waiting, the colonel and his wife are subject to a "slow death." Almost to the end, they maintain their patience, however much it is tested as they squabble over strategies to keep their bodies at least seminourished. Should they sell or keep the clock, and above all the rooster whose fight could lead to a big payout? Finally, the couple are reduced to bare life, at a loss even as to what to eat. And yet, strangely, this near-abject condition, as they lose any hope for transcendence, ushers in an almost ecstatic ascesis. After all his hesitation and anxiety, after so long being ignored or taken advantage of by the state and local notables alike, somehow the colonel's waiting is over: "It had taken the colonel seventy-five years—the seventy-five years of his life, minute by minute—to reach this moment. He felt pure, explicit, invincible at the moment that he replied: 'Shit.'"[20] The ambivalence of the colonel's expletive is that it can be read both as the ultimate in resignation, a willingness even to eat shit; and also as a refusal, the first stirrings of resistance.

There is, then, a politics of habit, which persists even as ideology wanes. We might consider it a micropolitics of affect, of a regularized low-intensity affect, closely associated with ethics. The decline of ideology is not the end of politics; a new politics is born, or rather the hidden truth of the old is finally revealed. Nor is it in fact the end of history; indeed habit is marked by and struggles with history and temporality, whereas ideology and hegemony claim to transcend and subsume our experience of time. In a sense, habit is life itself: as the nineteenth-century philosopher and psychologist William James noted, "living creatures . . . are bundles of habits."[21] But habit is also a source of life in that it is more than mere repetition. For Bourdieu, "one of the reasons for the use of the term habitus," a word that is the Latin for habit, "is the wish to set aside the common conception of habit as a mechanical assembly or preformed programme."[22] Habitus is generative: "An endless capacity to engender products," it is a force for "invention," even though its "conditioned and conditional freedom . . . is as remote from a creation of unpredictable novelty as it is from a simple mechanical reproduction of the initial conditionings."[23] It is in the gap, the temporal or geographical lag, between initial conditionings and habitual practice, that a politics opens up, albeit unseen and unrecognized. The politics of habit has long been misrecognized, its workings misattributed to ideological factors and hegemonic projects. In this misattribution, the role of habit is ignored and politics is (again) rendered opaque. Or rather, the fact that politics itself works opaquely, beneath discourse and representation, is hidden by an insistence on clarity and transparency.

Theorists of habit also often focus on the everyday. For feminist cultural critic Rita Felski, "the everyday is synonymous with habit, sameness, routine. . . . The idea of habit crystallises this experience of dailiness." Habit is associated, then, with "everyday life." As Felski puts it, "Everyday life simply *is* the routine act of conducting one's day to day existence without making it an object of conscious attention."[24] Habit drives and is driven by the unseen and barely audible hum of micropolitics that pervades our daily routines; it is like background noise in that we are almost oblivious to its ongoing importance, the ways in which it structures our all too familiar, endlessly repeated quotidian activities. Habit comprises the immanent micropolitics that Michel Foucault theorizes as governmentality or biopower. Habit is an instance of a power that has "invest[ed] life through and through." But it is therefore enabling as well as regulating or repressive. Without our habits, we would be paralyzed in the face of the myriad decisions that we otherwise take for granted. The power that sustains our mundane routines is also a power directed to the production of life; it is a "power capable of optimizing forces, aptitudes, and life in general."[25]

The everyday, routine, and almost invisible politics of habit contrasts with the often spectacular display that characterizes politics as it is more usually understood. The politics of habit is not the clash of ideologies within a theater of representation. It is a politics that is immanent and corporeal, that works directly through the body. Yet habit is primary; it is not an effect or a consequence of political processes that take place elsewhere. Rather, other forms of politics depend upon the dispositions and attitudes that habit inculcates. If we were to think of habit as ideology (and I agree with Bourdieu that we would be better off calling it something else), it would be closer to Louis Althusser's "ideology in general" than to ideology as the "system of ideas and representations which dominate the mind of a man or a social group."[26] Ideology in general precedes and underwrites specific ideologies, in that it constitutes the subjects who then conform to or recognize a system of representations. For Althusser, ideology in general consists in the mechanism of interpellation whereby Ideological State Apparatuses such as the school or the family call subjects into being, subjects whose condition of existence is that they recognize the power of some other, transcendent Subject (capitalized by Althusser) that is reciprocally produced in the same operation. Hence, although interpellation is material, in that it takes place in institutions and through practice (in his illustration, the subject comes into being by turning to face a police officer who hails him or her, and who comes to incarnate the Subject), what it produces is ideal. Physical gestures and attitudes such as kneeling at mass or standing at school assembly construct a doubled subjectivity, in which many subjects turn to face the one, transcendent Subject that appears to be mediated though ideas and representations. But the display, the theatrical (or cinematic) separation of Subject from subjects, is a product of the process that it subsequently appears to have produced. It is an effect that is taken to be cause; a quasi cause that arises through habit.

The habits that structure ideology in general constitute the state and its institutions, and also establish a relation to those institutions that appears to be ideological. The subjects that emerge through interpellation act as though they were following their consciences, as though ideas governed actions. Hegemony theory discloses that these ideas are not free, that they are orchestrated elsewhere. But it still stresses belief and consent. This does not go far enough: it does not recognize that belief arises from habit. Althusser cites the dictum of seventeenth-century philosopher Blaise Pascal: "Kneel down, move your lips in prayer, and you will believe." A Catholic will go to mass, a school pupil sing in assembly, a citizen enter the voting booth, and it can appear as though these practices were an effect of free will or, alternatively, of willing if deluded consent to a hegemonic project. Althusser insists, by contrast, that interpellation is a practice, and therefore already corporeal: always already acted out or performed, a subject's ideas are "material actions inserted into material practices governed by material rituals which are themselves defined by the material ideological apparatus from which derive the ideas of that subject." The ideal is at best contingent: its content irrelevant, it is effect rather than cause. Belief in the power of ideology is itself ideological; ideology is at best a quasi cause in that everything happens (only) *as though* ideology were in fact determinant. Hence "the ideology of ideology" is the conviction that ideology matters, that our actions follow on from the ideas that we hold or even from the ideas that hold us and so from the ruses of some hegemonic project.[27] And when this ideology of ideology wanes, when it becomes apparent that subjects "know very well what they are doing" but are still doing it, we have entered posthegemonic times.

My case study here is Chile from the heyday of resistance to Augusto Pinochet's dictatorship in the 1980s, to the relative quiescence of the so-called transition to democracy in the 1990s. Between 1983 and 1986, new social movements organized a rolling campaign of protest against the Pinochet regime. These movements included women's groups, the families of the detained and disappeared, and neighborhood associations, all of which emerged in the vacuum left after parties and unions were proscribed. A loose popular alliance, this "multi-form opposition" led to much discussion of the power of civil society and manifested, it was said, a widespread "cry for change" constrained only by "the Junta's massive efforts to hold down the opposition."[28] The protests later fed into the broad coalition that agitated for a "no" vote in the 1988 referendum that finally put paid to the dictatorship. This coalition was figured as a *concertación,* or pact, binding civil society in a rejection of authoritarianism and in a desire for reconciliation. The divisions that had been characteristic of Chilean society, aggravated and underlined both by Salvador Allende's left-wing Unidad Popular (1970 to 1973) and by Pinochet's dictatorship (1973 to 1990), would be replaced by a broad culture of consensus. Yet, as anthropologist Julia Paley puts it, the "paradox in the Chilean transition" is that social movements "largely diminished with the onset of postdictatorship democracy in the 1990s. This quieting of social movement activity at what appeared to be a moment of openness for political activity is striking."[29] As the Concertación came to power, with democratically elected president Patricio Aylwin in 1990, Chileans abandoned the protests and mobilizations of previous years. If the Concertación was the culmination of the social movements, it also finished them off more effectively than Pinochet ever could. So the question that plagues any analysis of these movements, greeted with such excitement when they burst onto the scene, is why did they disappear so easily, absorbed within a transition that ultimately left untouched most of the key aspects of Pinochet's social policy. Why did they "stop short half-way along the road"? Why did "none of them [find] themselves in a position to put forward a coherent project for transformation in whose embrace all the antisystemic referents could conjugate and combine"?[30]

A classic celebratory account of the social movements is political scientist Cathy Schneider's *Shantytown Protest in Pinochet's Chile.* Schneider has much to say about the height of the protests. But faced with apparent depoliticization and what she calls (quoting Aristide Zolberg) a "restoration of boredom" after the dictatorship, she merely suggests that "the deeply rooted opposition political culture and the networks of resistance that allowed Chileans to mobilize against authoritarian rule may only be in hiatus." She therefore concludes with the presentiment, perhaps no more than the hope, that

"Chile will again be shaken by an apocalypse of popular rebellion."[31] By contrast, Dutch anthropologist Ton Salman's *The Diffident Movement* is, as its title indicates, a more disenchanted take on the social movement experience. Salman concludes that "it is improbable that the *pobladores* [shantytown residents] will emerge as a strong social movement any time in the near future."[32] Political scientist Kenneth Roberts is likewise pessimistic, opening his book *Deepening Democracy?* with "mixed emotions" and the wish that he could be "more optimistic regarding the prospects for social reform and the deepening of democracy in Latin America." Roberts puts the blame for this unsatisfactory state of affairs on a failure to establish "a participatory civil society."[33] But Paley shows that the rhetoric of civil society and the discourse of participation are part of the problem, rather than the solution. She points out how, "while framed as a way of bolstering democracy by strengthening civil society, this kind of participation subsidized and fortified neoliberal economic reforms."[34] A similar emphasis on the continuities between dictatorship and transition can be found in Franco-Chilean theorist Nelly Richard's *Cultural Residues,* which also provides the best introduction to the culture of the postdictatorship period in Chile.

Rather than seeing the anti-Pinochet protests as a struggle for consent in the face of dictatorial coercion, I argue that it is habit that best describes both the protests and the quiescence that followed. Habit persists as ideology wanes in what is almost a textbook example of a postideological society. Ideology figures within Chilean public discourse only as an ugly holdover from the past: the Concertación claims to supercede the ideological divisions that allegedly once plagued an overly politicized society. Even critics of the regime agree with the proposition that Chileans have historically taken ideology too seriously, and that Chile's weakness is that "ideas constitute the principle dynamic force in [Chilean] culture."[35] The premise of the Concertación, therefore, is that political ideas are no longer up for discussion. If the Pinochet coup was facilitated by the political system's collapse under the weight of ever more polarized divisions during Allende's Unidad Popular, governability is now ensured by forestalling or warding off ideological debate. In place of ideological antagonism, the Concertación offers the pragmatics of consensus and a practice of cooperation in the service of (mostly economic) goals that are taken to be objective. Neoliberal technocracy promises an everyday life characterized by uncontroversial routine. So the postdictatorial transition, insofar as it draws lessons from the past, looks as much to the Unidad Popular as to the dictatorship: if "never again" should the state routinely resort to coercion and violence, equally "never again," it is implied, should the public sphere be rent by disagreement as it was in the early 1970s. This is a consensus that no longer depends upon consent. The Concertación refuses both coercion and consent, as though in recognition that the struggle to win consent, to achieve hegemony, would always be incomplete, would always leave a remainder whose very existence would make alternatives, of either the left or the right, imaginable. The transition from authoritarian rule orchestrates public life as though neither the Unidad Popular nor the dictatorship had ever happened, making socialism and dictatorship equally unimaginable. The transition aims to erase its status as transition: to become a permanent interregnum, an unshakeable habit, dissolving history and ideology at one and the same time.

Imagination is best curtailed if the past can be forgotten. Chilean democracy refuses any foundational narratives, preferring an amnesia that resists language itself. The political sphere in postdictatorial society is founded upon what sociologist Tomás Moulián terms a "compulsion to forget" what immediately preceded that foundation.[36] In response, some have advocated a politics of memory: Moulián, for one, in *Conversación interrumpida con Allende,* which aims to recover a dialogue and a political project cut short by the coup; or the contributors to Nelly Richard's collection *Políticas y estéticas de la memoria,* whose focus is on the atrocities committed by the dictatorship. Memory is at the center also of the continued struggles by families of the disappeared and the series of court cases through which human rights groups pursued Pinochet following his 1998 arrest in London and right up until his death in 2006. Further, Patricio Guzmán's documentary *Chile, la memoria obstinada* (1997) and Andrés Wood's feature *Machuca* (2004) are films that, in different ways, attempt a visual dialogue with the past. In all these cases, the politics of memory invokes the marginal, or what has been marginalized first by the dictatorship and then by the transition: they elaborate upon what Richard terms the "cultural residues" of Chile's turbulent recent history. Yet this call to the margins both presupposes and reconstructs a vanished center. It recovers historical memory in order to reconstruct common narratives and shared (if contested, but contested because shared) projects of sense making. As such, the appeal to memory is an attempt to reestablish hegemony and at the same time a melancholic recognition of hegemony's impossibility. Even Richard, who recognizes the impossibility of recovering any lost totality except as a specter haunting the fragments that persist into the present, occasionally succumbs to nostalgia for the totalizing projects of yesteryear. Her discussion of a collection of sidewalk portrait photographs from the 1970s, for example, is strangely in thrall to an era in which women's bodies were "still subjected to the unity of a central axis of temporal and geographic organization of the gaze."[37] The attempt to put memory into words invokes unity, fixity, and a striated space that puts the subject in the crosshairs of the gaze. Yet given that such unity has been lost, fixity undone, and the center is lacking or hollow (the Plaza Italia where the portraits Richard discusses were taken is today the unvisited axis of a traffic roundabout), it is not just the mad or the sick or the criminal who constitute some subaltern outside. We are all marginal now. Marginality is no privileged position, around which a progressive politics could construct a new hegemony. Chilean writer Diamela Eltit's work illustrates this predicament: the vagrant in her semitestimonial book *El padre mío,* for instance, or the forlorn protagonist of her novel *Lumpérica* are not atypical figures, for all their eccentricities. It is not that they inhabit some subaltern outside, at society's margin; rather, they *are* the social, they condense and incarnate the whole of society, even or especially in their odd habits and distracted ramblings through which they act out or ventriloquize multitudes.

The generalization, and so banalization or habituation, of marginality in Chile has its correlate in voter apathy: "The number of voters who indicate 'no preference' or who nullify their vote has . . . continued to increase, surpassing all historical precedents and climbing well beyond the average for Western democracies."[38] The 2000 presidential election showed a slight reversal of this trend, in part because of the furor surrounding Pinochet's extradition hearings in London, but over the long term, voter participation continues to decline.[39] Even the prospect of the country's first woman president, in the 2006 election won by Michelle Bachelet, failed to stem the tide.[40] Nor do other modes of political mobilization compensate: Chilean protest styles have been exported elsewhere (the *cacerolazo,* or pot-banging, so much a feature of the Argentine and Venezuelan crises of 2001 and 2002, can be traced back to anti-Allende mobilizations of the early 1970s), but in tandem with divestment from protest within the country itself. From cauldron of ideological dissent to cool, clean model of neoliberal quiescence over two decades: in culture as in economics, Chile converted to posthegemonic neoliberalism quicker and sooner than most. Where protest has flared up again, it has been around very everyday issues: urban transport, for instance, or the rising costs of education.

It is often claimed that we are witnessing ideology's decline, although differing explanations are offered for the fact. For instance it is argued that, with the end of the Cold War, liberal–democratic capitalism is common sense and socialism a bankrupt dogma. But the end of ideology is also taken to mean that people are now less interested in politics; falling electoral turnouts show that political narratives no longer have mobilizing force. For still others, the end of ideology follows from a general distrust of master narratives associated with postmodernity. Finally, debates around concepts such as "control societies" and governmentality suggest that neoliberalism ushers in a new form of rule for which ideology no longer plays a significant role — less the evacuation of politics than its more sinister insinuation into every pore of society as biopolitics. All these arguments have their merits, but they describe not so much the decline of ideology as the end of the ideology of ideology. For ideology has not vanished; after all, even many of the obituaries to ideology can be read as ideological statements. The state continues to inhabit a double inscription, in structures of representation as well as in bodies. But ideology itself has lost its hold, and yet everything continues regardless. Contemporary capitalism does not need to weave ideology into an outwardly coherent system that would gain consent and secure the reproduction of its specific social order. Hegemony theory, premised on the social efficacy of ideology, loses its power to persuade us that hegemony is the sine qua non of social organization. But was it ever? If hegemony is unpersuasive now, and yet its disappearance does not make for radical social change, then it can hardly have been the key factor in social domination earlier! Ideology's apparent decline is no more than the symptom of a preexisting condition; it reveals the persistence of habit.

Habit secures social order. Even in its best-case scenario, hegemony never sufficiently explains how order is secured and maintained. Bourdieu's theorization of habit as an immanent structuring structure indicates that power's most successful strategies are precisely those that never emerge into discourse, that go without saying in everyday life's routine rhythms. The state and its institutions function all the more effectively because they operate behind the backs of their own functionaries, whatever their best intentions. So in what follows I develop Bourdieu's conceptualization of habitus as reproduction. He describes how the habitus generates a practical reason that lies not "in the realm of *representations*" but at "the level of the most profound corporeal dispositions."[41] These "cognitive structures inscribed in bodies" constitute what Deleuze would term a "virtual" logic that generates actual practices in harmony with the institutions and experiences that shaped those structures in the first place. Habitus operates immediately (unmediatedly), but also historically and spatially: it forms our sense of time and place, our bearing in the world. Through habitus, power is invested in the production of life itself, in the everyday affects of ordinary encounters. At times Bourdieu struggles to explain resistance or to imagine possibilities for radical social change. But he does observe that habit can give rise to novelty and creativity. Its embodied memory motivates ethical resistance as well as political conformity. Moreover, in that habitus is a *collective* disposition, it suggests mechanisms for the formation of collective subjectivities whose cohesive principle is resonance rather than identity, expansive inclusion rather than demarcated difference. As Michael Hardt and Antonio Negri note, "habits constitute our shared nature" and so "look not only backward but also forward."[42]

Habit as Immanence

Bourdieu's concept of habitus is central to his intervention into the debate about structure and agency, "one of the key faultlines that runs through social theory."[43] Some theories stress the ways in which social structures determine individual or social agency. Marxism and psychoanalysis, for instance, tend to view agency as constrained by structures that are, respectively, material and psychic. Others emphasize that agents can resist or overcome these structural determinants. Cultural studies, for example, often points to the slippages by which (say) consumers eke out a measure of agency even within contemporary capitalism. As British sociologist Anthony Giddens (whose theory of structuration is an alternative bid to resolve the debate) puts it, those for whom "structure (in the divergent senses attributed to that concept) has primacy over action and the constraining qualities of structure are strongly accentuated" are arrayed against those for whom "action and meaning are accorded primacy in the explication of human conduct; structural concepts are not notably prominent, and there is not much talk of constraint." Giddens goes on to characterize this difference as an "imperialism of the social object" set against "an imperialism of the object."[44] In short, these are two competing claims to transcendence; what is at stake, Giddens argues, is as much ontological as it is epistemological, as much about divergent models of what society actually is as about conflicting perspectives on the same model.

Bourdieu's intervention is therefore also ontological, substituting immanence for the dueling imperial transcendences of structure and agency. He refuses both "mechanism" (an emphasis on structure) and "finalism" (a stress on agency), arguing that the debate between the two is "a false dilemma." We should certainly "abandon all theories which explicitly or implicitly treat practice as a mechanical reaction" shaped by rules or structures alone, but "rejection of mechanistic theories in no way implies that... we should reduce the objective intentions and constituted significations of actions and works to the conscious and deliberate intentions of their authors."[45] Mechanism and finalism, structure and agency, are equally reductionist, seeking causes always elsewhere, in some other dimension, either the "transcendent, permanent existence" of objective social constraints or the "transcendence of the ego" supposedly equipped to make its own rules.[46] So Bourdieu turns to habit, or habitus, an embodied set of dispositions immanent to practice itself, to give "back to history and to society what was given to a transcendence or a transcendent subject."[47] Habitus is a system "of durable, transposable dispositions, structured structures predisposed to function as structuring structures, that is, as principles which generate and organize practices and representations."[48] These dispositions are "objectively 'regulated' and 'regular' without in any way being the product of obedience to rules, objectively adapted to their goals without presupposing a conscious aiming at ends." Habit, everyday activity, is therefore the product of a "*scheme* (or principle) immanent in practice, which... exists in a practical state in agents' practice and not in their consciousness, or rather, their discourse."[49] Regulation and practice are immanent to each other, rather than mediated either by consciousness or by external structures. Habitus is an attitude of the body. It is an unspoken and unspeakable feel for the social game that generates the positions and actions that agents adopt in given situations, in regular if not fully predictable ways. Because it is immanent, habitus is embedded, and so structured; and it is also generative, an immediate rather than external motor of action.

There are many overlaps between Bourdieu's habitus and Deleuze's conception of the virtual. Both are immanent and productive, intensive and affective, corporeal and immediate. The relation between habitus and practice is not unlike that between virtual and actual: habitus leads to practice through an unfolding or differentiation that takes place in the event of an encounter with other bodies. Habitus and the virtual alike describe an ontology that underlies but is of a different order from the realm of representation, discourse, and ideology. Habitus, Bourdieu states, is like the work of art in that it "always contains something *ineffable*, not by excess . . . but by default, something which communicates, so to speak, from body to body, i.e., on the hither side of words and concepts," while the virtual, Brian Massumi explains, is "the *unsaid* of the statement, the unthought of thought."[50] Hence both theorists' distaste for ideology: for Deleuze and Guattari, "there is no ideology and never has been"; for Bourdieu, "I have little by little come to shun the use of the word 'ideology.' "[51] Despite these similarities, however, the tenor of Bourdieu's work differs markedly from Deleuze's. Where Deleuze emphasizes escape and a flight toward the immanent virtuality of affect as an empowering realization of what the body can do, for Bourdieu the immanence of habitus is characterized above all by inertia. Bourdieu shows how habit leads to social reproduction and works against radical social change, so much so that (as Bourdieu and his collaborator Loïc Wacquant note) some even accuse him of "a politically sterile hyperfunctionalism."[52] Though this "functionalist tenor" does not exhaust Bourdieu's account of habit, the contrast with the voluntarist tendency of Deleuze's theorization of affect is dramatic.[53] Yet the difference is not, as Massumi claims, that habitus is an "ideological notion" whereas Deleuze's account "emphasizes that [habit] belongs as much to the organic stratum, to the productive, physiological capacities of the flesh."[54] Bourdieu's habitus is fully as corporeal as Deleuze's affect. One way of seeing the contrast between Bourdieu and Deleuze, then, is that it replicates the debate between structure and agency, but now as a contest between two versions of immanence rather than two forms of transcendence.

The key to the difference between Bourdieu and Deleuze, and so to the specificity of the concept of habitus, consists in Bourdieu's related concepts of "field" and "symbolic capital." For Bourdieu, habitus is always embedded in a prior social field, which itself is structured by symbolic power. In some ways Bourdieu takes more seriously than Deleuze himself, then, the notion encapsulated in Deleuze and Guattari's own affirmation that "politics precedes being."[55] For if habitus is a set of "structured structures predisposed to function as structuring structures," it is not only generative but also generated.[56] It is the product of a given state of power relations: the social field as a whole and its distinct subfields, such as the artistic field, the journalistic field, the academic field, and so on. Hence, in Wacquant's words, "a field consists of a set of objective, historical relations between positions anchored in certain forms of power (or capital), while habitus consists of a set of historical relations 'deposited' within individual bodies."[57] The *dis*positions of habitus are also *de*positions, both in that they constitute a record of the state of the field that formed them, and in that they are the sediments that build up within a particular landscape of power. They are "conditionings associated with a particular class of conditions of existence."[58] And the social field that they generate or structure in turn tends therefore to reproduce the structures that constituted it, in that it generates practices that call those structures into being by silently taking them for granted.

Every particular field is shaped by a competition for domination and capital, its structure "determined by the structure of the distribution of the distinct forms of capital that are active in it."[59] For there are different forms of capital, whose relative weight depends upon the field in question. The shape of the field of culture, for instance, is determined by its differential distribution of cultural capital, while it is financial capital that counts in the market for economic goods. Yet Bourdieu downplays financial capital in favor of the various forms of symbolic capital that are the object of struggle, the ways in which the value accorded each form of capital is at stake in these struggles, as well as the mechanisms by which one form is converted into another. Power is most effective when it is symbolic, which does not mean that it is representational or "merely" symbolic, but that it is a mode of domination whose legitimacy derives from the fact that its arbitrariness is misrecognized, so much so that it goes without saying. Bourdieu and coauthor Jean-Claude Passeron's axiom of social reproduction is that "every power which manages to impose meanings and to impose them as legitimate by concealing the power relations which are the basis of its force, adds its own specifically symbolic force to those power relations."[60] What habitus reproduces is our corporeal assent to power's legitimacy and to the unequal distribution of capital that it secures.

Habitus is reflex and relay, product and producer, assuring social continuity by literally incarnating the principles of social order. In Bourdieu's words, "it ensures the active presence of past experiences, which, deposited in each organism in the form of schemes of perception, thought and action, tend to guarantee the 'correctness' of practices and their constancy over time."[61] It ensures that social agents are attuned to their circumstances. It fosters the self-confidence of the "inheritor" who, rich in cultural capital, exhibits a confidence and flair that is rewarded with further social and cultural capital; and it further ensures that those dispossessed of cultural capital assent to their dispossession by rejecting what is culturally consecrated (be it higher education or high art) with the sentiment that it is not for them. The dispossessed are often the first to suggest that they have only themselves to blame for their predicament. Privilege is naturalized as though it were simply a "gift"; and subordination is taken for granted as though social difference were a question of talent or taste. And all this is legitimated and arbitrated by institutions and officials who need not be aware of what they are doing, who can be committed to or even (increasingly) entirely cynical about the ideals they are upholding. For ideals are not at stake. Academic diplomas, for instance, attest to "gifts" and "merits," and can do so objectively with no hint of bias, because the real work has already been done in the conversion and so dissimulation of privilege as attitude. The source of these dispositions is concealed all the more effectively in that the habits they generate are second nature. Hence "the supreme privilege" of the privileged is "not seeing themselves as privileged," which in turn "manages the more easily to convince the disinherited that they owe their scholastic and social destiny to their lack of gifts and merits, because in matters of culture absolute dispossession excludes awareness of being dispossessed."[62]

There is no conspiracy because there is no hidden knowledge: the game's winners, losers, and arbitrators can all wholeheartedly act in perfectly good faith. The judgments that lead to social promotion or exclusion, driven by feelings such as "he's a good chap" or "she's not one of us," can be justified by transcendent principles whose legitimacy is assured by the fact of their mute resonance with immanent habits.

Authoritarian regimes rely neither on persuasion nor on censorship but on the silent harmonization that they establish in everyday routines. Such regimes are often described as "states of exception," a term associated with Carl Schmitt, whose *Political Theology* defines the sovereign as "he who decides on the exception."[63] For an analysis of the history of states of exception in Latin America, see political scientist Brian Loveman's *The Constitution of Tyranny,* which outlines the constitutional precedents on which Pinochet drew to justify his coup when the military junta declared that "the armed forces have taken on themselves the moral duty, which the country imposes on them, of deposing the government."[64] The Chilean constitutions of 1925, 1980, and 1985 codified the instances in which states of exception could be enforced, and Pinochet meticulously obeyed the letter of this authority in his promulgation of states of emergency and states of siege. His regime instituted its own Law of the States of Exception in 1985, further codifying and regularizing exceptionality. This combination of old and new legislation "created a complex hierarchy of states of exception, which could be declared by the government in cases of internal disturbance, subversion, or public calamity."[65] But amid this increasingly complex typology and perhaps surprising adherence to the rule of law, what is important is how such exceptionality soon becomes normal: "The states of exception were renewed constantly, with the state of emergency in force from 1973 until 1988 when the plebiscite was held."[66] Exceptionality became the norm, as indeed it was in much of Latin America during this period: the state of emergency in Paraguay under Alfredo Stroessner, for instance, lasted from 1954 to 1988. Exception became routine while protest became exceptional.

Despite the understandable attention paid to resistance against the Pinochet dictatorship, what should be noted, because it otherwise goes without saying, is how limited it was. Little has been written about "everyday" authoritarianism in Chile, the long periods of relative calm (however uneasy) that predominated in most of the country, most of the time. (Perhaps we could find such accounts in the novel or the chronicle rather than in social scientific studies.) For instance, journalist Samuel Chavkin's *Storm over Chile* takes its subtitle "The Junta under Siege" from a chapter describing the protests of 1983 and 1984, but has almost nothing to say about either the period from 1974 to 1983, from the coup's consolidation to the outbreak of protest, or the stretch from 1984 to 1988, from the height of the protests to the plebiscite that eventually brought down Pinochet. Indeed, the entirety of Chavkin's account of the period from 1984 to 1988 is contained in the following sentence: "For yet another four years Pinochet continued to hang on to power by torture and murder of his opponents."[67] Hence Chavkin hardly explains either the quiescence that was the rule or indeed why that quiescence should be broken, however briefly, by mobilization and resistance. By contrast, Schneider's fuller account of the protests is more thoughtful about the reason for their abeyance in the mid-1980s. She quotes one activist, Leo, recalling that "people left their homes, were beaten, saw no clear purpose to endure the abuse, grew bored with the protests, and returned to their homes." Beyond state-sponsored opposition, Leo points to a fatigue and a boredom that took over even in the most radicalized of barrios, a tiredness echoed elsewhere in Schneider's text: "Activists grew weary," she notes, commenting on a 1986 survey that showed the remarkable percentage of Chileans who felt tense, "resigned and disappointed," or "sad"; she remarks on the "state of numbness" that psychologists diagnosed even among activists; and she endorses Zolberg's argument that "movements of political enthusiasm are followed . . . always by the restoration of boredom."[68] In this panorama of a movement that has worn itself out, a low-level anxiety comes to the fore as ideological concerns recede. Schneider quotes another commentator's observation that the new generation of Chilean workers is "a collection of anxious individualists" who are no longer, now in Schneider's words, "ideologically predisposed." A general state of "physical and mental exhaustion" prevails.[69] Tiredness and waiting. Schneider depicts a population that, by the end of the dictatorship, is afflicted body and mind by the affects that Spinoza categorizes as sad passions: the "sadness [that] diminishes or restrains a man's powers of acting."[70] In Bourdieu's terms, this is the "resignation to necessity" that, he argues, characterizes the habitus of the dominated classes.[71]

It is in this context of exhaustion, and against the celebration of popular resistance found for example in Kenneth Aman and Cristián Parker's *Popular Culture in Chile,* that Salman emphasizes that the explosion of energy and enthusiasm in the revolt of Chile's new social movements was "an exceptional episode." Salman points to "lengthy periods of 'normalcy'" during which "what is involved are dispositions that do not solely play a role at the level of consciousness." He employs Bourdieu's concept of habitus to explain the delay in the emergence of *poblador* militancy in terms of the prevalence of a "class unconsciousness" incarnating a "sensitivity to authority" and "a wider and deeper tendency to reject deviancy."[72] The *pobladores'* dispositions were "fragmentary and pragmatic and not politically articulated." Protest only erupted once "the specific habitual and internalized ways of interpreting and perceiving Chilean reality and one's own position and options within it became inadequate." Even then, the ensuing mobilization was essentially conservative. For instance, women became active in the name of family and community survival, fostering "a practical, non-ideological politicization of the disrupted linkages in the traditional family, and in the traditional *poblador* strategies."[73] Salman emphasizes habitus as inertia, as the embodied sedimentation of a collective history that "resists change and guarantees the continuity of subjects." Politics, in its traditional conception as a spectacular and articulate attempt to set or change the public agenda through discourse, arises only when there is a breakdown in the relation between the expectations incarnated in habitus and the objective conditions of the moment; that is, when traditional (unspoken, unconscious) strategies fail because the field that molded them has changed. Thus the protests' emergence and their decline had the very same cause: a radical disenchantment. In the first instance, the call to mobilization in 1983 and 1984 catalyzed, especially for women and the young, a "disillusioned optimism" that arose from the failure of inherited strategies that had enabled survival and the prospect of social betterment for an earlier generation of male workers.[74] But as the protests became routine, they became subject to the same disenchantment: disappointment itself became embodied within the *pobladores'* habitus. So it is less that the protests "set the stage," as Schneider suggests, "for a negotiated transition to democracy" than that they were the visible symptom of a deeper transition in the regime of affect, from a sense of expectation nurtured by the state to the all-pervasive low-level anxiety that characterizes a postdictatorial order in which the market sets the tone for social interaction.[75] The period of the new social movements, in other words, effected a change within the habitus of the majority of Chile's population, who were habituated to the order that would come fully into its own only after the end of the dictatorship, with the institutionalization of the state of exception under neoliberalism.

Belief is a matter of the body: "To speak of 'ideologies' is to locate in the realm of *representations*... what in fact belongs to the order of *belief*, that is, to the level of the most profound corporeal dispositions."[76] It is also therefore immediate. Bourdieu adapts and radicalizes the Pascalianism on which Althusser also draws. For Pascal, belief arises from corporeal dispositions, but for Bourdieu it is located in those dispositions themselves and need never rise to consciousness. Though he praises Pascal's challenge to "all those who insist on seeing belief in terms of representations," Bourdieu argues that for Pascal consciousness is still preeminent, "as if will and consciousness were the basis of the disposition which 'with no violence, art or argument makes us believe.' "[77] For Bourdieu, dispositions are always primary: "What is essential *goes without saying because it comes without saying.*" There is no prior decision, and so no wager. Institutions work directly on the body; social order produces no rationale so long as it needs none, and "the principles embodied in this way are placed beyond the grasp of consciousness."[78] Everything passes through the corporeal, as we are habituated to subjection. We are steeped in *doxa*, "the relationship of immediate adherence that is established in practice between a *habitus* and the field to which it is attuned, the preverbal taking-for-granted that flows from practical sense."[79] Despite its immediacy, however, there is always some slippage between habitus and social order. Something always escapes. For as a deposit of the power relations that structure a given social field, habitus is also a residue, an embodied memory of a previous state of that field. And because fields are always in flux, in that their contours are determined only in the course of a permanent struggle between social agents by means of their continual position takings, habitus and field are never fully synchronized. Hence the historicity of habitus, or rather its "double historicity" in that it is both the product of history and the force that, by generating practice, produces history.[80] More fundamentally still, habitus generates time itself, for "time is what practical activity produces in the very act whereby it produces itself.... Time is engendered in the actualization of the act." History and time, in short, are fully immanent: "The theory of practice condensed in the notions of field and habitus allows us to do away with the metaphysical representation of time and history as realities in themselves, external and anterior to practice."[81]

The historicity of habitus secures social reproduction, but at the same time it allows for the possibility of resistance. It is because the practices it generates express dispositions structured by a previous state of the field that habitus enables historical structures to be reproduced in the present. But when the dispositions shaped by history interact with the field in its current state, the inevitable slippage, however slight, between the two makes for unpredictable effects and so the possibility of a new history. Habitus ensures resonance but also leads to dissonance. Hence what Bourdieu terms the "*hysteresis effect* necessarily implied in the logic of habitus," which means that "practices are always liable to incur negative sanctions when the environment with which they are actually confronted is too distant from that to which they are objectively fitted."[82] Hysteresis accounts for missed opportunities, for clumsy or unsuccessful moves by which individuals or groups confirm, despite themselves, their social decline by continuing with their outmoded habits in the face of social change. Equally, however, it can function as an embodied memory that provides a resource for resistance, just as cultural theorist Paul Gilroy argues that the "structures of feeling which underpin black expressive cultures" derive from memories of both "the once forbidden drum" and "a terror which has moved beyond the grasp of ideal, grammatical speech."[83] In either case, the gap between embodied structures and actual practices opens up a time for strategy. It is the strategic aspect of practice that means we can speak of a social *game* rather than a mechanistic structure. In any game or sport, there is always the chance of an upset. So it is with the interactions that constitute the reproduction of social hierarchy: though the playing field is never level, structured as it is by symbolic domination and the unequal distribution of capital, still the result of each move played is always partly in doubt. Time enables strategy, which in turn depends upon timing. As Bourdieu observes in his analysis of gift exchange, what counts is not some transcendent structure or invariable rules, but "the tempo of action" and "the interval between actions," such that success comes only with the skillful management of time, by acting neither too precipitately nor too late.[84]

Habitus provides us with a feeling for historicity and time, but it also unfolds in space. "Inhabited space," Bourdieu argues, "is the principal locus for the objectification of the generative schemes" of the habitus.[85] The basic spatial oppositions between left and right, or high and low, and the way they combine with sensual oppositions such as light and shade, or dry and damp, codify social oppositions such as the distinctions between male and female, public and private, sacred and profane. Bourdieu's analysis of a Kabyle house in Algeria shows how the structured divisions between spaces for cooking, for guests, for leisure, for work, and so on, all embody a set of arbitrary beliefs and habituate the house's inhabitants to the corresponding power relations. Inhabiting space becomes second nature, so the way in which that space orders practice is taken for granted, its lessons absorbed directly: "The 'book' from which the children learn their vision of the world is read through the body, in and through the movements and displacements which make the space within which they are enacted."[86] A similar pedagogy structures the social architecture of contemporary life. Museums, for instance, establish social meaning through a series of oppositions embedded in the modes of spatial navigation and bodily discipline that they demand: "untouchable–touchable; noise–contemplative silence; swift and haphazard exploration–slow and orderly procession" and so on. The museum induces a "total attitude change," directly affecting visitors' physical and mental orientation, simultaneously and immediately.[87] Likewise for the university lecture, at first sight a paradigm of communicative rationality, "the particularities of the space . . . (the platform, the professorial chair at the focal point on which all gazes converge)" provide the lecturer with the "material and symbolic conditions which enable him to keep the students at a respectful distance and would oblige him to do so even if he did not wish to."[88] Habitus is temporal and spatial, and in turn it provides us with our bearings in time and space, so that we comprehend the world as if by instinct.

The paradigmatic space of contemporary neoliberalism is the shopping mall. Mall space is simultaneously local and universal, situated in a particular geographical location yet also hermetically sealed from local context, part of a world of commodities that knows no national borders. Moreover, as Argentine critic Beatriz Sarlo notes, the mall "creates new habits . . . familiarizing people with the ways in which they should function in the mall."[89] In Chile during the dictatorship, a quite distinctive version of the mall flourished in capital Santiago's upscale neighborhoods such as Providencia: the *caracol* or "shell," so-called because of its seashell shape, with shops lining a spiral walkway surrounding a central atrium.[90] First to be built was the Caracol Los Leones, in 1975; other examples include Dos Caracoles (1976), La Rampa de las Flores (1979), and Caracol Vips (1982). Though their popularity has since declined, the *caracoles* were all the rage in the late 1970s, the early years of the dictatorship: "Every Saturday, as was the habit at the time, Providencia was the big draw for shopping."[91] Unlike the typical North American mall, which tends to be no more than two stories high, and to be built to an "L" or "T" plan with major department stores at each extremity, *caracoles* have no such "anchor" stores, but rather are occupied by up to two hundred more or less equally small retail outlets strung out over the equivalent of five or six stories. Moreover, they also lack the meeting points characteristic of other mall architecture. These common areas, usually at the intersection of the mall's main thoroughfares, are a legacy of the philosophy of pioneering architect Victor Gruen, the "inventor of the shopping mall," who designed Detroit's Northland Mall (the first U.S. multifunctional regional shopping center) in 1954, and Minnesota's Southdale Center mall near Minneapolis (the first fully enclosed, climate-controlled shopping center) in 1956. Gruen, "a fervent socialist," hoped that malls would counteract the increasing atomization of 1950s U.S. suburbia by uniting city center functions and services under a single roof and serving as the modern version of the ancient Greek agora or medieval city square.[92]

The Chilean malls, by contrast, accentuate atomizing tendencies. In the *caracol,* even the atrium floor is usually at basement level, and therefore bypassed by shoppers. There are no areas of special intensity and no points for downtime to break up the shopping experience; the *caracoles* construct a smooth space which is relatively undifferentiated along the whole length of its gently sloping gradient. These malls can only be successfully negotiated by very small groups or by individuals:

Christmas decorations hang in the central atrium of the Dos Caracoles mall, Santiago de Chile. Photograph by Jon Beasley-Murray.

any larger congregation of bodies would cause congestion on the narrow ramps. Shoppers are separated out by the gaping void of the atrium. Processes encouraged elsewhere by the dictatorship, such as the dissolution of group identities, are thereby facilitated in the course of reverent interaction with boutique-packaged commodification. No wonder that the North American building the *caracoles* most resemble should be Frank Lloyd Wright's New York Guggenheim museum: both are secular shrines whose centrifugal force draws people away from each other and toward a collection of riches to be venerated. In the malls, a state logic of disassociation combines immediately and immanently with the market presentation of seemingly limitless choice lining a prescribed but otherwise aimless path, to generate a cultural practice of anomic consumerism. The endless, spiralling drift up and down that they encourage is a postideological disaggregation of potentially subversive bodies; there is neither outside nor inside, only a moebius strip of commerce winding round a central abyss.

Like Deleuze, Bourdieu stresses immanence, immediacy, and corporeality. Habitus consists in the impersonal correlation of bodies and powers, determining the capacity to affect and to be affected (to structure and to be structured by social interaction) beneath the level of discourse. For Bourdieu as much as for Deleuze, "the social order is simply the order of bodies."[93] But rather than the violent and asocial intensity of affective experience emphasized by Deleuze, an intensity incarnated in nomadic escape or in terror, Bourdieu points to a low-intensity resonance that tends to preserve, transmit, and reproduce social order in everyday life. Bourdieu complicates the notion of affect's autonomy. Habitus is indeed separate from the order of discourse and representation, but for Bourdieu this means not a revolutionary break from a transcendent state, but rather that we are immersed in a state logic that is, in the end, itself immanent: "The construction of the state is accompanied by the construction of a sort of common historical transcendental, immanent to all its 'subjects.'... It thereby creates the conditions for a kind of immediate orchestration of habitus."[94] It is not that a transcendent state illegitimately imposes upon or blocks an unbound affect; instead, the state gains legitimacy through the habitual resonances that structure immanence itself.

Everything takes place in the ordinary everyday. Bourdieu focuses on quotidian, low-level, and apparently insignificant modes of incorporation, such as "the values given body, *made* body, by the hidden persuasion of an implicit pedagogy which can instil a whole cosmology through injunctions as insignificant as 'sit up straight' or 'don't hold your knife in your left hand.' "[95] These familiar practices anchor the values they inculcate "beyond the reach of consciousness and explicit statement," constituting a *doxa* that is the "universe of the undiscussed" subtending the "universe of discourse (or argument)."[96] It is in the everyday that the social arbitrary is naturalized, made second nature, as "political mythology is realized, *em-bodied*, turned into a permanent disposition, a durable way of standing, speaking, walking, and thereby of feeling and thinking."[97] We stand, speak, walk, feel, and think to collective rhythms synchronized and orchestrated at a pace set by social institutions. But it is also in these everyday practices that we might realize the potential opened up by the temporal slippage inherent in habitus and by the dissonances that result. Even in the most routine activities, a new autonomy arises, and new habits.

Life

Habit's rhythmic regularity structures life itself. Like a heart beating within the social body, its quiet pulses go without saying but without them life would be unimaginable. Unlike a beating heart, however, there is nothing particularly natural about habit. Everyday life resonates to a tempo fully invested by arbitrary power relations. As Althusser's anecdote of interpellation reveals, power is first of all a matter of encounters between bodies, here between police officer and pedestrian. Only retrospectively, after the street-level hailing in which the subject comes into being, can the idea of the state take hold, positing some unified center and source of power. Instead of top-down command, then, power functions from the ground up, molding and shaping daily life in increasingly impersonal ways. Today the cop on the beat is replaced by closed-circuit television, x-ray machines, speed cameras, and biometric passports, each of which regulates the flows of human bodies, speeding them up or slowing them down, separating them out or bringing them together. Regulation no longer is simply a matter of prohibition (what you can and cannot do), but rather actively encourages and fine-tunes particular performances (the roles you should play). In an era characterized by what Foucault terms "biopower," entire populations are endlessly animated, provoked to perform in regular ways if with sometimes unpredictable results. For life itself is now a terrain of struggle. A biopolitics emerges in which what is at stake is the creation of new habits and the persistence of old ones, the variability and intensity of daily rhythms, and the ways in which habit always outstrips the state. None of this is a matter of ideology or hidden agendas: literalism prevails. Power's tactics can be read directly from its public statements; there is no point to a hermeneutics of suspicion, which only conjures up imaginary enemies while ignoring what is on plain view. But a new clarity is required. Biopower and biopolitics too easily become indistinct. In itself, habit does not distinguish between life and liveliness.

Periodicity is fundamental for biological definitions of life: from the metabolic reactions that produce and burn energy, to reproduction and self-replication, circadian oscillations, or the myriad regularities (digestion, gestation, migration, hibernation) that pattern more complex forms, life is a series of repetitions. Hence, as Deleuze notes, "this living present, and with it all of organic and psychic life, rests on habit."[98] Nowhere is this more visible than in the everyday, indeed in the very fact that we can speak of an "every" day. So French theorist Henri Lefebvre observes that "the link between the everyday and cyclic patterns and timescales, the time of day and night, week and month, season and year, is obvious."[99] We wake up, get out of bed, drag a comb across our heads. Nothing could appear more natural. But equally, nothing is more engrained with the effects of socialization: the alarm clock sounds, we make ourselves presentable, head for the bus or the car, commute into work, take tea break, coffee break, lunch break. Then back home in time for the football, the pub, the TV. Life comprises a series of performances to a preset tempo. No wonder that for Karl Marx, the first and most basic struggle against capital is the campaign to reduce the working day, and more fundamentally still to abolish the category of socially necessary labor time.[100] We need to reclaim our time from its measurement by everything from the schoolroom bell to the factory whistle or the beep of a Blackberry. So Marx's brief depiction of postcapitalist society invokes a world in which people set their own pace, able "to hunt in the morning, fish in the afternoon, rear cattle in the evening, criticize after dinner."[101] Part and parcel of our exploitation is that our habits are not our own.

Even in disciplinary society, power is already diffuse and productive, infiltrating everyday life. Foucault describes how policing is more than "the form of a State apparatus . . . linked directly to the centre of political sovereignty"; it is also "an apparatus that must be coextensive with the entire social body."[102] Disciplinary society is characterized by the exercise of power directly on the body, coordinated through discursive formations: "It is in discourse that power and knowledge are joined together." But discursive form rather than content matters most. What is at stake is not "what ideology — dominant or dominated — [these discourses] represent," but their "tactical productivity . . . and their strategic integration."[103] Discourse is material: it is a particular way of arranging bodies. Hence Foucault refuses to distinguish between coercion and consent: "To analyse the political investment of the body presupposes . . . that one abandons — where power is concerned — the violence-ideology opposition."[104] Moreover, discourses constitute mutually reinforcing networks whose regularities and redundancies correspond to a particular historical *epistème* or regime of knowledge. Thus penology, psychology, pathology, and so on follow a similar logic; this logic then characterizes the social system as a whole and comes to seem the natural way of being in and understanding the world. Encoded in our "common sense" understandings of criminality, madness, and health is a way of thinking about the world organized by a power so diffuse (because we are incorporated within its all-pervasive structures) that it seems to disappear. Yet from a standpoint outside of a particular *epistème*, what was once everyday and quasi-natural (because naturalized, incorporated) appears senseless and barbarous: for example, the (now) apparently excessive system of punishment characteristic of the Middle Ages. Foucault's historical studies excavate the embodied logics that structured, for instance, the "classical age" (from the seventeenth century to the French Revolution), and, by implication, defamiliarize the naturalness of our own age.

What prevents us from understanding how habit functions in everyday life is that its power is invisible, because it is simply too familiar, too much a part of us. Foucauldian historicism is one strategy of critique or resistance through defamiliarization; artistic production can be another. For the Russian formalists, estrangement defined the aesthetic. As critic Victor Shklovsky argues, "the technique of art is to make objects 'unfamiliar,' to make forms difficult." And defamiliarization rescues life from a "habitualization [that] devours work, clothes, furniture, one's wife, and the fear of war." Habit, for Shklovsky, numbs the senses and leads to a kind of death in life, in which everything from the most intimate of relationships ("one's wife") to world historical events ("the fear of war") is devoured "and so life is reckoned as nothing." Defamiliarization counteracts this tendency by disrupting habit and opening up a space for affect once again, which in turn leads to a revival of cognition in contrast to the mere utilitarian perception or *re*cognition that clouds our repetitive, everyday vision: "After we see an object several times we begin to recognize it. The object is in front of us and we know about it, but we do not see it. . . . Art removes objects from the automatism of perception."[105] Shklovsky's point is that ultimately even representation is but a habit; his argument is that the shock of estrangement makes the work present or immediate once again. And though Bourdieu would hardly side with either formalism or what he terms the "aesthetic point of view," in part because he contends that they, too, abstract from everyday life, he would concur with the injunction to refocus on what is in plain view.[106] For however implicitly power operates, its explicit statements are not to be disregarded. If anything, the point is to examine discourse all the more carefully: to analyze the immanent effectivity of everyday statements and actions, rather than to indulge in the interpretative fever that assumes that the real action is always elsewhere. For it is not as though the workings of power are hidden. They can go without saying only because they have become a matter of habit, because they are all too evident.

What matters is how things present themselves to us, not what they may *re*present. Ideology critique rereads texts (reads them "against the grain") on the assumption that they contain a distorted representation of the world. Its purpose is to reveal the underlying truth that they misrepresent and to expose the distortions to which that truth has been subjected. As Sloterdijk observes, however, this approach is fruitless when faced with discourses whose function is not distortion. Instead of inspired revelation, what is required is a patient literalism. German theorist Klaus Theweleit, for instance, insists on taking at face value the writings of the "soldier males" he studies in *Male Fantasies*. These men were members of the Weimar-era Freikorps, volunteers whose mission was to put down working-class revolt in the aftermath of the First World War, who were later hailed by the Nazis as the "First Soldiers of the Third Reich." For Theweleit they embody something like the truth of Nazism, all the more emphatically in that they predate Hitler's rise to power. Nazism is not simply an ideological discourse that wins over the masses, still less one man's manipulation of the political and cultural spheres: ideology comes afterwards; hegemony is always belated. The Freikorps literature hides no coded ideological meaning. Everything is stated clearly, on the surface. Hence Theweleit's extravagant use of quotation, his declared aim simply "to present typical specimens of the writings of soldier males, sticking closely to the text in every case." For Theweleit, "the material has taken precedence over interpretations."[107]

Relation trumps interpretation. Anthropology has always manifested an interest in the patterns that structure everyday relations, such as kinship or marriage strategies, and also the ways in which informants relate their experience of life. Bourdieu carries over this interest to his analyses of twentieth-century France. In part, like Theweleit's faux-naïve reading of social actors' statements, his methodology consists in extended quotation (particularly in *Distinction* or *The Weight of the World*); but primarily it outlines the statistical regularities and patterns that structure discourses and institutions alike. The content of a particular utterance is of less interest than the way in which that content is a placeholder in a series of oppositions that mark out social positions and position takings within a given field. In *Distinction*, Bourdieu analyzes the taste for (say) classical music or abstract art as a marker for its holders' distinction from other members of society, who may favor (say) pop music or handicrafts. He constructs three-dimensional maps of social space by analyzing the results of surveys on everyday cultural preferences and then correlating their relations. For Bourdieu, there is no real difference between his respondents' statements and their social status: each is incarnated in the other. Hence "the first precept of method . . . requires us to resist by all means available our primary inclination to think the social world in a substantialist manner. . . . One must *think relationally*." As Wacquant observes, "habitus and field designate bundles of relations."[108] A focus on relation displaces preoccupation with meaning. Relationality is life itself. Everything is on the surface, to be read at face value.

The turn to neoliberalism that Pinochet's regime inaugurated has been termed a "silent revolution," as in the book titles of both Chilean politician Joaquín Lavín's apologia and British researcher Duncan Green's leftist critique. But Pinochet, despite hiding behind his shades, arms rigidly folded, in the famous photograph that is now an icon of dictatorial authority, was often ready to speak, at times too openly for his advisors' comfort. There is much to be seen in the reflections provided by dark glasses. One notable incident of Pinochet's volubility took place when he was in Spain in 1975, for Spanish dictator Francisco Franco's funeral. On his last day in the country, the general took the opportunity to clarify a few things to the international press. In journalist Ernesto Ekaizer's words, the event turned into "more than a press conference; it was an accelerated course in Pinochetism." Asked about the existence of political prisoners and disappearances in Chile, Pinochet was a little more revealing than diplomacy would have counseled: "We haven't kil... (you realize that he's about to conjugate the verb 'to kill').... Down in Chile the number who have died ... in combat... is no more than 2,500 people. The number who have died is... let's say no more than 3,000, then."[109] The dictatorship is continually on the point of letting slip its dirty not-so-secrets. Everybody knows, after all. Hence Luis Salinas's *The London Clinic* demonstrates the benefits of listening to the general speak: Salinas aims to explain Pinochet primarily by collecting and presenting the general's own words. This collection of quotations impresses upon us the general's astonishing confidence, his refusal to apologize, but also highlights a certain candor. The most famous example of Pinochet's blunt honesty is his remark that "burying two corpses in the same grave makes for great economies." In case we missed it, he later confirmed the bon mot, declaring "That is what I meant.... I never regret what I say." Manuel Contreras, former chief of Pinochet's secret service, tells us that his only regret is "not having been harder on the Marxists."[110] What becomes clear is that if Pinochet and company have nothing to regret, they also have nothing to hide. This is why Pinochet's words are so damning: he feels no need to justify his actions or to persuade us of his methods or his goals. Everything is on the surface. Perhaps there are some details that are not worth exploring, some areas best left unexamined; but these are all rather inconsequential. In a 1984 interview, Pinochet is asked (once more) about the disappeared: "Have you ever had any interest in finding out where all those people ended up?" He responds with condescension: "Señorita, no one knows. Look, if there are right now thirteen million Chileans, let's say twelve million, out of twelve million, two thousand are nothing (he makes a hand gesture to indicate a very small number).... In this country, señorita, things need to be forgotten." Pinochet produces effects rather than arguments. His ideological deficit is if anything flaunted rather than feared. The general has no clothes, but he is happy to parade naked. There is no real pretense that he is anything but guilty. As the Spanish newspaper *La Vanguardia* comments regarding the 1998 extradition process in the British courts, after the general's detention in London, "No one speaks of Pinochet as if he were innocent."[111] His defense rested instead upon technicalities. So a transparent neoliberalism employs technocrats in place of ideologues, whose métier is economic statistics rather than political rhetoric, and who concern themselves with the management of populations rather than with the singular victims whom the families of the disappeared hope to uncover.

A relational analysis, in place of hermeneutic interpretation, can be brought to bear also on the left and its leaders. Political scientist Katherine Hite's *When the Romance Ended* studies Chilean left leaders and the positions they took before, during, and after the dictatorship. It is a study in nostalgia, disillusion, and even cynicism. Hite quotes José Antonio Viera-Gallo, formerly of MAPU (a radical Catholic left group), undersecretary in Allende's Ministry of Justice, later speaker of the House under Aylwin: "Politics has little probability of touching the world of the economy. Here businessmen couldn't care less about politics... and many people, whether they're professionals or well-paid workers, why should they care?"[112] Her book is full of similar statements from those who were once radicals, often former members of the Unidad Popular, who have had to come to terms with the Pinochet coup, the long years of dictatorship and exile, and the effects of neoliberal transformation. Hite outlines the accommodations each has made to the changes that Chile and the world have undergone since the 1960s. On this basis, she categorizes her interviewees into four groups: party loyalists, personal loyalists, political thinkers, and political entrepreneurs. She suggests that these are "cognitive frameworks" that remain relatively stable over time.[113] Changes in Chilean political society result not from any conversion of political identities, but from the ways that events favor one cognitive type over another: whereas the 1960s saw the ascendancy of party loyalists, today political entrepreneurs have the advantage, but this balance of forces may (and, Hite suggests, will) shift.

Hite fails to show, however, that these cognitive types are analytic rather than descriptive categories, that her subjects' actions derive from their (enduring) dispositions, and that her labels are more than just ways of classifying their (variable) actions. Moreover, though Hite's reading, like Theweleit's and Bourdieu's, depends upon extended quotation, her quasi-psychological approach assumes that the confessing subject speaks the truth of his or her inner self. Her book is presented as a collective biography of the Chilean left; however, categorizing respondents according to psychological type dismantles any sense that they are immanently part of a society or social group. They are presented as figures who, by reflecting upon the field in which they engage, are also detached from it, transcendent. In the end, Hite hardly upsets a rational actor theory that separates actors from the positions they take, seeing agents as (ideally at least) devoid of any quality but rationality, the propensity to maximize personal benefit. She does grant different agents distinct propensities to choose one way rather than the other, according to "cognitive type," but she pays little attention to how these propensities emerge or to how they change according to the results of the choices these agents make. She ignores, in short, the habits that underlie or arise from the act of taking a position in a specific field whose shape is determined in part by the positions that are already staked out. By contrast, a focus on habitus (which lies on the same, preconscious level as Hite's cognitive types) helps us understand differential positions and position takings in all their dynamism. Habitus allows us to go beyond a decontextualized account of agents and actions, to see instead how positions are staked out and defined in the embodied and always fluid social context of life itself.

With biopower, any distinction between life and power fades. The state takes an immediate interest in the regularities that order and shape everyday existence. Foucault develops this concept in his first, introductory, volume to *The History of Sexuality*, where he argues that over the course of the classical age, power is invested ever more in managing life directly, via "an explosion of numerous and diverse techniques for achieving the subjugation of bodies and the control of the population, marking the beginning of an era of 'bio-power.' "[114] Regulation is no longer merely a matter of establishing limits (between sickness and health, madness and sanity, for instance) or of determining the sanctions and negations that are to enforce those limits, stigmatizing what lies beyond as the "other" of normality. Biopower is an active intervention into the production and morphology of the everyday. Power and the body are ever more intimately joined, the one instantiated in the other, and the vestiges of (state or discursive) transcendence are ever more redundant: "Power would no longer be dealing simply with legal subjects over whom the ultimate dominion was death, but with living beings, and the mastery it would be able to exercise over them would have to be applied at the level of life itself." Hence biopower "brought life and its mechanisms into the realm of explicit calculations and made knowledge-power an agent of transformation of human life."[115] With biopower, any distinction between nature and politics, or culture and the state, disappears altogether. Biopower is the absolute colonization, and production or incitement, of everyday life.

Biopower is positive and active: it provokes and engenders rather than restricts or negates; it encourages agency and fosters life. Its watchword is performance: with biopower, we are urged to "be all we can be," as the U.S. Army's recruitment slogan has it. In Italian theorist Paolo Virno's words, labor becomes "a virtuosic performance (without end product)."[116] Especially with the rise of so-called affective labor, we are encouraged to think that we are expressing ourselves in work as in play: restaurant workers in Mike Judge's film *Office Space* (1999), for instance, are required to wear "pieces of flair," the material signs of their supposedly bubbly and outgoing personalities that they are to mobilize to provide atmosphere and attitude for their customers. "That's what the flair's about," the restaurant manager berates a recalcitrant waitress. "It's about fun." The performance of enjoyment is to suffuse all of life. Indeed, if Taylorism and Fordism in the early twentieth century set out to shape and improve our habits at work, now for post-Fordist biopower there is little difference between work and play. The boundaries between the two disappear as corporations such as Google encourage an ethos of play at work, while everyday life itself becomes productive for capital. Habits likewise are performances through which we are encouraged both to realize ourselves and to become increasingly efficient, aided by "self-help" guides from Stephen Covey's mega-best-selling *The 7 Habits of Highly Effective People* to (say) Jim Canterucci's *Personal Brilliance: Mastering the Everyday Habits That Create a Lifetime of Success*. But there is something ambivalent about such performativity, in that it is both orchestrated by power and also constitutive of subjectivity. Are its subjects only subject to power, or is there some space for autonomy or resistance? In promising to teach us new habits, self-help guides and other agents of biopower admit the possibility of a dehabituation or rehabituation. Habits, too, are mutable and might enable new subjectivities that outstrip the everyday demands of neoliberal excellence. Self-help hints at the potential cultivation of a new collective self.

The Pinochet dictatorship oversaw an extraordinarily rapid transition from spectacular and disciplinary power to the biopower of a post-disciplinary age. Rather than heralding a conservative reaction, it instituted a wholesale, and in some ways progressive (because modernizing), shift in the way in which power organized the Chilean collective body. Given the rushed timetable of this transition, the regime was a particularly hybrid and somewhat ad hoc arrangement. More generally, as Moulián notes, "revolutionary dictatorships, which attempt to destroy preexisting forms of life with the aim of imposing a new, rational, order, make use simultaneously of silence and the austere economy of disciplinary power along with the stridency and visibility of repressive power." As a result, "this type of dictatorship unites power's invisible functioning, seen only in its effects, with the rage of punishment, which would appear to be simply a matter of passion."[117] But it would be a mistake to see the dictatorship as simply repressive. On the one hand, the use of Chile's National Stadium as a detention center in the coup's early days could be a metaphor for the visual display of authority, as indeed was the bombardment of the National Palace, the Moneda, on September 11, 1973. Such displays function by irradiation: exemplary acts at the center of the gaze generate effects elsewhere, promoting a pedagogical relationship with the people. So cultural critic Diana Taylor argues, in her analysis of the performativity of repression, that torture takes hold by means of an "amplification . . . through which twenty victims can paralyze an entire community or country."[118] On the other hand, power is all the more effective if the onus for performativity is more widely distributed. And Moulián argues that this is precisely what has taken place in Chile. He points to the way in which financial credit, intangible but all-pervasive, now fashions and distributes subjectivity: consumption becomes "a field for the exercise of power" by which "society seems to have habituated itself to the neoliberal order that emerged from a bloody dictatorship," all in the context of "a total absence of any dimension of transcendence."[119] If disciplinary power works at a distance, biopower is always immediately present. Yet too much of the resistance to Pinochet failed to learn the lessons of biopower. Exiled left-wing dissidents and their clandestine proxies within the country, such as the Manuel Rodríguez Patriotic Front, sought to achieve spectacular actions, notably the assassination of Pinochet himself. Their failure should not be attributed solely to the regime's repression or the efficiency of its security forces. Such militancy took no account of the fact that the form of power itself had changed. More promising, then, were protests whose motor was habit, activating a biopolitics that outperformed biopower.

The Chilean *arpilleristas,* for instance, were women who (like their counterparts, the Argentine "Mothers of the Disappeared") came together as they regularly encountered each other performing the same dreary routine of checking in the various state offices and morgues in search of their missing relatives. The Pinochet dictatorship, in disappearing their husbands or sons and daughters, forced new habits upon a group who previously had often enough been relatively apolitical housewives. Building on the companionship that they encountered with each other, and prodded also by the Catholic Church's Vicariate of Solidarity, the women began collectively sewing *arpilleras,* patchwork scenes of everyday life under the dictatorship. Though these tapestries were (mainly) representational, depicting human rights abuses and the women's own struggles to seek information and justice, perhaps more important was their mode of production: first, as an artisanal activity that drew on familiar and everyday skills, "a diary of life written with scraps of cloth, wool, needle and apron," often directly incorporating snippets of clothing and even hair that came from their loved ones or the women themselves; and second, as a communal practice by which "the women joined forces and the individual cause was regularly transformed into a collective one."[120] Hence cultural critic Marjorie Agosín argues that "the *arpillera* comes to life under the hands of its creator; more than that, it is the life of the creator."[121] And the creator is a collective subject that emerges from a process of, first, a dehabituation that brought together women who had previously been relatively isolated individuals, and then a rehabituation that forged new habits in resistance to the dictatorship's life management that even went beyond it. The *arpilleristas* established new connections, both among themselves in their regular meetings with needles and cloth, and as their "utterly silent social art" became one of "the most effective clandestine means of communication to resist the military dictatorship."[122]

The very notion of performance implies the possibility of breakdown. The difference between watching a film and going to the theater or the circus, say, resides in a certain unpredictability: this time, unlike almost every other time, an actor may fluff his or her lines, or the trapeze artist may lose his or her grip and fall. Because a performance is "live," we are always half holding our breath, wondering what could go wrong. The beauty of a live event is its imperfection, the rough edges that constitute its singularity and the fact that it is never an entirely flawless reproduction. Flawlessness is deadening: the liveliness of a concert or show derives from its elements of spontaneity or creativity, whether that be the jazz musician's improvisation in which new resonances, riffs, and rhythms are explored, the banter between a stand-up comic and his or her audience, or an inspired performance by an actor who goes beyond what the script demands. For performance is never fully representational: even if it reproduces some original source (a script or score), what is essential is the difference between copy and model, not the similarity. Reiteration allows for, even requires, difference. If life is constituted by habit, *liveliness* is inherent in the resistance that arises when the regularity and predictability of habit is interrupted. In everyday life, habit can always be waylaid by the friction that results as bodies are repeatedly in contact, whether that be the way in which a repeated performance or a stuck record starts to grate on our nerves, the "culture shock" as old habits meet new circumstances, or the static electricity that builds as surfaces rub against each other, leading to explosive discharge. So habit can lead to outpourings of resistance. As the waitress exclaims to her boss in *Office Space*, showing a spark of life as her performance of enjoyment breaks down: "Y'know what? . . . I *do* want to express myself. . . . And I don't need thirty-seven pieces of flair to do it." She gives him the finger and continues: "There's my flair! And this is me expressing myself. . . . I hate this job! I hate this goddamn job and I don't need it!"

Social reproduction is never truly flawless. It is always somewhat hit and miss. Philosopher Judith Butler's theorization of performativity as the embodied enactment of identity roles stresses the ways in which such roles can be "queered": bent out of shape if not fully avoided. She takes issue with Althusser's notion of interpellation, insisting on the possibilities of failed interpellation (only glimpsed in Althusser's brief reference to "bad subjects") to show that the voice of power, the state's "hailing," and the order of bodies are not fully synchronized. The body always falls short of or exceeds the voice. Hence she argues that "useful as it is, Althusser's scheme . . . attribut[es] a creative power to the voice that recalls and reconsolidates the figure of the divine voice in its ability to bring about what it names."[123] Although Althusser's essay is a critique of the fetishism that imagines that the state alone authorizes subjectivity, Butler suggests that he remains within precisely this paradigm. For Althusser, not only is "ideology in general" necessary and eternal; so therefore is the state that acts as the essential lynchpin of the double circuit of ideology, command, and habit. Butler points, on the one hand, to interpellation's citational quality: the fact that the state endlessly has to return to previous instances of interpellation so as to legitimate its attempts to constitute subjects reveals that it can never fully establish its claim to originality; the fact that it continually has to repeat itself shows that it is forever incomplete. On the other hand, Butler is also concerned with what remains unvoiced and unspoken. Censorship, for instance, "produces discursive regimes through the production of the unspeakable," and more generally the gap between what may and may not be spoken determines "the conditions of intelligibility" of any regime of power. "This normative exercise of power," she argues, "is rarely acknowledged as an operation of power at all. Indeed, we may classify it among the most implicit forms of power. . . . That power continues to act in illegible ways is one source of its relative invulnerability." Here, then, Butler turns to Bourdieu, theorist of "a bodily understanding, or *habitus*" that does not depend upon the voice or upon speech. For habit describes what exceeds interpellation, whether that be the state's biopower or an insurgent biopolitics.[124]

As life itself becomes fully subject to power, it becomes the terrain of political struggle, the site of a differentiation between distinct forms of vivacity, ways of life that are at odds with each other. For Agamben, for instance, with totalitarianism "life and politics... begin to become one," and what is now at stake is the increasingly blurred distinction between biopolitics and a "thanatopolitics" that plays out in the space of "bare life," pure potential or habit, in which we all find ourselves.[125] Biopolitics describes then both the apogee of politics, its ubiquity and immediacy, and also the effort to preserve a space for politics against its dissolution, to show that there is a life beyond the law. In Agamben's words, "to show law in its nonrelation to life and life in its nonrelation to law means to open a space between them for human action, which once claimed for itself the name of 'politics.' "[126] This "nonrelation" is the struggle by which biopolitics opposes biopower; it is a gamble on autonomy even within immanence, on a detotalization that unlocks the power of creativity. It is the deployment of what theorist Michel de Certeau terms the "tactics" implicit within "the practice of everyday life." Habitual but far from routine, against the functionalist tone of Bourdieu's theorization of habitus but in line with the allowance that he makes for unpredictability, a tactic is a "guileful ruse" by means of which agents carve out spaces of autonomy immanent to but just off kilter from the norm, "mak[ing] use of the cracks that particular conjunctions open in the surveillance of the proprietary powers."[127] Or in Hardt and Negri's words, "playing different tactical games in the continuity of strategy" opens up "two conflicting recognitions: one organizing the desire of life and the other the fear of death, biopolitics against biopower." Liveliness breaks from life as usual. But can biopolitics and biopower be so easily distinguished? Not, at least, from the perspective of habit, which is why a further step is required. A path leads from the friction of resistance, that is, the strategy of refusal and tactics of differentiation, to the "multitude" as "a diverse set of singularities that produce a common life."[128]

Toward the Multitude

We have seen how, in defining habit as an embodied disposition to act shaped by the social field, Bourdieu explains the workings of social control without recourse to ideology. Tiredness and waiting. Habitus is conservative: it is history, literally, incarnate; it ensures the tired repetitions of social reproduction; it encourages us to wait for the familiar rituals of everyday life. And yet Bourdieu's theory is premised on the assumption that social change is ceaseless and unstoppable. Habitus is historical only because social conditions have inevitably changed since the moment of its formation. Its repetitions are always slightly different. And in our waiting lies the hope of perhaps radical change. For there is always a lag between the time incarnated in habitus as disposition and the time of the event that disposition has to confront. Bourdieu's materialism is grounded in a conception of the interplay between social dynamism and the inertia inherent to bound affective states, with all the friction or resistance that results. Theories of ideology tend to be static; even when they incorporate notions of contestation, they imply a deadlock that can be broken only by forces that come from the outside. The classical architectural metaphor of base and superstructure comprises just such a static conception, for which change arises only as the base (the development of the forces of production) moves beneath the superstructure's feet. By contrast, Bourdieu's is a dynamic theory, for which change is immanent to all aspects of social production and reproduction. The texture of daily life is defined by our resistance as we are continually pressed to learn new habits and unlearn old ones. Even as biopower subsumes life itself, there is some space for an insurgent biopolitics.

Still, Bourdieu's functionalist tendencies are not quickly dispatched. De Certeau argues that there is a tension in Bourdieu's work, between a meticulous attention to everyday "practices and their logic," and the invocation of "a mystical reality, the *habitus*, which is to bring them under the law of reproduction."[129] And for critic Jeremy Lane, Bourdieu too often ignores the fact that the "process of incorporation" whereby the logic of a field is taken up by habitus is "always subject to failure; it could always go awry." Lane points also to the tensions between particular social contexts, smoothed over in "Bourdieu's assumption as to the existence of straightforward homologies between the different fields."[130] After all, each field is subject to different pressures and responds to distinct stimuli and so reciprocally shapes habits in different ways, raising the possibility of pockets of resistance, areas of social life at odds with the rest. Indeed, some of the most notable social disturbances arise when habits acquired in one context are blocked or denied in another: the ensuing disillusion can lead to a generalized rejection of the social game itself, a sort of absolute negation in which suddenly everything is up for grabs. Finally, however, habit can also play a constitutive role. Bourdieu's invocations of the concept of *conatus*, which describes an instinct for survival or increase, suggest ways in which a subjectivity formed immanently through habitus can threaten to displace the social order and may offer new forms of community. But Bourdieu fails to note that habit can be revolutionary, that revolutionaries must have their own habits, and that there is an ambivalence to habit in that at the same time as it ensures social reproduction it also enables creative constitution. So we move toward the concept of the multitude, a subjectivity that consolidates itself through habit.

For all his emphasis on reproduction, Bourdieu's work revolves around two of the most traumatic disruptions to postwar French society: the Algerian struggle for independence and the "events" of May 1968. While Bourdieu makes few explicit references to the violence of decolonization, still less to its repercussions in the metropolis, Lane argues that his early fieldwork in North Africa was "a significant gesture of solidarity with the Algerian independence movement" and that its analysis of the modernization process that transformed "peasants into revolutionaries" was "something of a model for Bourdieu's later theorisations of socio-cultural change in France."[131] *Outline of a Theory of Practice*, for instance, centers around the transition encapsulated in the scandalous tale of the mason "who had learnt his trade in France" and demanded to be paid in cash rather than accept the traditional gift economy of Kabyle society.[132] It describes the way in which an entire society is restructured with the arrival of an explicit logic of financial exchange. Similarly, *Reproduction*, *Distinction*, and *Homo Academicus* are concerned with the massive changes in French postwar society and the disturbances of the late 1960s that seemed to threaten the entire social order. Perhaps despite himself, Bourdieu is as much a theorist of crisis as of reproduction. Indeed it is crisis, Bourdieu and Passeron suggest, that reveals the truth of the social reproduction that it interrupts, however briefly: "The moment of transition from ruthless methods of imposition to more subtle methods is doubtless the most favourable moment for bringing to light the objective truth of that imposition."[133] And of May 1968, Bourdieu claims that "such a moment of awareness constitutes in itself an objective change, liable to make the whole mechanism grind to a halt."[134] The gap between habit and event allows for an awakening that can self-reflexively transform even the most settled habits. Equally, the development of new habits can open up a gap between subject and field that precipitates a transformative event.

There is nothing necessarily spontaneous or unconscious about the disruption of habit, and dehabituation can be a conscious strategy. Indeed, it is the avant-garde gesture par excellence. During the Pinochet dictatorship, the Colectivo Acciones de Arte (Art Action Collective or CADA), comprising several prominent Chilean artists and writers such as novelist Diamela Eltit, poet Raúl Zurita, and visual artist Lotty Rosenfeld, staged a series of performances designed to intervene in and interrupt the everyday habits of neoliberal consumerism. As critic Robert Neustadt's *CADA día* (literally, "Every Day") documents, these actions included the October 1979 "Inversion of Scene" that aimed to "underline the transparency of everyday repression" by cloaking Santiago's Museum of Fine Arts with a white sheet on the one hand, and renting ten milk trucks on the other, while taking out an advertisement in a daily newspaper that was nothing more than a blank page.[135] CADA's purpose was literally to screen off the museum while touching upon familiar objects and practices (the newspaper, drinking milk) so as, in Nelly Richard's words, "to modify both the customary perceptions of the city . . . and the social norms which regulate the behaviour of the citizen."[136] Other CADA actions included showering the city with 400,000 flyers dropped from the air, in the name of "a fusion of 'art' with 'life,'" and Lotty Rosenfeld's conversion of the broken white line in the middle of streets and highways into a series of crosses.[137] These are classic shock tactics of artistic defamiliarization, undertaken on a massive scale. Especially in their willful disarticulation of the signs of normality that the dictatorship wanted to convey for both national and external consumption, they set out to force "the gaze to unlearn what the press habitually teaches it."[138] And yet, beyond the fact that the artistic avant-garde is all too easily recuperated into a familiar tradition of provocation that can never quite escape the aestheticizing gaze, surely any artistic shock tactic could be no more than pale reflection of the effects of the coup itself. If art is defamiliarization, then like it or not Pinochet was its greatest Chilean practitioner. In philosopher Willy Thayer's words, "The coup d'état fulfilled the yearning for an event, epitome of the avant-garde."[139]

Bourdieu never fully makes up his mind about the source of resistance to power. He sometimes prioritizes intellectual, above all sociological, reflection as the means by which to grasp what otherwise goes without saying. Sociology is a "science ... of the hidden" that follows social crisis.[140] But such enlightenment is never the cause of the original crisis. Bourdieu's analyses of social action highlight instead a practical reason far removed from scientific rationality. Hence the tension between Bourdieu's own political program on the one hand, especially in his later work where he champions a "rational utopia" in which "scientists are no doubt the ones who have to shoulder the primary role," and on the other hand his descriptions of social movements, in which ethical protest generated by habit trumps political action motivated by rational deliberation.[141] Given the gap between practice and politics, no wonder that Bourdieu complains that social scientists are out of touch, though his conclusion that it is the "social movements" rather than the scientists that "have a lot of ground to make up" is unpersuasive.[142] For Bourdieu demonstrates that resistance arises semispontaneously at the interface of habit and social field after there have been significant changes to the rules of the game. He shows not only the ways in which power is secured beyond and despite ideology, but also how protest builds by means other than the construction of so-called counterhegemonic projects. Moreover, the dissent engendered by and in habitus undermines any putative hegemony or other political articulations. Politics is a restricted practice of representation, counterposed to an expansive ethics embodied in habitual practices.

There is, for Bourdieu, a significant distinction between politics and ethics. Politics concerns opinion; ethics involves affect and habit. Moreover, politics is subordinate to or grounded in ethics, albeit an ethics that is (in the terms discussed above) *bio*political in that what is at stake is life itself rather than the forms in which events are represented. Politics as the inclination to articulate "political principles to answer a problem that is presented as political" is unevenly distributed, and concentrated among the dominant class. Beyond this dominant class, and "for problems that have not been brought into a personal or party 'line,' agents are thrown back on their ethos." Ethos expresses the embodied experience of the habitus, and contrasts with the discursive realm of hegemonic articulation: "There is every difference in the world between the conscious, quasi-forced systematicity of a political 'line' and the systematicity 'in-itself' of the practices and judgements engendered by the unconscious principles of the ethos."[143] Ethical dispositions underlie but are never equivalent to political positions. So political struggle is never quite commensurate with ethical protest, with the heartfelt if sometimes inchoate resistance that comes from a sense of disruption to a subject's very way of life. The conservatism of habitus and its material ontology of embodied subjectivity means that ethical protest is similar to Foucault's conception of ethics as care of the self, the constitution and maintenance of a subject "defined by the relationship of self to self" that goes beyond any "juridical conception of the subject of right."[144] Recourse to an ethos rooted in the practices of the habitus suggests the possibility of an ethics that would be an immanent and postpolitical biopolitics of self-sustaining subjectivity.

Bourdieu argues that the May 1968 student protests were the result of ethical self-protection in the face of the inadvertent effects of increased access to the French educational system in the 1950s and 1960s. The expansion of secondary and tertiary education had led to "diploma inflation" and the devaluation of scholarly certification, such that educational success could no longer be converted straightforwardly into social mobility. Yet "newcomers to secondary education [we]re led . . . to expect it to give them what it gave others at a time when they themselves were excluded from it." Whereas "in an earlier period and for other classes, those aspirations were perfectly realistic, since they corresponded to objective probabilities," in the wake of systemic expansion "they are often quickly deflated by the verdicts of the scholastic market or the labour market." The social field had changed, shattering habitual expectation and provoking an ethical refusal that questioned the very rules of the game: "A whole generation, finding it has been taken for a ride, is inclined to extend to all institutions the mixture of revolt and resentment it feels toward the educational system." Hence the "anti-institutional cast of mind" that "point[ed] toward a denunciation of the tacit assumptions of the social order, a practical suspension of doxic adherence to the prizes it offers and the values it professes, and a withholding of the investments which are a necessary condition of its functioning." However much the events of 1968 drew "strength from ideological and scientific critiques," they were not themselves ideological; rather they constituted a suspension of (practical, embodied) belief in the wake of an interruption to the smooth functioning of social reproduction.[145] They were part of an ethical revolt that drew on habitual inclinations to confront the social order.

We have seen how Salman analyzes Chile's 1983 to 1984 protests as a "non-ideological politicization" of the new social movements. Young people's participation in particular arose from a collective disenchantment: they were "confronted with socialization patterns they felt were anachronistic.... Going to school would not get them a good job, the survival organizations would not enable them to express themselves, and the parties had nothing at all to give them." What provoked the revolt, then, was the radical discontinuity between a habitus produced under one set of social conditions, and a social field transformed by dictatorship. As an inherited habitus attuned to predictatorship conditions failed to prepare a new generation to survive and progress under the military regime, the result was a wholesale rejection of the rules of the game, and a "rejection of any kind of authoritarian control altogether." Likewise abandoning conventional politics ("for them there was almost a taboo on the political"), they experimented not with projects for counterhegemony, but with autonomous social structures and modes of valorization. As "they put more and more effort into setting up their own organizations in these years," this autovalorization constituted an exodus from the logic of authoritarianism rather than direct opposition.[146] It was the invention of new, nonideological forms of politics and new, nonidentitarian modes of subjectivity.

Exodus is not simply flight; it is also the construction of new habits of existence. Nelly Richard makes this clear in her discussion of the helicopter flight that liberated four militants of the Manuel Rodríguez Patriotic Front from Santiago's high-security prison in 1996. Her analysis plays on the connection between "fuga" (flight in the sense of "escape") and "vuelo" (flight as a mode of transport): the militants' escape was also a creative transportation that broke with any stale dichotomy of repression and resistance. The Front, the armed wing of the Communist Party, had earned a name for itself for its spectacular if sporadic armed actions in the latter days of the Pinochet regime, not least the assassination attempt on the general's motorcade in 1986 that had been a hair's breadth from success. As such, it radicalized the impulse that drove the new social movements' protests. By 1996, such militant attacks had lost most of their rationale, but the prison breakout pointed to the possibility of sustaining militancy on into the era of democratic transition by transforming struggle into flight. Richard focuses particularly on the way in which this escape became an aesthetic performance, as it was accompanied by a *testimonio*-style narrative smuggled out of prison (yet another escape) whose self-consciously literary style produced "signs of figurative obliqueness that speak to us of the allusive and elusive vocation of the metaphor that desubstantiates the truth with its 'art of flight.' "[147] The prison break was also then an experiment in creativity that conjured up a vision of new realities that go beyond neoliberalism's deadening rationalizations. More than just a break with the old rules of the game, flight plays with or even defies those rules, suggesting that other games are possible.

Similar experimentation is at work in Eltit's *Sacred Cow,* a novel set during an era of antiauthoritarian protest in which "all the signs [had begun] to disintegrate" and "reality shift[ed] to the margins." The book's narrator is a shifting, uncertain, multiple voice that moves from first- to second- to third-person address: an experiment in subjectivity. At one point she joins a movement of women workers, whose mark of belonging is a distinctive tattoo. These women incarnate a constituent power in that they are "drawing up the basis of a new constitution" to press "a demand that is neither conditional nor negotiable" for an expanded space of deterritorialized life: "How are we supposed to live if our bodies are cramped up against the walls? How can we go on living like that? We, the tattooed workers, insist our demand for living space is absolutely justified. The country must allow us to live with room enough to breathe." The narrator finds a temporary sense of community within this movement in which "nothing was in the least personal while at the same time it all belonged to us. I had attained the conviction that came with my tattoo."[148] So the bodily brand precedes and founds her belief, which in turn echoes a form of cooperation in which singularity and commonality are fused. At the same time, *Sacred Cow* registers a profound ambivalence around the difficulty of distinguishing good and bad habits, good and bad lines of flight. Nowhere is this more marked than with the birds that haunt the novel's action and flock together at its conclusion. The birds are in flight, "migrating, screeching with happiness or with pride or with panic, all singing different tunes." But it is unclear if this is a cacophony or a symphony, in that their screeching "was, none the less, harmonious, one of those contemporary harmonies where every solo is in fact carefully orchestrated." The narrator concludes that "above all the squawks were of pleasure, a guttural savage pleasure that put things human to shame." Yet she also recognizes "the murderousness of their flight.... The flock was criminal, it was obsessive" even as it transformed "cowardly flight" into "an epic of deliverance."[149] This ambivalence of joy and death, ecstasy and terror, indicates that the ethical response to authoritarianism also poses a specifically ethical problem, to which I will return in my conclusion: how to distinguish between good multitudes and bad.

Care for the self need not be solely conservative. Indeed, "cultivation of the self" implies growth nurtured through the adoption of good habits, "procedures, practices, and formulas," and the promotion of good encounters, "exchanges and communications, and at times even... institutions." Nor therefore is care for the self individualistic: it is "at once personal and social."[150] Foucault describes a dynamic concern for political community and the "practice of freedom" that takes place beyond the social pact for which all that counts is "a subject who has or does not have rights, who has had these rights either granted or removed by the institution of political society."[151] The care of the self is an ontological self-fashioning through habit. The persistence of habit becomes the insistence of an ever more expansive immanent subjectivity. It is what Foucault elsewhere terms "a historico-practical test of the limits we may go beyond... work carried out by ourselves upon ourselves as free beings."[152] It is also therefore a daily performance, or rather the drive to outperform the limits set by any given social field. It is the underside of biopower: an instance of the creativity and performativity to which we are all now enjoined, but no longer in the service of state or capital. Care for the self is the autonomy of habit.

Habits never fully coincide with the institutions and norms that structure society. But that is not simply because they are the passive residues of a past state of the field. Another way of thinking about "care for the self" is to observe that habits express *conatus*, that is, a subject's insistence on its own powers of existence. *Conatus* is the Latin for "endeavor" or "striving," and is part of a long philosophical tradition that includes Descartes, Hobbes, and perhaps particularly (as I will discuss in my conclusion) Spinoza. Bourdieu picks up on the term and defines it as "that combination of dispositions and interests associated with a particular class or social position which inclines agents to strive to reproduce at a constant or an increasing rate the properties constituting their social identity, without even needing to do this deliberately or consciously."[153] It is therefore an unconscious or habitual striving not only to reproduce but also to expand and fortify the self. Or as Bourdieu puts it in an explanation of his "historicist ontology," and as yet another riposte against the charge of determinism, "both habitus and field . . . are the site of a sort of *conatus*, of a tendency to perpetuate themselves in their being, to reproduce themselves in that which constitutes their existence and their identity." Hence, Bourdieu concludes, "it is not true to say that everything that people do or say is aimed at maximizing their social profit; but one may say that they do it to perpetuate or to augment their social being."[154] Whereas Bourdieu's constant discussion of capital in its various forms (cultural, symbolic, social, or financial) sometimes makes it seem as though he is unable to imagine forces beyond market interactions, here he points to *conatus* as a tendency that precedes and underwrites, or perhaps goes against, the principles of exchange. And insofar as a group or subject struggles "to perpetuate or to augment [its] social being," it is constantly struggling against the countervailing tendency of the field toward its own reproduction. The constant asymmetry between habitus and field indicates therefore a constant struggle between the two, even as habitus is also the vehicle by which a field is reproduced.

Bourdieu suggests that both habitus and field seek their own reproduction. But surely only habit expresses *conatus*. Ascribing such a subjectivity to the social field would be hyperfunctionalism indeed. Better, then, to see this asymmetrical struggle as pitting a *conatus* expressed through habit against the inertia of social institutions. This is the reverse of the picture Bourdieu otherwise seems to paint elsewhere: in this version of hysteresis, it is the field that lags behind habit. Habit is now the means by which a dynamic social subject seeks its own perpetuation or augmentation; and the institutions that structure the field have then to react to this subjectivity, to ensure their own reproduction and survival. Moreover, habit is also the vehicle by which that subject seeks (again, consciously or not) to change the social order, even to liberate itself from the constraints of a purported contractualism. The social game is a series of encounters or relations through which habit expresses a biopolitical struggle to constitute a social subject that would outperform or outstrip the institutions within which it is inscribed. On the one hand, we have the everyday life of repetitions and embodied periodicity; on the other, there is the liveliness of a creative striving, a *conatus* that goes beyond mere repetition. So, in short, the encounter between habitus and field is deeply ambivalent: it is where social order is reproduced; but it also comprises events that lead to what Bourdieu terms "a positive or negative surprise," to joyful or sad passions that in turn either strengthen or weaken the power of an oppositional subjectivity.[155] Biopower confronted by biopolitics. At this point, however, we must leave Bourdieu behind: a focus on habit alone cannot resolve this ambivalence. We have to examine the kinds of subjectivity constituted through habitus, and the possible transformation of *conatus* from "the drive of every individual being to the production of itself and the world" to what Negri envisages as "a general *conatus* of the organization of the freedom of all."[156] We need to understand habit as part of the constituent power of the multitude. The multitude is the subject of constituent power and also perhaps the agent of a revolution that would dissolve all structures of command and control.

Conclusion

Negri and Multitude

I am not going to die. I'm departing now,
on this day full of volcanoes,
for the multitude, for life.
Here I've settled these matters
...
At last, I'm free within beings.

Amid beings, like live air,
and from corralled solitude
I set forth to the multitude of combats,
free because my hand holds your hand,
conquering indomitable happiness.

—Pablo Neruda, *Canto General*

The question of the multitude is a thorn in the side of Western political thought.... However, this anguish and malaise are also ours. Our answer to the questions posed by constituent power is neither peaceful nor optimistic.

—Antonio Negri, *Insurgencies*

The Multitude as Subject

Cultural studies and civil society theory purport to be progressive projects, liberatory alternatives to the dominant social order. Yet cultural studies' notion of "counterhegemony" only reinforces all the populist assumptions upon which hegemony rests, leaving the state unquestioned. Likewise, for all its talk of "society against the state," civil society theory also merely entrenches state power by excluding other logics that might unsettle sovereign claims to legitimacy and universality. In short, both of these influential intellectual traditions appeal to and uphold constituted power, instantiated in and exercised through representation. Constituted power is the transcendent power of the sovereign subject, but it is a delegated power: it is the result of the prior articulation (in cultural studies' terms), mediation (for civil society theory), or, better, capture of a force that both anticipates and escapes it. Constituted power draws its strength from an immanent constituent power that precedes it, and which it claims to represent. Hence the power that a political order exercises is always derivative, and that order is itself the creation of constituent power. In the words of French thinker and politician the Abbé Sieyès, who first formulated this distinction in the context of France's 1789 Constituent Assembly, "in each of its parts a constitution is not the work of a constituted power but a constituent power. No type of delegated power can modify the conditions of its delegation."[1] For Sieyès, the constituent assembly was to harmonize these two modalities of power: to ensure that government was well constituted. But the very notion of good constitution presupposes a distinction between the constituent and the constituted; it assumes that the two are not necessarily or normally in harmony. Indeed, the split between them is at the heart of the "paradox of constitutionality": that the people, the presumed subject of power, are denied access to it; "the power they possess, it would appear, can only be exercised through constitutional forms already established or in the process of being established."[2]

Gilles Deleuze signals the discrepancy between constituent and constituted power in his examination of deterritorialized affect as an index of an immanent power that lies beyond hegemony. Affect precedes and resists the process of subjection that gives us stable emotions and bounded identities. The state's representational claims are ungrounded by an exodus that flees from the demands of categorical order to construct and inhabit a plane of immanence for which transcendence would be no more than a dead letter. Something always escapes. But affect is ambivalent: increasingly the state itself is becoming affective, not only in its suicidal plunges into terror, but also in the everyday modulations of biopower. As habit, affect continually encodes structures of domination, even immanently. Pierre Bourdieu's theorization of habitus outlines the mechanisms by which a practical, corporeal logic perpetuates an arbitrary social order "on the hither side of words and concepts" and so regardless of the presence or absence of ideological mechanisms. Assumptions and injunctions that go without saying can appear so engrained that Bourdieu tends toward functionalism. But history always intervenes, and crises reveal the asymmetry between habitus and field. For, like affect, habit in turn is ambivalent: it expresses a *conatus* that threatens to outstrip the structures that it constitutes. Affect and habit are both therefore components of a constituent power that escapes and exceeds constituted power; they hint at a subject that goes beyond the sovereign people posited by constitutionalism. Affect and habit are the first two concepts of a theory of posthegemony, but they lead on to a third: the multitude.

The multitude is a collective subject that gathers on affect's line of flight, consolidates in habit, and expresses itself through constituent power. So the concept of the multitude reclaims subjectivity from its disrepute in much twentieth-century political theory. For Louis Althusser, for instance, history is "a process without a subject."[3] But by contrast Antonio Negri, in an analysis first presented on Althusser's invitation, stresses subjectivity as a key element in his reinvigoration of Marxism, his "Marx beyond Marx." In an implicit rebuke to Althusser and coauthor Etienne Balibar's focus on "reading *Capital*," Negri criticizes "the objectification of categories in *Capital*" and praises instead "the *Grundrisse* [as] a text dedicated to revolutionary subjectivity."[4] But the multitude is a subject of a very particular kind: it is not the traditional working class, whose identity derives from its place in the process of production and hence its relation to capital; nor is it either the rational individual beloved of the social sciences or one of the delimited identities of cultural studies' multicultural alliance. The multitude is immanent, and it spills out of transcendent categories. As Paolo Virno notes in his discussion of "multitude as subjectivity," this is "an amphibian subject" that is neither individual nor the site of individuality's dissolution.[5] Rather, the multitude is preindividual in that it is rooted in affect and habit, in "the sensory organs, motor skills apparatus, perception abilities"; but it also constitutes a dynamic "social individual" whose principle of commonality is "general intellect," the virtuoso performance of communicative collaboration. The multitude forms as bodies come together through resonances established by good encounters, but it is always open to new encounters, and so to new transformations. In the multitude, "the 'many' persevere as 'many' without aspiring to the unity of the state."[6]

The term "multitude" is taken from early modern political philosophy, and above all from Benedict de Spinoza. But the concept's contemporary use is also rooted in the Italian workerist and autonomist traditions from which both Virno and Negri derive. Workerism stresses the independent agency of the working class. It argues that the dynamic of capitalist development is driven by proletarian subjectivity, which generates crises that threaten the process by which surplus value is appropriated. In response, capital reconfigures the labor process, introduces new technologies, provides circumscribed concessions to labor demands, and thereby transforms the composition of the working class. But this class recomposition allows for even more expansive expressions of insurgent subjectivity that go on to provoke deeper crises. In Michael Hardt's words, "worker subjectivity, then, is determined in the specific mode of production and the composition of this subjectivity, in turn, provides the model for revolutionary organization."[7] From this perspective, the multitude is the culmination of a long history of struggle; it is the form of subjectivity that presses revolutionary demands on all fronts, presaging capitalism's terminal crisis. Hardt and Negri argue that the multitude is the final stage in the sequence of struggles, that it is an insurgent subject with the capacity for full autonomy: "The multitude provides us with a social subject and a logic of social organization that makes possible today, for the very first time, the realization of democracy."[8] Hence Hardt describes Negri's Marxism as "projective" rather than "critical."[9] It affirms the emergence of this new subject, the multitude.

The recourse to Spinoza, however, shows another side to the multitude's subjectivity, one more in tune with critical Marxism and more agnostic about prospects for liberation today. For Spinoza's theorization of the multitude comes from a very different context: the seventeenth-century bourgeois revolution and capitalism's ascendance, rather than its demise. The multitude can therefore be seen as a historical subject: less the emergence of the new, the culmination of a process coming to its end, than the return of the same, the continuation of a cycle. The multitude, too, is ambivalent. Historically, constituent leads to constituted power. Though the multitude initiates revolution, all too soon something goes wrong. What begins as immanence and liberation, as innovation and creativity, ends up as transcendence and normalization, as the state form and its repressive apparatuses. Constituent power makes and remakes society, but the fruit of its labors to date is the world we see around us, characterized by oppression and exploitation. In Negri's words, constituted power "feeds on" constituent power; "without this strength it could not exist." And though the multitude resists domination, "this resistance is dissolved in the dialectic, over and over again." Its status as subject, the subject of history, is consistently denied: "the multitude is always objectified. Its name is reduced to a curse: *vulgus*, or worse, *Pöbel*. Its strength is expropriated.... Modernity is therefore the negation of any possibility that the multitude may express itself as subjectivity."[10] The multitude is like the proletarian: creator of the social world, but alienated within it. And why should we believe that the conditions are now ripe for autonomy, for a liberation of constituent power in and for itself? It would seem more likely that the multitude will simply call forth a new state form, perhaps all the more repressive and insidious than before. Indeed, is this not already happening with the rise of the decentered and diffuse sovereignty that Negri and Hardt term "Empire"? Moreover, even were it achievable, Negri's utopia of a self-realized multitude, "the most extreme deterritorialization" and "the revolution of the eternal," is perhaps too invested in a theological chiliasm whose vision of eternal life is scarcely distinguishable from eternal death.[11] For if all objectivity and constituted power are abolished, history itself comes to an end.

The multitude runs like a red thread through the history of Latin America, but its ambivalence is visible at every turn. From the conquest, and even before, to the current so-called political "left turns," the multitude constitutes the particular "New World" that we call the Americas. Recovering this hidden history both shows the asymmetry between constituent and constituted power, the ways in which the multitude as subject always exceeds the object of its constitution, and also demonstrates the dangers that attend its insurgent subjectivity. What, for instance, could be more cataclysmic than the conquistadors' rampage through the region? The legacy of their wholesale destruction of indigenous civilizations and the impact of ethnocentric subalternization continue into the present. But it would be wrong to see the conquest simply as the imposition of colonial order from above, or to identify resistance solely with the natives' defense of their territories. Pre-Columbian states incarnated their own forms of constituted power, while at the heart of the imperial project was a rebellious subjectivity that constantly threatened to outstrip and destabilize the order that it itself constituted. From the attempted mutiny on Columbus's first voyage to the bloody disorder that characterized the Spanish settlements on Hispaniola or in Peru, the energy that imperialism unleashed always rebounded against the regime that sponsored it. The tale of conquistador Lope de Aguirre is exemplary: sent down the Amazon in search of El Dorado, Aguirre overthrew his expedition leader and declared himself "the Wrath of God, Prince of Freedom... Lord of all South America."[12] But this great usurper felt that it was he who had been betrayed by the Spanish state. Aguirre was merely taking the logic of colonialism to its apocalyptic consequences, keeping faith with the insurgent impulses that drove its voracious expansion. He asserted the subjectivity of those whom the king regarded as subject to royal sovereignty, and so questioned the legitimacy of the Empire's appropriation of constituent power. As his 1561 letter to King Philip II puts it: "You cannot rightfully draw any revenue from these lands, where you yourself have risked nothing, until those who have laboured here have been rewarded."[13]

Colonial and postcolonial states had to adapt and to recompose their constituted power in response to the various instantiations of multitudinous subjectivity. So, for instance, to regulate conquistador excesses the Spanish crown proposed the "New Laws of the Indies" (1542) and the Toledo Reforms (1569 to 1581). To ensure regular supply chains and guarantee trade contracts in the face of corruption, fraud, and piracy, it instituted the formidable imperial bureaucracy that was the Casa de Contratación. In the eighteenth century, creole dissatisfaction and indigenous rebellions prompted the Bourbon Reforms. Then the so-called liberators in turn struggled to arrest the forces they had set loose in the nineteenth-century wars of independence, a task whose futility was memorably encapsulated in liberator Simón Bolívar's exasperated declaration that "those who serve a revolution plough the sea."[14] Subsequent founding fictions of the postcolonial nation-states, such as the Argentine Domingo Sarmiento's *Facundo,* set to forging a nation in the face of the unruly energies of brigands and gauchos who roamed its territory. And so on into the twentieth century: state-sponsored indigenism in Mexico aimed to compensate for the failures of nineteenth-century technocracy; populism in the Southern Cone purported to order the seething mass of migrants who provoked new crises while apparently solving the old ones; national liberation movements were torn between the twin impulses of liberation and nation formation; and neoliberalism arose as an antipolitical response to the profoundly political challenges posed by Guevarism, third worldism, and student radicalism in the 1960s and early 1970s. Finally, the turns to the left that usher in leaders such as Venezuela's Hugo Chávez and Bolivia's Evo Morales, Brazil's Luiz Inácio Lula da Silva and Argentina's Néstor and Cristina Kirchner, are simply the latest response on the part of constituted power to the ever more expansive demands of the multitude as expressed for example in the São Paulo labor radicalism of the 1980s, the Caracazo of 1989, the Argentine rebellion of 2001, or the Bolivian gas protests of 2004.

Throughout Latin American history, the multitude comes first. As Negri and coauthor Giuseppe Cocco put it, even "the so-called antimodern elements found in the cultural histories and oppositional traditions of each of the great areas of underdevelopment... can be understood not as burdensome legacies of the past but rather as creative elements of another modernity, another modernization." Hence "liberation takes place beforehand," expressed in a "thousand forms of Exodus."[15] This is the productive subjectivity that kick-starts development. Against dependency theory, Negri and Cocco argue that it is the state and its protectionist impulses that have blocked the region's economic and social progress. At the same time, the state is the beneficiary of the multitude's productivity. A history of the Latin American multitude is also therefore an account of the numerous attempts by state functionaries and social elites to construct the fiction of a pact that would bind culture to politics, and subordinate constituent to constituted power. Hence I am more cautious than Negri and Cocco about any "new pact" that results from the election of left-wing governments, such as in Brazil and Argentina, over the past few years. They claim that "this constituent New Deal organizes the strength of the subaltern classes such that they are presented, nationally and internationally, as multitudes—that is, no longer as objects of representation but as subjects."[16] I am skeptical about the radicalism of Lula or the Kirchners, or even Morales or Chávez. Indeed, the 2006 squabble between Néstor Kirchner and his Uruguayan counterpart, former Tupamaro Tabaré Vázquez, over a paper mill allegedly polluting the River Uruguay, which divides their two countries, showed that both were still happy to make populist moves in defense of national sovereignty. Likewise, and for all their internationalist gestures, the governments of Brazil, Bolivia, and Venezuela are no less dedicated to upholding constituted power.

In this chapter, I return to my previous case studies: Peronism, Sendero Luminoso, Central American national liberation struggles, and new social movements in Chile. Previously I showed how the paradigms of cultural studies and civil society break down in the context of an examination of Latin American political and cultural history, and I argued for a focus on affect and habit. This final chapter sketches the physiognomy of the Latin American multitude and outlines how a theory of posthegemony reframes analysis of the region. I revisit these case studies to highlight the relationship of constituent to constituted power, and therefore the double inscription of power in posthegemony, as well as the points at which that constitution starts to dissolve. In the epilogue that follows, I add a final reflection on the situation in Venezuela: events there demonstrate both the failure of the contemporary state form and the urgent need for new theoretical tools to take us beyond impasses that are practical as much as they are conceptual. Twentieth- and twenty-first-century Latin America has been a cauldron of social and political experimentation and creativity, a veritable laboratory of rebellion, mobilization, and counterinsurgency. It is a spur and a challenge to political theory.

As the subject of constituent power, the multitude is productive. Hence its centrality and its ambivalence from the point of view of constituted power. The multitude is not only economically productive but also socially productive: indeed, the multitude produces everyday life itself; its activity is immediately biopolitical. Biopower's parasitical relationship to this productive power is like capital's relationship to labor, characterized both by indebtedness and by an anxiety that leads to denial. The multitude cannot be acknowledged directly but has to be misrepresented as a dependent subject in an inversion that posits the state as the sole source of power and civil and political society as the only arenas for its exercise. The state is fetishized, hegemony is substituted for any other conception of politics, and civil society is instituted as a steering mechanism for the efficient control of state power. All the errors of cultural studies and civil society follow on. The multitude is recast in identitarian terms: as people, as class, or as a set of discrete social identities. But these categories are unstable, and they break down as the nomad takes flight in exodus, while in the persistence of *conatus* the multitude constitutes a resonant community through quotidian encounters.

Insistently productive and self-organizing, the multitude is more than some mere subaltern remainder or excess. Like the multitude, the subaltern is beyond representation, an insurgent betrayal of constituted power. Moreover, as Alberto Moreiras puts it, "subaltern negation" is posthegemonic in that it is a "refusal to submit to hegemonic interpellation, an exodus from hegemony."[17] But the subaltern is a limit concept, "the absolute limit of the place where history is narrativized into logic," in postcolonial theorist Gayatri Spivak's words, whereas for Negri the multitude is both central and beyond limit.[18] Subalternity is defined negatively: for Indian historian Ranajit Guha, it is the "demographic difference" or what is left when the elite are subtracted from the total population.[19] The multitude, by contrast, is defined positively: it is "the ontological name of fullness against emptiness, of production against parasitical leftovers."[20] The subaltern is more abject than subject; indeed, Moreiras describes subalternity as "the non-subject of the political."[21] But despite these differences, subaltern excess is an index of the presence of the multitude, indicating the repeated failures of representation and so the asymmetry between constituent and constituted power. Subaltern remainder points to the surplus of constituent power, which can never be fully captured by the state. And so subaltern insurgency can be a gateway to the multitude, whose positive sense of commonality often starts as negation, as what Marxist theorist John Holloway calls "a scream of refusal."[22]

Subaltern studies splits subalternity off from hegemony, but this insistence on radical difference only reinforces the hegemonic project to establish a limit between inside and outside, between people and nonpeople, civilization and barbarism. The concept of the multitude offers a way out of such false dichotomies by leaving hegemony behind altogether. But how is the multitude's subjectivity produced, and how does it organize (and care for) itself? In the rest of this chapter, I outline the principles of the multitude's subjective constitution and self-organization that break decisively with hegemony and subalternity alike. I also show, however, that these principles introduce their own ambivalences. First, the multitude is radically *open:* it tends toward the absolute immanence of what Spinoza terms Substance itself, and so undoes any distinction between social identity and otherness. As Hardt and Negri comment, the multitude is at least "potentially all-inclusive."[23] Second, refusing the contractual demands of state claims to transcendence, the multitude's immanent expansion proceeds by means of *contiguity* and contact, in resonances established through affective encounter. It develops through what Negri calls a "physics of society," experimental conjunctions and aleatory events whose outcomes can never be fully predicted.[24] Indeed, there can be no guarantee that what results is not a bad multitude, a truly monstrous and corrupt figure of devastation and destruction. Third, then, any analysis of the multitude has to attend to the play between *commonality* and corruption. Hardt and Negri make polyvalent commonality a defining feature of the multitude, and corruption the key characteristic of what they term Empire. But it can be hard to distinguish between corruption and commonality, especially in that they both express a similar propensity to connection. For, fourth, the multitude is also defined by the links and *continuities* that it establishes. Whereas the state incarnates a series of discontinuous forms, the multitude manifests itself in the crises that attend these forms' dissolution and reconstitution. Hardt and Negri argue that the preconditions are now present for the multitude's final liberation from all state strictures, for the emergence of a pure subjectivity, "a constituent power that no longer produces constitutions separate from itself, but rather is itself constitution."[25] This is their political project. An end to separation would call forth the Kingdom of God on Earth, the actualization of a Spinozan paradise of blessed communion between nature and divinity. Perhaps. But we might hesitate before such a teleo-theological vision. Posthegemony theory is poised in the tension between this project and its critique.

Open

The multitude is open and expansive. In Hardt and Negri's definition, "the multitude is a multiplicity, a plane of singularities, an open set of relations, which is not homogeneous or identical with itself and bears an indistinct, inclusive relation to those outside of it." Hence it differs from "the people," which by contrast "tends toward identity and homogeneity internally while posing its difference from and excluding what remains outside of it. Whereas the multitude is an inconclusive constituent relation, the people is a constituted synthesis that is prepared for sovereignty."[26] The multitude makes its presence felt with the rupture of social order that characterizes constituent power, "a force that bursts apart, breaks, interrupts, unhinges any preexisting equilibrium and any possible continuity."[27] Even when constituted power has closed off constituent power, to delimit the multitude and to convert it into a people, to establish an inside and an outside, the multitude presses against and transgresses those limits in its constant tendency toward exodus, deterritorialization, and flight. The multitude is the turbulence that forever threatens to destabilize popular identifications and loyalties. Thanks to this dynamic tendency, the multitude is never pregiven or preformed. It is a subject that continually creates and re-creates itself; its expansion is also a manifestation of care for the social self. But this recursiveness is far from solipsistic: indeed, the multitude's radical openness means that it tends, Negri suggests, toward the absolute and so toward a democracy that Hardt and Negri claim will likewise be "full and absolute."[28]

The multitude breaks with any contract or compact that would limit its expansiveness and close off constituent power. It therefore goes against the dominant tradition of modern political philosophy that for Negri is represented by Hobbes, Rousseau, and Hegel. Against these theorists of a contract mediated by transcendence, Negri turns to Spinoza's "constitutive ontology" for "a theory of the political composition of subjectivity" whose only limit is "perfection" itself.[29] In Virno's words, the multitude's reemergence opens an "old dispute" that had seemed lost: "It was the notion of the 'people' which prevailed. 'Multitude' is the losing term, the concept which got the worst of it." But now "this once defeated notion" may well be "taking its dramatic revenge."[30] Posthegemony is more than what comes after hegemony's patent demise; it is also a critical examination of the epoch in which hegemony apparently held sway. Negri argues that "the perspective of constituent power puts the contractualist position under attack and recognizes in it the inevitable deferral to transcendence, to constituted power and its apology."[31] In place of the contract's enclosures, and its separation of people from power, subaltern from hegemon, the multitude opens up the immanent frontier that is *kairòs*, the temporality of what is to come.

The contract converts constituent into constituted power, multitude into people. This is modernity's grand narrative: a series of defeats for constituent power. For looking around us we see that, reconfigured and recomposed, sovereignty appears to lie at the end of every road. Hence the classic paradox of political theory, most famously expressed in the first lines of eighteenth-century Enlightenment philosopher Jean-Jacques Rousseau's *The Social Contract:* "Man was born free, and everywhere he is in chains. . . . How has this change come about? I do not know."[32] The free subjectivity of the multitude is constantly superseded by the constituted power of the state. Openness and expansiveness are replaced by closure, interiority, and boundedness. Even the most revolutionary beginnings seem to go wrong, get bogged down, or transmute into totalitarianism. For every Constituent Assembly, there is a Terror and a Thermidor; for every Winter Palace stormed, a subsequent Purge. So revolution comes to appear impossible, naïve at best and dangerous at worst. And yet the fact that the impulse to liberation endlessly returns, that constituent power reemerges and constituted power frays at the edges, means that the question has to be posed again: What goes wrong? What happens to the moment of liberation that is so soon closed down? Liberalism's answer to this question is the contract, presented as the happy and safely inviolate resolution at the origin of society itself.

In answer to his own question, Rousseau posits the "assumption" of an originary contract that is embedded within society and never up for renegotiation: "The slightest modification" of its clauses "would make them empty and ineffectual." Indeed, the contract is never even discussed because it is "the same everywhere, and everywhere tacitly recognized and accepted"; it has become a matter of habit. In these first few pages of *The Social Contract*'s opening section, then, freedom quickly mutates from a birthright to something always already relinquished in "the complete transfer of each associate, with all his rights, to the whole community."[33] The contract explains and justifies the shift from freedom to total alienation, from constituent to constituted power. In and through the contract, individuals are assumed to have transferred their rights to a higher order. But paradoxically it is only through the contract that they become individuals, bearers of civil rights (as well as responsibilities). A sovereign power on the one hand and civil rights on the other are the twin pillars presumed by the contractualist tradition, which stretches from Rousseau back to Thomas Hobbes in the seventeenth century, and forward to U.S. philosopher John Rawls in the twentieth. And Rawls argues that a "veil of ignorance" has to be drawn over the moment in which agreement to these fundamental principles is first secured.[34] For contract theory, the basis of social order is an unquestionable consent to which we are now habituated.

The social contract separates at the same time that it unites. It marks off the civil from the natural. For those who are assumed to be party to it, the contract is envisaged as absolute and without remainder. Rousseau argues that "the transfer [of rights] being carried out unreservedly, the union between the associates is as perfect as can be, and none of them has any further requirements to add." But the notion of a transfer of rights presupposes a sphere of nature that predates the institution of the contract: the "human race . . . change[s] its mode of existence" as through the contract it overcomes "the obstacles to men's self-preservation in the state of nature."[35] So civil society and civil rights are defined negatively, in opposition to this state of nature that Hobbes famously portrays as a "warre . . . of every man against every man" in which the "life of man [is] solitary, poore, nasty, brutish, and short." The contract marks off the social from the natural, and demarcates civilized community in its contrast to the "continuall feare, and danger of violent death" that preceded it.[36] Only in the relative safety provided by the contract can industry, science, and the arts prosper. But the notion of an outside lingers, and the contract is legitimated by the fear of that fear that it purports to have banished. Civil society depends upon its outside, upon the affect that the outside is said to instill.

The limit established through the contract is spatial, and so geopolitical, as well as temporal, and so historical. In addition to a mythic narrative of origin, contract theory posits a distinction between coevals, or rather between peoples with history and peoples without. At the global periphery, the state of nature persists, and there is no better instance of this than the native peoples of the Americas: "For the savage people of *America* . . . have no government at all; and live today in that brutish manner."[37] As well as anchoring a fictional foundation for civil society, the contract also sets off a civilized interiority from a subaltern exterior in the present. Even Rousseau, theorist of the "noble savage," agrees that only with the establishment of a "civil state" are man's "faculties exercised and improved, his ideas amplified, his feelings ennobled." Within the terms of the social contract the citizen can be "an intelligent being and a man"; outside, he is a noncitizen, "a limited and stupid animal."[38] And just as the historical narrative tells of a transition that is absolute and without remainder, so for geopolitics there can strictly be no relation between civilized and savage save that the latter agrees to the total alienation of his (or her) natural right, in other words, gives up his (or her) savage "nature." In a nutshell, this is the justification for the Spanish *Requerimiento*.

Within the social order that it defines, the contract effects a further double articulation of separation and unification: it establishes a state that rises transcendent over a people. Whereas the subaltern outside is abject and voiceless, the hegemonic inside is organized as a hierarchy that redistributes subjectivity in line with the principles of representation. A single institution, Hobbes's Leviathan, stands in for the multitude that enters into the contract, and assumes the status of a transcendent subject. This is, for Hobbes, "the Essence of the Common-wealth," that there be "One Person, of whose Acts a great Multitude, by mutuall Covenants one with another, have made themselves every one the Author, to the end he may use the strength and means of them all, as he shall think expedient, for their Peace and Common Defence." And though this account seems to position the state as the beneficiary of the multitude's constituent power, contract theory maintains that constituted power is in fact society's great benefactor. We are all in debt to the state. For Hobbes, the best comparison is with the divine: the contract enables "the Generation of that great LEVIATHAN, or rather (to speake more reverently) of that *Mortall God*, to which we owe under the *Immortall God*, our peace and defence."[39] A civil society is also a civic religion in which the product of the multitude's contraction is fetishized as a benevolent deity.

To represent the multitude is also to eliminate it. In place of a fluid mass of variable singularities, the contract shapes a people composed of individual citizens. In principle equally subject to the law, citizens are, notionally at least, therefore equal in both rights and responsibilities. Differences in power and affect, the correlate of distinctions between singular bodies, are no longer relevant. All power has been transferred to the sovereign, and affect has been banished in the name of a rationality that deals in disembodied subjects rather than embodied subjectivity. What is more, citizens have no need to fear each other, and so are able to work together constructively and industriously. Hence the contract is also envisaged as marking the emergence of the people, a body of individuals united and homogenized by their common relation to the state, a collective identity that can thus be regarded as a single juridical individual. The multitude's multiplicity is transformed into the unity that characterizes the people. Hobbes explains in *De Cive* ("On the Citizen") how the establishment of a single transcendent power retrospectively constructs a unified people; how, in other words, the circuit of constituent and constituted power folds back on the multitude to eliminate it from civil society. For "if the . . . multitude do contract one with another, that the will of one man, or the agreeing wills of the major part of them, shall be received for the will of all; then it becomes one person." As a result, "it is oftener called the people, than the multitude."[40] Insofar, therefore, as the multitude contracts, and is represented, it becomes the people. Yet all this leaves the multitude peculiarly dislocated: like the subaltern, it is outside civil society in that it preexists the contract that constitutes juridical persons; but it also stands on the threshold of civility in that the people arise from the multitude, or rather the dyad of people and state replaces an immanent multitude; moreover, it threatens to arise again within the polity, with every movement to reopen the constituent process. The multitude is inside and outside as well as at the border. It confounds the very distinctions that the contract is meant to institute, and yet it founds the contract itself. Contractualism both reacts to and depends upon the multitude, even as it tries to eliminate it.

The multitude is never fully banished from the social; the contract is never fully effective. However much contract theorists wish to expel the multitude to a subaltern exterior, Spinoza argues that natural rights are never entirely abandoned: "Every man retains some part of his right, in dependence on his own decision, and no one else's." This is Spinoza's break with contract theory, his challenge to the purported absolutism of the state. Spinoza claims that there can be no absolute transfer of rights, that constituent power can never be fully alienated: "For men have never so far ceded their power as to cease to be an object of fear to the rulers who received such power and right."[41] Constituent power lurks behind any constitution and can always return to upset and undermine it. Hence in his *Political Treatise* Spinoza argues that aristocracy, any system in which the few purport to rule over the many, is "in practice . . . not absolute [because] the multitude is a cause of fear to the rulers, and therefore succeeds in retaining for itself some liberty, which it asserts and holds as its own, if not by an express law, yet on a tacit understanding." The multitude constantly disrupts and unsettles claims to sovereignty and to closure. The only absolute is absolute immanence: "If there be any absolute dominion, it is, in fact, that which is held by an entire multitude."[42] Constituent power is always in some measure retained by the multitude, which therefore resists becoming people and tends instead toward what Negri describes as "a general horizon of power" and "life, always open."[43]

The social contract cannot simply be assumed as originary and settled; it has continually to be made and remade in everyday life. The contract is not foundational. It is, rather, an effect of the state. The state declares the contract settled in order retrospectively to conjure up the people as the cornerstone of social organization. In Hardt and Negri's words, "the modern conception of the people is in fact a product of the nation-state."[44] And the people are merely the multitude misrecognized, delimited, and so alienated from itself. Virno therefore describes the multitude as modernity's "defining concept." The multitude grounds the constitution of popular citizenship, but its constituent power has to be denied in the name of a community imagined in terms of lineage and enclosure rather than rupture and openness. The contract purports to establish a bounded social order, but the multitude always escapes: it "shuns political unity, is recalcitrant to obedience, never achieves the status of juridical personage, and is thus unable to make promises, to make pacts, or to acquire and transfer rights." Society's founding tension between constituent and constituted power translates into an opposition between multitude and people: "The citizens, when they rebel against the State, are 'the *Multitude* against the *People*.' "[45] But such rebellions are not confrontations between inside and outside: rather, the inside opens up to the outside; the people desert their role as people; the multitude escapes *from* the people. No promises, no pacts, and no consent: this is an uncertain world of treachery and deceit, of disarticulation and exodus. The multitude is essentially untrustworthy, an immeasurable force exercising what Spinoza sees as its unshakeable right "to act deceitfully, and to break . . . compacts."[46] Throughout modernity, the state's aim has been to convert the multitude into the people, to remind its citizens of their promises, and to establish consent to consent, the hegemony of hegemony. The apogee of this stratagem is populism, one of the most effective of state discourses. Populism posits the people as a homogenous mass bound to institutional authority by an affective relationship to some transcendent fetish. But a latent distrust still surrounds the concept of the popular, as though to acknowledge that behind the people lurks the multitude, and that the risk of appealing to popular forces is that the multitude may break out and overwhelm the state.

Peronism shows how populism's invocation and suppression of the multitude runs the risk of disaster. In October 1950, at Peronism's height, an article in the magazine *Mundo Argentino* entitled "The Multitude Is the People" rehearses the gesture that simultaneously appeals to the multitude and converts it into a people: "Until a short while ago," it states, "we Argentines did not know what the multitude was. We would talk about the people, and others would talk about the people, without anyone having seen its face." An unknown (indeed, unknowable) multitude has to be converted into the expected people. This slippage between multitude and people is resolved only by reference to some defining event, here the demonstration of October 17, 1945, that brought Peronism to power: "In October 1945 the multitude in the street took us by surprise – a multitude that was the people – and we saw its face. And a few months later, in February 1946, we saw it act in the elections."[47] The people, then, is constituted in a retroactive act of naming that puts the multitude in a relation with the state. The Peronist multitude can be equated with the people once it is identified with a leader, Perón, and reframed within a hegemonic process, here the 1946 elections. The multitude comes as if from nowhere, but its arrival is articulated as though it were long expected, predestined. Except that it is the people who have been expected, and the multitude is invoked only to provide evidence for popular will and agency, as the body to which the people will put a face. The multitude threatens personal identity: the article's anonymous author writes, "I too forgot myself, confused among the multitude." Memory returns only once identity can be recast in terms of the nation-state, forming a nexus of individualism, patriotism, and the popular, bound by the low-intensity affect of contentment: "At nightfall I escaped back home, very content with myself, with my fatherland, and with its people."[48]

Populism is a meditation upon constituent power: it identifies, appropriates, and then disavows the multitude in the name of the people, but remains anxiously aware that the multitude always returns. In Peronism's case, this anxiety centers on the October 17 demonstration mentioned above, as though in recognition that the regime's founding moment did not, in fact, accord with its own imaginary. Peronism's primal scene was only gradually, retroactively, brought into line with Peronist self-representation by being reimagined and recast in the yearly anniversaries re-creating the 1945 events. Annual celebrations produced a succession of copies ever closer to the original as it was (and had to be) imagined by Peronism. But the effort of re-creation reveals the preoccupation that the initial demonstration, and thus Peronism itself, belonged less to the people than to the multitude. Peronism's portrayal of October 17 and its subsequent anniversaries cast the multitude as unrepresentable, overwhelming, and fanatical, but by channeling these attributes through the figures of Perón and Evita attempted to represent, subsume, and pacify these energies as, now, belonging to a people celebrating what came to be called a "day of loyalty." Hence *Mundo Argentino*'s account of the 1948 celebration invokes a "huge multitude" that the magazine's photographic spread can only fail to represent, as its captions make clear: "The photograph shows only a partial aspect of the multitude" taking part in "scenes of indescribable enthusiasm."[49] Any attempt to convey the experience of the event is subsumed by sublime awe prompted by a power that could overwhelm the political and geographical landscape of the state: the multitude is everywhere, picnicking on the grass and stopping traffic, its waves of energy and affect lapping at the walls of the presidential palace. To prevent the multitude from swamping the state's own position of enunciation, it has to be put into a determinable (representable, reproducible) relation with the state. Populism's "balcony effect" insinuates a limit between multitude and state, substituting a social contract for the social *contact* that the multitude desires and threatens, and thus recomposes the multitude as the people.

Populism's balcony effect consists in the classic cinematic device of shot and reverse shot applied to public spectacle: the multitude and the Peróns are not represented together; rather, a (partial, inadequate) vision of the multitude is followed by an image of the balcony from which Juan and Evita address them. The cut from multitude to balcony (and vice versa) presents each as in meaningful (logical rather than accidental) relation with the other. These are the classic images of Peronism: the medium shot view (from in front and slightly below) of Evita on the balcony, her arms raised in salute, coupled with a long shot from above of the crowds in the plaza. *Mundo Argentino* and other print publications of the time mimic this cinematic effect in photographic spreads juxtaposing these two perspectives, making the accompanying commentary almost redundant: the multitude is gathered "to listen attentively to what the president of the republic and his lady wife have to say"; Evita's speech provokes "repeated demonstrations of warm enthusiasm." Enthusiasm is given meaning (is now described and qualified, and so domesticated) by her discourse. What exactly she says goes unreported; it is enough that affect be subordinated to the word. Pairing the eminently representable Peróns with the otherwise unrepresentable multitude gives meaning and visibility to what had been unintelligible: the multitude becomes people. The cut established in the sequence taking us from the plaza to the balcony (and back again) both joins and separates: the multitude's heterogeneity becomes homogeneity as its various partial aspects (all that can be represented conventionally) are joined in what Ernesto Laclau terms a "chain of equivalence," dependent upon their relation with those on the balcony. So contemporary newsreel footage presents a narrative in which a demonstration gathers and builds from groups originating in the most diverse locations. These singular bodies emerge from the hidden recesses of the city and its suburbs and encounter each other en route, forming an increasingly monstrous throng. Once Evita and Perón step onto the stage, however, the balcony effect takes hold: shot, reverse shot; this multitude is represented (literally, presented again) as the people whose gathering is retroactively intelligible by reference to the balcony, and to the state. And as this relation is established and the multitude reduced to a homogenous (hegemonic) bloc, properties of the multitude can be transferred to the figures on high: the Peróns acquire their own sublimity as, larger than life, they now dominate the frame with a power borrowed from the thousands thronging the square who give their presence meaning.

When the balcony effect is derailed, populism threatens to collapse as the multitude reemerges as an open, insurrectionary presence. This is the risk populism takes, and it is nowhere more apparent than in the trauma of Evita Perón's renunciation on August 22, 1951. At this tumultuous open meeting, in front of a crowd two million strong, Evita fended off demands that she stand for election as vice president. In his novel *Santa Evita,* Argentine author Tomás Eloy Martínez narrates this episode as a film script pieced together from newsreel depictions. Indeed, the demonstration's staging was perhaps the most fully cinematic of all of Peronism's set pieces. Scaffolding set up in the broad Avenida 9 de Julio held a platform flanked by two enormous photographs of Juan and Evita. Juan Schroeder's documentary *Evita* (1974?) has footage of the events, and shows how newsreel cameras cut from this huge screen to the multitude frantically waving handkerchiefs below.[50] Eloy Martínez describes "the ebb and flow of the multitude, dangerous surges to get closer to the idol"; in the newsreels, the balcony effect is maintained for some time, but the images become increasingly agitated, with fewer cuts and more pans as the camera darts from crowd to platform. Eloy Martínez writes that "Perón looks dwarfed," but it is when Evita comes out, as daylight fades, that the spectacle truly disintegrates.[51] The newsreels show Evita's image compressed into one corner of the frame as the camera simultaneously tries to take in as much of the multitude as possible. Evita seems lost, about to disappear from the *mise en scène.* Peronism's mechanisms of control fail as the crowds demand that Evita accept her nomination. Evita can only defer a decision, but her attempts to impose a contract on the multitude (asking them to wait four days, twenty-four hours, a few hours) are overwhelmed by their demands for immediacy and contact.

Through Evita, Peronism operates a particularly powerful conversion mechanism, framing multitude as people and thereby setting bounds and establishing transcendence, giving birth to the state in its double articulation. But Peronism enters into crisis at the very moment of its greatest success: populism promises immediacy and welcomes affective investment, but only so long as a line is drawn, a limit establishing the people as the body whose representability depends upon its distance from its leaders. Without this distance, populism finds its "own" people strictly incomprehensible. Alive, Evita fails finally to maintain that separation and has to renounce and be renounced: the balcony becomes "the altar on which she [is] sacrificed."[52] Dead, of course, Evita is another matter; dead, she helps to ensure Peronism's continued meaningfulness. Echoing a similar declaration by the famed eighteenth-century indigenous rebel Túpac Amaru, the inscription on Evita's tomb still promises, "I will return and be millions."

The contract sets limits. It separates the civil from the subaltern; it establishes a hierarchy in which a unitary people are subject to and represented by a sovereign state; and it simultaneously invokes and displaces the multitude as the subjectivity that stands on the threshold of civility. All this is legitimated by the assumption of prior consent to sovereignty. Hence Negri argues that the contractualist tradition is "the inevitable deferral to transcendence, to constituted power, and its apology."[53] By contrast, the multitude insists on immanence and materiality and on a constituent power that is "the utter limit of any politics," or alternatively a vision of a "politics that survives the dissolution of governments, the disruption of legal systems, and the collapse of instituted powers."[54] The only limit to constituent power is the ever-shifting voyage into the future, or what Negri terms the "to-come." This is *kairòs:* "the moment of rupture and opening of temporality . . . the modality of time through which being opens itself, attracted by the void at the limit of time, and it thus decides to fill that void." Open to the to-come, constituent power generates being itself: "In becoming power, the multitude generates. . . . The generation of the multitude innovates being."[55] Hence for Negri, following Spinoza, the multitude tends toward the absolute, absolute immanence, a true absolute rather than the pernicious and false absolutism of the contract. Its generation proceeds through the contiguity of singular encounters, the commonality of collective constitution, and the continuity of historical tendency. But at each stage, ambivalence abounds.

Contiguous

The multitude comprises a multiplicity of singular bodies organized in a nonhierarchical, open network in which each body is in touch with every other body. Its principle of organization is contiguity: contact rather than contract; affect rather than effect. Whereas a contract fixes discrete identities that are stable over time, whose relations are governed by an appeal to transcendent law, the multitude is fluid, its relations structured by immanent affect and habit. The multitude is always in generation: *kairòs*, the temporality of the event and of constitution, straddles past, present, and future. Its singular bodies are perpetually encountering and reencountering each other (and others), contingently and contiguously. But for all its fluidity and mutability, this generative process need not be chaotic; constituent power gains force according to principles of self-organization, care for the self. The contacts between the bodies that compose, or come to compose, the multitude follow an immanent ethics of the encounter. Spinoza's account of such an ethics outlines a social physics in which there are both good and bad encounters: good encounters are associated with joy, expand the body's power to affect and be affected, and construct and reveal the common; the bad, by contrast, are associated with sadness, cause a diminution of the body's power, and lead to division and destruction. But Spinoza and Negri both subscribe to a teleology in which the multitude tends toward perfection. A more complex account would stress that there are good multitudes and bad: bodies that resonate and expand versus dissonant bodies or bodies whose resonance hits a peak that leads to collapse.

In the same way that the multitude undoes the spatial logic of hegemony, because it is inside, outside, and on the border at same time, so likewise it problematizes linear temporality. For the multitude is simultaneously historic presupposition, future goal, and present constitution. On the one hand, the multitude's constituent power lies at the origin of all social order. Moreover, the historical multitude reappears at every point at which the constituent process is opened up, in all the revolutions and insurrections that pockmark modernity and give the lie to its narrative of linear progress. On the other hand, this multitude is evanescent, and its full actualization in history is still to come. Hardt and Negri argue that it is only with the contemporary prevalence of post-Fordist immaterial labor, the expansion of global communication networks, and the emergence of the "general intellect" (production through cooperation and communication) that the multitude can reveal itself empowered for the first time, to usher in the absolute democracy of the Communist project. In their words, then, the multitude has "a strange, double temporality: always-already and not-yet."[56] But as a result, the multitude is also always in-between: it is a becoming, a tendency. It inhabits the time of *kairòs*, in which history, project, and event meet in what Negri describes as "the instant in which the 'archer looses the arrow.' "[57] If the dynamic encounters that constitute the multitude were to cease, time itself would come to an end.

The time of the contract, by contrast, is the empty time of chronology, of an abstraction governed by transcendent categories. Contract law sets strict standards and limits to what can and cannot count as a binding contract. A contract refers to the future and requires what common-law codes describe as "adequate consideration": an unconditional promise is unenforceable, hence each side must pledge something; and "past consideration is no consideration," so a timetable for future action should be agreed in advance.[58] The contract is an instant in time and space, and the precise limits of the before and the after, the moment of offer and acceptance, as well as the appropriate jurisdiction, all have to be meticulously determined. An acceptance by mail, for example, is valid from the moment it is posted; an acceptance by email or fax comes into force once it is read or received.[59] Above all, a contract establishes particular relations between defined entities. Only certain legal subjects in given conditions can enter into a binding contract. Minors and the insane, for instance, cannot contract, nor can anyone incapacitated by drink or duress. A contract must also be public and invoke an intention to enter into legal relations: agreements within the family are not legally binding. So a contract presumes or (better) establishes distance and difference, and presents itself as the premeditated attempt to bring those differences together, to establish a "meeting of the minds."[60] To put this another way: contracts (and contract law) establish the abstract time that enables the legal fictions of exchange, equivalence, and consent.

The empty time of the legal contract is, however, parasitical upon the intimacy of the contact that constitutes the multitude. Contact generates social ties immediately and affectively, rather than waiting for the deferred satisfaction promised by the contract. Contact is the moment of the encounter, the brush or grip of body upon body. Contact comes from contiguity and contingency, words sharing the same Latin root. It is not that there is no reciprocity or obligation inscribed within contact. A gift implies or calls forth an exchange; but there is no fixed timetable, only the sensuous feel or intuition for the right moment.[61] Unlike the contract with all its predeterminations, contact is always somehow surprising, and therefore innovative. Where contract closes down, contact opens up. However much it is ritualized, contact is still unexpected.

Every encounter is subtly different, involving new bodies, or new combinations of bodies, affectively charged in novel ways. Contact, in short, concerns affect; contract, effect. If the multitude's expansiveness breaks down the boundary between inside and outside, its affective tactility also reconfigures the relations between its constituent elements.

Contracts formalize and encode affect. This is true as much of juridical contracts as of the social contract. They rely for their effectiveness on the fact that they are backed by the force of law. They obey a series of rules that determine which contracts are enforceable; or rather, which agreements are, by virtue of their legal enforceability, contracts, and which are not. With the threat of legal intervention should the promise they encode be unfulfilled, contracts abstract from the contact and affective investment that first motivate the contracting parties. Paradigmatically, marriage is a legal contract formalizing what is primarily an affective relation. It is true that marriage is often regarded as an exceptional type of contract, in that the contracting parties are legally prevented from dissolving their obligations of their own accord — a marriage can be dissolved only in a court of law. But the fact that the state is a "third party" to every marriage only reveals the way in which civil contracts always imply potential intervention by the state. Contracts capture contact by imposing conditions: if this, then that, or else. The state is poised like a sword of Damocles over every social relation. Difference becomes a distance that requires mediation, rather than a matter of social cohabitation in which we adjust our habits to others'. Yet juridical contracts depend upon the affective contact and habitual practices that they subsequently encode to produce social order. The handshake that traditionally seals an agreement (or the priest's injunction that "you may now kiss the bride" in a marriage ceremony) indicates at least one way in which the contract is premised on the contact that it purports to supersede. Indeed, the very notion that a contract has to be sealed with the imprint of contact signals that contract can never fully escape its dependence on the tactile. At stake in the distinction between contract and contact are two forms of difference: an immanent and substantial difference, between singularities that encounter each other in affect and habit, versus the formal distinction between juridical equals mediated by a transcendent state. As well as converting multitude into people, a bounded unity, the contract also represents the individuals that constitute the people as distinct and distant; they are distinguished from each other, even as they are imagined to be formally equal before the law. The people envelops formally distinct individuals whose relationship is maintained and mediated by the law; the multitude is a set of mobile singularities contingently aligned through immanent interaction.

The multitude is "a perpetual mass mobilization."[62] It is a *perpetuum mobile*, a "permanent in-between movement" that endlessly resists juridical formalization.[63] It incarnates "a politics of permanent revolution . . . in which social stability must always be recreated through a constant reorganization of social life."[64] Yet it is not formless anarchy; its motion is not random, though it may be guided by (and affirm) the role of chance. Indeed, chance is the very principle of the life of the multitude, which is open to the contingent, the fortuitous, and the unexpected. In the encounter with what life places in one's path, resisting the predestination of some originary contract, patterns emerge, and the multitude takes shape. Like the sea, the multitude forms sinuous waves: restless and apparently chaotic, but with their own logic and power. The immanent, guiding principle of the multitude's self-constitution is fluidity and flux, but this is not a seething mass of atomized individuals; instead, mobility and motility maximize opportunities for contact and encourage the formation of habitual patterns shaped by affect rather than the force of law. The multitude is eminently sociable: as the subject of constituent power, it produces society itself. Rebellious but not anomic, the multitude combines and recombines, unfolding and enfolding, in increasingly complex instances of self-organization: sometimes these are unstable, transient, and delicate, but in each case they are driven by a *conatus* that expresses a striving to persevere; they also often benefit from the feedback loops that elicit order from chaos. The multitude comes into being at what scientists such as theoretical biologist Stuart Kauffman call "the poised edge between order and chaos."[65]

The multitude is resonant. What Negri terms Spinoza's "physics of society" is, he says, "a mechanics of individual pressures and a dynamics of associative relationships, which characteristically are never closed in the absolute but, rather, proceed by ontological dislocations."[66] The universe is made up of an infinite number of bodies, each of which expresses some part of the whole ("God or Nature," in Spinoza's famous formulation). These bodies are "distinguished from one another," Spinoza tells us, "by reason of motion and rest, speed and slowness, and not by reason of substance." They are predisposed to combine and to form "composite bodies" that, in turn, are distinguished by their own patterns of motion or rest, that is, by their capacity to affect and be affected. Simple bodies and compound bodies alike combine by establishing a mutual resonance through chance encounters, when they are "so constrained by other bodies that they lie upon one another, or if they so move, whether with the same degree or with different degrees of speed, that they communicate their motions to each other in a certain fixed manner." Spinoza says that the resulting "bodies . . . united with one another . . . all together compose one body *or* individual, which is distinguished from the others by this union of bodies."[67] Hence the "ontological dislocations": everybody (every body) comprises a singular combination of simpler bodies that resonate to produce a new being, a body that is ever more open to new encounters, and so new transformations. This "dynamics of associative relationships" proceeds on the basis of the affect generated in these myriad encounters. The good encounters that lead to association and enhance a body's power (producing a body with a greater power to affect and be affected) are marked by joy; bad encounters, which lead to disassociation and dissonance, are clouded by sadness. In Spinoza's words, "joy is an affect by which the body's power of acting is increased or aided. Sadness, on the other hand, is an affect by which the body's power of acting is diminished or restrained."[68]

The multitude is a compound body made up of many diverse bodies (both compound and simple) whose common principle is immanent rather than transcendent. For Negri, this is the key to the *Ethics:* "The entire thematic of idealistic thought . . . is denied. The materialism of the mode is foundational."[69] However, the mode (the individual body) is merely the expression of divine or natural substance: the multitude is both virtual and actual. The universe has, for Spinoza (and by extension, Negri), an essential order toward which the multitude tends; the multitude expresses ever more fully the order of essences as it organizes itself in line with their fundamental harmony. Hence the multitude is both "always already" and perpetually "not yet." As bodies combine and exercise their increasing power, they become more virtuous and tend toward "greater perfection."[70] This empowerment is ensured socially, as opportunities for contiguity and contact multiply. For Negri and Hardt, contemporary global communications networks are both the result of the multitude's self-organization, which "produces cooperation, communication, forms of life, and social relationships," and also the long-awaited preconditions for its further expansion.[71] Drawing parallels from cybernetics and open-source programming, they argue that democracy is "possible for the first time today" thanks to the contemporary importance of such networks, which actualize a rhizomatic form of organization in which, now in Deleuze and Guattari's words, "any point . . . can be connected to anything other, and must be."[72] As the multitude constitutes society, it opens the ground for still further constitution. It generates the common: Spinoza charts a path from affective encounters (the joyful or sad passions generated as bodies associate or disassociate) through to what he terms "freedom," passing through the active affections that increase a body's power and enable the constitution of "common notions" rather than knowledge based merely on signs.[73]

Ethics, for Spinoza, is grounded in everyday pragmatics: of how to maximize good encounters (and so pleasure) and minimize the bad (and so pain). But ethics soon becomes politics: "It is especially useful to men that they harness their habits together, to draw themselves close by those bonds most apt to make one individual of them."[74] Common habits need no mediating transcendent instance, and therefore found a political principle that rejects anarchy (that is, unformed chaos), market principles (of rational actors), and state organization alike. Immanent positive feedback enables "a process that sees the human individuality construct itself as a collective entity."[75] The multitude takes shape. It pervades modernity as a virtual presence, a potential inherent in the enhanced possibilities for contact and communication that the modern world provides. Again, there is a feedback loop: pressing for contact, the pleasure of good encounters, and further expansion, the multitude impels modernity on. It calls forth the modern. But can it escape modernity's presuppositions? After all, Spinoza and Negri both affirm a strikingly linear teleology. Spinoza believes in the ultimate perfectibility of humankind, "help[ing] himself," philosopher Jonathan Bennett argues, "to a teleological version of self-preservation."[76] And Negri's affirmation of contiguity and contingency is premised on the faith that the multitude is destined to constitute a Communist society. What he elsewhere terms "a veritable *thermodynamics of society*" takes surprisingly little account of the unpredictability stressed by contemporary theorists of complexity.[77] Negri only rarely acknowledges the multitude's ambivalence, as for instance when he recognizes that Spinoza's materialist utopia conjures up "a terrible storm, now on the verge of explosion."[78]

Sendero Luminoso undoubtedly unleashed a storm in the Andes, and an almost entirely unexpected one at that: Carlos Iván Degregori describes its "vertiginous expansion" as over the course of only a couple of years it developed from a group of university professors and students to a force that almost entirely displaced the state in much of the Ayacucho countryside.[79] Despite its significance and impact, however, Sendero remains, years after its downfall, surprisingly mysterious. Journalist Santiago Roncagliolo's best-selling 2007 biography of leader Abimael Guzmán constantly reminds us that its account is necessarily incomplete, that Sendero somehow still evades representation. Moreover, Roncagliolo also reports that the very effort of writing about the group was profoundly disconcerting: "Over the course of this entire investigation, my state of mind itself has been at stake.... What used to seem terrible but familiar now fills me with guilt and rage. I feel ashamed of who I am." Roncagliolo is constantly driven, to the point of obsession, to return to the mystery of Sendero, as though to a primal trauma in which he hopes to find himself, if only by losing himself in the process. His earliest memory of Peru is the image of dead dogs hung on Lima lampposts at the outset of Sendero's uprising; as a child, he and the other children of leftist exiles living in Mexico City would play games of "people's war"; and yet, returning to Lima in order to write the book, despite this intimate history and his preparatory research, he tells us "I touch down in my city with the sensation that I've got myself into a scrape. For a start, really I know nothing."[80] Sendero continues to provoke bafflement and to infect those who write about it with unwelcome affects that disturb their sense of self. U.S. journalist Robin Kirk, writing about women militants, points to "something overwhelming, that confers on Sendero Luminoso a strange power, out of this world. Something beyond all understanding." Kirk immediately adds "I, too, fail to understand it." All her presumptions about progressive politics, social movements, and even her own identity as a woman and feminist, are put into question by a movement whose women members become "an alter ego, a photographic negative of the ideal woman imagined by contemporary feminists."[81] When she meets this other self, Kirk feels that she has reached the absolute limit of sisterhood while recognizing that something, strangely, has drawn these women to Sendero and away from her own conception of the political.

The study of (in Kirk's words) "how Sendero came to form itself" has been hampered by the difficulty of gaining access to militants and by their reluctance to talk.[82] Strikingly, Senderistas remain mute: unlike almost every other guerrilla movement in Latin America, there are hardly any Sendero *testimonios.* Guzmán famously gave what was touted as the "Interview of the Century" to a sympathetic journalist in 1988, but this only "added to the mystery and the mystique."[83] Perhaps the closest to a *testimonio* from a figure close to Sendero's inner circle is rural sociologist Antonio Díaz Martínez's *Ayacucho: Hambre y esperanza.* Díaz Martínez was a colleague of Guzmán's at the University of Huamanga in the 1960s and 1970s, and by the time he died, in a prison massacre in 1986, was reputedly number three in the organization.[84] His book on Ayacucho, first published in 1969, is for the most part a fairly dry account of the land tenure system in the Peruvian highlands, but it also shows clear frustration at a landowning class that preferred inefficient but profitable capital underinvestment, and superexploitation of the peasantry, to changing the habits of a colonial lifetime. Díaz Martínez offers technical advice but above all stresses the need to "get to know the native community, their social organization, to get close to them, work with them, distance yourself from the *mistis* [the rural elite] for as long as they remain distanced from the community." Quoting the noted indigenist historian Luis Valcárcel, whose most famous book is *Tempestad en los Andes* ("Storm in the Andes"), he adds the reminder that Peru is "a country of 'Indians,' a fact that remains as pertinent as ever."[85] Yet anthropologist Orin Starn commends Díaz Martínez's nuanced take on what Starn calls "Andeanism": "He never lost a sense of mixture and movement"; he accurately reported the "fluidity and uncertain future" of indigenous communities and the "sense of interconnection" of a population that "was constantly on the move." For the book's second edition in 1985, however, by which time Díaz Martínez was a declared Senderista, imprisoned in Lurigancho jail and, as Starn notes, "clearly . . . a hardliner," the author added a concluding essay.[86] This updated ending shows little of the subtlety and attention to either mobility or affect manifested by the (now) fifteen-year-old text to which it is appended. Instead, it repeats almost verbatim Senderista slogans and an affirmation of faith in Guzmán, the Revolution's "Presidente Gonzalo, mentor and guide to the Red Faction of the Communist Party of Peru who, by means of determined struggle against revisionism and rightward drift, managed to reconstitute the Party of the working class, a Revolutionary Party of a new type." It is thanks to "the armed struggle directed by the Communist Party" that the peasant masses "will organize themselves, will overflow," and "will arise like a tempest, a hurricane, a force so impetuous and violent that nothing can contain it," so as to "bury all the imperialists, the military *caudillos,* the corrupt functionaries, the local despots, and the evil landlords."[87] Something has transformed Díaz Martínez's language: what was flexible has become rigid; what was fluid has reached boiling point.

Senderismo paradoxically manifests both extreme rigidity and extreme volatility. In a kind of reverse of *gatopardismo,* nothing changes and yet everything is different. Senderista militant Rosa Murinache's *Tiempos de guerra,* discussed by cultural critic Victor Vich, manifests this paradox in heightened form. As Vich explains, Murinache's text is "a clandestine book of poetry that circulated during the harshest years of Peru's dirty war... [whose] aim is to expound upon the necessity for armed struggle and for a radically revolutionary change in the country's social structure." Against conventional notions of lyric voice, however, this particular poetry reveals little about its author. "The curious thing," Vich continues, "is that Rosa is the author of the book but not of the poems, which are rather the product of an 'editing' operation performed on the political discourse of Abimael Guzmán." Murinache has taken Guzmán's pronouncements and presented them as poetry; she is at pains to point out that she has neither added nor subtracted a single word from his work. "All" she has done is rearrange it on the page, introducing line breaks, indentations, and stanza divisions. Murinache's intervention, then, is purely formal. Its apparent minimalism, which changes nothing but transforms everything, both fascinates and frustrates Vich: it is superfluous; it means nothing; it is "a gesture at best, a simple movement, the useless attempt to arrange the words (of the Other) in some other way."[88] But Murinache has drawn out the formal properties of Guzmán's political discourse. She challenges us to read Sendero ideology as form rather than content, as aesthetics or affect rather than politics or ideology.

She has made his discourse sing, vibrate, and resonate; at least, she has tried to indicate how it sings for her. By recasting Guzmán as poet, Murinache warns against the interpretations, engrossed with content and signification, that have dominated and stymied most readings of Sendero, Vich's included. She suggests that Guzmán's followers were less interested in what their leader meant than in the ways in which Sendero allowed them to find form, to construct their own forms (their own habits) from the affective building blocks supplied by a discourse of blood and revolution, reorganization and (literally) reformation.

Analyses of Sendero that stress its ideological rigidity fail to explain its remarkable influence. Sociologist Gonzalo Portocarrero notes the group's religious aspects, arguing that it was a moralistic sect dedicated to a hyperrational cult of violence. But most such sects remain tiny and insignificant. Portocarrero is closer to the mark when he further observes that Sendero also had "a cult of movement, an unlimited fascination for the capacity to act," and when he quotes Guzmán's paean to "perpetual activity" and "the intensity of the creative impulse." Joining Sendero meant sacrificing individuality in the name of "an unconditional surrender to the collective," but this was a chance to participate in an empowered subjectivity destined (its adherents believed) to constitute a "new power."[89] Degregori comments that in Sendero "power appeared in all its fearful splendor" and Senderistas felt that they were its direct agents: "We blew it up just to blow it up, nothing else," as one of them reports.[90] Moreover, the movement was remarkably open: for instance, as Kirk observes, a strikingly high proportion (up to 40 percent) of its militants were women, including the group's early martyr, nineteen-year-old Edith Lagos, whose 1982 funeral filled Ayacucho's main square with a "multitude" of over ten thousand, the largest such assembly the city had ever seen.[91] Perhaps more importantly still, as Degregori documents, Sendero welcomed provincial students caught up in the explosion of secondary and higher education during the 1960s, who were otherwise in a "no man's land" between the Andean customs they had left behind and the urban creole elites that discriminated against them for their supposed backwardness.[92] Sendero latched on to this flow of young people whose desires so resonated with its promise that together, a disparate mass could become strong. Over the course of the 1970s, Sendero's fortunes waxed and waned, but with each wave of mobilization and retrenchment the intensity of its organization and gravitational pull increased until it ended up, Degregori suggests, "becoming a type of dwarf star, one of those in which matter is so compressed that there is hardly any space between its constituent atoms, such that it achieves an enormous weight, disproportionate to its size."[93] It had taken contiguity to its limit.

The multitude has multiple points of equilibrium, some more stable than others; immanent processes can lead to transitions by which the multitude suddenly changes its aspect. There are combinations of bodies that prove singularly explosive, however much their internal operations correspond to the logic of the good encounter. A social thermodynamics should account for such nonlinearity. An ethics of the encounter should take note of the ever-present potential for dissolution as much as resonance. We need to distinguish between multitudes, between different expressions of constituent power. The multitude's expansion can hit a limit, however contingent, and bring death rather than life, setting off a chain reaction. Not all pain can be attributed to the state. There are immanent processes that obey the logic of resonance until they hit a tipping point, at which they become precipitously dissonant. Dissonance is death: as Spinoza puts it, "I understand the body to die when its parts are so disposed that they acquire a different proportion of motion and rest to one another."[94] Such, surely, is the case with al-Qaida: an immanent, unrepresentable, and fluid network, it is a multitudinous movement that is also spectacularly destructive. The multitude, always monstrous from the point of view of constituted power, can threaten constituent power too; it can become a bad multitude. Sometimes the sea is whipped up into a hurricane, a frighteningly unstable equilibrium. Contiguity all too easily leads to corruption.

Common

The multitude is common. It is ordinary and everyday, and it is both the product and the producer of shared resources. It comprises what historians Peter Linebaugh and Marcus Rediker term the "hewers of wood and drawers of water": a "motley crew" of apparently disorganized labor.[95] Though Negri sometimes flirts with an almost Leninist vanguardism, the multitude rebels against party organization or the privileging of so-called advanced sectors. The exercise of constituent power is a matter of habit, not training, indoctrination, or even will. The multitude seeks connections based on what we already hold in common; its polyvalent powers of connection open up new bases for commonality. Negri and Hardt reverse the narrative that claims that capitalism has already destroyed the commons and that privatization is now rampant, especially after neoliberalism. They argue that we have more in common now than ever before and that the stage is set for the "common name" of a Communist liberty to come. The love of the common people is to ensure the transformation of what is now either private interest or public command into an immanent utopia. And yet it can be hard to distinguish the multitude from the actual dystopia of Empire. Hardt and Negri oppose the multitude's commonality to Empire's corruption, but their analysis of corruption is confused and contradictory. Indeed, the common and the corrupt often overlap: both are products of informal and unsupervised networks. Again, the multitude is ambivalent and the state has no monopoly on corruption. The principle of commonality suggests that there can be no categorical distinction between multitude and Empire: if constituted power is merely a particular (de)formation of the constituent, the point is rather to distinguish between such formations, to find a protocol by which to tell bad from good rather than to affirm the multitude at every turn. When it comes to the multitude, Negri's projective Marxism too quickly renounces critique.

Naomi Klein notes that in recent years there has been "something of a rediscovery" of the commons, with increasing interest in and attention to "the public sphere, the public good, the non-corporate."[96] In part, this is a backlash against neoliberalism and the perceived excesses of Reaganism and Thatcherism in the 1980s; in part, it stems from specifically environmental concerns about global warming and diminishing natural resources; and in part, Klein argues, it comes from anxiety and sympathy after the attacks of September 11, 2001, symbolized in renewed appreciation for public workers such as the firefighters and police officers who died in the collapse of New York's twin towers. In academia, too, the topic has prompted fresh interest: introducing the *International Journal of the Commons* in 2007, its editors Frank van Laerhoven and Elinor Ostrom argue that "the study of the commons has experienced substantial growth and development over the past decades."[97] At first sight such attention is counterintuitive. More standard accounts, both popular and scholarly, lament a precipitous decline in common feeling and common holdings. Capitalism's first move is always enclosure, by means of so-called primitive accumulation, to turn the common into private property. And as Marxist geographer David Harvey points out, the pace of what he terms "accumulation by dispossession" has if anything intensified, not slackened: he sees it as the heart of the "new imperialism" that led the United States to war in Afghanistan and Iraq. Philosopher George Caffentzis likewise identifies "new enclosures" not only in the Middle East but also in official responses to Hurricane Katrina in New Orleans. Moreover, primitive accumulation proceeds apace in the biopolitical terrain with, for instance, virus and gene patents. Even Klein is more reserved in her latest book, which focuses rather more on catastrophe than on commonality.[98]

Hardt and Negri acknowledge the wave of privatizations, even in areas (such as genetics) that had previously been off-limits to capital. But they argue that such attempts to expand property rights are a reaction to "the rising biopolitical productivity of the multitude."[99] It is only in response to transformations in the productive process, as innovation and production increasingly take place in common, that capital takes stock in new ways, to reimagine its mechanisms of measure and attribution. Economic processes, they argue, are ever more characterized by their commonality: "immaterial labor," by which they mean "labor that creates immaterial products, such as knowledge, information, communication, a relationship, or an emotional response," depends upon the common relations already established. In turn, it "creates common relationships and common social forms in a way more pronounced than ever before"; the "production of the common" is now "central to every form of social production . . . and it is, in fact, the primary characteristic of the new dominant forms of labor today."[100] The same is true in other spheres, such as politics, where the common has taken on "a new intensity" as "the common antagonism and common wealth of the exploited and expropriated are translated into common conduct, habits, and performativity." Resonance is established as habits tend to converge and as we are encouraged to perform in similar ways albeit in diverse circumstances. Behind management and educational buzzwords such as "transferable skills" are communicative and "problem-solving" practices that are increasingly demanded over a wide range of distinct fields. What emerges is a "spiral, expansive relationship" as the multitude produces the common and the common enables the multitude to produce further: "The common is produced and it is also productive," which is the "key to understanding all social and economic activity." Capital's new enclosures are no more than a symptom of the immense productivity that commonality is now starting to unlock; "becoming common . . . is the biopolitical condition of the multitude."[101] Contrasting the common with both the public and the private, Hardt and Negri argue for communism as "the institution of the common as a social institution."[102]

Hardt and Negri's stress on immaterial labor, and so on the production of knowledge and communication, can seem to privilege certain economic sectors, and so certain classes of workers, over others. They acknowledge that industrial labor remains important, and even quantitatively dominant, not least in large parts of the third world. Nonetheless, they identify a passage "from the domination of industry to that of services and information, a process of economic *postmodernization*, or better, *informatization.*"[103] Many have criticized their analysis of immaterial labor, and their apparent focus on so-called "knowledge work." Labor sociologist Paul Thompson, for example, points out that even in countries such as the United States and Great Britain, knowledge workers account for less than 15 percent of the working population. He goes on to argue that the "move from immaterial labour to the multitude" is achieved only "by sleight of hand" and concludes by lambasting Hardt and Negri for what he calls their "infantile vanguardism."[104] As Caffentzis notes, moreover, their privileging of "computer programmers and their ilk" is, rather ironically, both "Leninist to the core" and surprisingly in sync with the much more pessimistic prognostications of a fairly mainstream economist such as Jeremy Rifkin, who warns against a "workerless world."[105]

If the multitude is common, it must be so also in the sense that it is demotic and everyday; it is "common or garden." Linebaugh and Rediker provide a better account of this than does Negri, who is indeed prone to idealizing knowledge work and the service sector. Linebaugh and Rediker's portrayal of the "revolutionary Atlantic" of the seventeenth and eighteenth centuries likewise stresses communication and commonality, in the name of what they call a "plebeian commonism" resolutely opposed to slavery. Yet the people who gave sermons or smuggled pamphlets, who spread rumors or sang songs of rebellion, and who generally fed the fires of resistance across the Atlantic world, were not the knowledge workers of their time but the lay preachers and stewards, the "sailors, pilots, felons, lovers, translators, musicians, mobile workers of all kinds [who] made new and unexpected connections, which variously appeared to be accidental, contingent, transient, even miraculous." This was the "motley crew," itself made up of "various crews and gangs that possessed their own motility and were often independent of leadership from above," that formed the "urban mob and the revolutionary crowd."[106] This is the multitude as a many-headed hydra, a disparate and mobile collection of ordinary men and women who struggle in common over common grievances and common desires. There is nothing exceptional about the common; it is not some prelapsarian paradise or rare remnant of a long-lost fullness. It is merely a matter of habit: "Habit is the common in practice," as Hardt and Negri argue; "habits are living practice, the site of creation and innovation."[107] There is also nothing, in this sense, special about the multitude, or about constituent power. Constituent power is not confined merely to the exceptional moments of rupture between constitutions; or rather, we are forever in-between, forever in a moment of exception or interregnum. The multitude is everywhere and anywhere, spilling out wherever and whenever you look around. The multitude is ordinary.

The common is "animated by love," Negri claims: "Love is the constitutive *praxis* of the common"; it is the "desire of the common."[108] Love, defined by Spinoza as "joy, accompanied by the idea of an external cause," provides the impetus for maximizing good encounters.[109] To see constituent power in these terms may seem odd, as Hardt acknowledges, but he has said that he and Negri "would like to make love a properly political concept."[110] The "revolutionary time" of constituent power is, he argues, "the time of love." Neither sentimental nor nostalgic, the love that Hardt and Negri celebrate is promiscuous and polyvalent; it is "the ultimate sign of exposure" to the other, to an unpredictable and perhaps hostile otherness.[111] Love is the desire to encounter other bodies, to enfold them and create new bodies with them, to constitute the multitude. It is "the ethical cement of collective life."[112] Love is what holds connections together; it is what transforms the habitual recognition of commonality into an active project of resistance and constitution. Love is, Negri argues, "the ontological power that constructs being."[113] Love, he seems to be saying, makes the world go round.

Money also makes the world go round. Indeed, there can be little to choose between love and money, as George Orwell's parody of 1 Corinthians 13 reminds us: "Though I speak with the tongues of men and of angels, and have not money, I am become as a sounding brass, or a tinkling cymbal."[114] Money, too, is polyvalent and promiscuous. Money, too, is ubiquitous and common; moreover, as the universal equivalent, it also produces commonality, connecting discrete singularities. It is dispersed and nonhierarchical: "Capital," Hardt and Negri argue, following Deleuze and Guattari, "operates on the plane of *immanence*... without reliance on a transcendent center of power." Capital, too, is expansive and boundary-breaking. Capital, too, rebels against "the transcendence of modern sovereignty."[115] In the epoch of Empire, sovereign transcendence is undercut and constituted power gives way, but not to constituent power or the multitude. In Hardt and Negri's words, with the arrival of postmodernity "the absoluteness of imperial power is the complementary term to its complete immanence to the ontological machine of production and reproduction." This is Empire: a postmodern, neoliberal, globalized form of power that succeeds the nation-state and its associated imperialism. Empire responds to the multitude, giving in to some of its pressure and so taking us a step further toward the Communist society that Hardt and Negri claim the multitude demands; hence "we must push through Empire to come out the other side.... We have to accelerate the process."[116] But the congruence between Empire and multitude means that it is hard to tell the two apart. As Alberto Moreiras asks, "what would keep us from suspecting that there is finally no difference between Empire and counter-Empire, once immanentization has run full course?"[117]

It is always hard to distinguish between constituent and constituted power. At the best of times, the distinction is only formal: constituted power is a form of constituent power; it is constituent power folded back upon itself. As political theorist Jodi Dean comments, *Empire* and *Insurgencies* alike propose an "impossibly clean division" between the two. Dean even argues that the division "makes no sense. Constituted power is of course constituent, productive, performative, generating new arrangements of bodies."[118] In Empire, however, the distinction becomes ever more moot, as what was once more clearly constituted power (the formal republican institutions of the modern nation-state) is transformed in favor of the fluidity and expansiveness typical of the constituent; as even the illusion of hegemony is replaced by posthegemony. And if Empire comes to approximate the multitude, in turn the multitude has taken on new and more disturbing forms, to become more destructive than ever. A test case for the distinction between the two, and for Hardt and Negri's constant affirmation of the multitude, came with the September 11 attacks on New York and Washington D.C. In the wake of the fall of the twin towers, there was no shortage of critics who declared that *Empire* could be read as apology, or even inspiration, for the attacks. Sociologist Michael Rustin, for example, argues that it is now "unfortunately clear" how one might read the book's praise for the "new barbarians" who "destroy with an affirmative violence" by reducing what exists to rubble.[119] Moreover, the impact of such criticisms was exacerbated by Negri's rather ambivalent reaction to the events: he commented to *Le Monde*, for instance, "I would have been a lot more pleased if, on 11th September, the Pentagon had been razed and they had not missed the White House."[120]

For Hardt and Negri, it is corruption that distinguishes Empire from the multitude. Corruption is the "simple negation" of the multitude's "power of generation."[121] Corruption has "become generalized"; "corruption triumphs."[122] "In Empire," they claim, "corruption is everywhere. It is the cornerstone and keystone of domination." Indeed, "corruption itself," they argue, "is the substance and totality of Empire." It is "not an aberration of imperial sovereignty but its very essence and modus operandi."[123] Corruption and command have, as Machiavelli predicted, become synonymous. The only way in which Empire holds itself at arm's length from the pressing insistence of the multitude is through myriad corrupt practices, in which the legal framework of the constitutional republic breaks down and "the weak form of governance make[s] it open season for the profit hunters." But this, too, is a sign of instability, of the fact that Empire is merely an "interregnum," a "passage from one regime to another."[124] With the expansion of the common, the emergence of the multitude in full force and actuality, and so the collapse of the law of value, or indeed any consistent system of legality, there is no longer any reason why constituent power should depend upon constituted power; it is only corruption that keeps the multitude from its goal.

Given the concept's key role in their work, it is surprising how laxly Hardt and Negri define corruption. Sometimes they use the word in a fairly ordinary sense, for instance in a discussion of the Enron scandal or in Negri's comments on contemporary Italy, whose politicians are "all unimaginably corrupt" and where "corruption has become a form of government."[125] *Empire*, however, stretches the term's meaning to the limit. First, corruption is something like egoism: "individual choice that is opposed to and violates the fundamental community and solidarity defined by biopolitical production." Second, it is the extraction of surplus value, "or really exploitation. This includes the fact that the values that derive from the collective cooperation of labor are expropriated." Third, ideological distortion is also corruption: "the perversion of the senses of linguistic communication." Fourth, corruption is political and military, when "the threat of terror becomes a weapon to resolve limited or regional conflicts." Later, corruption and command are practically conflated: "Corruption is the pure exercise of command, without proportion or adequate reference to the world of life."[126] When the concept is first introduced, however, it is more ambivalent: corruption is "omni-crisis"; it is a symptom of Empire's hybridity and shows "that imperial rule functions by breaking down. (Here the Latin etymology is precise: *com-rumpere*, to break.)" Corruption is both the sign of an "ontological vacuum" and a process, "a reverse process of generation and composition, a moment of metamorphosis" that therefore "potentially frees spaces for change."[127] With all these iterations, no wonder that "the forms in which corruption appears are so numerous that trying to list them is like pouring the sea into a teacup."[128] Like the sea, corruption becomes fluid and escapes definition; the concept of corruption, in Hardt and Negri, itself becomes corrupted. Moreover, if corruption is like the sea, boundless and unrepresentable in the many shifting singular forms it adopts, could it be just another name for the multitude?

Latin American *testimonio* thrives on commonality. It promises to give the reader contact, more or less directly, with ordinary men and women whose voices and lives are not usually recorded. *Testimonio* has little ambition toward literary distinction. It rejects the notion that its protagonists are exceptional; they are "notable only by their shared ordinariness."[129] Moreover, its readers prize a simple style; it is *testimonio's* unaffectedness, in part, that makes it so affecting. Its ordinariness enables what cultural critic John Beverley terms "new forms of subject identification of the personal-in-the-collective."[130] *Testimonio* stages an encounter between the testimonial subject, the editor who frames his or her words, and the reader. Beverley notes that the "trick" of *testimonio* is "finding a commonality in singularity," although he then goes on to argue that such commonality should be "the basis for a new hegemonic bloc."[131] But on the face of it, this is a strange demand indeed, as hegemony and *testimonio* are, in fact, more often at odds. Whereas commonality preserves singularity and difference, hegemonic projects stress equivalence in the name of state-centered unity. The entire discourse of solidarity and hegemony, didacticism and the national–popular, flattens out testimonial literature by transforming commonality into identity. This then is the tension at the heart of *testimonio:* between multiplicity and unity, between the multitudinous production of the common and its capture by the monopolistic state. Perhaps this is why *testimonio* so often provokes a scandal: it is the site of a double corruption, as would-be hegemonic actors try to force it into the mold of national liberation, while its expansive and promiscuous tendencies always betray such pretensions, showing their ultimate hollowness.

Within Central American *testimonio,* an example of the tension between commonality and solidarity, the multitude and a would-be hegemon, can be found in Nicaraguan Omar Cabezas's *Fire from the Mountain.* This documents Cabezas's life as a guerrilla with the Sandinistas, though it stops short of describing the movement's triumph, when in 1979 the rebel army finally overthrew the Somoza dictatorship, or Cabezas's subsequent career within the revolutionary government. Indeed, turning from triumphalism, the book is strangely suffused with dissatisfaction. Cabezas stresses the disorientation and anxiety of what seems to be an interminable campaign: his original ideological certitude deserts him as, out in the countryside, he feels hungry, ill, and constantly lost; his girlfriend leaves him, and he feels his "world coming apart"; he loses his sense of self altogether, as well as his "sense of space, [his] equilibrium, all sense of gravity and inertia"; he feels a temporal disjunction as "the organic unity of [his] past and present" is "shattered"; finally, he comes to believe that "we were living in a society of the absurd and our life was the life of the absurd."[132] But the day after this ultimate expression of the struggle's meaninglessness, Cabezas encounters an aged *campesino,* Don Leandro, who, it transpires, had fought with Augusto Sandino forty years earlier. Listening to the old man's story, Cabezas is suddenly able to construct a narrative of Nicaragua's long search for freedom. He can imagine himself heir to this national history, with Don Leandro as hitherto absent father: "I felt I really was his son, the son of Sandino, the son of history. I understood my own past; I knew where I stood; I had a country, a historical identity." *Anomie* is replaced by filiation, entitlement, and empowerment. At precisely this moment, however, the book abruptly ends: Cabezas's own narrative proves insufficient. The implication is that the narrator's voice has to be supplemented by that of the peasant informant, who would finally give sense to the struggle of the intellectual turned guerrilla. Cabezas therefore invokes another genre that would, he imagines, fully represent "the essence of Nicaragua." As Don Leandro speaks, Cabezas exclaims: "How I wished I had a tape recorder right then, because what he was telling me was so wonderful."[133] The novel is cast as a poor substitute for *testimonio,* whose "recording and/or transcription and editing of an oral account by an interlocutor" can alone properly flesh out a fantasy of personal and national fulfillment.[134]

When Cabezas's narrator transforms himself into a would-be editor of a *testimonio,* the accidental encounter with the single individual (Don Leandro) who stands in for an entire people comes retrospectively to justify the hierarchical structures (intellectual versus peasant, city versus countryside, present versus past) that this narrative trick allegedly displaces. Appealing to the authenticity of its contact with bodies described in affective terms ("We took hold of the campesinos' hands, broad, powerful, roughened hands"; the *campesino* has "a whole series of characteristic emotions . . . a very special sort of affection"), *testimonio* constructs the fiction of an organic link between historical tradition and political project, between everyday culture and nation-state.[135] Though *testimonio* is presented as the *cri de coeur* of the oppressed, Cabezas shows how it becomes the means by which a committed intelligentsia seeks to resolve its own sense of isolation and affliction. *Testimonio* consolidates a revolutionary movement's claim to legitimacy by appealing to the mediation of subaltern interlocution. It reinvents Latin American populism, constructing a people, and so also the effect of a state, not through mass mobilizations, but through dialogues with exemplary individual interlocutors; the tape recorder replaces the balcony as the instrument by which transcendence is asserted. For the Salvadoran case, Roque Dalton's *Miguel Mármol* corresponds most closely to Cabezas's ideal type: leftist poet Dalton met the former Communist leader Mármol at a café in Czechoslovakia, and in the conversations that followed, written up as *testimonio,* he establishes a historical narrative linking Mármol's attempted Communist rebellion of the 1930s with the organizing that would later become the FMLN. Or consider the subtitle of Alegría's *They Won't Take Me Alive:* "Salvadorean Women in Struggle for Liberation" suggests that the book's subject, Comandante Eugenia, is an exemplary figure who can stand in for an entire national type. No wonder that Beverley links *testimonio* so closely to hegemony: the genre too often rehearses the articulatory strategies characteristic of classical populism but now by means of a narrative strategy founded on the chance encounter. Narrating the encounter is *testimonio's* key trope. Venezuelan anthropologist Elisabeth Burgos-Debray, for instance, describes in detail her first meeting with Rigoberta Menchú: "I remember it being a particularly cold night.... The first thing that struck me about her was her open, almost childlike smile."[136] Even what is arguably the very first Latin American *testimonio,* Argentine journalist Rodolfo Walsh's *Operación masacre,* opens with an extended account of a chance meeting in a café. Accidental contact paves the way for the invention of a people, and *testimonio* becomes univalent, flattened, fixated on the fantasy of a revolutionary state. Committed intellectuals corrupt the genre's potential for difference and diversity, by single-mindedly channeling subaltern affect into projects for national unity. And they present this process as some kind of accident.

Still, however many hegemonic projects seek to capture *testimonio* and to make it a vehicle by which to convert multitude into people, *testimonio* itself always corrupts these efforts. The scandal over the most famous instance of the genre, *I, Rigoberta Menchú,* was not ultimately about the book's referentiality: whatever her story's inaccuracies, anthropologist David Stoll concedes that Menchú was "a legitimate Maya voice" and that her story was at least "poetically true"; but he criticizes the way in which she was presented as "a representative of the revolutionary movement," and the melodramatic move by which the book "turned a nightmarish experience into a morality play."[137] At issue in Stoll's account is how a story about a range of affective experiences common to "all poor Guatemalans" was hijacked by movements seeking hegemony, whether that be the guerrilla URNG in Guatemala, or leftist academics fighting culture wars in the United States. Stoll seeks to reinsert difference into the narrative, emphasizing for instance land conflicts between rural indigenous people as well as what he calls "the plasticity of stories about the Menchús." It is this fluidity that allows both Rigoberta and her father, Vicente, to become mythic figures who are to "stand above internecine feuds"; but by the same token, this is what undermines and corrupts such hegemonic projects.[138] *Testimonio's* polyvalence is both the condition for attempts at hegemonic articulation and also what finally makes them unsustainable. Here, as elsewhere, something always escapes, not least the many secrets that Menchú herself continually proffers and withdraws, to construct what critic Doris Sommer terms a "flexible and fluid subject" that teaches us "the kind of love that takes care not to simply appropriate its object."[139]

The testimonial encounter has little to do with representation; it is a singular opening to the common. *Testimonio* does anything but lead to the national-popular; it touches directly on the global and its real impact has always been outside any national or even Latin American context. *Testimonio* was read more by North American undergraduates than by Central American *campesinos.* However much it was celebrated for fomenting national–popular rebellion within Latin America, in fact the genre was above all a point of contact for the construction of a transnational common. Understanding this opens up new modes of reading *testimonio* no longer within the straightjacket of the desire for organic tradition. Rather than reading *testimonio* as the authentic voice of a particular Latin American people, it is better to see how it connects with a much more disparate global network, with cultural effects that cannot so easily be mapped on to any individual state formation. In this sense, the genre actively resists the reductionism that hegemonic projects promote: it tends to proliferation rather than unity, as is suggested by the original Spanish title of the Salvadoran *testimonio Rebel Radio,* which translates as "The Thousand and One Stories of Radio Venceremos." *Rebel Radio's* editor writes that "these are chronicles of the thousand and one adventures lived by the *compas* [comrades] who made this radio station possible. Stories that aren't intended to prove anything."[140] Like a radio transmission, *testimonio* propagates via waves that cross national borders with ease, resonating or meeting interference depending on the terrain or the other waves that cross its path. A territorializing desire for lineage such as Cabezas's gives way to the self-consciously globalizing use of technology by a figure such as the Zapatistas' Subcomandante Marcos, who welcomes identity loss and polyvalent flexibility. Asked about rumors of his homosexuality, Marcos replied that he was "gay in San Francisco," following up with the declaration that he was also "a black person in South Africa" as well as "an indigenous person on the streets of San Cristóbal... an artist without a gallery or portfolio, a housewife in whatever neighbourhood in whatever city in whatever Mexico on a Saturday night.... In short, Marcos is a whatever human being in this world."[141] The epitome of the "whatever," everyday and indefinite, *testimonio* is singular (a myriad singularities) and universal at the same time. The genre can emerge from the shadow of hegemony, to become a vehicle for the multitude's pursuit of good encounters.

Hardt and Negri exclaim "Long live movement! Long live carnival! Long live the common!"[142] But there is a fine line between the common and the corrupt, and sometimes little to choose between the two. Both are complex networks that depend upon connections and contacts rather than contracts regulated by a higher power. Both are subterranean and immanent, resisting representation until their public exposure in either insurgency or scandal. Corruption sidesteps regulations and substitutes informal habitual arrangements for formal hierarchies and principles; it undermines the constitution and prompts other modes of self-organization. Of course, there are many different forms of corruption, but then the multitude also takes on various forms, not all of which can or should be uniformly affirmed. As the multitude expands or comes under particular pressure, it can reach critical points of instability that mark phase transitions (as when a liquid becomes a gas, water becomes steam) in which it becomes suddenly destructive or self-destructive. A line of flight can, as Deleuze and Guattari observe, take on "an odor of death and immolation, a state of war from which one returns broken."[143] Or, to use another image, it may resonate with such intensity that it tears itself apart, like a suspension bridge swaying in the wind at a pitch that makes the entire structure oscillate with increasing amplitude until it collapses into the waters below. Negri suggests that the multitude can develop continuously until it achieves the absolute democracy of a Communist utopia. But we may question the possibility, and even the desirability, of that end.

The Tacoma Narrows suspension bridge, November 7, 1940. The midsection twists shortly before the bridge's final collapse. Film still; courtesy of the University of Washington Libraries, Special Collections, negative no. UW 21427. Image restoration by Lise Diane Broer.

Continuous

The multitude persists, continually extending its sphere of influence and contact as it opens up to the common. Expansive, tactile, and polyvalent, it provokes discontinuous responses and recompositions from constituted power. The multitude, in short, is active while the state is reactive. This insight is already implicit in the Italian workerist and autonomist theoretical traditions in which Negri won his spurs during the 1960s and 1970s. Theorists such as Mario Tronti argued that the working class was dominant within capitalism: labor struggles impel capitalist development and immediately impact the political order. In reply, capital and the state force class recomposition upon their revolutionary antagonist. But each struggle lost is also a struggle won, as a new and more expansive subject is forged in the fire of combat. The skilled worker, labor's aristocracy, had by the late 1960s given way to the mass worker with Fordism and Taylorism. In the 1970s, autonomists claimed to see the emergence of a new social subject, the socialized worker. But despite Negri's high hopes, it too was beaten back, as neoliberal globalization instituted a dramatic counterrevolution in the 1980s and 1990s, and the welfare state ceded to the warfare state. A parade of state formations reshapes space and time to ward off or contain the multitude. Yet Negri argues that we have reached a new stage: proletarian insurgency continues, and its common name is now the multitude. The multitude will bring history to a close; Negri's fundamentalism envisages the Kingdom of God here on earth. For Negri, this leap of faith anchors his entire political project. But we might want to disarticulate this project from its associated critique, or at least inhabit the space in-between.

Constituent power is continuous and everyday. Appearances, however, are deceptive: in appearance, constituent power emerges only in moments of crisis, in the transition from one political order to another, soon thereafter to disappear. As Negri notes, "once the exceptional moment of innovation is over, constituent power seems to exhaust its effects." The normative regulations of constituted power are more familiar to us than the uproarious intensity associated with constitutional assemblies, when constituent power is glimpsed in full force as it intervenes decisively on the political stage. But for Negri, this "appearance of exhaustion" is simply "mystification"; in fact, "the only limits on constituent power are the limits of the world of life."[144] Constituent power "persists": once a constitution is declared, it goes underground; unseen, it continues to expand until it erupts once more to interrupt constituted power, forcing drastic changes in social relations. Capital responds with a series of class recompositions that it presents as natural; the state reacts with periodic refoundations that it presents as simple renegotiations of some original social pact. At each stage, the multitude is beaten back, temporarily defeated, "absorbed into the mechanism of representation" and so misrecognized as class, people, mass, or some other docile political subject. But even such misrecognitions, Negri claims, signal an "ontological accumulation." Being itself is transformed through the "continuous and unrestrainable practice" that is the multitude's everyday, permanent revolution. A focus on constituent power, then, rather than on the different forms taken by constituted power, opens up "a new substratum" of history, "an ontological level on which productive humanity anticipate[s] the concrete becoming, forcing it or being blocked by it."[145]

In the Italian workerist and autonomist traditions, with which Negri was associated in the 1960s and 1970s, this tension between continuity and discontinuity was theorized in terms of class recomposition, which analyst Steve Wright calls workerism's "most novel and important" contribution to political theory and practice. Indeed, Wright notes that it came to "assume the role played within Italian Communist thought by *hegemony*."[146] Workerism's insight is that the working class is active while capital is reactive: capitalist transformation is always a reaction to working-class demands or subversion. In workerist pioneer Mario Tronti's words, "We have worked with a concept that puts capitalist development first, and workers second. This is a mistake. And now we have to put the problem on its head . . . and start again from the beginning." The "true secret" of left-wing strategy is that workers have "the political ability to force capital into reformism, and then to blatantly make use of that reformism for the working class revolution."[147] In other words, capital retrofits and improves the production process only after labor strategies have made the existing regime untenable. In response, for instance, to demands for a shorter working day, which generate a political reaction in the form of factory legislation, capital introduces efficiencies by means of mechanization, so in fact increasing the rate of exploitation.[148] Later, innovations such as Taylorism will also be capital's forced response to worker militancy. Capital answers working-class demands with revolutionary change, but in a way that consolidates and broadens its own command. Yet this is a Pyrrhic victory for capital, in that as a result the sphere of struggle expands, communication and commonality become more important, and so the working class becomes stronger and more united. Class struggle is followed by class recomposition, which in turn is the basis for further struggle. The perhaps surprising conclusion is that "the capitalist class, from its birth, is in fact subordinate to the working class." This realization, moreover, necessitates a new approach to history, a "working class history of capitalist society."[149]

Workerism stresses the centrality of working-class subjectivity. But it also points out how that subjectivity continually mutates, and its needs and demands change. As the cycle of struggle and recomposition develops, the insurgent subject expands and its demands become increasingly political. Workerists were particularly interested in the shift from the "skilled" to the "mass" worker. Skilled (or professional) workers had been the backbone of the organized labor movement and had led nineteenth- and early twentieth-century labor struggles. In response, capital introduced the assembly line, Fordism, and Taylorism, which meant a thorough deskilling of the workforce as well as improved productivity and efficiency. But this engendered a new and more powerful threat in the resulting huge factories such as FIAT's Mirafiori plant: the mass worker, an unpredictable and apparently disorganized subject that expressed itself not so much through unionism as through the everyday resistance of absenteeism, go-slows, and wildcat strikes. The mass worker comprised the "common" workers who became, as sociologist Emilio Reyneri puts it, "direct protagonists of struggle" in the unrest that shook Italian society in the late 1960s.[150] But no sooner had the mass worker emerged (in Italy's relatively late industrialization of the 1950s and 1960s), than it too was defeated as the efflorescence of the 1960s turned into the mass unemployment, austerity, repression, and "years of lead" of the 1970s. Autonomism, however, with Negri as its leading theorist, picked up where workerism had left off and identified a still more expansive social subject forged in this apparent defeat: the "socialized" worker. With the factory system disassembled in response to the mass worker's struggles, work was "diffused throughout the entire society" and the laboring subject became likewise immediately social. The struggles of the 1970s therefore brought together the unemployed, students, housewives, and others who had previously been at the margins of class antagonism: the socialized worker broke out of the factory walls to become "the producer of the social cooperation necessary for work" and even, Negri argued, "a kind of actualization of communism, its developed condition."[151]

The socialized worker did not, however, lead to communism. In fact, as Virno notes, the 1970s saw the start of a "counterrevolution" that continued on to the mid-1990s. Virno defines counterrevolution as "an impetuous innovation of modes of production, forms of life, and social relations that, however, consolidate and set again in motion capitalist command."[152] In short, it is another case of reactive development and class recomposition. The "movement of '77," the broad front of social movements that Negri identified with the "socialized worker," refused factory discipline and the idea of a job for life, demanding instead flexibility and the freedom to drop out or change jobs at will; but capital responded with lay-offs and structural unemployment that led to "the rapid alternation of superexploitation and inactivity." Where protesters valued "self-sufficiency . . . individual autonomy and experimentation," this was "put to work" with the 1980s rise of microbusinesses and diffuse entrepreneurialism that coincided with "extremely high levels of self-exploitation."[153] So post-Fordism and neoliberalism were also a response to insurgent subjectivity. We might add that globalization, too, can be seen as a reaction to similar demands for transnational mobility and to an exodus not only from the factory but also from the nation-state. Moreover, as for politics, Virno notes that the social movements of the 1970s "removed themselves from the logic of political representation" and positioned themselves at best "at the edges of the political parties, considering them nothing more than the ventriloquists of cheap identities"; in response, however, those parties initiated "a tendential restriction of political participation," finding in "the crisis of representation . . . the legitimation of an authoritarian reorganization of the state." Hence the "new Right" (Virno specifically refers to Silvio Berlusconi's Forza Italia, but we have seen similar developments elsewhere, and not merely in parties self-identified as right-wing) "recognizes, and temporarily makes its own, elements that would ultimately be worthy of our highest hopes: anti-Statism, collective practices that elude political representation, and the power of mass intellectual labor." These ideals are distorted and reduced to an "evil caricature," as constituted power folds back on the constituent, but they define the next stage of struggle. In Virno's words, "That act is over — let the next begin!"[154]

The various incarnations of what workerists termed working-class subjectivity, but which with the socialized worker and the movement of '77 increasingly spilled out of traditional class categories, all had direct social and political effects. For Tronti, the state has to intervene in industrial and social disputes because labor is dominant within the process of production itself: out of "economic necessity," capitalists resort to "force to make the working class abandon its proper social role as the dominant class. . . . In order to exist, the class of capitalists needs the mediation of a formal political level."[155] As Negri put it in the late 1960s, "the only way to understand our present state-form is to highlight the dramatic impact of the working class on the structures of capitalism." Negri argued that "the state-form has to register the impact of the working class on society" and showed how proletarian militancy led first to the rise of the "planning-based state" or "planner-state" of Keynesianism and the New Deal, and then to its crisis in the 1960s as "the state more openly asserts its monstrous role as the technical organ of domination."[156] In the 1970s, the planner-state gives way to the "crisis-state," the welfare state to the "warfare state." But the fact that the state is in crisis does not make it any the less functional: it means rather "a definitive point of rupture with any possible social contract for planned development"; any pretense to hegemony is replaced by simple command "ever more emptied of any rationale other than the reproduction of its own effectiveness."[157]

The history of the state is punctuated by spectacular ruptures, revolutions, and coups that force dramatic political reorganization. Every interruption prompts a fresh attempt to set limits to constituent power, to impose finality, and (in philosopher Peter Hallward's metaphor) to "dam the flood."[158] Each incarnation of state power has its topography: the state is a spatial arrangement, rather than a temporal one, though it also overcodes time by trying to give it measure. Twentieth-century technologies of containment range from the cinematic scenography of populism to the televisual ubiquity of neoliberalism. At no point, however, is hegemony at issue: constituted power folds in on constituent power to (re)compose its characteristic structures of affect and habit; it establishes a holding pattern, an apparatus of capture, to produce the effect of transcendence and sovereignty. Negri points out that the concept of hegemony lacks the "materialist consistency" required to understand such efforts to reshape being itself. The concept grants too much dynamism and authority to the "petrified and illusory command" wielded by the state form.[159] And hegemony passes over the mobility and flexibility of the multiple resistances that "escape the increasingly confining enclosures of misery and Power."[160] Above all, hegemony simply takes the state for granted, assuming that counterpower should seek to take over the state, to establish its own hegemony. By contrast, Negri argues for what he terms a "constituent Republic," that is, "a Republic that comes before the State, that comes outside of the State." This would be a social form in which "the constituent process never closes,...the revolution does not come to an end."[161] The dams would be definitively breached; continuity would be all.

The multitude is both an extension of the lineage outlined by workerism and autonomism, and its precondition. It is an extension in that it refines and further develops the concept of the socialized worker. The multitude is the socialized worker now that the terrain of struggle has become global and biopolitical. It is the product of capital's response to the socialized worker, a subject born (or still being born) out of neoliberalism and globalization. The baton of revolutionary subjectivity passes from the socialized worker to the multitude, which will only be fully incarnated once capitalism has been finally defeated. On the other hand, the multitude is the precondition of the entire sequence from skilled worker to mass and socialized worker inasmuch as it incarnates a virtual potential that is gradually actualized in history. The multitude is continuous variation: its constituent power is what is common to all the various struggles for liberation from union militancy to student unrest, as well as, for instance, colonial and postcolonial subaltern insurgency. Hence the multitude is past, present, and future at the same time. The multitude drives temporality, and constitutes time itself, a "liberated time" that is beyond all measure; "the love of time," Negri argues, "is the soul of constituent power because this makes of the world of life a dynamic essence."[162] But the multitude will bring time to an end, as it prefigures the end of history, the imminence of a Communist utopia. Hardt and Negri insist that the choice is between life and death, between "a present that is already dead and a future that is already living."[163] Theirs is a quasi-religious call to the promised land; but what if that future brought its own form of death?

At first sight, recent Chilean history is pitted with discontinuities. The country seems to have lurched from center to left to right and back to center and then left again over the course of its successive regimes since the mid-1960s: Eduardo Frei Montalva's progressive Christian Democracy (1964 to 1970); Salvador Allende's socialist Unidad Popular (1970 to 1973); Augusto Pinochet's dictatorship (1973 to 1990), and the Concertación (1990 to 2010).[164] Even the Concertación presidencies have shown marked differences, from Patricio Aylwin and Eduardo Frei Ruiz-Tagle's Christian Democracy to the Socialists Ricardo Lagos and Michelle Bachelet. Indeed Bachelet's 2006 victory is often counted among Latin America's left turns, although it involved a handover between two presidents belonging to the same party in the same coalition that has been in power for over a quarter of a century. The fact that the electorate voted for a woman (a single mother, what is more) once tortured by the dictatorship was taken to be yet another shift in the country's political sensibilities. Political scientist Lois Hecht Oppenheim highlights Chile's "turbulent history as a social laboratory" and "the dramatic changes that have taken place over the past forty years"; she argues for "Chile's exceptionalism," in light of "the fact that it has served as the site for quite diverse political experiments over the course of its history."[165] That the country has nonetheless also won a reputation for stability, both economic and political, is due to the "compulsion to forget" that sociologist Tomás Moulián identifies at the heart of its post-Pinochet transition to democracy.[166] But even this forced oblivion itself indicates another refoundation (the transition) that, as with any such new beginning, claims to be a self-realization for which all traces of the past can be erased. The "whitewash" that establishes the idea that Chile has had a "perfect transition" is engineered by a series of social transformations attendant on "a change in the state form." Chile has moved, Moulián argues, from a welfare state to a "mercantile state," from citizen rights to market liberty.[167] But the new regime passes itself off as inevitable, as the product of a prior agreement that separates the natural from the social: "Society is thought to have taken on its definitive stage or state, lacking all historicity, the product of a type of 'atavistic pact.'" For the Chilean transition and its interminable interregnum, actuality is all; its consensus is "the higher stage of forgetfulness."[168]

Dramatic changes in the Chilean state form conceal deeper historical continuities. Moulián, for instance, notes that "this new type of State, which we will call neoliberal, can take either democratic or authoritarian forms." So there is a fundamental unity of purpose shared by the dictatorship and the democratic transition that followed it: the "primordial objective" of the contemporary state is "to ensure that the economic and social order created by authoritarianism can be reproduced." The dictatorship succeeded in subordinating politics to economics, and in its constitutional phase, after promulgating a new constitution in 1980, legitimated these changes and finally managed "to absorb the opposition within the game of alternatives defined by the regime itself."[169] For Moulián, the dictatorship effected a shift in the mode in which power was exercised, from a dependence on ideology to a postideological integration of atomized individuals into the marketplace. But in sum, in the transition from dictatorship to democracy, "those who wielded power changed, but society did not. This has accomplished the central principle of so-called *gatopardismo:* everything has to change, so that everything can stay the same." This is the "counterrevolution" that aims to negate the legacy of the Unidad Popular.[170] Or in philosopher Willy Thayer's words, "It is not the passage from Dictatorship to democracy to which we should give the name 'transition'; rather, the transition was the transformation effected by the Dictatorship itself, in displacing the State as national history's subject and center, in favor of the ex-centric post-state market." The most profound effect of the transition, for Thayer, is a "change in the mode of production of representation." Even the word "transition" is misleading, in that it suggests "movement and transformation" when reality is "stationary and intransitive." Transition is the "perfect host" in that anything and everything is welcome; but in transition, "nothing new happens." It is "the very definition of boredom."[171] To extend Thayer's metaphor: it throws a party to which everyone is welcome, but which no one would want to attend.

For both Moulián and Thayer, the only definitive break in recent Chilean history is the 1973 coup. For Moulián, the left is complicit in the historical amnesia that has erased this most violent of state refoundations; his *Conversación interrumpida con Allende* is intended to bridge that void. For Thayer, the left has yet to take stock of the magnitude of the caesura; by failing to see that the coup did not simply take place within history, that it affected history itself, even the most radical of its critics become structurally complicit as they reiterate, in their very criticism, "the Dictatorship's foundational *state of exception* that suspends the Constitution and then refounds the Constitution." So Thayer also wants to rescue something from the previous epoch: a "purely destructive critique, which neither conserved nor founded rights," that he finds in "the popular practices of Salvador Allende's Government" and its *"anasemic performance,* disjunctive, mute, unjudgemental." This anasemic or antisemantic performance "was activated without concern for its success, as a *'revolutionary general strike.'"* However, Allende's government "inscribed the destruction of representation within the enclosures of Republican representation." In the end, the general strike failed to destroy the republic; the republic was undone, rather, by the "sovereign Coup that was Globalization's 'Big Bang.' "[172] Thayer emphasizes the destructive aspects of the revolutionary general strike which, following German philosopher Walter Benjamin's reading of French anarcho-syndicalist Georges Sorel, he distinguishes from the "political general strike," whose aim is to strengthen state power. But surely the general strike is also affirmative: it is an instance of what Benjamin terms messianic or "divine" violence, that is, "pure power over all life for the sake of the living."[173] The performance (or pure performativity) to which Thayer points is constituent power, and it precedes, traverses, and outlasts the rise and fall of Allende's Unidad Popular.

Instead of ruptures and discontinuities in Chilean history, sociologists Javier Martínez and Alvaro Díaz argue in *Chile: The Great Transformation* that the continuities are more striking, over a period that reaches back to the mid-1960s. They go beyond "the strictly episodic aspects of the Chilean experience," tracking long-term processes that explain Pinochet's success and the transition to neoliberalism that he ushered in. For instance, land in Chile (as indeed in much of Latin America) was traditionally concentrated very unequally in the hands of a small class of rural landholders. From the late 1950s, some large estates, known as *latifundios,* began to be divided. But still by the early 1960s, many believed that "the responsibility for all national ills – real or imaginary – could be laid at the door of the *latifundio.*" Under Frei's Social Democratic government, therefore, and even more rapidly under Allende's Unidad Popular, vast swathes of Chile's farmland were nationalized and redistributed: "Between 1964 and 1973, more than 5,000 holdings were expropriated, covering 10 million hectares, equivalent to 60 percent of the country's arable land."[174] This tendency continued under Pinochet: "Despite expectations, the military coup did not bring about a return of the *latifundio.*" Instead, the dictatorship gave "a new twist to the process": it made land a fungible commodity, enabling sales, rentals, auctions, and private corporations.[175] Ten years of social democracy and socialism had already broken the back of the rural oligarchy; Pinochet's government took the opportunity to accelerate the pace of change, but in the name of the market rather than the state. More generally, Martínez and Díaz stress that the three successive administrations "were all revolutionary governments"; Social Democracy paved the way for the Unidad Popular, which in turn enabled the dictatorship to complete the tasks it left pending, always with a "twist."

"The neoliberal project's radicalism," Martínez and Díaz argue, "was possible because the attempts that had preceded it were also radical. Given the dimension of the changes that took place, it would seem appropriate to talk of a revolutionary epoch." Or rather, the Pinochet counterrevolution continued (and even accelerated) revolutionary processes that were already in train, but it took them in a new direction. Under Frei and Allende, Chile underwent an "advanced socialization" in which new social movements "questioned the social order and modified the logic of programs for social change" while "the ruling classes saw their power gravely weakened."[176] Constituent power transformed the social order, forcing creative adjustment from the state.

The multitude is the key to Chile's underlying continuities. Social democracy and the Unidad Popular, too, were responses to its constituent power. Martínez and Díaz's narrative of social change obscures this fact because of their narrow focus on government. Regarding land reform, for instance, they pass over in silence the numerous land seizures or *tomas de terreno* through which peasants and urban migrants took matters into their own hands. Cathy Schneider points to the massive migration to Santiago over the 1950s and the consequent increasing numbers of homeless people in the capital city: "Before the end of the decade," she reports, they grew to "about 150,000 people, or 8 percent of the population." A series of seizures followed, notably the 1957 occupation of the land that would become the neighborhood of La Victoria: for two months, police besieged 3,000 illegal settlers, until the government gave in and awarded the squatters housing rights. This, however, was only the beginning, as "in the next few decades illegal land seizures would account for over 40 percent of Santiago's growth."[177] In the countryside, meanwhile, political scientist Patricio Silva notes that the late 1960s saw an "explosive expansion of rural unionism . . . accompanied by a dramatic increase in the number of strikes and *tomas* (land seizures)." In 1964, only 1,800 peasants belonged to a union; in 1967, there were 54,418; and three years later, by the end of the Frei administration, the number had risen to 140,293, or "around a third of all Chilean agrarian workers." Increased unionization resulted in part from government attempts to incorporate the peasantry with a 1967 "Law on Agrarian Unionization," but it "produced a deep split between the ruling Christian Democrats and the right-wing parties, making possible the victory of the Unidad Popular in the 1970 presidential elections." Under Allende, peasant radicalization increased still further, union membership doubled yet again, and there was an "enormous increase in the number of strikes and land seizures."[178] The Unidad Popular was torn between its radical or messianic elements, which incarnated what Thayer terms the revolutionary general strike, and its lawmaking, constitutional tendencies. The so-called government of "popular unity" could not contain the multitude with and against which it moved; it was ultimately neither popular nor unified. In Moulián's words, it was wracked by an internal conflict between revolution and counterrevolution, "licentiousness 'festive' and conspiratorial."[179] The dictatorship stepped in to quell the disorder and to install a new constitution; but it only continued the revolutionary process, albeit in cruel and bloody caricature. And no sooner had the constitution been declared, than the social movements of the 1980s erupted. These movements were demobilized and absorbed into the renewed pact forged by the postdictatorial Concertación. But as Bachelet discovered within weeks of assuming office in 2006, when students took to the streets to demand educational reform and free public transportation, and corruption scandals hit the heart of her administration, the multitude continues.

With the declaration that communism is imminent, analysis shades into project. Negri has repeatedly announced that we are on the verge of revolution, or even that the revolution has already taken place. In the 1970s, the socialized worker in post-Fordist Italy had achieved "a kind of actualization of communism."[180] In the 1980s, Negri heralded Parisian student protests as incarnating the "actuality of communism" and "the unfurled consciousness of the socialized worker."[181] In the 1990s, with *Labor of Dionysus*, Negri and Hardt declared that the "prerequisites of communism" were now present, part of an "irreversible" tendency. Indeed they argued that "we are living a revolution that is already developed and only a death threat stops it from being declared."[182] In their subsequent work, Hardt and Negri are more circumspect: *Multitude* cautions that "a philosophical book like this . . . is not the place for us to evaluate whether the time of revolutionary political decision is imminent. . . . There is no need for eschatology or utopianism here."[183] Yet the promise of revolution suffuses both *Empire* and *Multitude*. Critic Marcia Landy says of Negri's earlier writings that "the conditions of possibility for revolution are uppermost."[184] This has not changed in the intervening years. Having identified the multitude as the subject of constituent power, Negri unabashedly celebrates and affirms its revolutionary potential. In his own terms, he is a militant, "posing against the misery of power the joy of being" in the name of "a revolution that no power will control."[185] Neither cultural studies nor civil society theory have any such pretensions to revolution. They cannot imagine life outside the contemporary social order (for both, exteriority is mute subalternity), still less that the barrier between inside and outside could break down, and with it the fiction of a social pact that passes through a transcendent center. Cultural studies merely calls for more hegemony: counterhegemony, working-class hegemony, national–popular hegemony. Hegemony upon hegemony! What kind of slogan is that? And civil society theory's demands for good management and transparency are naïve at best, antipolitical technocracy at worst. Negri's posthegemonic proclamation of multitudinous liberation is perhaps the sole remaining revolutionary project with any credence. And it depends fully on credence, on faith.

The promise of communism is necessary for Negri's analysis: it motivates the call to pass through Empire to the other side. Without it, there would be no reason to go further into Empire, a form of rule more vicious and arbitrary (corrupt, Negri and Hardt tell us) than any before. If Empire has in fact no other side, then at best we can aim for reactive resistance, perhaps the establishment of what anarchist theorist Hakim Bey terms "temporary autonomous zones," an exodus with no promised land in sight.[186] At worst, we end up with mere redescription: new words (affect, habit, multitude) for old problems, but no solutions; in the case of theorist Manuel De Landa's "new philosophy of society," a similar redescription in terms of assemblages, intensities, and flows ends up legitimating the complexity of contemporary capitalism, encouraging a "positive, even joyful conception of reality."[187] For Hardt and Negri, by contrast, "joy" comes from "being communist" and from the belief that "Empire creates a greater potential for revolution" than did previous regimes of power, because it "presents us . . . [with] a multitude that is directly opposed to Empire, with no mediation between them."[188] Faced with this alternative, between the millenarianism of Negri's *multitudo fidelium* and a cynicism that identifies what is with what ought to be, I prefer to hesitate, to remain agnostic, to affiliate myself however uneasily with Latin Americanist critic Gareth Williams's "perhaps."[189] The multitude is already here and now; *perhaps* it is also to come. In the meantime (and these are indeed mean times), in a potentially interminable in-between, we can continue to seek good encounters, habits, and affects. In the meantime, we must strive to persist, guided by a *conatus* forever impatient with the current order.

Negri posits the multitude as a modern god. "The poor," he and Hardt claim, "is god on earth."[190] In the best tradition of fundamentalism, he calls for the kingdom of God on earth to start here and now. Spinoza, too, cannot help but be a fundamentalist: what made Spinoza the great atheist was also what made him the great (if heretic) theist. For Spinoza, eliminating transcendence allows us to become immediately one with God: *Deus sive Natura*. He envisages a fully achieved immanence as the privilege of universal divinity, perfect and eternal. *Sub specie aeternitatis,* that is, from the perspective of eternity, every difference is resolved, and harmony and knowledge are all. The ultimate aim of Spinoza's ethics is to achieve blessedness, what he terms the third kind of knowledge, which follows and completes the knowledge revealed through signs or representation and the knowledge revealed in the joyfulness of immanent commonality. Blessedness is communion with God in eternity; it is the end of history. "The wise man," Spinoza declares at the conclusion to the *Ethics*, "is hardly troubled in spirit, but being, by a certain eternal necessity, conscious of himself, and of God, and of things, he never ceases to be, but always possesses true peace of mind."[191] This is what Negri terms "the revolution of the eternal."[192] But absolute immanence would not only end history; it would also end the play of encounter, the series of events that give rise to either pleasure or pain. All contingency and accident would be abolished in favor of absolute necessity, for Spinoza coterminous with absolute freedom. There would be no encounter because everything would be already in its place. What would endure would be pure intensity, outside of time or, better, of time (a time without measure) rather than in time. Should the multitude come into its own, unfettered by constituted power, and the state and transcendence disappear, there would be no objectivity, only the pure subjectivity of the divine presence and power. Heaven is a place where nothing ever happens. Future Perfect or *perfectum est:* It would be perfect, but it would be dead.

Epilogue

April 13, 2002

[Demystifying] the notion that technology is a dark science fit only for specialists and that the production of information is the sole preserve of "professionals" ... leads us to a new model of social communication, in which communication is no longer instrumentalized and commodified but becomes once more the human faculty of exchanging affects, desires, and knowledges. A communication that would be the expression of the multitude, of diversity, of liberty.

—Asociación Nacional de Medios, Comunitarios, Libres y Alternativos (Venezuela), "Somos expresión de la multitud"

The Multitude Breaks the Pact

The fiction of hegemony is more threadbare than ever. The myth of the social contract is over. In place of coercion or consent, both of which depend upon granting transcendence to the state, posthegemony substitutes affect, habit, and an immanent multitude. Politics is biopolitics: in fact, it always has been, but today more clearly than before neither civil society nor the state are sites of struggle or objects of negotiation. At stake is life itself. On the one hand, increasingly corrupt forces of command and control modulate and intervene directly on the bodies of ordinary men and women. On the other hand, everyday insurgencies of constituent power reveal a multitude that betrays and corrodes constituted power from the inside, overflowing and escaping its bounds. The outcome of this confrontation is uncertain: constituent power may still fold back against itself; the line of flight that escapes may become suicidal; the multitude may turn bad and become monstrous; or perhaps, just perhaps, exodus may lead to what Negri terms "the time of common freedom."[1]

It is in Latin America that the failure of modernity's social contract is most evident. And Latin America, too, is the setting for the most promising experiments in common freedom. Veteran activist and critic Tariq Ali claims that "South America is on the march again, offering hope to a world either deep in neo-liberal torpor or suffering daily from the military and economic depredations of the New Order."[2] For Ali, "Venezuela and the Bolivarian dream" are at the center of an "axis of hope."[3] He offers a rosy view of what have been called the Latin American "left turns" or "pink tide," in which a series of left-leaning governments have been elected to power in the region: from Hugo Chávez in Venezuela in 1998, Luiz Inácio "Lula" da Silva in Brazil in 2002, and Evo Morales in Bolivia in 2005, to Fernando Lugo in Paraguay in 2008, the left has dominated the continent's politics over the past decade. But these electoral victories are at best a symptom, at worst a reaction. They follow an even more surprising series of social protests and multitudinous mobilizations: from the Venezuelan Caracazo of 1989, Mexico's Zapatista insurgency since 1994, and the Argentine crisis of 2001, to the Bolivian gas protests of 2004, Latin America has been shaken by myriad struggles that have ushered in a new era of political flux. From carnivalesque revolt to neighborhood assemblies, from highway pickets to barter economies, novel forms of collective action have shattered the theater of political representation and marked the emergence of a multitude. In response, the region's left-wing regimes usher in a "new governability," more precarious if also more propitious than before.[4]

The Caracazo was the first of the social ruptures that indicated the end of the social pact and presaged the left turns. It began with an instance of what in 1970s Italy was called self-valorization or autoreduction. As sociologists Eddy Cherki and Michel Wieviorka explain, autoreduction is "the act by which consumers, in the area of consumption, and workers, in the area of production, take it upon themselves to reduce, at a *collectively* determined level, the price of public services, housing, electricity."[5] Cherki and Wieviorka discuss Turin workers' refusal to pay increased bus fares in 1974. In almost identical fashion, on the morning of February 27, 1989, commuters in and around Venezuela's capital refused to pay the higher prices that transport companies demanded of them in the wake of newly elected President Carlos Andrés Pérez's packet of neoliberal reforms. But whereas in Turin, this fare strike was soon "organized... by unions which brought their active support and simultaneously imposed a coherent line of struggle,"[6] in Caracas no leaders emerged, no party line was enforced.

Within hours, protest spread across the country and especially all over the capital city in what was an apparently "anarchic movement, without direction, totally spontaneous, in no way preconceived by any subversive organizations."[7] By midmorning, people had built barricades and started to stop trucks, especially all those thought to carry food, and empty them of their merchandise, as well as looting shops and malls. Outrage was provoked by the discovery that shopkeepers had hoarded goods in anticipation of imminent price rises. In Caracas, the main squares and highways were blockaded. Cars were set on fire. Motorcycle dispatch riders spread news, communicated rebellion, and ferried personnel.[8] A protest against bus fares had turned into a general revolt against neoliberal structural adjustment! Moreover, the riot took on colors of carnival as the police were powerless to intervene and, in some cases, even sympathized with the movement and helped to ensure that the plunder took place with some order and fair distribution between young and old, men and women. What anthropologists Fernando Coronil and Julie Skurski call a "loose organization" emerged as groceries and clothing were taken to those who were unable to participate in the pillage themselves, and large sides of beef and pork were carved up and shared out. A barter economy flourished and "looting dissolved momentarily money's ability to regulate collective life." In the end, an estimated one million people took part in the disturbances, "in effect erasing state control of the street."[9] That night, even as tanks started to roll in to put down what was by now a full-scale insurrection, in the poor barrios high up on the hills overlooking Caracas "a party was underway, with champagne, steak, and imported whisky, all products of the looting."[10] Salsa and merengue music blared from stolen hi-fi equipment. Common unrest had become shared celebration.

The state was slow to react. The president was traveling and—only half-aware of what was going on—told "that nothing out of the ordinary was happening."[11] It was not until the afternoon of the following day that a government official even tried to address the nation. When eventually the minister of the interior appeared on the television, he was halfway through his appeal for calm when he "was overcome by nervous exhaustion and rendered speechless on camera. Disney cartoons replaced him without explanation." The state was quite literally struck dumb by events. It failed to articulate even the thinnest of hegemonic fictions. The social pact was almost completely ruptured. And any tenuous notion of a contract with a benevolent and protective state that might have survived the initial uprising was shattered by the government's eventual response. For when the state finally moved, it moved with force against its own citizenry. A state of exception was declared, the constitution suspended, freedom of the press curtailed, and a curfew imposed. As Coronil and Skurski observe, the "traditional language of populism" was abruptly abandoned, as it failed to "represent the state" let alone the people. Indeed, Pérez was now a president "without a people."[12] The multitude had taken its place. Unable to convert multitude into people, with all its representational strategies now bankrupt, the state responded only with massive repression. Over the next few days, the center of Caracas was a war zone. For at least one reporter, "Caracas was Beirut": a city at the epicenter of a civil war.[13] As Coronil and Skurski put it, "the government's armed agencies deployed violence in multiple forms, communicating in practice to the poor the distinct forms of otherness by which they could be encompassed."[14] Up to a thousand people were killed. Firefights rang out in the downtown. The military fired artillery rounds almost indiscriminately at tower blocks, seeking out snipers but also in general fear at what might lie within their walls: in the words of another journalist, "behind that silent cement the multitude is hidden. Thousands of eyes observe our movements."[15]

What was most disquieting and unexpected about the Caracazo was that it broke the peace of what had been South America's most stable democracy. Venezuela had even been "the 'center' of world democracy" as it celebrated a spectacular presidential inauguration, attended by an unprecedented gathering of world leaders from 108 countries, less than a month previously.[16] More generally, for much of the twentieth century the country had avoided the political violence that had blighted so much of Latin America. While nations such as Argentina, Chile, and Brazil were under military rule in the 1970s, Venezuela boomed thanks to its oil wealth and the rising price of crude. It had long been regarded as an "exceptional democracy," exempt from the conflicts that afflicted the rest of the region; it was touted as "a model democracy for Latin America."[17] The country apparently demonstrated the benefits and viability of a formal social pact: in 1958, its major political parties had signed a written accord, the "Pact of Punto Fijo." They agreed to defend the constitution and to respect electoral results; they established a minimum common program and a promise to share power with electoral rivals; and they incorporated elements of so-called civil society, such as labor unions and professional associations. The pact aimed to ensure stability and continuity and to marginalize more radical forces such as, notably, Venezuela's Communist Party. It was under the auspices of *puntofijismo* that, in the subsequent three decades, the country garnered its reputation as a democratic paradise, and became known for baseball and beauty queens rather than coups or revolutions. But the Pact of Punto Fijo broke down in the Caracazo. The "fixed point" was overwhelmed first by the tidal surge of an irrepressible multitude, and then by the state's vicious abandonment of even the pretense of hegemony.

Habits and Affects

The trigger for the Caracazo was no more (and no less) than habit. Commuters were accustomed to paying one price for public transport; they protested when they were suddenly forced to pay another. In response to the shock doctrine of neoliberal reform, sprung on the nation without warning after President Pérez had run for office on a broadly populist platform, the Venezuelan population took violent umbrage. There was something conservative about their response: the uprising was an expression of habitus, as well as of *conatus*, of an instinct for self-preservation or survival. The impulse to demonstrate also drew on traditional habits. Historian Margarita López Maya emphasizes the continuities between the 1989 rebellion and previous moments of social protest: a 1902 British and German blockade of Venezuela's ports, for instance, had provoked "protests whose protagonists were multitudes whose organization and leadership were unknown." Further disturbances accompanied the death of the dictator Juan Vicente Gómez in 1935, in response to which General José López Contreras, Gómez's successor, "regarding the multitude, . . . moved in clear pursuit of winning the *people* to his side." But unrest continued through to 1936, leading to the growth of "political organizations that would seek in the following years to channel the force lodged in these multitudes toward more stable and fluid forms of communication, so that they could dialogue with power."[18]

Slowly, López Contreras's project of converting multitude into people was realized. Over the course of the 1940s and 1950s, despite outbreaks of protest in 1945 (marked by a particularly "festive tone") and 1948, not to mention January 1958 with the fall of the country's last dictatorial regime, gradually "the protagonism of the multitude gave way to that of social and political organizations."[19] In short, Venezuela's rapid modernization and urbanization in the first half of the twentieth century (as oil was discovered and the economy shifted from agriculture to hydrocarbons) had been characterized by a series of multitudinous protests and demonstrations. But these were eventually absorbed and disarmed by so-called civil society. The Pact of Punto Fijo in 1958 was merely the culmination of a long process of state reaction to this ever-present multitude. In the thirty years of exceptional democracy that followed, the multitude rarely appeared: "The political institutions of mediation first replaced the multitudes and then excluded them from the political system." But the Caracazo revealed their continued presence, now more expansive and stronger than ever. Since 1989, "the multitudes have taken to the street once more."[20]

The Caracazo was both new and old. It was old in that it was the resumption of habits of protest long dormant yet never entirely forgotten. It was the return of affects long repressed yet never fully eliminated. For Coronil and Skurski, it was the latest incarnation of the "river of instinctual energy" that has been coded as "barbarism" in Venezuelan cultural discourse, not least in the nation's founding fiction, the 1929 novel *Doña Bárbara*. Its author, Rómulo Gallegos, briefly became president in the late 1940s, and so contributed to the project of taming the multitude's "energy" and "passion" through politics as well as literature. And yet the Caracazo was also new: it was a watershed in Venezuelan history, and for Coronil and Skurski part of a "worldwide reordering of body politics."[21] A sign of its novelty, and of the way in which it fractured the frame of political and social representation, was the fact that for a long time nobody even knew what to call it. The events "disrupted established interpretive schemes, resisting the efforts of official and opposition forces to fix them with a name." They were "27–F" or *los sucesos* ("the events"); "the disturbances" or *el sacudón* ("the big jolt"); a "social explosion," a *poblada* (popular uprising), or *el masacrón* ("the big massacre"); or they were simply "the war."[22] Language could not contain what had taken place. The Caracazo was affect.

On the sidelines, a small group of young military officers were also trying to make sense of what had happened. The Bolivarian Revolutionary Movement (Movimiento Bolivariano Revolucionario, or MBR) was a clandestine organization, founded in 1982, that brought together would-be revolutionaries who had sworn fidelity to a vague set of ideals based loosely on the Enlightenment political philosophy of Simón Bolívar. They became convinced that the only way to achieve significant change in Venezuela was through a coup d'état. Not much had come of their plotting, however, and the Caracazo with its sudden explosion of violence on the streets took them, as much as anyone else, by surprise: they "felt aggrieved that the moment and the opportunity that they had been half expecting had passed them by without any possibility of taking action." Before their eyes they felt they saw something like an emerging historic movement threatening the old order, but these young Turks were in no position to impose any kind of hegemonic leadership; they were "not remotely prepared."[23] The most disappointed of all at the MBR's failure to seize this opportunity would have been the movement's founder: a young army lieutenant who spent the morning of February 27 lying ill in bed. His name was Hugo Chávez Frías.

Chávez recognized that the Caracazo was an expression of constituent power. In its wake, he and his group accelerated their plans to take over the state and began putting "forward the argument for a constituent assembly as the only path out of the trap" of a now bankrupt *puntofijismo*.[24] Three years later, in February 1992, they finally acted. Yet their attempted coup was a short-lived failure. Rebel forces took provincial cities, but in Caracas Chávez was unable to detain President Pérez as planned, and he found himself surrounded and cut off in the city's historical museum. He confessed later that "the civilians didn't show up."[25] The people were missing. Forced to turn himself in, the would-be coup leader asked only for a minute of airtime on national television so as to tell his allies elsewhere that they too should surrender. It was this brief broadcast that made his name, as Chávez declared to the country that "for now" the attempt to overthrow the regime had failed. On TV, speaking directly to the nation without the mediation of the MBR or any other organization, at last Chávez found his métier. Though he would soon be jailed for his leading role in the conspiracy, in the space of an instant, with a two-word phrase evoking change to come, he had identified himself with a messianic promise.

By 1994, Chávez was pardoned and released (Pérez had been impeached for corruption and thrown out of office). No longer a clandestine organization, the MBR focused on "its fundamental political strategy of demanding the convocation of a National Constituent Assembly."[26] In the build-up to the 1998 presidential race, it was transformed into a political party: the Movement for the Fifth Republic. Running on a manifesto to build a new republic, Chávez was handsomely elected into power, winning 56 percent of the vote. A constituent assembly followed in 1999, and a new constitution was approved in December of that year. The constitution called for a one-time "mega-election" in which all elected officials, from city council members to president, would have to stand to be relegitimated. On July 30, 2000, as over thirty-three thousand candidates competed for more than six thousand posts, in a stroke the election "eliminated the country's old political elite almost entirely from the upper reaches of Venezuela's public institutions."[27] The old guard had gone; but in each electoral race a new guard took its place. The old pact had ruptured; a new pact, in which the state would now appeal directly to the multitude over the airwaves, had just begun.

The Insistence of Posthegemony

Television has been instrumental in Chávez's capture of the nation, from the 1992 coup attempt onward. In power, Chávez's folksy televised appearances and his weekly call-in talk show, *Aló, Presidente,* have been cornerstones of his neopopulist appeal. Writing in 2007 and reporting on an edition of the show that lasted over eight hours, journalist Rory Carroll quotes Venezuelan political scientist Arturo Serrano's observation that "Chávez governs from *Aló Presidente.*" But Serrano focuses on the way in which this "television chatshow like no other" is a vehicle for communication between the president and his colleagues and subordinates: "It is on this show that ministers find out if they have been fired or hired; it is here where mayors and governors are reprimanded for anything they have done wrong."[28] But far more important is the way in which

Chávez, "wizard of the emotions," employs television to construct a new form of social pact, however precarious and ambivalent.[29]

In April 2002, the overthrow and then precipitate reinstatement of Chávez's regime revealed the limits of this televisual pact and of mediated politics as a whole.[30] The coup was the all too predictable culmination of a battle for the airwaves; in the countercoup, a mere two days later, the multitude emerged unheralded, but undisguised. In February, Chávez had sacked the president and most of the directors of the state oil company, PDVSA. Management responded with a production slowdown and then a strike; in turn, Chávez fired nineteen managers. During March and early April, constant news coverage of a gathering crisis gripped Caracas. The press and the television networks launched an open and concerted assault on the government, happily giving space to Chávez's opponents. Only the one state-owned TV channel was unashamedly for the regime. Chávez took to decreeing *cadenas,* or "chains," in which he obliged all the networks to broadcast his long addresses to the nation. One set of televisual discourses fought another. The commercial media redoubled their opposition, subverting the *cadenas* by superimposing text protesting this "abuse" of media freedom, or splitting the screen between images of Chávez's speech on one side and images of antigovernment demonstrations on the other. The struggle for dominance was incarnated in split-screen TV.

Chávez opponents banged pots and pans to drown out the president's broadcasts and demonstrated outside PDVSA's headquarters; his supporters gathered in televised rallies at the presidential palace. The opposition called a general strike, which became indefinite on April 10. An opposition march, heavily promoted by the commercial stations, was announced for the morning of Thursday April 11. That day, two hundred thousand demonstrators continued beyond their stated destination, heading for downtown. The regime's final moments began as the president tried to turn off the television networks literally as well as symbolically. As the march approached the national palace, around 1:30 in the afternoon, a *cadena* was announced and Chávez appeared on the screen, broadcasting from his office in front of a portrait of Bolívar, downplaying any disturbance. While he talked, one by one the terrestrial channels disappeared from the air, leaving only the government station. A surreal dialogue ensued: the private channels (now visible only to cable subscribers) split their screens once more, showing mute

Hugo Chávez broadcasts from the Miraflores palace, April 11, 2002. The television station has split the screen to show disturbances outside at the same time. Still from *Crónica de un golpe de estado: El secuestro de la verdad,* venezuelapolitica.org, 2002.

and confused images of riots outside the palace, superimposing their own commentary, and Chávez responded live to what the TV stations were adding to the official discourse. Then the chain broke and the game was up. The networks abandoned Chávez and dedicated themselves to the footage (repeated, out of sync) of earlier events: disorganized images of stone-throwing youths; injured people on stretchers; Chávez loyalists with firearms; bodies. Troops and tanks mobilizing and military communiqués marked a coup in progress. As the night wore on, state television screened nature documentaries, and then shut down entirely while the private channels returned to the airwaves in full force. A narrative emerged: that Chávez had ordered police to fire on the demonstrators. But the images never quite added up. Something always escapes. Eventually the military high command came out against the president and, at 1:30 a.m., the sound of pots and pans and fireworks greeted the news that Chávez was in custody. Businessman Pedro Carmona appeared on television as the new president.

Twelve hours later, the previous day's choppy and incoherent images had been played over and over, settling if only by virtue of their ordered repetition into the linear, coherent story provided by the newspapers. Glimpsed scenes of men shooting pistols from a bridge, their guns circled and digitally enhanced, were given context by diagrams and firsthand accounts provided by print journalists.

The morning of Saturday April 13, headlines declared "A Step in the Right Direction." President Carmona was sworn in and named his "transitional" government, whose first policies were announced. All traces of the previous regime were to be erased. Even the country's name changed: from the 1999 Constitution's "Bolivarian Republic of Venezuela" to, once more, simply "The Republic of Venezuela." Cultural critic Luis Duno Gottberg shows how, during this interregnum "a certain sort of collectivity — understood as mob, horde, rabble, lumpen — was displaced by contrast to acceptable, democratic and organised rationalities."[31] Elsewhere, however, another story was afoot, and fragments of news circulated by word of mouth or cell phone. Rumors spread of disturbances in the streets; of a parachute regiment and a section of the air force rebelling; of an imminent state of siege. As if from nowhere, ragged processions started advancing on downtown, converging on the national palace, chanting pro-Chávez slogans and carrying portraits of the deposed president. They distributed amateurish flyers. Other chavistas commandeered buses, calling on passersby to join this unexpected protest.

Some radio reports told of the crowds on the streets, but mainly the news media broadcast official pronouncements. President Carmona declared that the situation was under control, downplaying any insubordination among the armed forces, but announced he might fire some of the high command. The pact between military and commerce was quietly unraveling. Commercial TV continued with normal programming: soap operas, imported U.S. sitcoms, game shows. The state-owned channel was still off the air. Only on cable, from BBC World and CNN en español, did reports arrive of disturbances in Caracas's working-class neighborhoods and of the parachute regiment's refusal to surrender arms. The BBC spoke of thousands outside the palace. Darkness fell, and still no word from the networks. The self-censorship of light entertainment blocked any acknowledgment of what was slowly emerging as a pro-Chávez multitude. Abruptly, however, one channel broke from its programming to show scenes of the street outside its own headquarters. A group of young and mobile demonstrators, on motorcycles and scooters, were agitating outside the plate glass windows. Rocks were thrown, glass cracked, graffiti sprayed, and a new chain materialized as all the networks switched to this same image of demonstrators "attacking" the building. The group moved on and the soap operas resumed. Until a similar group turned up at another channel's headquarters, then another, and another. No more stones were thrown, but the demonstrations could now at least be glimpsed, in fragments, outside the TV stations. The channels split their screens into three, and, as one image was of the television screen itself, the picture fragmented further still into an endless regress of distorted images snatched through cracked windows. No camera teams ventured out.

Suddenly, around 10:30 that night, the state television station returned to the airwaves. Those who had retaken the station were improvising, desperately. But they gave a version of the previous Thursday's events that was very different from the narrative that had been put forward to justify the coup: the snipers firing on the crowds had been shooting at chavistas, not opposition protesters. Chávez had not resigned; he was forcibly detained. President Carmona was the illegitimate head of a de facto regime. Thousands of people were on the streets demanding Chávez's return. Over the next few hours, technical problems meant that the channel would go on and off the air several times. Repeatedly the channel attempted to show images from inside the presidential palace. Around 1:00 a.m., amid confusion and elation, Chávez's vice president, Diosdado Cabello, was sworn in as president. Venezuela now had three presidents simultaneously: Chávez, Carmona, and Cabello. The only question, posed by the crowds at the gates of the presidential palace and still besieging the private television stations, where was Chávez?

So the unthinkable happened. As the palace was effectively returned to those loyal to the deposed regime, shortly before three in the morning, a helicopter brought Hugo Chávez back, mobbed by thousands of near-delirious supporters. All the television stations were now running the images provided by the state channel without further comment; a new chain had formed, as commercial television lapsed into stunned silence. The president returned to the office from which he had been broadcasting as the coup was unfolding. Now, however, he was no longer alone, but flanked by his ministers in a crowded room buzzing with excitement. The coup had been overthrown almost invisibly, at the margins of the media. Democracy had returned despite a self-imposed media blackout of astonishing proportions. A massive revolt had erupted while the country's middle classes watched soap operas and game shows; television networks took notice only in the final moments, and when compelled to do so. Thereafter they simply bore mute witness to an event almost without precedent, as the coup was brought down less than forty-eight hours after its initial triumph. With nothing to say, the following day's newspapers simply failed to appear.

The alliance between military and business that engineered the coup was weak and could survive only through repression or apathy. The military were reluctant to turn to repression, and the coup plotters were received not with apathy, but with an extraordinary and near-spontaneous multitudinous insurrection. The coup's overthrow was also a revolt against a televisual regime in which Chávez himself was fully complicit. Chávez's government depended all too much on the figure of the president himself, whose promise of a direct contract through televisual means was shown to be remarkably insubstantial. *Chavismo* created the political vacuum that briefly allowed a far-right pact of arms and commerce to take control. In the event, however, the multitude came to fill that vacuum. The April 13 insurrection showed that Chávez's regime is not ultimately a product of either television or charisma, but is constituted by that multitude. The president thought he could serve as a substitute, masquerading the multitude's agency as his own. But Chávez himself is far from indispensable. In the tumultuous two days in which the president was detained, *chavismo* without Chávez demonstrated a power all its own, wrong-footing confused attempts at representation. The countercoup points once more toward a politics beyond systematic substitutions of people for multitude, emotion for affect, hegemony for habit. It points to posthegemony.

Acknowledgments

This book has been a long time coming. Along the way I have accumulated a great number of debts. *Posthegemony* originated as a Ph.D. dissertation, and I owe profound gratitude and respect first to my advisor and friend Alberto Moreiras. Alberto provides a model of intellectual engagement as a collective project that is both serious and fun. Second, to my committee: Michael Hardt, Danny James, Peter Lange, Gabriela Nouzeilles, Ken Surin, and, for much of the process, Fred Jameson. They offered valuable feedback and astute criticism.

I thank the Ford Foundation exchange between the Duke–UNC Program in Latin American Studies and the Instituto de Estudios Peruanos in Lima for funding research in Peru. The Rockefeller-funded seminar on postdictatorship culture for supporting research in Chile, and Duke's Center for International Studies for funding travel to Italy. Grants from the universities of Aberdeen and Manchester and from the Social Sciences and Humanities Research Council of Canada enabled me to be in Latin America at significant moments, as well as to attend conferences to present aspects of this work in gestation. I thank the Peter Wall Institute for Advanced Studies for providing an intellectual oasis during the final stages. Also, the various organizations that have invited me to present portions of the argument over the years.

A multitude more influenced and aided me while this book was brewing. In the space available I can do little more than list their names, but each has been the source of many good encounters: Angus Alton, Steve Baker, Bill Duggan, Charles Hart, Jacy Kilvert, and Linda Kirkham; while I was at Cambridge, Joe Bamberg, Maurice Biriotti, Jeanette Blair, Charlie Blake, Linnie Blake, Brendan Burke, Jenny Clarke, Matt Cockerill, Sarah Corry Roberts, Dave Cunningham, Pete de Bolla, Markman Ellis, Josep-Anton Fernàndez, Richard Hamblyn, Nick Land, Gavin Larner, Cressida Leyshon, Helen MacDonald, Judith Ross, and Jill Whalley;

in El Salvador, Salvador Alcántara, Tom Gibb, Mike Lanchin, and David and Rachel Quinney Mee; in Milwaukee, Malgosia Askanas, Nikki Cunningham, Andy Daitsman, Gareth Evans, Jane Gallop, Kathy Green, Amelie Hastie, Lynne Joyrich, Andy Martin, Tara McPherson, Patrice Petro, and Art Redding; at Duke University, Idelber Avelar, Roger Beebe, Anne Curtis, Tracy Devine, Greg Dobbins, Ulrik Ekman, Grant Farred, Alessandro Fornazzari, John French, Paul Gormley, Larry Grossberg, Natalie Hartman (special thanks!), Mark Healey, Barbara Herrnstein Smith, Adriana Johnson, John Kraniauskas, Horacio Legras, Brett Levinson, Ryan Long, Peter Osborne, Jody Pavilak, Rob Sikorski, Imre Szeman, Silvia Tandeciarz, Pam Terterian, Teresa Vilarós, Gareth Williams, and Caroline Yezer; in Peru, Natalia Ames, Patty Ames, Juan Fernando Bossio, Ignacio Cancino, Olga González, Carmen Ilizarbe, Patty Oliart, Aldo Panfichi, Ponciano del Pino, Gonzalo Portocarrero, Guillermo Rochabrún, Janine Soenens, and Tania Vásquez; in Chile, Diamela Eltit, Federico Galende, Kate Jenckes, Sergio Parra, Nelly Richard, Willy Thayer, and Sergio Villalobos; in Argentina, Ana Amado, Adriana Brodsky, Ana Longoni, Mario Santucho, Beatriz Sarlo, Horacio Tarcus, and Keith Zahniser; at Aberdeen, Bruce Adams, Jennifer Arnold, Julia Biggane, Pilar Escabias, Fidelma Farley, Kaarina Hollo, Ian Maclachlan, and Phil Swanson; at Manchester, Lucy Burke, Catherine Davies, James Dunkerley, Paul Henley, Ken Hirschkop, Ella Howard, Richard Kirkland, Jeremy Lawrance, Sasha Schell, Pete Wade, and Natalie Zacek; in Venezuela, Jeffrey Cedeño, Sergio Chefjec, Luis Duno, and Juan Antonio Hernández; in Vancouver, Alejandra Bronfman, Richard Cavell, Peter Dickinson, Marisol Fernández Utrera, Adam Frank, Derek Gregory, Eric Hershberg, Fiona Jeffries, Brian Lamb, Pablo Méndez, Cristina Moreiras, Alessandra Santos, Terri Tomsky, Sebastián Touza, Rafael Wainer, and Sandra Youssef. I thank my research assistants, Camilo Suárez, Camille Sutton, and Ana Vivaldi, and my students, from Milwaukee to British Columbia.

For help with the illustrations, thanks to Lise Diane Broer, Jeff Miller, and Novak Rogic. For reading and commenting on significant sections of the manuscript, I thank Benjamin Arditi, Gastón Gordillo, Jeremy Lane, Maria Rosales, Freya Schiwy, Jason Tockman, and Andy Willis. For reading the entire text and for incisive comments and constant encouragement, my special thanks to Chris Bongie, Alec Dawson, and James Scorer. For friendship and love when I needed it most, heartfelt thanks to Max Cameron and family, Katherine Cox, Linda Price, and above all to Ofelia Ros and Jaume Subirana. Thanks to my family for their patience, and to Jemima, Felix, Raphael, and Clara. I owe particular thanks to Susan Brook, who was with me almost every step of the way. And last but far from least, to Fiona Hanington, the best of copy editors (among other things).

Notes

Introduction

1. See Keohane, *After Hegemony*.
2. Spinoza, *Ethics*, 71.
3. Lash, "Power after Hegemony," 55.
4. Thoburn, "Patterns of Production."
5. Arditi, "Post-Hegemony," 215, 209.
6. Larsen, *Modernism and Hegemony*, 97.
7. Yúdice, "Civil Society," 4.
8. See Hardt, "The Withering of Civil Society."
9. Guha, "The Prose of Counter-Insurgency," 83.
10. Guha, *Dominance without Hegemony*, xi.
11. See Spivak, "Can the Subaltern Speak?"
12. Williams, *The Other Side of the Popular*, 327 n. 7.
13. Moreiras, *The Exhaustion of Difference*, 263.
14. Negri, *El exilio*, 38.
15. Roseberry, "Hegemony and the Language of Contention," 364. Roseberry's version of hegemony is rather similar to Bourdieu's conception of a divide between discourse and "doxa": between "the universe of the thinkable" and "the universe of the unthinkable . . . what cannot be said for lack of an available discourse" (*Outline of a Theory of Practice*, 170). But Bourdieu would be the first to note that power works also through the unthinkable and the unsayable (in other words, through habit), not simply through establishing a framework for what can be said.
16. Perec, *W*, [vii].
17. Beasley-Murray, "Latin America and the Global System."
18. See again Beasley-Murray, "Latin America and the Global System."
19. See, for instance, Holloway, *Change the World without Taking Power*, and Mentinis, *Zapatistas*.

Prologue

1. Gramsci, *Selections from Prison Notebooks*, 12.
2. Quoted in Hanke, *History of Latin American Civilization*, 1:125.
3. Kamen, *Empire*, 97.
4. Quoted in Williams, *The American Indian in Western Legal Thought*, 92.

5. Hoffer, *Law and People in Colonial America*, 56.
6. Kamen, *Empire*, 97.
7. Quoted in Kamen, *Empire*, 97.
8. Beezley et al., "Introduction," xiii.
9. Las Casas, *A Short Account of the Destruction of the Indies*, 33.
10. Moreiras, "Spanish Nation Formation," 9.
11. Seed, *Ceremonies of Possession*, 88.
12. Cornejo Polar, *Escribir en el aire*, 40.
13. Seed, *Ceremonies of Possession*, 88.
14. See Castro, *Another Face of Empire*.
15. Las Casas, *A Short Account of the Destruction of the Indies*, 96.
16. Guha, *Dominance without Hegemony*, 72.
17. Kamen, *Empire*, 87.
18. Morison, *Admiral of the Ocean Sea*, 148.
19. Fernández-Armesto, *Columbus*, 46.
20. Morison, *Admiral of the Ocean Sea*, 142.
21. Phillips and Phillips, *The Worlds of Christopher Columbus*, 138.
22. Cummins, *The Voyage of Christopher Columbus*, 55–56.
23. Columbus, *The Four Voyages*, 39.
24. Quoted in Fernández-Armesto, *Columbus*, 76; see also Bedini, *Christopher Columbus*, 695.
25. Columbus, *The Four Voyages*, 47, 41.
26. Ibid., 42, 43, 47, 49.
27. Phillips and Phillips, *The Worlds of Christopher Columbus*, 150.
28. Columbus, *The Four Voyages*, 48.
29. Morison, *Admiral of the Ocean Sea*, 208, 210.
30. Fernández-Armesto, *Columbus*, 50.
31. Fuson, *The Log of Christopher Columbus*, 71.
32. See Phillips and Phillips, *The Worlds of Christopher Columbus*, 150–51.
33. Columbus, *The Four Voyages*, 51.
34. Morison, *Admiral of the Ocean Sea*, 214, 215; Columbus, *The Four Voyages*, 51.
35. Phillips and Phillips, *The Worlds of Christopher Columbus*, 152.
36. Ibid., 152–53.
37. See Morison, *Admiral of the Ocean Sea*, 216–20.
38. Fernández-Armesto, *Columbus*, 109.

1. Argentina 1972

1. Nelson et al., "Cultural Studies," 3.
2. Hall, "Cultural Studies and Its Theoretical Legacies," 263, 262.
3. Nelson et al., "Cultural Studies," 10.
4. Johnson, "Reinventing Cultural Studies," 452.

5. Nelson et al., "Cultural Studies," 10.

6. Chun, *The British New Left*, 26.

7. Williams, "Culture Is Ordinary," 4; Thompson, "The Long Revolution," 33.

8. See Centre for Contemporary Cultural Studies, *The Empire Strikes Back*, and Women's Study Group, *Women Take Issue*.

9. Hall, "Cultural Studies and Its Theoretical Legacies," 274.

10. Rifkin, "Inventing Recollection," 108.

11. Johnson, "Reinventing Cultural Studies," 457.

12. Sarlo, *Scenes from Postmodern Life*, 55.

13. Moreiras, *The Exhaustion of Difference*, 8.

14. Ibid., 247, 251, 241.

15. Critchley, "Why I Love Cultural Studies," 64.

16. Grossberg, "History, Politics, and Postmodernism," 162, 163.

17. Slack, "The Theory and Method of Articulation in Cultural Studies," 117, 125.

18. See Grossberg, *Dancing in Spite of Myself*.

19. Grossberg, *We Gotta Get Out of This Place*, 78.

20. Johnson, "Alternative," 4.

21. Nelson et al., "Cultural Studies," 5.

22. Crassweller, *Perón*, 10.

23. "La fiesta del monstruo" is included, along with many other such stories, in Olguín, *Perón vuelve*.

24. Romero, *A History of Argentina*, 97, 118.

25. Critchley, "Why I Love Cultural Studies," 74.

26. Beasley-Murray, "Peronism and the Secret History of Cultural Studies."

27. McGuigan, *Cultural Populism*, 13, 32.

28. Beasley-Murray, "Towards an Unpopular Cultural Studies."

29. Bourdieu, *Outline of a Theory of Practice*, 188.

30. Taggart, *Populism*, 115, 116, 3.

31. Mény and Surel, "The Constitutive Ambiguity of Populism," 3, 13.

32. Ibid., 12, 13.

33. Bell, *Populism and Elitism*, 3.

34. Ibid., 190, 175.

35. Williams, "Culture Is Ordinary," 12.

36. Castañeda, *Utopia Unarmed*, 44.

37. Conniff, "Introduction," 1.

38. Quoted in Castañeda, *Utopia Unarmed*, 43.

39. Torres Ballesteros, "El populismo," 173.

40. Quoted in Iturrieta, *El pensamiento peronista*, 42.

41. Ibid., 41.

42. Perón, *El pensamiento político de Perón*, 121–23.
43. Perón, *Los vendepatria*, 310, 311, 315.
44. Ibid., 181, 109–13, 317.
45. Perón, "Lecciones para las Fuerzas Armadas," 404, 407, 406.
46. Iturrieta, *El pensamiento peronista*, 42.
47. Perón, *Los vendepatria*, 318, 319.
48. Iturrieta, *El pensamiento peronista*, 42.
49. Perón, *Los vendepatria*, 318–19, 319.
50. Iturrieta, *El pensamiento peronista*, 36.
51. McGuigan, *Cultural Populism*, 4.
52. Williams, "Culture Is Ordinary," 3; Arnold, *Culture and Anarchy*, 6.
53. Hall and Whannel, *The Popular Arts*, 73.
54. See, for instance, Hawkes, *That Shakesperherian Rag*.
55. Hartley, *A Short History of Cultural Studies*, 48.
56. Williams, *Culture and Society*, 328.
57. Grossberg, *We Gotta Get Out of This Place*, 106.
58. Hall, "Notes on Deconstructing the 'Popular,'" 239.
59. Grossberg, *We Gotta Get Out of This Place*, 78.
60. Williams, *Culture and Society*, 328, 333.
61. Gilroy, *Postcolonial Melancholia*, 131, 72.
62. Willis, *Learning to Labor*, 197.
63. Hall, "Cultural Studies and Its Theoretical Legacies," 267.
64. Williams, *Culture and Society*, 332; Hall, "Cultural Studies and Its Theoretical Legacies," 267–78; Grossberg, *We Gotta Get Out of This Place*, 376.
65. Grossberg, *We Gotta Get Out of This Place*, 394.
66. Laclau, *Politics and Ideology*, 173.
67. Quoted in Stratton and Ang, "On the Impossibility of a Global Cultural Studies," 370.
68. Laclau and Mouffe, *Hegemony and Socialist Strategy*, 127.
69. Quoted in Ciria, *Política y cultura popular*, 311. See also Perón, *El pensamiento político*, 123–25.
70. Laclau, *Emancipation(s)*, 36, 55.
71. Taylor, *Eva Perón*, 141.
72. Laclau, *Emancipation(s)*, 56.
73. See di Tella, *Argentina under Perón*, 66.
74. Moreiras, "Pastiche Identity," 207.
75. Frow, *Cultural Studies and Cultural Value*, 79.
76. Belsey, "From Cultural Studies to Cultural Criticism?" 19.
77. Hall, "The 'First' New Left," 36, 32, 36.
78. See, for instance, Jameson, "On 'Cultural Studies,'" or Szeman, "The Limits of Culture."

79. Hirschkop, "A Complex Populism," 18.
80. McGuigan, *Cultural Populism*, 5, 244.
81. Agger, *Cultural Studies as Critical Theory*, 194.
82. Hall, "The Toad in the Garden," 40.
83. Hall, "Cultural Studies and Its Theoretical Legacies," 268.
84. Hall, "The Toad in the Garden," 53, 61.
85. Hall, *The Hard Road to Renewal*, 165.
86. Hall, "The Toad in the Garden," 53.
87. Hebdige, *Subculture*, 15. See Jameson, "On 'Cultural Studies,'" 51 n. 3.
88. Critchley, "Why I Love Cultural Studies," 64.
89. Harris, *From Class Struggle to the Politics of Pleasure*, 3, 5. See also Lee, *Life and Times of Cultural Studies*, 142.
90. Hall, "Cultural Studies and Its Theoretical Legacies," 267.
91. Turner, *British Cultural Studies*, 177.
92. Quoted in Brennan, *Wars of Position*, 240.
93. Hall, "Cultural Studies," 48.
94. Sparks, "Stuart Hall," 95.
95. Critchley and Marchant, "Introduction," 3; Brennan, *Wars of Position*, 245.
96. Hall, "On Postmodernism and Articulation," 146.
97. McRobbie, "Post-Marxism and Cultural Studies," 724.
98. Laclau, *New Reflections*, 200.
99. Marchant, "Politics and the Ontological Difference," 55.
100. Laclau and Mouffe, *Hegemony and Socialist Strategy*, 131, 169–70.
101. Laclau, *On Populist Reason*, 43.
102. Laclau and Mouffe, *Hegemony and Socialist Strategy*, 7, 69.
103. Ibid., 75, 85, 136.
104. Laclau, *Politics and Ideology*, 159, 158.
105. Laclau, *On Populist Reason*, 4, 17.
106. Laclau, *Politics and Ideology*, 160, 161, 162.
107. Ibid., 160; Laclau and Mouffe, *Hegemony and Socialist Strategy*, 127.
108. Laclau, *Politics and Ideology*, 166, 174, 173.
109. Ibid., 131, 130.
110. Laclau, "Populism," 42.
111. Laclau, *On Populist Reason*, 153, 154.
112. Laclau, *Politics and Ideology*, 172–73.
113. Laclau, *On Populist Reason*, 225; Laclau, "Populism," 47.
114. Laclau, *Politics and Ideology*, 181, 186, 187.
115. Ibid., 189, 190, 191.
116. Laclau, *Emancipation(s)*, 54, 55, 56.

117. Laclau, *On Populist Reason*, 214, 215, 216.
118. Ibid., 217, 221.
119. Ibid., 193.
120. Ibid., 217.
121. Laclau, *Politics and Ideology*, 167, 173.
122. Ibid., 174, 196.
123. Laclau and Mouffe, *Hegemony and Socialist Strategy*, 159–60, 167.
124. Ibid., 167, 138, 139.
125. Critchley, "Is There a Normative Deficit in the Theory of Hegemony?" 116, 117.
126. See Sarlo, *Una modernidad periférica*.
127. James, *Doña María's Story*, 220.
128. Auyero, *Poor People's Politics*, 182–204.
129. Ibid., 202.
130. Laclau, "Populism," 45.
131. Ibid.
132. Laclau, *On Populist Reason*, 73, 89, 116, 125.
133. Ibid., 73; Laclau, "Populism," 36.
134. Laclau, *On Populist Reason*, 86.
135. Laclau, "Populism," 36.
136. Laclau, *On Populist Reason*, 127, 128, 74.
137. Ibid., 86, 97, 105.
138. Ibid., 100, 170.
139. Laclau, *Politics and Ideology*, 196, 172–73, 173.
140. Ibid., 196.
141. Ibid.
142. Abrams, "Notes on the Difficulty of Studying the State," 75, 76.
143. Frow, *Cultural Studies and Cultural Value*, 78, 80.
144. Laclau, *Politics and Ideology*, 197.
145. Ibid., 198.
146. Di Tella, *Argentina under Perón*, 18.
147. Sebreli, *Los deseos imaginarios del peronismo*, 64–67; Romero, *A History of Argentina*, 108.
148. Luna, *Perón y su tiempo*, 1:408.
149. Romero, *A History of Argentina*, 111.
150. Portantiero and de Ipola, "Lo nacional popular," 209.
151. De Ipola, "Populismo e ideología," 949, 960.
152. See, most notably, Geras, "Post-Marxism?"
153. Kraniauskas, "Rodolfo Walsh y Eva Perón," 113.
154. Laclau, "Teorías marxistas del estado," 54.
155. Jameson, *Postmodernism*, ix.
156. James, *Resistance and Integration*, 264, 262.

157. Ibid., 264, 259, 97, 30.
158. James, *Doña María's Story*, 16, 211, 212, 254–55.
159. Auyero, *Poor People's Politics*, 145, 147.
160. Kraniauskas, "Political Puig," 129.
161. Quoted in Poneman, *Argentina*, caption to plate 2.
162. Taylor, *Eva Perón*, 67.
163. Kraniauskas, "Political Puig," 126, 123, 131.
164. Plotkin, *Mañana es San Perón*, 81.

2. Ayacucho 1982

1. Edwards, *Civil Society*, 4, 112, vi.
2. Aristotle, *The Politics*, 53.
3. Colas, *Civil Society and Fanaticism;* Ehrenberg, *Civil Society*.
4. Edwards, *Civil Society*, 10.
5. Cahoone, *Civil Society*, 219.
6. Keane, *Civil Society*, 32.
7. Edwards, *Civil Society*, 14.
8. Putnam, *Bowling Alone*, 338.
9. Touraine, *What Is Democracy?* 58.
10. Touraine, *Beyond Neoliberalism*, 99.
11. Stepan, *Rethinking Military Politics*, 5.
12. O'Donnell and Schmitter, *Tentative Conclusions about Uncertain Democracies*, 48.
13. "Plan of Action of Santiago," 10.
14. Frei, "Preface," vii, viii.
15. Alvarez et al., "Introduction," 17.
16. Hopenhayn, *No Apocalypse, No Integration*, 86–87.
17. Ibid., 68.
18. Touraine, *Beyond Neoliberalism*, 99.
19. See Franco, "A Ghost Dance on the Fields of the Cold War" and *The Decline and Fall of the Lettered City*, 108–11.
20. Green, *Silent Revolution*, 191.
21. Castañeda, *Utopia Unarmed*, 372.
22. Cohen and Arato, *Civil Society and Political Theory*, 493 and passim.
23. Castañeda, *Utopia Unarmed*, 488, 448.
24. Stern, *Shining and Other Paths*, 8.
25. Gorriti, *The Shining Path*, xv.
26. Stern, *Shining and Other Paths*, 1.
27. Knight et al., *Reviving Democracy*, 1, 59.
28. Korten, *Globalizing Civil Society*, 5, 72–73.
29. Klein, "Killing Democracy in Iraq."

30. Edwards, *Civil Society*, 111–12.
31. Castañeda, *Utopia Unarmed*, 372.
32. Robinson, "The São Paulo Forum," 6.
33. See McClintock, *Revolutionary Movements in Latin America*, 64–65.
34. Comisión de la Verdad y Reconciliación, *Informe final*, 2:14, 17, 22.
35. Gorriti, *The Shining Path*, 32.
36. Foweraker, *Theorizing Social Movements*, 91.
37. Keane, *Civil Society*, 171–72.
38. Cahoone, *Civil Society*, 205.
39. Robinson, "The São Paulo Forum," 6.
40. Cohen and Arato, *Civil Society and Political Theory*, 492.
41. World Social Forum, "Charter of Principles," June 10, 2001, Fórum Social Mundial, www.forumsocialmundial.org.br/.
42. Touraine, *The Voice and the Eye*, 6, 7.
43. Kriesi et al., *New Social Movements in Western Europe*, xviii.
44. Touraine, *The Voice and the Eye*, 22.
45. Guidry et al., "Globalizations and Social Movements," 15.
46. Calderón et al., "Social Movements," 30.
47. Touraine, *What Is Democracy?* 38.
48. Cohen and Arato, *Civil Society and Political Theory*, 531.
49. Escobar and Alvarez, "Introduction," 3.
50. Starn, "To Revolt against the Revolution," 558.
51. Eckstein, "Power and Popular Protest," 9.
52. Starn, "To Revolt against the Revolution," 558, 561.
53. Slater, "Social Movements," 25 n. 43.
54. See Degregori et al., *Las rondas campesinas*.
55. Gorriti, *The Shining Path*, 76.
56. Manrique, "La década de la violencia," 137.
57. Gianotten et al., "The Impact of Sendero Luminoso," 198.
58. McClintock, "Peru's Sendero Luminoso Rebellion," 96.
59. Zirakzadeh, *Social Movements in Politics*, 219.
60. Calderón et al., "Social Movements," 21.
61. Smith, *Entre dos fuegos*, 54–55.
62. Knight et al., *Reviving Democracy*, 166, 164, 165.
63. Cohen and Arato, *Civil Society and Political Theory,* 451, 3.
64. Ibid., 3, 523.
65. Ibid., 48, 487.
66. Ibid., 346, 561, 423.
67. Ibid., ix.
68. Ibid., 346.
69. Ibid., 423, 425, x.

70. Ibid., 442, 532, 531.
71. Ibid., 456, 454.
72. Ibid., 549, 451, 454.
73. Ibid., 713 n. 134, 532, 454, 469.
74. Ibid., 415, 539.
75. See Klein, *Fences and Windows.*
76. Cohen and Arato, *Civil Society and Political Theory,* 24, 565, 453, 24–25, 422, 453.
77. Ibid., 16, 561, 422.
78. Ibid., 421, 422, 421.
79. Colas, *Civil Society and Fanaticism*, 280, 23, 288.
80. Ibid., 355, 351, 353, 103.
81. Ibid., 122.
82. Yúdice, "Translator's Introduction," xxxvi.
83. García Canclini, *Hybrid Cultures*, 39.
84. Yúdice, "Civil Society," 18, 19.
85. García Canclini, *Consumers and Citizens*, 27, 28.
86. Ibid., 126, 79.
87. García Canclini, *Hybrid Cultures*, 281.
88. I thank Alberto Moreiras for drawing my attention to this aspect of the film.
89. Gorriti, *The Shining Path*, 167, 169, 259.
90. Ibid., 258, 253.
91. Cohen and Arato, *Civil Society and Political Theory,* 455, 451.
92. Ibid., 415, 741 n. 80.
93. Ibid., 479, 50.
94. Green, *Silent Revolution*, 4–5.
95. See Klein, *The Shock Doctrine.*
96. Weber, *From Max Weber*, 82.
97. Agamben, *State of Exception*, 2.
98. Weber, *From Max Weber*, 78.
99. Deleuze and Guattari, *Anti-Oedipus*, 217.
100. Mauceri, "The Transition to 'Democracy,' " 35, 36.
101. Gonzales de Olarte, *El neoliberalismo a la peruana*, 41, 97, 106.
102. Degregori, *La década de la antipolítica*, 53, 60, 62, 63.
103. Quoted in Degregori, *La década de la antipolítica*, 252.
104. Degregori, *La década de la antipolítica*, 252.
105. Cotler and Grompone, *El fujimorismo*, 116, 140.
106. Agamben, *State of Exception*, 4.
107. Poole and Rénique, *Peru*, 62.
108. Tello, *Perú*, 116.

109. Michel Camdessus, "The IMF and Good Governance," address to Transparency International, January 21, 1998, International Monetary Fund, http://internationalmonetaryfund.com/.

110. Transparency International, "About Us," Transparency International: The Global Coalition against Corruption, www.transparency.org/.

111. Bourdieu, *Distinction*, 460.

112. Ibid., 461.

113. Deleuze and Guattari, *A Thousand Plateaus*, 445.

114. Mauceri, "State Reform, Coalitions, and the Neoliberal *Autogolpe* in Peru," 32.

115. Poole and Rénique, *Peru*, 161.

116. Conaghan, "Polls, Political Discourse, and the Public Sphere," 242.

117. Poole and Rénique, *Peru*, 161.

118. Interview with Fernando Tuesta Soldevilla, Lima, August 14, 1997.

119. Oficina de Prensa de la Corte Superior de Justicia de Lima, "Ratifican que en campaña re reeleccionista de Fujimori se gastó más de US$4 millones," Corte Superior de Justicia de Lima, March 20, 2006, www.pj.gob.pe/.

120. Jochamowitz, *Ciudadano Fujimori*, 277.

121. Grompone, *Fujimori, neopopulismo y comunicación política*, 26.

122. Quoted in Chávez Toro, *Susy Díaz*, 103.

123. Ibid., 104.

124. Degregori, *La década de la antipolítica*, 206.

125. Ibid., 377.

126. Virno, "Do You Remember Counterrevolution?" 240.

127. Conaghan and Malloy, *Unsettling Statecraft*, 224.

128. Degregori, *La década de la antipolítica*, 110.

129. Salcedo, *Terremoto*, 68, 72.

130. Gorriti, *The Shining Path*, 229.

131. Shakespeare, *The Dancer Upstairs*, 39, 36–37.

132. Apter, "Political Violence in Analytical Perspective," 5.

133. Degregori, "The Maturation of a Cosmocrat," 55.

134. Degregori, *Que difícil es ser Dios*, 20.

135. Degregori, "The Maturation of a Cosmocrat," 52, 53.

136. Guzmán, "We Are the Initiators," 313.

137. Didion, *Salvador*, 36; Strong, *Shining Path*.

138. Flores Galindo, "Muerte en Haquira," 196.

139. Starn, "Maoism in the Andes," 405.

3. Escalón 1989

1. Jameson, "Postmodernism," 61, 64.
2. Jameson, *Postmodernism*, 313, 316.

3. Robin, *Fear: The History of a Political Idea;* Bourke, *Fear: A Cultural History;* Brennan, *The Transmission of Affect;* Damasio, *Looking for Spinoza;* Massumi, *Parables for the Virtual;* Sedgwick, *Touching, Feeling.*

4. See Ticineto Clough, *The Affective Turn.*

5. Jameson, "Postmodernism," 64.

6. Brennan, *The Transmission of Affect*, 6, 5.

7. Damasio, *Looking for Spinoza*, 28.

8. Massumi, *Parables for the Virtual*, 28.

9. Sedgwick, *Touching, Feeling*, 18, 19.

10. Massumi, *Parables for the Virtual*, 42, 43.

11. Spinoza, *Ethics*, 69, 43, 44.

12. Deleuze, *Spinoza*, 49, 39, 50.

13. Massumi, *Parables for the Virtual*, 35, 16, 35.

14. Deleuze and Guattari, *A Thousand Plateaus*, 341.

15. Massumi, *Parables for the Virtual*, 41.

16. Ibid., 42, 49, 40, 41.

17. Ibid., 62, 45, 218, 217.

18. López, "Are All Latins from Manhattan?" 77.

19. Ortiz, *Cuban Counterpoint*, 206.

20. Massumi, *Parables for the Virtual*, 218.

21. Deleuze and Guattari, *A Thousand Plateaus*, 430.

22. Jameson, *The Political Unconscious*, 102.

23. See Linebaugh, *The London Hanged.*

24. Holloway, *Change the World*, 1.

25. Massumi, *Parables for the Virtual*, 35.

26. Ibid.

27. Deleuze, "On Philosophy," 137.

28. Massumi, *User's Guide*, 93.

29. Lauria-Santiago and Binford, "Local History, Politics, and the State," 9, 2.

30. Binford, "Peasants, Catechists, Revolutionaries," 108.

31. Bracamonte and Spencer, *Strategy and Tactics of the Salvadoran FMLN Guerrillas*, 16.

32. Byrne, *El Salvador's Civil War*, 79, 87, 104.

33. Dunkerley, *The Long War*, 189.

34. Bracamonte and Spencer, *Strategy and Tactics of the Salvadoran FMLN Guerrillas*, 37. Bracamonte is the pseudonym of an ex-combatant; Spencer is a freelance analyst and writer who has also taught at the U.S. Air Force Special Operations School and the Security Studies Institute of the U.S. Army War College.

35. Byrne, *El Salvador's Civil War*, 104, 135.

36. Espinaza, "Preliminar," 11.

37. Massumi, "Fear (The Spectrum Said)," 34.

38. Deleuze and Guattari, *A Thousand Plateaus*, 420.
39. Hardt, *Gilles Deleuze*, xiii.
40. Deleuze and Guattari, *What Is Philosophy?* 48.
41. Seigworth, "From Affection to Soul," 160, 162, 167, 168.
42. Deleuze and Guattari, *Anti-Oedipus*, 10.
43. Deleuze and Guattari, *A Thousand Plateaus*, 448, 400.
44. Ibid., 352, 357.
45. Ibid., 400, 356.
46. Bracamonte and Spencer, *Strategy and Tactics of the Salvadoran FMLN Guerrillas*, 8.
47. Alegría, *They Won't Take Me Alive*, 72.
48. Ibid., translation modified.
49. Clements, *Witness to War*, 30, 221.
50. Metzi, *Por los caminos de Chalatenango*, 165.
51. López Vigil, *Muerte y vida en Morazán*, 73–74.
52. López Vigil, *Rebel Radio*, 45.
53. Henríquez Consalvi, *La terquedad del Izote*, 95.
54. López Vigil, *Rebel Radio*, 46.
55. Foucault, *Abnormal*, 325.
56. Todorov, *The Conquest of America*, 50.
57. Torgovnick, *Primitive Passions*, 14.
58. Ibid., 15, 109, 103.
59. See, for instance, Bongie, *Exotic Memories*, for a compelling critique.
60. Deleuze, *Difference and Repetition*, 208; Deleuze and Guattari, *Anti-Oedipus*, 321.
61. Alegría, *They Won't Take Me Alive*, 145, translation modified.
62. Ayala, *El tope y más allá*, 60, 277.
63. Ibid., 276. The original Spanish is "Salí de la multitud para acercarme a una persona."
64. Danner, *The Massacre at El Mozote*, 10.
65. López Vigil, *Muerte y vida en Morazán*, 94.
66. López Vigil, *Rebel Radio*, 134.
67. Mena Sandoval, *Del ejército nacional al ejército guerrillero*, 344, 349.
68. López Vigil, *Muerte y vida en Morazán*, 74, 88, 89.
69. López Vigil, *Las mil y una historias de Radio Venceremos*, 259.
70. Lievens, *El quinto piso de la alegría*.
71. On air power, see Lindqvist, *A History of Bombing*.
72. See Multimedia Development Corporation: Driving Transformation, www.mdc.com.my/msc/, and MSC Malaysia: Spearheading Transformation, www.mscmalaysia.my/.
73. López Vigil, *Rebel Radio*, 229.

74. Simon Tisdall, "Green Berets Walk Free from Salvador Siege," *The Guardian*, November 23, 1989.

75. Tom Gibb, "Sheraton Siege Ends as Rebels Withdraw," *The Times* (London), November 23, 1989.

76. Tom Gibb, "U.S. Alert as Rebels Hold Four in Hotel," *The Times* (London), November 22, 1989.

77. Gilbert and Guhar, *The Madwoman in the Attic*, 77.

78. Eagleton, *The Ideology of the Aesthetic*, 20, 28.

79. Khanna, *Dark Continents*, x.

80. Torgovnick, *Primitive Passion*, 217.

81. Furedi, *Politics of Fear*, 132, 169.

82. There is no better or more disturbing meditation on the mute logic of violence in Northern Ireland (or even, perhaps, anywhere else) than Alan Clarke's film, *Elephant* (1989). See Kirkland, "The Spectacle of Terrorism in Northern Irish Culture."

83. Stoll, *Rigoberta Menchú and the Story of All Poor Guatemalans;* Beverley, *Testimonio*, 84.

84. Quoted in Simpson, "Naming the Dead," 6.

85. Berger, "America under Attack."

86. Scarry, *The Body in Pain*, 4.

87. Norris, "Giorgio Agamben and the Politics of the Living Dead," 41.

88. Thornton, "The Peculiar Temporality of Violence," 44, 43.

89. Colectivo "Huitzilipochtli," *El "Cipitío" en el Salvador Sheraton*, 7, 9, 11; ellipses in original.

90. Ibid., 11, 48, 33, 36.

91. Ibid., 62, 14–15, 14, 63; ellipses in original.

92. Taussig, *Shamanism, Colonialism, and the Wild Man*, 132, 134–35, 135.

93. Ibid., 128, 132, 134.

94. Taussig, *The Magic of the State*, 169, 186.

95. Ibid., 187.

96. Ibid., 174.

97. Jameson, "Postmodernism," 5.

98. Foucault, *The History of Sexuality*, 1:92.

99. Deleuze and Guattari, *Anti-Oedipus*, 321.

100. Deleuze and Parnet, *Dialogues*, 144, 140.

101. Deleuze and Guattari, *A Thousand Plateaus*, 229, 230f.

102. Land, "Making It with Death," 75.

103. Land, "Meltdown."

104. Redding, *Raids on Human Consciousness*, 204, 211.

105. Massumi, *Parables for the Virtual*, 220.

106. Hamblyn, *The Invention of Clouds*, 203.

107. Clements, *Witness to War*, 115, 116.
108. Henríquez Consalvi, *La terquedad del Izote*, 48.
109. Williams, *The Other Side of the Popular*, 193, 194, 192.
110. Ibid., 193, 213.
111. Massumi, "Everywhere You Want to Be," 24, 12.
112. Althusser, "Ideology and Ideological State Apparatuses," 48.
113. Massumi, "Everywhere You Want to Be," 10–11.
114. Agamben, *The Open*, 64.
115. Massumi, "Everywhere You Want to Be," 27.
116. López Vigil, *Muerte y vida en Morazán*, 89.
117. Moodie, " 'El Capitán Cinchazo,' " 227.
118. Hume, *Armed Violence and Poverty in El Salvador*, 2, 11, 12.
119. McClintock, *Revolutionary Movements in Latin America*, 84.
120. Deleuze, "Postscript on Control Societies," 178, 177, 182.
121. Ibid., 178.
122. Ibid., 181.
123. Virilio, *Ground Zero*, 37, 82.
124. Deleuze, *Difference and Repetition*, 73, 78.
125. Deleuze, *Foucault*, 104.
126. Whelan, "Appropriat(e)ing Wavelength," 132.

4. Chile 1992

1. Deleuze, *Cinema 2*, 189, 192, 194.
2. Ibid., 189; Deleuze, *Spinoza*, 124–25.
3. Agamben, *The Open*, 47, 68.
4. Ibid., 76, 70.
5. See The Trojan Room Coffee Machine, www.cl.cam.ac.uk/coffee/coffee.html, and Watching Paint Dry! www.watching-paint-dry.com/.
6. Sloterdijk, *Critique of Cynical Reason*, 3, 4, 6.
7. Chaloupka, *Everybody Knows*, 5.
8. Bewes, *Cynicism and Postmodernity*, 3. Barack Obama's 2008 election to the U.S. presidency seemed briefly perhaps to have galvanized many and heralded the return of belief: "Yes, we can!" But Obama stands out against a backdrop of ever-more pervasive cynicism, now directed equally at the stock market wizards and bankers who allowed the financial system to collapse while reaping copious rewards for themselves.
9. Chaloupka, *Everybody Knows*, 15.
10. Redding, *Raids on Human Consciousness*, 211.
11. Sloterdijk, *Critique of Cynical Reason*, 3.
12. Deleuze and Guattari, *A Thousand Plateaus*, 89.
13. Žižek, *The Sublime Object of Ideology*, 28, 29, 21, 30.
14. Deleuze and Guattari, *A Thousand Plateaus*, 4.
15. Bourdieu and Wacquant, *An Invitation to Reflexive Sociology*, 250.

16. Ibid., 127, 128.
17. García Márquez, *One Hundred Years of Solitude*, 265.
18. García Márquez, "No One Writes to the Colonel," 109, 110.
19. Ibid., 112, 127.
20. Ibid., 165, 166.
21. James, *Habit*, 3.
22. Bourdieu, *Outline of a Theory of Practice*, 218 n. 47.
23. Ibid., 95.
24. Felski, "The Invention of Everyday Life," 26, 27.
25. Foucault, *The History of Sexuality*, 1:139, 141.
26. Althusser, "Ideology and Ideological State Apparatuses," 32.
27. Ibid., 42, 43, 42.
28. Guillaudat and Mouterde, *Los movimientos sociales in Chile*, 143; Chavkin, *Storm over Chile*, 264.
29. Paley, *Marketing Democracy*, 5.
30. Guillaudat and Mouterde, *Los movimientos sociales en Chile*, 233.
31. Schneider, *Shantytown Protest in Pinochet's Chile*, 211, 213.
32. Salman, *The Diffident Movement*, 225.
33. Roberts, *Deepening Democracy?* vii, 281.
34. Paley, *Marketing Democracy*, 6.
35. Subercaseaux, *Chile*, 49.
36. Moulián, *Chile actual*, 31.
37. Richard, *Cultural Residues*, 69.
38. Riquelme, "Voting for Nobody," 31.
39. See Drake and Winn, "The Presidential Election of 1999/2000."
40. See the International Institute for Democracy and Electoral Assistance's statistics at www.idea.int/; in the 2002 edition of the publication *Voter Turnout since 1945: A Global Report* (by Rafael López Pintor and Maria Gratschew), the IDEA locates Chile 145th in the world for voter turnout as a proportion of the voting age population, sandwiched between Ghana and Mauritania.
41. Bourdieu, *Practical Reason*, 55.
42. Hardt and Negri, *Multitude*, 197.
43. Korczynski, Hodson, and Edwards, "Introduction," 12.
44. Giddens, *The Constitution of Society*, 2.
45. Bourdieu, *Outline of a Theory of Practice*, 72, 73.
46. Ibid., 27, 75.
47. Bourdieu, *Pascalian Meditations*, 115.
48. Bourdieu, *The Logic of Practice*, 53.
49. Bourdieu, *Outline of a Theory of Practice*, 72, 27.
50. Ibid., 2; Massumi, *A User's Guide*, 46.
51. Deleuze and Guattari, *A Thousand Plateaus*, 4; Bourdieu, *Pascalian Meditations*, 181.

52. See Bourdieu and Wacquant, *An Invitation to Reflexive Sociology*, 52.

53. For Bourdieu's "functionalist tenor," see Lane, *Bourdieu's Politics*, 116.

54. Massumi, "Introduction," xxxvii.

55. Deleuze and Guattari, *A Thousand Plateaus*, 203.

56. Bourdieu, *The Logic of Practice*, 53.

57. Bourdieu and Wacquant, *An Invitation to Reflexive Sociology*, 16.

58. Bourdieu, *The Logic of Practice*, 53.

59. Bourdieu and Wacquant, *An Invitation to Reflexive Sociology*, 108.

60. Bourdieu and Passeron, *Reproduction*, 4.

61. Bourdieu, *The Logic of Practice*, 54.

62. Bourdieu and Passeron, *Reproduction*, 210.

63. Schmitt, *Political Theology*, 5.

64. Quoted in Loveman, *The Constitution of Tyranny*, 15.

65. Snyder, "The Dirty Legal War," 264.

66. Ibid., 264.

67. Chavkin, *Storm over Chile*, 278.

68. Schneider, *Shantytown Protest in Pinochet's Chile*, 187, 187–88, 202, 211.

69. Ibid., 206.

70. Spinoza, *Ethics*, 89.

71. Bourdieu, *Distinction*, 380.

72. Salman, *The Diffident Movement*, 4, 146, 147.

73. Ibid., 153, 207, 212.

74. Ibid., 49, 193.

75. Schneider, *Shantytown Protest in Pinochet's Chile*, 194.

76. Bourdieu, *Practical Reason*, 55.

77. Bourdieu, *The Logic of Practice*, 49.

78. Bourdieu, *Outline of a Theory of Practice*, 157, 94.

79. Bourdieu, *The Logic of Practice*, 68.

80. Bourdieu and Wacquant, *An Invitation to Reflexive Sociology*, 139; see also Bourdieu, *Outline of a Theory of Practice*, 82.

81. Bourdieu and Wacquant, *An Invitation to Reflexive Sociology*, 138.

82. Bourdieu, *Outline of a Theory of Practice*, 78.

83. Gilroy, *The Black Atlantic*, 77, 76, 71.

84. Bourdieu, *The Logic of Practice*, 106.

85. Bourdieu, *Outline of a Theory of Practice*, 89.

86. Ibid., 90.

87. Bourdieu and Darbel, *The Love of Art*, 51.

88. Bourdieu and Passeron, *Reproduction*, 109.

89. Sarlo, *Scenes from Postmodern Life*, 13.

90. I thank Jean Franco for drawing my attention to Chile's *caracoles*.

91. Cecilia Gutiérrez Ronda, "Caracoles están perdiendo la pelea por sobrevivir," *La Tercera*, June 28, 1998, www.tercera.cl/.

92. Harden, *Mall Maker*, 3.

93. Bourdieu, *Pascalian Meditations*, 168.

94. Bourdieu, *Practical Reason*, 54.

95. Bourdieu, *The Logic of Practice*, 69.

96. Bourdieu, *The Logic of Practice*, 60; Bourdieu, *Outline of a Theory of Practice*, 168.

97. Bourdieu, *The Logic of Practice*, 69–70.

98. Deleuze, *Difference and Repetition*, 78.

99. Lefebvre, *Critique of Everyday Life*, 2:14.

100. See Postone, *Time, Labor, and Social Domination*.

101. Marx, *Selected Writings*, 169.

102. Foucault, *Discipline and Punish*, 209, 213.

103. Foucault, *The History of Sexuality*, 1:100, 102.

104. Foucault, *Discipline and Punish*, 28.

105. Shklovsky, "Art as Technique," 16.

106. Bourdieu, *Distinction*, 40.

107. Theweleit, *Male Fantasies*, 22, 57, 24.

108. Bourdieu and Wacquant, *An Invitation to Reflexive Sociology*, 228, 16.

109. Ekaizer, *Yo, Augusto*, 272, 274; ellipses in original. The original Spanish is "No hemos mat... [se da cuenta de que va a conjugar el verbo matar]... No se ha muerto allá en Chile más... en combate... más de dos mil quinientas personas. No han muerto... Póngale tres mil, pues."

110. Salinas, *The London Clinic*, 28, 107, 104.

111. Ibid., 112–13, 95.

112. Hite, *When the Romance Ended*, 193.

113. Ibid., xv.

114. Foucault, *The History of Sexuality*, 1:140.

115. Ibid., 142–43, 143.

116. Virno, *A Grammar of the Multitude*, 55.

117. Moulián, *Chile actual*, 174.

118. Taylor, *Disappearing Acts*, 130.

119. Moulián, *El consumo me consume*, 69, 45, 67.

120. Sepúlveda, "Introduction," 31, 32.

121. Agosín, *Tapestries of Hope*, 23.

122. Sepúlveda, "Introduction," 25.

123. Butler, *Excitable Speech*, 32; see Althusser, "Ideology and Ideological State Apparatuses," 55.

124. Butler, *Excitable Speech*, 139, 134.

125. Agamben, *Homo Sacer*, 148, 122.

126. Agamben, *State of Exception*, 88.

127. De Certeau, *The Practice of Everyday Life*, 37.

128. Hardt and Negri, *Multitude*, 356, 349; see also Lazzarato, "From Biopower to Biopolitics."

129. De Certeau, *The Practice of Everyday Life*, 59.

130. Lane, *Bourdieu's Politics*, 118.

131. Lane, *Pierre Bourdieu*, 13, 15.

132. Bourdieu, *Outline of a Theory of Practice*, 173.

133. Bourdieu and Passeron, *Reproduction*, xxi.

134. Bourdieu, *Homo Academicus*, 147.

135. Neustadt, *CADA día*, 31.

136. Richard, *Margins and Institutions*, 55.

137. For the "fusion of 'art' with 'life,' " see Neustadt, *CADA día*, 35.

138. Richard, *Margins and Institutions*, 56.

139. Thayer, *El fragmento repetido*, 16.

140. Bourdieu and Passeron, *Reproduction*, xxi.

141. Bourdieu, *Firing Back*, 63, 25.

142. Bourdieu, *Acts of Resistance*, 57.

143. Bourdieu, *Distinction*, 398, 420.

144. Foucault, *The Hermeneutics of the Subject*, 252.

145. Bourdieu, *Distinction*, 143, 144.

146. Salman, *The Diffident Movement*, 212, 200.

147. Richard, *Cultural Residues*, 156.

148. Eltit, *Sacred Cow*, 15, 70, 71, 71–72.

149. Ibid., 102, 103.

150. Foucault, *The History of Sexuality*, 3:45, 58.

151. Foucault, "The Ethics of the Concern for Self as a Practice of Freedom," 500.

152. Foucault, "What Is Enlightenment?" 316.

153. Bourdieu, *Homo Academicus*, 176.

154. Bourdieu, "Concluding Remarks," 274.

155. Bourdieu, *Pascalian Meditations*, 149.

156. Negri, *Subversive Spinoza*, 12, 37.

Conclusion

1. Sieyès, "What Is the Third Estate?" 136.
2. Loughlin and Walker, "Introduction," 1.
3. Althusser, *Essays in Self-Criticism*, 51, and also 94–99.
4. Negri, *Marx beyond Marx*, 8.
5. Virno, *A Grammar of the Multitude*, 78.
6. Ibid., 76, 80, 66, 80.
7. Hardt, "Into the Factory," 18.
8. Hardt and Negri, *Multitude*, 219.
9. Hardt, "Into the Factory," 9.

10. Negri, *Insurgencies*, 325.
11. Negri, *Time for Revolution*, 260, 261.
12. Minta, *Aguirre*, 155.
13. Quoted in Minta, *Aguirre*, 181.
14. Quoted in Lynch, *Simón Bolívar*, 276.
15. Negri and Cocco, *GlobAL*, 52, 106.
16. Ibid., 226, 227.
17. Moreiras, *The Exhaustion of Difference*, 126.
18. Spivak, "Subaltern Studies," 16.
19. Guha, "On Some Aspects of the Colonial Historiography of Colonial India," 44.
20. Negri, "Towards an Ontological Definition of the Multitude," 125.
21. Moreiras, "Children of Light I," 12.
22. Holloway, *Change the World without Taking Power*, 1.
23. Hardt and Negri, *Multitude*, 226.
24. Negri, *The Savage Anomaly*, 109.
25. Hardt and Negri, *Labor of Dionysus*, 309.
26. Hardt and Negri, *Empire*, 103.
27. Negri, *Insurgencies*, 11.
28. Hardt and Negri, *Multitude*, 353.
29. Negri, *The Savage Anomaly*, 265, 227.
30. Virno, *A Grammar of the Multitude*, 21.
31. Negri, *Insurgencies*, 28–29.
32. Rousseau, *The Social Contract*, 45.
33. Ibid., 54, 55. The original French phrase here translated as "complete transfer" is "aliénation totale."
34. Rawls, *A Theory of Justice*, 11.
35. Rousseau, *The Social Contract*, 55, 54.
36. Hobbes, *Leviathan*, 185, 186.
37. Ibid., 187.
38. Rousseau, *The Social Contract*, 59.
39. Hobbes, *Leviathan*, 228, 227.
40. Hobbes, *Man and Citizen*, 174.
41. Spinoza, *A Theologico-Political Treatise and A Political Treatise*, 215, 214.
42. Ibid., 347.
43. Negri, "*Reliqua Desiderantur*," 225, 226.
44. Hardt and Negri, *Empire*, 102.
45. Virno, "Virtuosity and Revolution," 201, 200, 201.
46. Spinoza, *A Theologico-Political Treatise and a Political Treatise*, 204.
47. "La multitud es el pueblo," *Mundo Argentino*, October 25, 1950, 27.

48. Ibid.

49. *Mundo Argentino*, October 27, 1948.

50. I thank Gabriela Nouzeilles for her comments on the imagery in this film.

51. Eloy Martínez, *Santa Evita*, 85 (translation modified), 87.

52. Ibid., 98.

53. Negri, *Insurgencies*, 29.

54. Kalyvas, "Popular Sovereignty, Democracy, and the Constituent Power," 227.

55. Negri, *Time for Revolution*, 152, 232.

56. Hardt and Negri, *Multitude*, 222.

57. Negri, *Time for Revolution*, 152.

58. Kreitner, "The Gift beyond the Grave," 1886.

59. Chen-Wishart, *Contract Law*, 88–89.

60. Dalton, "An Essay in the Deconstruction of Contract Doctrine," 1042.

61. See Bourdieu, *Outline of a Theory of Practice*, 6.

62. Montag, *Bodies, Masses, Power*, 84–85.

63. Colombat, "Deleuze and the Three Powers of Literature and Philosophy," 208.

64. Montag, *Bodies, Masses, Power*, 84.

65. Kauffman, *At Home in the Universe*, 29.

66. Negri, *The Savage Anomaly*, 109.

67. Spinoza, *Ethics*, 41, 42.

68. Ibid., 138.

69. Negri, *The Savage Anomaly*, 65.

70. Spinoza, *Ethics*, 125.

71. Hardt and Negri, *Multitude*, 339.

72. Ibid., 340; Deleuze and Guattari, *A Thousand Plateaus*, 7.

73. Spinoza, *Ethics*, 160, 54–58.

74. Ibid., 156, translation modified. The original Latin is: "Hominibus apprime utile est, *consuetudines* iungere, seseque iis vinculis astringere, quibus aptius de se omnibus unum efficiant."

75. Negri, *The Savage Anomaly*, 135.

76. Bennett, *A Study of Spinoza's "Ethics,"* 245.

77. Negri, *Time for Revolution*, 50

78. Negri, *The Savage Anomaly*, 67.

79. Degregori, "Harvesting Storms," 128.

80. Roncagliolo, *La cuarta espada*, 190, 22, 24.

81. Kirk, *Grabado en piedra*, 19, 10.

82. Ibid., 11.

83. Palmer, "The Revolutionary Terrorism of Peru's Shining Path," 278.

84. Starn, "Missing the Revolution," 65.
85. Díaz Martínez, *Ayacucho*, 116.
86. Starn, "Missing the Revolution," 73, 75, 84.
87. Díaz Martínez, *Ayacucho*, 199, 200.
88. Vich, *El caníbal es el Otro*, 13–14, 14, 35.
89. Portocarrero, *Razones de sangre*, 60, 61.
90. Degregori, "Harvesting Storms," 130.
91. Kirk, *Grabado en piedra*, 14, 37.
92. Degregori, *El surgimiento de Sendero Luminoso*, 186.
93. Degregori, *"Sendero Luminoso,"* 37–38.
94. Spinoza, *Ethics*, 137.
95. Linebaugh and Rediker, *The Many-Headed Hydra*, 40, 212.
96. Klein, *Fences and Windows*, 242.
97. Van Laerhoven and Ostrom, "Traditions and Trends," 3.
98. Harvey, *The New Imperialism;* Caffentzis, "Acts of God and Enclosures in New Orleans"; Klein, *The Shock Doctrine.*
99. Hardt and Negri, *Multitude*, 186.
100. Ibid., 108, 113, xv.
101. Ibid., 213, 212–13, 197, 114.
102. Michael Hardt and Remi Nilsen, "We Need to Broaden Our Political Possibilities: Interview with Michael Hardt," *Eurozine*, November 2008, www.eurozine.com. Hardt and Negri expand on their conception of the common in *Commonwealth.*
103. Hardt and Negri, *Empire*, 280.
104. Thompson, "Foundation and Empire," 85, 90, 92.
105. Caffentzis, "The End of Work."
106. Linebaugh and Rediker, *The Many-Headed Hydra*, 24, 6, 213.
107. Hardt and Negri, *Multitude*, 197, 198.
108. Negri, *Time for Revolution*, 223, 209.
109. Spinoza, *Ethics*, 139.
110. Hardt, with Smith and Minardi, "The Collaborator and the Multitude."
111. Hardt, "Prison Time," 79, 69.
112. Hardt and Negri, *Empire*, 78.
113. Negri, *Time for Revolution*, 210.
114. Orwell, *Keep the Aspidistra Flying*, 5.
115. Hardt and Negri, *Empire*, 326, 327.
116. Ibid., 41, 206.
117. Moreiras, "A Line of Shadow," 225.
118. Dean, "The Networked Empire," 284.
119. Rustin, "*Empire*," 14.
120. "Toni Negri Interviewed by *Le Monde*," October 3, 2001, Interactivist Info Exchange, http://info.interactivist.net/node/373. Translated

from Caroline Monnot and Nicolas Weill, "C'est la lutte des talibans du dollar contre les talibans du pétrole."

121. Hardt and Negri, *Empire*, 389, 388.
122. Hardt and Negri, *Multitude*, 178.
123. Hardt and Negri, *Empire*, 389, 391, 202.
124. Hardt and Negri, *Multitude*, 50, 178.
125. Ibid., 178; Negri, *Negri on Negri*, 55, 56.
126. Hardt and Negri, *Empire*, 390, 391.
127. Ibid., 201, 202, 201.
128. Ibid., 390.
129. Craft, *Novels of Testimony and Resistance*, 21.
130. Beverley, *Against Literature*, 113.
131. Beverley, *Testimonio*, 27.
132. Cabezas, *Fire from the Mountain*, 198, 215, 216.
133. Ibid., 221, 218.
134. Beverley and Zimmerman, *Literature and Politics in the Central American Revolutions*, 173.
135. Cabezas, *Fire from the Mountain*, 210, 210–11.
136. Burgos-Debray, "Introduction," xiv.
137. Stoll, *Rigoberta Menchú and the Story of All Poor Guatemalans*, 247, 262, 246, 235.
138. Ibid., 104, 105.
139. Sommer, "No Secrets," 157.
140. López Vigil, *Rebel Radio*, 1.
141. *Zapatistas!* 312–13, translation modified.
142. Hardt and Negri, *Multitude*, 211.
143. Deleuze and Guattari, *A Thousand Plateaus*, 229.
144. Negri, *Insurgencies*, 327, 328.
145. Ibid., 3, 334, 232.
146. Wright, *Storming Heaven*, 4, 4–5.
147. Tronti, "Lenin in England," 1, 3.
148. Tronti, *Obreros y capital*, 51–56.
149. Tronti, "The Strategy of the Refusal," 10, 13.
150. Quoted in Wright, *Storming Heaven*, 120.
151. Negri, "From the Mass Worker to the Socialized Worker," 77, 80, 81.
152. Virno, "Do You Remember Counterrevolution?" 242, 241.
153. Ibid., 249, 250.
154. Ibid., 256, 259.
155. Tronti, "The Strategy of the Refusal," 10, 11.
156. Negri, "Keynes and the Capitalist Theory of the State," 30; Negri, "Crisis of the Planner-State," 101.
157. Negri, "Crisis of the Crisis-State," 181, 186, 190.

158. Hallward, *Damming the Flood.*
159. Negri, "Crisis of the Crisis-State," 196.
160. Negri, *Time for Revolution*, 200–201.
161. Negri, "Constituent Republic," 222.
162. Negri, *Time for Revolution*, 120–26; Negri, *Insurgencies*, 334.
163. Hardt and Negri, *Multitude*, 358.
164. Sebastián Piñera's victory in the presidential election of 2010 seems to usher in yet another stage, of course. Perhaps appropriately, his inauguration was rocked by an aftershock from the devastating earthquake that had caused widespread destruction the month before.
165. Hecht Oppenheim, *Politics in Chile*, xvii, 4.
166. Moulián, *Chile actual*, 31.
167. Ibid., 33, 116.
168. Ibid., 46, 37.
169. Ibid., 362, 364, 146.
170. Ibid., 358, 25.
171. Thayer, *El fragmento repetido*, 124, 128, 129, 130.
172. Ibid., 77, 80, 44.
173. Benjamin, "Critique of Violence," 291, 297.
174. Martínez and Díaz, *Chile*, 2, 61, 61–62.
175. Ibid., 62, 61.
176. Ibid., 130, 131, 135.
177. Schneider, *Shantytown Protest in Pinochet's Chile*, 41, 45.
178. Silva, "The State, Politics and Peasant Unions in Chile," 436, 437.
179. Moulián, *Conversación interrumpida con Allende*, 86.
180. Negri, "From the Mass Worker to the Socialized Worker," 81.
181. Negri, "Paris 1986," 56.
182. Hardt and Negri, *Labor of Dionysus*, 275, 276, 313.
183. Hardt and Negri, *Multitude*, 357.
184. Landy, "Gramsci beyond Gramsci," 68.
185. Hardt and Negri, *Empire*, 413.
186. Bey, *T.A.Z.*
187. De Landa, *A Thousand Years of Nonlinear History*, 274.
188. Hardt and Negri, *Empire*, 413, 393.
189. Williams, *The Other Side of the Popular*, 208; for the *multitudo fidelium*, see Brennan, "The Italian Ideology," 115.
190. Hardt and Negri, *Empire*, 157.
191. Spinoza, *Ethics*, 181.
192. Negri, *Time for Revolution*, 261.

Epilogue

1. Negri, *The Porcelain Workshop*, 161.
2. Ali, *Pirates of the Caribbean*, 138.

3. Tariq Ali, "Axis of Hope: Venezuela and the Bolivarian Dream," *Counterpunch*, November 30, 2006, www.counterpunch.org/.

4. Colectivo Situaciones, "¿Hay una 'nueva gobernabilidad'?"

5. Cherki and Wieviorka, "Autoreduction Movements in Turin," 72.

6. Ibid., 74.

7. Giusti, "El día en que bajaron los cerros," 37.

8. López Maya, "The Venezuelan *Caracazo*," 125.

9. Coronil and Skurski, "Dismembering and Remembering the Nation," 317, 291.

10. Ojeda, "Paz a punto de cañones," 43.

11. López Maya, "The Venezuelan *Caracazo*," 134.

12. Coronil and Skurski, "Dismembering and Remembering the Nation," 321.

13. Ojeda, "Beirut en Caracas," 33.

14. Coronil and Skurski, "Dismembering and Remembering the Nation," 323.

15. Giusti, "Noche de queda," 75.

16. Ojeda, "Beirut en Caracas," 33.

17. Ellner and Tinker Salas, "Introduction," xiii.

18. López Maya, "¡Se rompieron las fuentes!" 78, 80, 84.

19. Ibid., 87, 85.

20. Ibid., 104, 101.

21. Coronil and Skurski, "Dismembering and Remembering the Nation," 299, 334.

22. Ibid., 311.

23. Gott, *In the Shadow of the Liberator*, 47, 43.

24. Chávez, *Understanding the Venezuelan Revolution*, 32.

25. Quoted in Gott, *In the Shadow of the Liberator*, 69.

26. López Maya, "New Avenues for Popular Representation," 90.

27. Wilpert, *Changing Venezuela by Taking Power*, 22.

28. Rory Carroll, "Government by TV: Chávez Sets 8-Hour Record," *The Guardian*, September 25, 2007, www.guardian.co.uk/media/.

29. See Uzcátegui, *Chávez, mago de las emociones*.

30. This description of the 2002 coup draws on my own personal experience of the event. See also Beasley-Murray, "Media and Multitude."

31. Duno Gottberg, "Mob Outrages," 118.

Bibliography

Abrams, Philip. "Notes on the Difficulty of Studying the State." *Journal of Historical Sociology* 1, no. 1 (March 1988): 58–89.

Agamben, Giorgio. *Homo Sacer: Sovereign Power and Bare Life*. Translated by Daniel Heller-Roazen. Stanford: Stanford University Press, 1998.

———. *The Open: Man and Animal.* Translated by Kevin Attell. Stanford: Stanford University Press, 2004.

———. *State of Exception.* Translated by Kevin Attell. Chicago: University of Chicago Press, 2005.

Agger, Ben. *Cultural Studies as Critical Theory*. London: Falmer, 1992.

Agosín, Marjorie. *Tapestries of Hope, Threads of Love: The "Arpillera" Movement in Chile, 1974–1994.* Albuquerque: University of New Mexico Press, 1996.

Alegría, Claribel. *They Won't Take Me Alive: Salvadorean Women in Struggle for Liberation.* Translated by Amanda Hopkinson. London: Women's Press, 1987.

Ali, Tariq. *Pirates of the Caribbean: Axis of Hope*. London: Verso, 2006.

Althusser, Louis. *Essays in Self-Criticism.* Translated by Graham Locke. London: New Left Books, 1976.

———. "Ideology and Ideological State Apparatuses (Notes Towards an Investigation)." In *Essays on Ideology*, 1–60. London: Verso, 1984.

Alvarez, Sonia, Evelina Dagnino, and Arturo Escobar, eds. *Cultures of Politics / Politics of Cultures: Re-Visioning Latin American Social Movements*. Boulder, Colo.: Westview, 1998.

———. "Introduction: The Cultural and the Political in Latin American Social Movements." In Alvarez et al., *Cultures of Politics / Politics of Cultures*, 1–29.

Aman, Kenneth, and Cristián Parker, eds. *Popular Culture in Chile: Resistance and Survival*. Boulder, Colo.: Westview, 1991.

Apter, David. "Political Violence in Analytical Perspective." In *The Legitimization of Violence*, ed. David Apter, 1–32. New York: New York University Press, 1997.

Arditi, Benjamin. "Post-Hegemony: Politics Outside the Usual Post-Marxist Paradigm." *Contemporary Politics* 13, no. 3 (September 2007): 205–26.

Aristotle. *The Politics*. Translated by T. A. Sinclair. London: Penguin, 1992.

Arnold, Matthew. *Culture and Anarchy*. Edited by J. Dover Wilson. Cambridge: Cambridge University Press, 1935.

Asociación Nacional de Medios Comunitarios, Libres y Alternativos. "Somos expresión de la multitud." Comunicación popular para el socialismo. www.medioscomunitarios.org/.

Auyero, Javier. *Poor People's Politics: Peronist Survival Networks and the Legacy of Evita*. Durham, N.C.: Duke University Press, 2000.

Ayala, Edwin Ernesto. *El tope y más allá: Desde la ofensiva del 89 a los acuerdos de paz; Testimonio de una guerrilla*. San Salvador: Sombrero Azul, 1997.

Beasley-Murray, Jon. "Peronism and the Secret History of Cultural Studies: Populism and the Substitution of Culture for State." *Cultural Critique*, no. 39 (Spring 1998): 189–224.

———. "Towards an Unpopular Cultural Studies: The Perspective of the Multitude." In *Cultura popular: Studies in Spanish and Latin American Popular Culture*, ed. Shelley Godsland and Anne White, 27–45. Oxford: Peter Lang, 2002.

———. "Media and Multitude: Chronicle of a Coup Unforetold." *JILAS: Journal of Iberian and Latin American Studies* (Melbourne) 8, no. 1 (July 2002): 105–16.

———. "Latin America and the Global System." In *The Companion to Latin American Studies*, ed. Philip Swanson, 222–38. London: Arnold, 2003.

Bedini, Silvio, ed. *Christopher Columbus and the Age of Exploration: An Encyclopedia*. New York: Da Capo, 1998.

Beezley, William H., Cheryl English Martin, and William E. French. "Introduction: Constructing Consent, Inciting Conflict." In *Rituals of Rule, Rituals of Resistance: Public Celebrations and Popular Culture in Mexico*, ed. William H. Beezley, Cheryl English Martin, and William E. French, xiii–xxxii. Wilmington, Del.: Scholarly Resources, 1994.

Bell, Jeffery. *Populism and Elitism: Politics in the Age of Elitism*. Washington, D.C.: Regnery Gateway, 1992.

Belsey, Catherine. "From Cultural Studies to Cultural Criticism?" In *Interrogating Cultural Studies: Theory, Politics, and Practice*, ed. Paul Bowman, 19–29. London: Pluto, 2003.

Benjamin, Walter. "Critique of Violence." In *Reflections*, ed. Peter Demetz, translated by Edmund Jephcott, 277–300. New York: Schocken, 1986.

Bennett, Jonathan. *A Study of Spinoza's "Ethics."* Indianapolis: Hackett, 1984.

Berger, Rony. "America under Attack: The Psychological Impacts of the Terror Attack on the Citizens of the USA." NATAL: Israel's Trauma Center for Victims of War and Terror, 2001. http://natal.org.il/english/.

Now available only from the Internet Archive: Wayback Machine, http://web.archive.org/web/20070109092115/http://www.natal.org.il/eng/publish/bergerwtc.html.

Beverley, John. *Against Literature*. Minneapolis: University of Minnesota Press, 1993.

———. *Testimonio: On the Politics of Truth*. Minneapolis: University of Minnesota Press, 2004.

Beverley, John, and Marc Zimmerman. *Literature and Politics in the Central American Revolutions*. Austin: University of Texas Press, 1990.

Bewes, Timothy. *Cynicism and Postmodernity*. London: Verso, 1997.

Bey, Hakim. *T.A.Z.: The Temporary Autonomous Zone, Ontological Anarchy, Poetic Terrorism*. Brooklyn, N.Y.: Autonomedia, 1991.

Binford, Leigh. "Peasants, Catechists, Revolutionaries: Organic Intellectuals in the Salvadoran Revolution, 1980–1992." In Lauria-Santiago and Binford, *Landscapes of Struggle*, 105–25.

Blissett, Luther. *Q*. Translated by Shaun Whiteside. London: William Heinemann, 2003.

Bongie, Chris. *Exotic Memories: Literature, Colonialism, and the Fin De Siècle*. Stanford: Stanford University Press, 1991.

Bourdieu, Pierre. *Outline of a Theory of Practice*. Translated by Richard Nice. Cambridge: Cambridge University Press, 1977.

———. *Distinction: A Social Critique of the Judgement of Taste*. Translated by Richard Nice. London: Routledge and Kegan Paul, 1984.

———. *Homo Academicus*. Translated by Peter Collier. Cambridge: Polity, 1988.

———. *The Logic of Practice*. Translated by Richard Nice. Cambridge: Polity, 1990.

———. "Concluding Remarks: For a Sociogenetic Understanding of Intellectual Works." Translated by Nicole Kaplan, Craig Calhoun, and Leah Florence. In *Bourdieu: Critical Perspectives*, ed. Craig Calhoun, Edward LiPuma, and Moishe Postone, 263–75. Cambridge: Polity, 1993.

———. *Practical Reason: On the Theory of Action*. Cambridge: Polity, 1998.

———. *Acts of Resistance: Against the New Myths of Our Time*. Translated by Richard Nice. Cambridge: Polity, 1998.

———. *Pascalian Meditations*. Translated by Richard Nice. Cambridge: Polity, 2000.

———. *Firing Back: Against the Tyranny of the Market 2*. Translated by Loïc Wacquant. New York: New Press, 2003.

Bourdieu, Pierre, and Alain Darbel, with Dominique Schnapper. *The Love of Art: European Art Museums and Their Public*. Translated by Caroline Beattie and Nick Merriman. Cambridge: Polity, 1991.

Bourdieu, Pierre, and Jean-Claude Passeron. *Reproduction in Education, Society, and Culture*. 2nd ed. Translated by Richard Nice. London: Sage, 1990.

Bourdieu, Pierre, and Loïc Wacquant. *An Invitation to Reflexive Sociology*. Chicago: University of Chicago Press, 1992.

Bourdieu, Pierre, et al. *The Weight of the World: Social Suffering in Contemporary Society*. Translated by Priscilla Parkhurst Ferguson et al. Cambridge: Polity, 1999.

Bourke, Joanna. *Fear: A Cultural History*. London: Virago, 2006.

Bracamonte, José Angel Moroni, and David E. Spencer. *Strategy and Tactics of the Salvadoran FMLN Guerrillas: Last Battle of the Cold War, Blueprint for Future Conflicts*. Westport, Conn.: Praeger, 1995.

Brennan, Teresa. *The Transmission of Affect*. Ithaca, N.Y.: Cornell University Press, 2004.

Brennan, Timothy. "The Italian Ideology." In *Debating Empire*, ed. Gopal Balakrishnan, 97–120. London: Verso, 2003.

———. *Wars of Position: The Cultural Politics of Left and Right*. New York: Columbia University Press, 2006.

Burgos-Debray, Elisabeth. "Introduction." In Menchú, *I, Rigoberta Menchú*, xi–xxi.

Butler, Judith. *Excitable Speech: A Politics of the Performative*. London: Routledge, 1997.

Byrne, Hugh. *El Salvador's Civil War: A Study of Revolution*. Boulder, Colo.: Lynne Rienner, 1996.

Cabezas, Omar. *Fire from the Mountain: The Making of a Sandinista*. Translated by Kathleen Weaver. New York: Plume, 1985.

Caffentzis, George. "The End of Work or the Renaissance of Slavery? A Critique of Rifkin and Negri." *Multitudes Web*, March 17, 2005. http://multitudes.samizdat.net/.

———. "Acts of God and Enclosures in New Orleans." *Mute Magazine* 2, no. 2 (May 2006): 78–87. *Mute: Culture and Politics after the Net*, May 24, 2006. http://www.metamute.org/.

Cahoone, Lawrence. *Civil Society: The Conservative Meaning of Liberal Politics*. Oxford: Blackwell, 2002.

Calderón, Fernando, Alejandro Piscitelli, and José Luis Reyna. "Social Movements: Actors, Theories, Expectations." In Escobar and Alvarez, *The Making of Social Movements in Latin America*, 19–36.

Caldwell, Wilber. *Cynicism and the Evolution of the American Dream*. Dulles, Va.: Potomac, 2006.

Canterucci, Jim. *Personal Brilliance: Mastering the Everyday Habits That Create a Lifetime of Success*. New York: AMACOM, 2005.

Castañeda, Jorge. *Utopia Unarmed: The Latin American Left after the Cold War*. New York: Vintage, 1993.

———. *Compañero: The Life and Death of Che Guevara*. Translated by Marina Castañeda. New York: Knopf, 1997.

Castro, Daniel. *Another Face of Empire: Bartolomé de Las Casas, Indigenous Rights, and Ecclesiastical Imperialism*. Durham, N.C.: Duke University Press, 2007.

Centre for Contemporary Cultural Studies. *The Empire Strikes Back: Race and Racism in 70s Britain*. London: Hutchinson, 1982.

Chaloupka, William. *Everybody Knows: Cynicism in America*. Minneapolis: University of Minnesota Press, 1999.

Chávez, Hugo. *Understanding the Venezuelan Revolution: Hugo Chávez Talks to Marta Harnecker*. Translated by Chesa Boudin. New York: Monthly Review, 2005.

Chávez Toro, Carlos. *Susy Díaz: Anatomía de una democracia*. Lima: Arteidea, 1995.

Chavkin, Samuel. *Storm over Chile: The Junta under Siege*. Rev. ed. Chicago: Lawrance Hill Books, 1989.

Chen-Wishart, Mindy. *Contract Law*. 2nd ed. Oxford: Oxford University Press, 2008.

Cherki, Eddy, and Michel Wieviorka. "Autoreduction Movements in Turin." In *Autonomia: Post-Political Politics*, ed. Sylvère Lotringer and Christian Marazzi, 72–78. 2nd ed. Los Angeles: Semiotext(e), 2007.

Chun, Lin. *The British New Left*. Edinburgh: Edinburgh University Press, 1993.

Ciria, Alberto. *Política y cultura popular: La Argentina peronista, 1946–1955*. Buenos Aires: Ediciones de la Flor, 1983.

Clements, Charles. *Witness to War: An American Doctor in El Salvador*. New York: Bantam, 1984.

Cohen, Jean, and Andrew Arato. *Civil Society and Political Theory*. Cambridge, Mass.: Massachusetts Institute of Technology Press, 1994.

Colas, Dominique. *Civil Society and Fanaticism: Conjoined Histories*. Translated by Amy Jacobs. Stanford: Stanford University Press, 1997.

Colectivo "Huitzilipochtli." *El "Cipitío" en el Salvador Sheraton: Un round de 11 días de 10 años de guerra*. San Salvador: Arcoiris, 1990.

Colectivo Situaciones. "¿Hay una 'nueva gobernabilidad'?" *La fogata*, no. 1 (March 2006). Situaciones: Colectivo de investigación militante. http://www.situaciones.org/.

Colombat, André Pierre. "Deleuze and the Three Powers of Literature and Philosophy: To Demystify, to Experiment, to Create." In *Deleuze and Guattari: Critical Assessments of Leading Philosophers*, ed. Gary Genosko, 207–22. London: Routledge, 2001.

Columbus, Christopher. *The Four Voyages*. Translated by J. M. Cohen. London: Penguin, 1969.

Comisión de la Verdad y Reconciliación. *Informe final*. 9 vols. Lima, 2003. Comisión de la Verdad y Reconciliación. http://www.cverdad.org.pe/.

Conaghan, Catherine. "Polls, Political Discourse, and the Public Sphere: The Spin on Peru's Fuji-golpe." In *Latin America in Comparative Perspective: New Approaches to Methods and Analysis*, ed. Peter H. Smith, 227–55. Boulder, Colo.: Westview, 1995.

Conaghan, Catherine, and James Malloy. *Unsettling Statecraft: Democracy and Neoliberalism in the Central Andes*. Pittsburgh: University of Pittsburgh Press, 1994.

Conniff, Michael. "Introduction." In *Populism in Latin America*, ed. Michael Conniff, 1–21. Tuscaloosa: University of Alabama Press, 1999.

Cornejo Polar, Antonio. *Escribir en el aire: Ensayo sobre la heterogeneidad socio-cultural en las literaturas andinas*. Lima: Latinoamericana, 2003.

Coronil, Fernando, and Julie Skurski. "Dismembering and Remembering the Nation: The Semantics of Political Violence in Venezuela." *Comparative Studies in Society and History* 33, no. 2 (April 1991): 288–337.

Cotler, Julio, and Romeo Grompone. *El fujimorismo: Ascenso y caída de un régimen autoritario*. Lima: Instituto de Estudios Peruanos, 2000.

Covey, Stephen. *The 7 Habits of Highly Effective People*. New York: Simon and Schuster, 1989.

Craft, Linda J. *Novels of Testimony and Resistance from Central America*. Gainesville: University Press of Florida, 1997.

Crassweller, Robert. *Perón and the Enigmas of Argentina*. New York: Norton, 1987.

Critchley, Simon. "Why I Love Cultural Studies." In *Interrogating Cultural Studies: Theory, Politics, and Practice*, ed. Paul Bowman, 59–75. London: Pluto, 2003.

———. "Is There a Normative Deficit in the Theory of Hegemony?" In Critchley and Marchant, *Laclau*, 113–22.

Critchley, Simon, and Oliver Marchant, eds. *Laclau: A Critical Reader*. London: Routledge, 2004.

———. "Introduction." In Critchley and Marchant, *Laclau*, 1–13.

Cummins, John. *The Voyage of Christopher Columbus: Columbus' Own Journal of Discovery Newly Restored and Translated*. London: Weidenfeld and Nicolson, 1992.

Dalton, Clare. "An Essay in the Deconstruction of Contract Doctrine." *The Yale Law Journal* 94, no. 5 (April 1985): 997–1114.

Dalton, Roque. *Miguel Mármol*. Translated by Kathleen Ross and Richard Schaaf. Boulder, Colo.: Curbstone, 1987.

Damasio, Antonio. *Looking for Spinoza: Joy, Sorrow, and the Feeling Brain*. Orlando, Fla.: Harcourt, 2003.

Danner, Mark. *The Massacre at El Mozote: A Parable of the Cold War*. New York: Vintage, 1994.

Dean, Jodi. "The Networked Empire: Communicative Capitalism and the Hope for Politics." In *Empire's New Clothes: Reading Hardt and Negri*, ed. Paul A. Passavant and Jodi Dean, 265–88. New York: Routledge, 2004.

de Certeau, Michel. *The Practice of Everyday Life*. Translated by Steven Rendall. Berkeley: University of California Press, 1984.

Degregori, Carlos Iván. *Que difícil es ser Dios: Ideología y violencia política en Sendero Luminoso*. Lima: El Zorro de Abajo, 1989.

———. *"Sendero Luminoso": 1. Los hondos y mortales desencuentros; 2. Lucha armada y utopia autoritaria*. Working Papers 4 and 6. Lima: Instituto de Estudios Peruanos, 1989.

———. *El surgimiento de Sendero Luminoso: Ayacucho, 1969–1979*. Lima: Instituto de Estudios Peruanos, 1990.

———. "The Maturation of a Cosmocrat and the Building of a Discourse Community: The Case of the Shining Path." In *The Legitimization of Violence*, ed. David Apter, 33–82. New York: New York University Press, 1997.

———. "Harvesting Storms: Peasant *Rondas* and the Defeat of Sendero Luminoso in Ayacucho." In Stern, *Shining and Other Paths*, 128–57.

———. *La década de la antipolítica: Auge y huida de Alberto Fujimori y Vladimiro Montesinos*. 2nd ed. Lima: Instituto de Estudios Peruanos, 2001.

Degregori, Carlos Iván, José Coronel, Ponciano del Pino, and Orin Starn. *Las rondas campesinas y la derrota de Sendero Luminoso*. Lima: Instituto de Estudios Peruanos, 1996.

De Ipola, Emilio. "Populismo e ideología. (A propósito de Ernesto Laclau: *Política e ideología en la teoría marxista*.)" *Revista Mexicana de Sociología* 41, no. 3 (1979): 925–60.

De Landa, Manuel. *A Thousand Years of Nonlinear History*. New York: Swerve, 1997.

Deleuze, Gilles. *Spinoza: Practical Philosophy*. Translated by Robert Hurley. San Francisco: City Lights, 1988.

———. *Foucault*. Translated by Seán Hand. Minneapolis: University of Minnesota Press, 1988.

———. *Cinema 2: The Time-Image*. Translated by Hugh Tomlinson and Robert Galeta. Minneapolis: University of Minnesota Press, 1989.

———. *Difference and Repetition*. Translated by Paul Patton. Columbia: Columbia University Press, 1994.

———. *Negotiations: 1972–1990*. Translated by Martin Joughlin. New York: Columbia University Press, 1995.

———. "On Philosophy." In *Negotiations*, 135–55.

———. "Postscript on Control Societies." In *Negotiations*, 177–82.

———. *Pure Immanence: Essays on A Life*. Translated by Anne Boyman. New York: Zone, 2001.

Deleuze, Gilles, and Félix Guattari. *Anti-Oedipus: Capitalism and Schizophrenia*. Translated by Robert Hurley, Mark Seem, and Helen Lane. London: Athlone, 1984.

———. *A Thousand Plateaus: Capitalism and Schizophrenia*. Translated by Brian Massumi. London: Athlone, 1988.

———. *What Is Philosophy?* Translated by Hugh Tomlinson and Graham Burchell. New York: Columbia University Press, 1996.

Deleuze, Gilles, and Claire Parnet. *Dialogues*. Translated by Hugh Tomlinson and Barbara Habberjam. New York: Columbia University Press, 1987.

Del Sarto, Ana, Alicia Ríos, and Abril Trigo, eds. *The Latin American Cultural Studies Reader*. Durham, N.C.: Duke University Press, 2004.

Díaz Martínez, Antonio. *Ayacucho: Hambre y esperanza*. 2nd ed. Lima: Mosca Azul, 1985.

Didion, Joan. *Salvador*. New York: Washington Square, 1983.

Di Tella, Guido. *Argentina under Perón, 1973–76: The Nation's Experience with a Labour-Based Government*. New York: St. Martin's, 1983.

Drake, Paul, and Peter Winn. "The Presidential Election of 1999/2000 and Chile's Transition to Democracy." *LASA Forum* 31, no. 1 (Spring 2000): 5–9.

Dunkerley, James. *The Long War: Dictatorship and Revolution in El Salvador*. London: Junction Books, 1982.

Duno Gottberg, Luis. "Mob Outrages: Reflections on the Media Construction of the Masses in Venezuela (April 2000–January 2003)." *Journal of Latin American Cultural Studies* 13, no. 1 (March 2004): 115–35.

Eagleton, Terry. *The Ideology of the Aesthetic*. Oxford: Blackwell, 1990.

Eckstein, Susan, ed. *Power and Popular Protest: Latin American Social Movements*. Berkeley: University of California Press, 1989.

———. "Power and Popular Protest in Latin America." In Eckstein, *Power and Popular Protest*, 1–60.

Edwards, Michael. *Civil Society*. Cambridge: Polity, 2004.

Ehrenberg, John. *Civil Society: The Critical History of an Idea*. New York: New York University Press, 1999.

Ekaizer, Ernesto. *Yo, Augusto*. Buenos Aires: Aguilar, 2003.

Ellner, Steve, and Miguel Tinker Salas. "Introduction: New Perspectives and the Chávez Phenomenon." In *Venezuela: Hugo Chávez and the Decline of an "Exceptional Democracy,"* ed. Steve Ellner and Miguel Tinker Salas, xiii–xvi. Lanham, Md.: Rowman and Littlefield, 2007.

Eloy Martínez, Tomás. *The Perón Novel.* Translated by Asa Zatz. New York: Pantheon, 1988.

———. *Santa Evita.* Translated by Helen Lane. New York: Vintage, 1997.

Eltit, Diamela. *Lumpérica.* Santiago, Chile: Ornitorrinco, 1983.

———. *El padre mío.* Santiago, Chile: Francisco Zegers, 1989.

———. *Sacred Cow.* Translated by Amanda Hopkinson. London: Serpent's Tail, 1995.

Escobar, Arturo, and Sonia E. Alvarez, eds. *The Making of Social Movements in Latin America: Identity, Strategy, and Democracy.* Boulder, Colo.: Westview, 1992.

———. "Introduction: Theory and Protest in Latin America Today." In Escobar and Alvarez, *The Making of Social Movements in Latin America,* 1–15.

Espinaza, José María. "Preliminar." In *La terquedad del Izote: El Salvador, crónica de una victoria; La historia de Radio Venceremos,* by Carlos Henríquez Consalvi (Santiago), 11–12. Mexico City: Diana, 1992.

Felski, Rita. "The Invention of Everyday Life." *New Formations,* no. 39 (Winter 1999–2000): 15–31.

Fernández-Armesto, Felipe. *Columbus.* London: Duckworth, 1996.

Flores Galindo, Alberto. "Muerte en Haquira, también . . . " *Márgenes,* no. 4 (December 1988): 196.

Foucault, Michel. *The History of Sexuality.* Vol. 3, *The Care of the Self,* translated by Robert Hurley. New York: Vintage, 1988.

———. *The History of Sexuality.* Vol. 1, *An Introduction,* translated by Robert Hurley. New York: Vintage, 1990.

———. *Discipline and Punish: The Birth of the Prison.* Translated by Alan Sheridan. London: Penguin, 1991.

———. "The Ethics of the Concern for Self as a Practice of Freedom." Translated by P. Aranov and D. McGrawth. In *Ethics: Subjectivity and Truth,* ed. Paul Rabinow, 281–301. New York: New Press, 1997.

———. "What Is Enlightenment?" Translated by Catherine Porter. In *Ethics: Subjectivity and Truth,* ed. Paul Rabinow, 303–19. New York: New Press, 1997.

———. *Abnormal: Lectures at the Collège de France, 1974–1975.* Translated by Graham Burchell. New York: Picador, 2003.

———. *The Hermeneutics of the Subject: Lectures at the Collège de France, 1981–1982.* Translated by Graham Burchell. New York: Palgrave, 2005.

Foweraker, Joe. *Theorizing Social Movements.* London: Pluto, 1995.

Franco, Jean. "A Ghost Dance on the Fields of the Cold War." Unpublished essay, 1998.

———. *The Decline and Fall of the Lettered City: Latin America in the Cold War*. Cambridge, Mass.: Harvard University Press, 2002.

Frei, Eduardo. "Preface." In *Civil Society and the Summit of the Americas: The 1998 Santiago Summit*, ed. Richard Feinberg and Robin Rosenberg, vii–viii. Coral Gables, Fla.: North-South Center Press, 1999.

Frow, John. *Cultural Studies and Cultural Value*. Oxford: Oxford University Press, 1995.

Furedi, Frank. *Politics of Fear: Beyond Left and Right*. London: Continuum, 2005.

Fuson, Robert. *The Log of Christopher Columbus*. Southampton: Ashford, 1987.

García Canclini, Néstor. *Hybrid Cultures: Strategies for Entering and Leaving Modernity*. Translated by Christopher Chiappari and Silvia López. Minneapolis: University of Minnesota Press, 1995.

———. *Consumers and Citizens: Globalization and Multicultural Conflicts*. Translated by George Yúdice. Minneapolis: University of Minnesota Press, 2001.

García Márquez, Gabriel. "No One Writes to the Colonel." Translated by J. S. Bernstein. In *Collected Novellas*, 107–66. New York: HarperCollins, 1990.

———. *One Hundred Years of Solitude*. Translated by Gregory Rabassa. New York: HarperCollins, 1992.

Geras, Norman. "Post-Marxism?" *New Left Review*, no. 163 (1987): 40–82.

Giddens, Anthony. *The Constitution of Society: Outline of the Theory of Stucturation*. Cambridge: Polity, 1986.

Gilbert, Sandra, and Susan Gubar. *The Madwoman in the Attic: The Woman Writer and the Nineteenth-Century Literary Imagination*. New Haven: Yale University Press, 1979.

Gilroy, Paul. *The Black Atlantic: Modernity and Double Consciousness*. Cambridge, Mass.: Harvard University Press, 1993.

———. *Postcolonial Melancholia*. New York: Columbia University Press, 2005.

Giusti, Roberto. "El día en que bajaron los cerros." In Ramia, *El día en que bajaron los cerros*, 36–38.

———. "Noche de queda." In Ramia, *El día en que bajaron los cerros*, 75–77.

Gonzales de Olarte, Efraín. *El neoliberalismo a la peruana: Economía política del ajuste estructural, 1990–1997*. Lima: Instituto de Estudios Peruanos, 1998.

Gorriti, Gustavo. *The Shining Path: A History of the Millenarian War in Peru*. Translated by Robin Kirk. Chapel Hill: University of North Carolina Press, 1999.

Gott, Richard. *In the Shadow of the Liberator: Hugo Chávez and the Transformation of Venezuela*. London: Verso, 2000.

Gramsci, Antonio. *Selections from Prison Notebooks*. Translated by Quintin Hoare and Geoffrey Nowell Smith. London: Lawrence and Wishart, 1971.

Green, Duncan. *Silent Revolution: The Rise of Market Economics in Latin America*. London: Cassell, 1995.

Grompone, Romeo. *Fujimori, neopopulismo y comunicación política*. Working Paper 93. Lima: Instituto de Estudios Peruanos, 1998.

Grossberg, Lawrence. *We Gotta Get Out of This Place: Popular Conservatism and Postmodern Culture*. London: Routledge, 1992.

———. "History, Politics, and Postmodernism: Stuart Hall and Cultural Studies." In Morley and Chen, *Stuart Hall*, 151–73.

———. *Dancing In Spite of Myself: Essays on Popular Culture*. Durham, N.C.: Duke University Press, 1997.

Guha, Ranajit. "On Some Aspects of the Historiography of Colonial India." In Guha and Spivak, *Selected Subaltern Studies*, 37–44.

———. "The Prose of Counter-Insurgency." In Guha and Spivak, *Selected Subaltern Studies*, 45–86.

———. *Dominance without Hegemony: History and Power in Colonial India*. Cambridge, Mass.: Harvard University Press, 1997.

Guha, Ranajit, and Gayatri Spivak, eds. *Selected Subaltern Studies*. Oxford: Oxford University Press, 1988.

Guidry, John, Michael Kennedy, and Mayer Zald. "Globalizations and Social Movements." In *Globalizations and Social Movements: Culture, Power, and the Transnational Public Sphere*, ed. John Guidry, Michael Kennedy, and Mayer Zald, 1–32. Ann Arbor: University of Michigan Press, 2000.

Guillaudat, Patrick, and Pierre Mouterde. *Los movimientos sociales en Chile, 1973–1993*. Translated by Juan Domingo Silva. Santiago, Chile: LOM, 1998.

Guzmán, Abimael. "We Are the Initiators." In *The Peru Reader: History, Culture, Politics*, ed. Orin Starn, Carlos Iván Degregori, and Robin Kirk, 310–15. Durham, N.C.: Duke University Press, 1995.

Hall, Stuart. "Notes on Deconstructing 'the Popular.'" In *People's History and Socialist Theory*, ed. Raphael Samuel, 227–40. London: Routledge, 1981.

———. "Cultural Studies: Two Paradigms." In *Media, Culture and Society: A Critical Reader*, ed. Richard Collins et al., 33–48. London: Sage, 1986.

———. *The Hard Road to Renewal: Thatcherism and the Crisis of the Left*. London: Verso, 1988.

———. "The Toad in the Garden: Thatcherism among the Theorists." In *Marxism and the Interpretation of Culture*, ed. Cary Nelson and Lawrence Grossberg, 35–73. Urbana: University of Illinois Press, 1988.

———. "The 'First' New Left: Life and Times." In *Out of Apathy: Voices of the New Left Thirty Years On*, ed. Robin Archer et al., 11–38. London: Verso, 1989.

———. "On Postmodernism and Articulation: An Interview with Stuart Hall." Edited by Lawrence Grossberg. In Morley and Chen, *Stuart Hall*, 131–50.

———. "Cultural Studies and Its Theoretical Legacies." In Morley and Chen, *Stuart Hall*, 262–75.

Hall, Stuart, and Paddy Whannel. *The Popular Arts*. London: Hutchinson, 1964.

Hallward, Peter. *Damming the Flood: Haiti, Aristide, and the Politics of Containment*. London: Verso, 2007.

Hamblyn, Richard. *The Invention of Clouds: How an Amateur Meteorologist Forged the Language of the Skies*. London: Picador, 2002.

Hanke, Lewis. *History of Latin American Civilization: Sources and Interpretations*. Vol. 1, *The Colonial Experience*. London: Methuen, 1969.

Hardt, Michael. *Gilles Deleuze: An Apprenticeship in Philosophy*. Minneapolis: University of Minnesota Press, 1993.

———. "The Withering of Civil Society." *Social Text*, no. 45 (Winter 1995): 27–44.

———. "Prison Time." *Yale French Studies*, no. 91 (1997): 64–79.

———. "Into the Factory: Negri's Lenin and the Subjective Caesura (1968–73)." In *The Philosophy of Antonio Negri: Resistance in Practice*, ed. Timothy S. Murphy and Abdul-Karim Mustapha, 7–37. London: Pluto, 2005.

Hardt, Michael, and Antonio Negri. *Labor of Dionysus: A Critique of the State-Form*. Minneapolis: University of Minnesota Press, 1994.

———. *Empire*. Cambridge, Mass.: Harvard University Press, 2000.

———. *Multitude: War and Democracy in the Age of Empire*. New York: Penguin, 2004.

———. *Commonwealth*. Cambridge, Mass.: Belknap, 2009.

Hardt, Michael, with Caleb Smith and Enrico Minardi. "The Collaborator and the Multitude: An Interview with Michael Hardt." *Minnesota Review*, nos. 61–62 (Spring 1994): 63–77. www.theminnesotareview.org/.

Hardwick, Jeffery. *Mall Maker: Victor Gruen, Architect of an American Dream*. Philadelphia: University of Pennsylvania Press, 2004.

Harris, David. *From Class Struggle to the Politics of Pleasure: The Effects of Gramscianism on Cultural Studies*. London: Routledge, 1992.

Hartley, John. *A Short History of Cultural Studies*. London: Sage, 2003.

Harvey, David. *The New Imperialism*. Oxford: Oxford University Press, 2005.

Hawkes, Terence. *That Shakespeherian Rag*. London: Routledge, 1986.

Hebdige, Dick. *Subculture: The Meaning of Style*. London: Routledge, 1991.

Hecht Oppenheim, Lois. *Politics in Chile: Socialism, Authoritarianism, and Market Democracy*. 3rd ed. Boulder, Colo.: Westview, 2007.

Henríquez Consalvi, Carlos (Santiago). *La terquedad del Izote: El Salvador, crónica de una victoria. La historia de Radio Venceremos*. Mexico City: Diana, 1992.

Hirschkop, Ken. "A Complex Populism: The Political Thought of Raymond Williams." *News from Nowhere*, no. 6 (February 1989): 12–22.

Hite, Katherine. *When the Romance Ended: Leaders of the Chilean Left, 1968–1998*. New York: Columbia University Press, 2000.

Hobbes, Thomas. *Leviathan*. Edited by C. B. Macpherson. London: Penguin, 1968.

———. *Man and Citizen ("De Homine" and "De Cive")*. Edited by Bernard Gert. Translated by Charles T. Wood et al. Indianapolis: Hackett, 1991.

Hoffer, Peter Charles. *Law and People in Colonial America*. Baltimore: Johns Hopkins University Press, 1998.

Hoggart, Richard. *The Uses of Literacy: Aspects of Working-Class Life with Special References to Publications and Entertainments*. London: Chatto and Windus, 1957.

Holloway, John. *Change the World without Taking Power: The Meaning of Revolution Today*. London: Pluto, 2002.

Hopenhayn, Martín. *No Apocalypse, No Integration: Modernism and Postmodernism in Latin America*. Translated by Cynthia Margarita Tompkins and Elizabeth Rosa Horan. Durham, N.C.: Duke University Press, 2001.

Hume, Mo. *Armed Violence and Poverty in El Salvador: A Mini Case Study for the Armed Violence and Poverty Initiative*. Bradford, U.K.: University of Bradford Centre for International Cooperation and Security, 2004.

Iturrieta, Aníbal, ed. *El pensamiento peronista*. Madrid: Ediciones de Cultura Hispánica, 1990.

James, Daniel. *Resistance and Integration: Peronism and the Argentine Working Class, 1946–1976*. Cambridge: Cambridge University Press, 1988.

———. *Doña María's Story: Life, History, and Political Identity*. Durham, N.C.: Duke University Press, 2000.

James, William. *Habit*. New York: H. Holt, 1890.

Jameson, Fredric. *The Political Unconscious: Narrative as a Socially Symbolic Act*. Ithaca: Cornell University Press, 1981.

———. "Postmodernism, or The Cultural Logic of Late Capitalism." *New Left Review*, no. 1/146 (July–August 1984): 53–92.

———. *Postmodernism, or, The Cultural Logic of Late Capitalism*. Durham, N.C.: Duke University Press, 1991.

———. "On 'Cultural Studies.'" *Social Text*, no. 34 (1993): 17–52.

Jochamowitz, Luis. *Ciudadano Fujimori: La construcción de un político*. 4th ed. Lima: Peisa, 1997.

Johnson, Richard. "Reinventing Cultural Studies: Remembering for the Best Version." In *From Sociology to Cultural Studies: New Perspectives*, ed. Elizabeth Long, 452–88. Oxford: Blackwell, 1997.

———. "Alternative." In *New Keywords: A Revised Vocabulary of Culture and Society*, ed. Tony Bennett, Lawrence Grossberg, and Meaghan Morris, 3–5. Oxford: Blackwell, 2005.

Kalyvas, Andreas. "Popular Sovereignty, Democracy, and the Constituent Power." *Constellations* 12, no. 2 (June 2005): 223–44.

Kamen, Henry. *Empire: How Spain Became a World Power, 1492–1763*. New York: HarperCollins, 2003.

Kaplan, Alice Yaeger. *Reproductions of Banality: Fascism, Literature, and French Intellectual Life*. Minneapolis: University of Minnesota Press, 1986.

Kauffman, Stuart A. *At Home in the Universe: The Search for Laws of Self-Organization and Complexity*. Oxford: Oxford University Press, 1995.

Keane, John. *Democracy and Civil Society: On the Predicaments of European Socialism, the Prospects for Democracy, and the Problem of Controlling Social and Political Power*. Rev. ed. London: University of Westminster Press, 1998.

———. *Civil Society: Old Images, New Visions*. Cambridge: Polity, 1998.

Keohane, Robert. *After Hegemony: Cooperation and Discord in the World Political Economy*. Princeton: Princeton University Press, 1984.

Kesey, Ken. *One Flew over the Cuckoo's Nest*. New York: Viking, 1962.

Khanna, Ranjana. *Dark Continents: Psychoanalysis and Colonialism*. Durham, N.C.: Duke University Press, 2003.

Kirk, Robin. *Grabado en piedra: Las mujeres de Sendero Luminoso*. Lima: Instituto de Estudios Peruanos, 1993.

Kirkland, Richard. "The Spectacle of Terrorism in Northern Irish Culture." *Critical Survey* 15, no. 1 (2003): 77–90.

Klein, Naomi. *Fences and Windows: Dispatches from the Front Lines of the Globalization Debate*. Toronto: Vintage Canada, 2002.

———. *The Shock Doctrine: The Rise of Disaster Capitalism*. Toronto: Alfred A. Knopf Canada, 2007.

Klein, Naomi, and Haifa Zangana. "Killing Democracy in Iraq." *Red Pepper*, no. 75 (December 2004). www.redpepper.org.uk/.

Knight, Barry, Hope Chigudu, and Rajesh Tandon. *Reviving Democracy: Citizens at the Heart of Governance*. London: Earthscan, 2002.

Korczynski, Marek, Randy Hodson, and Paul Edwards. "Introduction: Competing, Collaborating, and Reinforcing Theories." In *Social Theory at Work*, ed. Marek Korczynski, Randy Hodson, and Paul Edwards, 1–25. Oxford: Oxford University Press, 2006.

Korten, David. *Globalizing Civil Society: Reclaiming Our Right to Power*. New York: Seven Stories, 1998.

Kraniauskas, John. "Rodolfo Walsh y Eva Perón: 'Esa Mujer.'" *Nuevo Texto Crítico* 6, nos. 12–13 (July 1993–June 1994): 105–19.

———. "Political Puig: Eva Perón and the Populist Negotiation of Modernity." In "Conservative Modernity," ed. C. Kaplan and D. Glover. Special issue, *New Formations*, no. 28 (Spring 1996): 121–31.

Kreitner, Roy. "The Gift beyond the Grave: Revisiting the Question of Consideration." *Columbia Law Review* 101, no. 8 (December 2001): 1876–1957.

Kriesi, Hanspeter, Ruud Koopmans, Jan Willem Duyvendak, and Marco Giugni. *New Social Movements in Western Europe: A Comparative Analysis*. Minneapolis: University of Minnesota Press, 1995.

Laclau, Ernesto. *Politics and Ideology in Marxist Theory: Capitalism—Fascism—Populism*. London: New Left Books, 1977.

———. "Teorías marxistas del estado: Debates y perspectivas." In *Estado y política en América Latina*, ed. Norbert Lechner, 25–59. Mexico City: Siglo Veintiuno, 1981.

———. *New Reflections on the Revolution of Our Time*. London: Verso, 1990.

———. *Emancipation(s)*. London: Verso, 1996.

———. "Populism: What's in a Name?" In *Populism and the Mirror of Democracy*, ed. Francisco Panizza, 32–49. London: Verso, 2005.

———. *On Populist Reason*. London: Verso, 2005.

Laclau, Ernesto, and Chantal Mouffe. *Hegemony and Socialist Strategy: Towards a Radical Democratic Politics*. London: Verso, 1985.

Land, Nick. *The Thirst for Annihilation: Georges Bataille and Virulent Nihilism*. London: Routledge, 1992.

———. "Making It with Death: Remarks on Thanatos and Desiring-Production." *Journal of the British Society for Phenomenology* 24, no. 1 (January 1993): 66–76.

———. "Meltdown." *Abstract Culture: Swarm 1* (Winter 1997). Cybernetic Culture Research Unit. www.ccru.net/.

Landy, Marcia. " 'Gramsci beyond Gramsci': The Writings of Toni Negri." *boundary 2* 21, no. 2 (1994): 63–97.

Lane, Jeremy. *Pierre Bourdieu: A Critical Introduction.* London: Pluto, 2000.

———. *Bourdieu's Politics: Problems and Possibilities.* London: Routledge, 2006.

Larsen, Neil. *Modernism and Hegemony: A Materialist Critique of Aesthetic Agencies.* Minneapolis: University of Minnesota Press, 1990.

Las Casas, Bartolomé de. *A Short Account of the Destruction of the Indies.* Translated by Nigel Griffin. London: Penguin, 1992.

Lash, Scott. "Power after Hegemony: Cultural Studies in Mutation?" *Theory, Culture and Society* 24, no. 3 (2007): 55–78.

Lauria-Santiago, Aldo, and Leigh Binford, eds. *Landscapes of Struggle: Politics, Society, and Community in El Salvador.* Pittsburgh: University of Pittsburgh Press, 2004.

———. "Local History, Politics, and the State in El Salvador." In Lauria-Santiago and Binford, *Landscapes of Struggle,* 1–11.

Lavín, Joaquín. *La revolución silenciosa.* Santiago, Chile: Zig-Zag, 1987.

Lazzarato, Maurizio. "From Biopower to Biopolitics." *Tailoring Biotechnologies* 2, no. 2 (Summer–Fall 2006): 11–20.

Lee, Richard. *Life and Times of Cultural Studies: The Politics and Transformation of the Structures of Knowledge.* Durham, N.C.: Duke University Press, 2003.

Lefebvre, Henri. *Critique of Everyday Life.* Vol. 2, *Foundations for a Sociology of the Everyday,* translated by John Moore. London: Verso, 2002.

Lievens, Karin. *El quinto piso de la alegría: Tres años con la guerrilla.* San Salvador: Sistema Radio Venceremos, 1988.

Lindqvist, Sven. *A History of Bombing.* London: Granta, 2001.

Linebaugh, Peter. *The London Hanged: Crime and Civil Society in the Eighteenth Century.* Cambridge: Cambridge University Press, 1992.

Linebaugh, Peter, and Marcus Rediker. *The Many-Headed Hydra: The Hidden History of the Revolutionary Atlantic.* London: Verso, 2000.

López, Ana M. "Are All Latins from Manhattan? Hollywood, Ethnography, and Cultural Colonialism." In *Mediating Two Worlds: Cinematic Encounters in the Americas,* ed. John King, Ana M. López, and Manuel Alvarado, 67–80. London: British Film Institute, 1993.

López Maya, Margarita. "New Avenues for Popular Representation in Venezuela: La Causa-R and the Movimiento Bolivariano 200." In *Reinventing Legitimacy: Democracy and Political Change in Venezuela,* ed. Damarys Canache and Michael R. Kulisheck, 83–95. Westport, Conn.: Greenwood, 1998.

———. "¡Se rompieron las fuentes! La política está en la calle." In *Venezuela Siglo XX: Visiones y testimonios*, ed. Adrúbal Baptista, 73–106. Caracas: Fundación Polar, 2000.

———. "The Venezuelan *Caracazo* of 1989: Popular Protest and Institutional Weakness." *Journal of Latin American Studies* 35, no. 1 (February 2003): 117–37.

López Vigil, José Ignacio. *Rebel Radio: The Story of El Salvador's Radio Venceremos*. Translated by Mark Fried. Willimantic, Conn.: Curbstone, 1994. Originally published as *Las mil y una historias de Radio Venceremos*. San Salvador: UCA Editores, 1991.

López Vigil, María. *Muerte y vida en Morazán: Testimonio de un sacerdote*. San Salvador: UCA Editores, 1987.

Loughlin, Martin, and Neil Walker. "Introduction." In *The Paradox of Constitutionalism: Constituent Power and Constitutional Form*, ed. Martin Loughlin and Neil Walker, 1–8. Oxford: Oxford University Press, 2007.

Loveman, Brian. *The Constitution of Tyranny: States of Exception in South America*. Pittsburgh: University of Pittsburgh Press, 1993.

Luna, Félix. *Perón y su tiempo*. 3 vols. Buenos Aires: Sudamericana, 1984–1986.

Lynch, John. *Simón Bolívar: A Life*. New Haven: Yale University Press, 2006.

Manrique, Nelson. "La década de la violencia." *Márgenes*, nos. 5–6 (December 1989): 137–82.

Marchant, Oliver. "Politics and the Ontological Difference: On the 'Strictly Philosophical' in Laclau's Work." In Critchley and Marchant, *Laclau*, 54–72.

Martínez, Javier, and Alvaro Díaz. *Chile: The Great Transformation*. Washington, D.C. and Geneva: Brookings Institute and United Nations Institute for Social Development, 1996.

Marx, Karl. *Selected Writings*. Edited by David McLellan. Oxford: Oxford University Press, 1977.

Massumi, Brian. *A User's Guide to Capitalism and Schizophrenia: Deviations from Deleuze and Guattari*. Cambridge, Mass.: Massachusetts Institute of Technology Press, 1992.

———. "Everywhere You Want to Be: Introduction to Fear." In *The Politics of Everyday Fear*, ed. Brian Massumi, 3–37. Minneapolis: University of Minnesota Press, 1993.

———. "Introduction: Like a Thought." In *A Shock to Thought: Expressions after Deleuze and Guattari*, ed. Brian Massumi, xiii–xxxix. London: Routledge, 2002.

———. *Parables for the Virtual: Movement, Affect, Sensation*. Durham, N.C.: Duke University Press, 2002.

———. “Fear (The Spectrum Said).” *Positions* 13, no. 1 (Spring 2005): 31–48.

Mauceri, Philip. “State Reform, Coalitions, and the Neoliberal Autogolpe in Peru.” *Latin American Research Review* 30, no. 1 (1995): 7–37.

———. “The Transition to ‘Democracy’ and the Failures of Institution Building.” In *The Peruvian Labyrinth: Polity, Society, Economy*, ed. Maxwell Cameron and Philip Mauceri, 13–36. University Park, Pa.: Pennsylvania State University Press, 1997.

McClintock, Cynthia. “Peru’s Sendero Luminoso Rebellion: Origins and Trajectory.” In Eckstein, *Power and Popular Protest*, 61–101.

———. *Revolutionary Movements in Latin America: El Salvador’s FMLN and Peru’s Shining Path*. Washington, D.C.: United States Institute of Peace Press, 1998.

McGuigan, Jim. *Cultural Populism*. London: Routledge, 1992.

McRobbie, Angela. “Post-Marxism and Cultural Studies: A Post-script.” In *Cultural Studies*, ed. Lawrence Grossberg, Cary Nelson, and Paula Treichler, 719–30. New York: Routledge, 1992.

Mena Sandoval, Capitán Francisco Emilio. *Del ejército nacional al ejército guerrillero*. San Salvador: Arcoiris, [1990?].

Menchú, Rigoberta. *I, Rigoberta Menchú: An Indian Woman in Guatemala*. Edited by Elisabeth Burgos-Debray. Translated by Ann Wright. London: Verso, 1984.

Mentinis, Mihalis. *Zapatistas: The Chiapas Revolt and What It Means for Radical Politics*. London: Pluto, 2006.

Mény, Yves, and Yves Surel. “The Constitutive Ambiguity of Populism.” In *Democracies and the Populist Challenge*, ed. Yves Mény and Yves Surel, 1–21. Basingstoke: Palgrave, 2002.

Mertes, Tom, ed. *A Movement of Movements: Is Another World Really Possible?* London: Verso, 2004.

Metzi, Francisco. *Por los caminos de Chalatenango con la salud en la mochila*. San Salvador: UCA Editores, 1988.

Minta, Stephen. *Aguirre: The Re-Creation of a Sixteenth-Century Journey across South America*. London: Jonathan Cape, 2003.

Monbiot, George. *The Age of Consent: A Manifesto for a New World Order*. London: Flamingo, 2003.

Montag, Warren. *Bodies, Masses, Power: Spinoza and His Contemporaries*. London: Verso, 1999.

Moodie, Ellen. “ ‘El Capitán Cinchazo’: Blood and Meaning in Postwar San Salvador.” In Lauria-Santiago and Binford, *Landscapes of Struggle*, 226–44.

Moraña, Mabel, ed. *Nuevas perspectivas desde/sobre América Latina: El desafío de los estudios culturales*. Santiago, Chile: Cuarto Propio, 2000.

Moreiras, Alberto. "Pastiche Identity, and Allegory of Allegory." In *Latin American Identity and Constructions of Difference*, ed. Amaryll Chanady, 204–38. Minneapolis: University of Minnesota Press, 1994.

———. *The Exhaustion of Difference: The Politics of Latin American Cultural Studies*. Durham, N.C.: Duke University Press, 2001.

———. "Spanish Nation Formation: An Introduction." *Journal of Spanish Cultural Studies* 2, no. 1 (2001): 5–11.

———. "A Line of Shadow: Metaphysics in Counter-Empire." *Rethinking Marxism* 13, nos. 3–4 (Fall–Winter 2001): 216–26.

———. "Children of Light: Neo-Paulinism and the Cathexis of Difference (Part I)." *The Bible and Critical Theory* 1, no. 1 (2004): 03-1-03-16.

———. *Línea de sombra: El no sujeto de la política*. Santiago, Chile: Palinodia, 2006.

Morison, Samuel Eliot. *Admiral of the Ocean Sea: A Life of Christopher Columbus*. Boston: Northeastern University Press, 1983.

Morley, David, and Kuan-Hsing Chen, eds. *Stuart Hall: Critical Dialogues in Cultural Studies*. London: Routledge, 1996.

Mouffe, Chantal, ed. *Gramsci and Marxist Theory*. London: Routledge, 1979.

Moulián, Tomás. *Chile actual: Anatomía de un mito*. Santiago, Chile: LOM/ARCIS, 1997.

———. *El consumo me consume*. Santiago, Chile: LOM, 1998.

———. *Conversación interrumpida con Allende*. Santiago, Chile: LOM/ARCIS, 1998.

Negri, Antonio. "Keynes and the Capitalist Theory of the State Post-1929." In *Revolution Retrieved: Selected Writings on Marx, Keynes, Capitalist Crisis and New Social Subjects, 1967–83*, 9–42. London: Red Notes, 1988.

———. "Crisis of the Planner-State: Communism and Revolutionary Organisation." In *Revolution Retrieved*, 97–148.

———. "Crisis of the Crisis-State." In *Revolution Retrieved*, 181–97.

———. "Paris 1986, 26 November–10 December." In *The Politics of Subversion: A Manifesto for the Twenty-First Century*, translated by James Newell, 47–60. Cambridge: Polity, 1989.

———. "From the Mass Worker to the Socialized Worker — and Beyond." In *The Politics of Subversion*, 75–88.

———. *The Savage Anomaly: The Power of Spinoza's Metaphysics and Politics*. Translated by Michael Hardt. Minneapolis: University of Minnesota Press, 1991.

———. *Marx beyond Marx: Lessons on the Grundrisse*. Edited by Jim Fleming. Translated by Harry Cleaver, Michael Ryan, and Maurizio Viano. Brooklyn, N.Y.: Autonomedia, 1991.

———. "Constituent Republic." Translated by Ed Emory. In Virno and Hardt, *Radical Thought in Italy*, 213–22.

———. "*Reliqua Desiderantur:* A Conjecture for a Definition of the Concept of Democracy in the Final Spinoza." Translated by Ted Stolze. In *The New Spinoza*, ed. Warren Montag and Ted Stolze, 219–47. Minneapolis: University of Minnesota Press, 1997.

———. *El exilio*. Translated by Raúl Sánchez. Barcelona: El Viejo Topo, 1998.

———. *Insurgencies: Constituent Power and the Modern State*. Translated by Maurizia Boscagli. Minneapolis: University of Minnesota Press, 1999.

———. *Time for Revolution*. Translated by Matteo Mandarini. New York: Continuum, 2003.

———. *Subversive Spinoza: (Un)contemporary Variations*. Edited by Timothy S. Murphy. Translated by Timothy S. Murphy et al. Manchester: Manchester University Press, 2004.

———. "Towards an Ontological Definition of the Multitude." In *Reflections on Empire*, translated by Ed Emery, 114–25. Cambridge: Polity, 2008.

———. *The Porcelain Workshop: For a New Grammar of Politics*. Translated by Noura Wedell. New York: Semiotext(e), 2008.

Negri, Antonio, and Giuseppe Cocco. *GlobAL: Biopoder y luchas en una América Latina globalizada*. Translated by Elena Bossi. Buenos Aires: Paidós, 2006.

Negri, Antonio, in conversation with Anne Dufourmantelle. *Negri on Negri*. Translated by M. B. DeBevoise. New York: Routledge, 2004.

Nelson, Cary, Paula Treichler, and Lawrence Grossberg. "Cultural Studies: An Introduction." In *Cultural Studies*, ed. Lawrence Grossberg, Cary Nelson, and Paula Treichler, 1–22. New York: Routledge, 1992.

Neruda, Pablo. *Canto General*. Translated by Jack Schmitt. Berkeley: University of California Press, 1991.

Neustadt, Robert. *CADA día: La creación de un arte social*. Santiago, Chile: Cuarto Propio, 2001.

Norris, Andrew. "Giorgio Agamben and the Politics of the Living Dead." *Diacritics* 30, no. 4 (Winter 2000): 38–58.

O'Brien, Flann. *At Swim-Two-Birds*. Harmondsworth: Penguin, 1967.

O'Donnell, Guillermo, and Philippe Schmitter. *Tentative Conclusions about Uncertain Democracies*. Vol. 4 of *Transitions from Authoritarian Rule:*

Prospects for Democracy, ed. Guillermo O'Donnell, Philippe Schmitter, and Laurence Whitehead. Baltimore: Johns Hopkins University Press, 1986.

Ojeda, Fabricio. "Paz a punto de cañones." In Ramia, *El día en que bajaron los cerros*, 33–35.

———. "Beirut en Caracas." In Ramia, *El día en que bajaron los cerros*, 43–46.

Olguín, Sergio. *Perón vuelve: Cuentos sobre peronismo*. Buenos Aires: Norma, 2000.

Ortiz, Fernando. *Cuban Counterpoint: Tobacco and Sugar*. Translated by Harriet de Onís. Durham, N.C.: Duke University Press, 1995.

Orwell, George. *Keep the Aspidistra Flying*. Harmondsworth: Penguin, 1936.

Paley, Julia. *Marketing Democracy: Power and Social Movements in Post-Dictatorship Chile*. Berkeley: University of California Press, 2001.

Palmer, David Scott. "The Revolutionary Terrorism of Peru's Shining Path." In *Terrorism in Context*, ed. Martha Crenshaw, 249–310. University Park: Pennsylvania State University Press, 1995.

Perec, Georges. *W, or, The Memory of Childhood*. Translated by David Bellos. London: Collins Harvill, 1989.

Perón, Juan Domingo. *El pensamiento político de Perón: Los más importantes discursos y mensajes, 1943–1973*. Edited by Abel del Río. Buenos Aires: Kikiyón, 1972.

———. *Obras completas*. Vol. 22, *Los vendepatria: Las pruebas de una traición*. Buenos Aires: Docencia, 1985.

———. "Lecciones para las Fuerzas Armadas." In *Obras completas*, 25: 401–11. Buenos Aires: Docencia, 1988.

Phillips, William, and Carla Phillips. *The Worlds of Christopher Columbus*. Cambridge: Cambridge University Press, 1992.

"Plan of Action of Santiago: Summit of the Americas." In *Civil Society and the Summit of the Americas: The 1998 Santiago Summit*, ed. Richard Feinberg and Robin Rosenberg, 7–22. Coral Gables, Fla.: North-South Center Press, 1999.

Plotkin, Mariano Ben. *Mañana es San Perón: A Cultural History of Perón's Argentina*. Translated by Keith Zahniser. Wilmington, Del.: Scholarly Resources, 2003.

Poneman, Daniel. *Argentina: Democracy on Trial*. New York: Paragon, 1987.

Poole, Deborah, and Gerardo Rénique. *Peru: Time of Fear*. London: Latin American Bureau, 1992.

Portantiero, Juan Carlos, and Emilio de Ipola. “Lo nacional popular y los populismos realmente existentes.” In *El estado periférico latinoamericano*, ed. Juan Carlos Rubinstein, 203–13. Buenos Aires: Tercer Mundo, 1988.

Portocarrero, Gonzalo. *Razones de sangre: Aproximaciones a la violencia política*. Lima: Pontificia Universidad Católica del Perú, 1998.

Postone, Moishe. *Time, Labor, and Social Domination: A Reinterpretation of Marx's Critical Theory*. Cambridge: Cambridge University Press, 1993.

Putnam, Robert. *Bowling Alone: The Collapse and Revival of American Community*. New York: Simon and Schuster, 2000.

Ramia, Carmen, ed. *El día en que bajaron los cerros: El saqueo de Caracas*. 2nd ed. Caracas: Ateneo, 1989.

Rawls, John. *A Theory of Justice*. Rev. ed. Cambridge, Mass.: Belknap, 1999.

Redding, Arthur. *Raids on Human Consciousness: Writing, Anarchism, and Violence*. Columbia: University of South Carolina Press, 1998.

Richard, Nelly. *Margins and Institutions: Art in Chile since 1973*. Special issue, *Art and Text* (Melbourne), no. 21 (May–July 1986).

———. *Cultural Residues: Chile in Transition*. Translated by Alan West-Durán and Theodore Quester. Minneapolis: University of Minnesota Press, 2004.

Richard, Nelly, ed. *Políticas y estéticas de la memoria*. Santiago, Chile: Cuarto Propio, 2000.

Rifkin, Adrian. “Inventing Recollection.” In *Interrogating Cultural Studies: Theory, Politics, and Practice*, ed. Paul Bowman, 101–24. London: Pluto, 2003.

Riquelme, Alfredo. “Voting for Nobody in Chile's New Democracy.” *NACLA: Report on the Americas* 32, no. 6 (May–June 1999): 31–33.

Roberts, Kenneth. *Deepening Democracy? The Modern Left and Social Movements in Chile and Peru*. Stanford: Stanford University Press, 1998.

Robin, Corey. *Fear: The History of a Political Idea*. Oxford: Oxford University Press, 2004.

Robinson, William. “The São Paulo Forum: Is There a New Latin American Left?” *Monthly Review* 44, no. 7 (December 1992): 1–12.

Romero, Luis Alberto. *A History of Argentina in the Twentieth Century*. Translated by James P. Brennan. University Park: Pennsylvania State University Press, 2002.

Roncagliolo, Santiago. *La cuarta espada: La historia de Abimael Guzmán y Sendero Luminoso*. Barcelona: Debate, 2007.

Roseberry, William. “Hegemony and the Language of Contention.” In *Everyday Forms of State Formation: Revolution and the Negotiation of Rule in Modern Mexico*, ed. Gilbert M. Joseph and Daniel Nugent, 355–66. Durham, N.C.: Duke University Press, 1994.

Rousseau, Jean-Jacques. *The Social Contract*. Translated by Christopher Betts. Oxford: Oxford University Press, 1994.

Rustin, Michael. "*Empire:* A Postmodern Theory of Revolution." In *Debating Empire*, ed. Gopal Balakrishnan, 1–18. London: Verso, 2003.

Sader, Emir. "Beyond Civil Society." In Mertes, *A Movement of Movements*, 248–61.

Salcedo, José María. *Terremoto: ¿Por qué ganó Fujimori?* Lima: Brasa, 1995.

Salinas, Luis Alejandro. *The London Clinic*. Santiago, Chile: LOM, 1999.

Salman, Ton. *The Diffident Movement: Disintegration, Ingenuity and Resistance of the Chilean Pobladores, 1973–1990*. Translated by Sheila Gogol. Amsterdam: Thela, 1997.

Sarlo, Beatriz. *Una modernidad periférica: Buenos Aires, 1920 y 1930*. Buenos Aires: Nueva Visión, 1988.

———. *Scenes from Postmodern Life*. Translated by Jon Beasley-Murray. Minneapolis: University of Minnesota Press, 2001.

Scarry, Elaine. *The Body in Pain: The Making and Unmaking of the World*. Oxford: Oxford University Press, 1985.

Schmitt, Carl. *Political Theology: Four Chapters on the Concept of Theology*. Translated by George Schwab. Chicago: University of Chicago Press, 2005.

Schneider, Cathy Lisa. *Shantytown Protest in Pinochet's Chile*. Philadelphia: Temple University Press, 1995.

Sebreli, Juan José. *Los deseos imaginarios del peronismo*. Buenos Aires: Legasa, 1983.

Sedgwick, Eve Kosofsky. *Touching, Feeling: Affect, Pedagogy, Performativity*. Durham, N.C.: Duke University Press, 2003.

Seed, Patricia. *Ceremonies of Possession in Europe's Conquest of the New World, 1492–1640*. Cambridge: Cambridge University Press, 1995.

Seigworth, Gregory. "From Affection to Soul." In *Gilles Deleuze: Key Concepts*, ed. Charles Stivale, 159–69. Chesham: Acumen, 2005.

Sepúlveda, Emma. "Introduction." In *We, Chile: Personal Testimonies of the Chilean Arpilleristas*, ed. Emma Sepúlveda, 19–38. Falls Church, Va.: Azul, 1996.

Shakespeare, Nicholas. *The Dancer Upstairs*. London: Picador, 1997.

Shklovsky, Victor. "Art as Technique." In *Literary Theory: An Anthology*, ed. Julie Rivkin and Michael Ryan, 15–21. 2nd ed. Oxford: Blackwell, 2004.

Sieyès, Emmanuel. "What Is the Third Estate?" In *Political Writings*, edited and translated by Michael Sonenscher, 92–162. Indianapolis: Hackett, 2003.

Silva, Patricio. "The State, Politics and Peasant Unions in Chile." *Journal of Latin American Studies* 20, no. 2 (November 1988): 433–52.

Simpson, David. "Naming the Dead." *London Review of Books* 23, no. 22 (November 15, 2001): 3–7.

Slack, Jennifer Daryl. "The Theory and Method of Articulation in Cultural Studies." In Morley and Chen, *Stuart Hall*, 112–27.

Slater, David, ed. *New Social Movements and the State in Latin America.* Amsterdam: CEDLA, 1985.

———. "Social Movements and a Recasting of the Political." In Slater, *New Social Movements*, 1–25.

Sloterdijk, Peter. *Critique of Cynical Reason.* Translated by Michael Eldred. Minneapolis: University of Minnesota Press, 1987.

Smith, Michael. *Entre dos fuegos: ONG, desarrollo rural y violencia política.* Lima: Instituto de Estudios Peruanos, 1992.

Snyder, Edward. "The Dirty Legal War: Human Rights and the Rule of Law in Chile 1973–1995." *Tulsa Journal of Comparative and International Law*, no. 2 (Spring 1995): 253–87.

Sommer, Doris. "No Secrets." In *The Real Thing: Testimonial Discourse and Latin America*, ed. Georg M. Gugelberger, 130–57. Durham, N.C.: Duke University Press, 1996.

Sparks, Colin. "Stuart Hall, Cultural Studies and Marxism." In Morley and Chen, *Stuart Hall*, 71–101.

Spinoza, Benedict de. *A Theologico-Political Treatise and a Political Treatise.* Translated by R. H. M. Elwes. New York: Dover, 1951.

———. *Ethics.* Translated by Edwin Curley. London: Penguin, 1996.

Spivak, Gayatri. "Subaltern Studies: Deconstructing Historiography." In Guha and Spivak, *Selected Subaltern Studies*, 3–32.

———. "Can the Subaltern Speak?" In *Marxism and the Interpretation of Culture*, ed. Lawrence Grossberg and Cary Nelson, 271–313. Urbana: University of Illinois Press, 1988.

Starn, Orin. "Missing the Revolution: Anthropologists and the War in Peru." *Cultural Anthropology* 6, no. 1 (February 1991): 63–91.

———. "Maoism in the Andes: The Communist Party of Peru-Shining Path and the Refusal of History." *Journal of Latin American Studies* 27, no. 2 (May 1995): 399–421.

———. "To Revolt against the Revolution: War and Resistance in Peru's Andes." *Cultural Anthropology* 10, no. 4 (November 1995): 547–80.

Stepan, Alfred. *Rethinking Military Politics: Brazil and the Southern Cone.* Princeton: Princeton University Press, 1988.

Stern, Steve, ed. *Shining and Other Paths: War and Society in Peru, 1980–1995*. Durham, N.C.: Duke University Press, 1998.

Stoll, David. *Rigoberta Menchú and the Story of All Poor Guatemalans*. Boulder, Colo.: Westview, 1999.

Stratton, Jon, and Ien Ang. "On the Impossibility of a Global Cultural Studies: 'British' Cultural Studies in an 'International' Frame." In Morley and Chen, *Stuart Hall*, 361–91.

Strong, Simon. *Shining Path: The World's Deadliest Revolutionary Force*. London: HarperCollins, 1992.

Subercaseaux, Bernardo. *Chile: ¿Un país moderno?* Santiago, Chile: Ediciones B, 1996.

Szeman, Imre. "The Limits of Culture: The Frankfurt School and/for Cultural Studies." In *Rethinking the Frankfurt School: Alternative Legacies of Cultural Critique*, ed. Caren Irr and Jeffrey Nealon, 59–80. Albany: State University of New York Press, 2002.

Taggart, Paul. *Populism*. Buckingham: Open University Press, 2000.

Taussig, Michael. *Shamanism, Colonialism, and the Wild Man: A Study in Terror and Healing*. Chicago: University of Chicago Press, 1987.

———. *The Magic of the State*. New York: Routledge, 1997.

———. *Defacement: Public Secrecy and the Labor of the Negative*. Stanford: Stanford University Press, 1999.

Taylor, Diana. *Disappearing Acts: Spectacles of Gender and Nationalism in Argentina's "Dirty War."* Durham, N.C.: Duke University Press, 1997.

Taylor, Julie. *Eva Perón: The Myths of a Woman*. Chicago: University of Chicago Press, 1979.

Tello, María del Pilar. *Perú: el precio de la paz*. Lima: PetroPeru, 1991.

Thayer, Willy. *El fragmento repetido: Escritos en estado de excepción*. Santiago, Chile: Metales Pesados, 2006.

Thoburn, Nicholas. "Patterns of Production: Cultural Studies after Hegemony." *Theory, Culture and Society* 24, no. 3 (2007): 79–94.

Thompson, E. P. "The Long Revolution I." *New Left Review*, no. 1/9 (May–June 1961): 24–33.

———. *The Making of the English Working Class*. London: Victor Gollancz, 1963.

Thompson, Paul. "Foundation and Empire: A Critique of Hardt and Negri." *Capital and Class*, no. 86 (Summer 2005): 73–98.

Thornton, Robert. "The Peculiar Temporality of Violence: A Source of Perplexity about Social Power." *KronoScope* 2, no. 1 (2002): 41–69.

Ticineto Clough, Patricia, with Jean Halley, eds. *The Affective Turn: Theorizing the Social*. Durham, N.C.: Duke University Press, 2007.

Todorov, Tzvetan. *The Conquest of America: The Question of the Other*. Translated by Richard Howard. New York: HarperCollins, 1984.

Torgovnick, Marianna. *Primitive Passions: Men, Women, and the Quest for Ecstasy*. Chicago: University of Chicago Press, 1998.

Torres Ballesteros, Sagrario. "El populismo. Un concepto escurridizo." In *Populismo, caudillaje y discurso demagógico*, ed. José Alvarez Junco, 159–80. Madrid: Siglo Veintiuno de España, 1987.

Touraine, Alain. *The Voice and the Eye: An Analysis of Social Movements*. Translated by Alan Duff. Cambridge: Cambridge University Press, 1981.

———. *What Is Democracy?* Translated by David Macey. Boulder, Colo.: Westview, 1997.

———. *Beyond Neoliberalism*. Translated by David Macey. Cambridge: Polity, 2001.

Tronti, Mario. "Lenin in England." In *Working Class Autonomy and the Crisis: Italian Marxist Texts of the Theory and Practice of a Class Movement, 1964–79*, ed. Red Notes, 1–6. London: Red Notes and CSE Books, 1979.

———. "The Strategy of the Refusal." In *Working Class Autonomy and the Crisis: Italian Marxist Texts of the Theory and Practice of a Class Movement, 1964–79*, ed. Red Notes, 7–21. London: Red Notes and CSE Books, 1979.

———. *Obreros y capital*. Translated by Oscar Chaves Hernández et al. Madrid: Akal, 2001.

Tuesta Soldevilla, Fernando. *No sabe/no opina: Encuestas políticas y medios*. Lima: Universidad de Lima, 1997.

Turner, Graeme. *British Cultural Studies: An Introduction*. 3rd ed. London: Routledge, 2003.

Uzcátegui, Luis José. *Chávez, mago de las emociones: Análisis psicosocial de un fenómeno político*. Caracas: Lithopolar Gráficas, 1999.

Valcárcel, Luis. *Tempestad en los Andes*. Lima: Universo, 1975.

Van Laerhoven, Frank, and Elinor Ostrom. "Traditions and Trends in the Study of the Commons." *International Journal of the Commons* 1, no. 1 (October 2007): 3–28.

Vargas Gutiérrez, José Luis. *Adiós a la vergüenza: Los talk shows en el Perú*. Arequipa: Editorial de la Universidad Nacional de San Agustín, 2000.

Virilio, Paul. *Ground Zero*. Translated by Chris Turner. London: Verso, 2002.

Virno, Paolo. "Virtuosity and Revolution: The Political Theory of Exodus." Translated by Ed Emory. In Virno and Hardt, *Radical Thought in Italy*, 189–210.

———. "Do You Remember Counterrevolution?" Translated by Michael Hardt. In Virno and Hardt, *Radical Thought in Italy*, 240–59.

———. *A Grammar of the Multitude*. Translated by Isabella Bertoletti, James Cascaito, and Andrea Casson. New York: Semiotext(e), 2004.

Virno, Paolo, and Michael Hardt, eds. *Radical Thought in Italy: A Potential Politics*. Minneapolis: University of Minnesota Press, 1996.

Walsh, Rodolfo. *Operación masacre*. Buenos Aires: Ediciones de la Flor, 1972.

Weber, Max. *From Max Weber: Essays in Sociology*. Edited and translated by H. H. Gerth and C. Wright Mills. New York: Oxford University Press, 1946.

Whelan, Glen. "Appropriat(e)ing Wavelength: On Bourdieu's *On Television*." *Ephemera* 2, no. 2 (2002): 131–48.

Williams, Gareth. *The Other Side of the Popular: Neoliberalism and Subalternity in Latin America*. Durham, N.C.: Duke University Press, 2002.

Williams, Raymond. "Base and Superstructure in Marxist Cultural Theory." In *Problems in Materialism and Culture: Selected Essays*, 31–49. London: Verso, 1980.

———. "Culture Is Ordinary." In *Resources of Hope: Culture, Democracy, Socialism*, ed. Robin Gable, 3–18. London: Verso, 1989.

———. *Culture and Society: Coleridge to Orwell*. London: Hogarth, 1990.

Williams, Robert A. *The American Indian in Western Legal Thought: The Discourses of Conquest*. Oxford: Oxford University Press, 1990.

Willis, Paul. *Learning to Labor: How Working Class Kids Get Working Class Jobs*. New York: Columbia University Press, 1981.

Wilpert, Gregory. *Changing Venezuela by Taking Power: The History and Policies of the Chávez Government*. London: Verso, 2007.

Women's Studies Group, Centre for Contemporary Cultural Studies. *Women Take Issue: Aspects of Women's Subordination*. London: Hutchinson, 1978.

Wright, Steve. *Storming Heaven: Class Composition and Struggle in Italian Autonomist Marxism*. London: Pluto, 2002.

Yúdice, George. "Civil Society, Consumption, and Governmentality in an Age of Global Restructuring: An Introduction." *Social Text*, no. 45 (Winter 1995): 1–25.

———. "Translator's Introduction." In *Consumers and Citizens: Globalization and Multicultural Conflicts*, by Néstor García Canclini, ix–xxxviii. Minneapolis: University of Minnesota Press, 2001.

Zapatistas! Documents of the New Mexican Revolution. New York: Autonomedia, 1994.

Zirakzadeh, Cyrus. *Social Movements in Politics: A Comparative Study*. London: Longman, 1997.

Žižek, Slavoj. *The Sublime Object of Ideology*. London: Verso, 1989.

Index